The Lost Children of *Wilder*

The Epic Struggle to Change Foster Care

Nina Bernstein

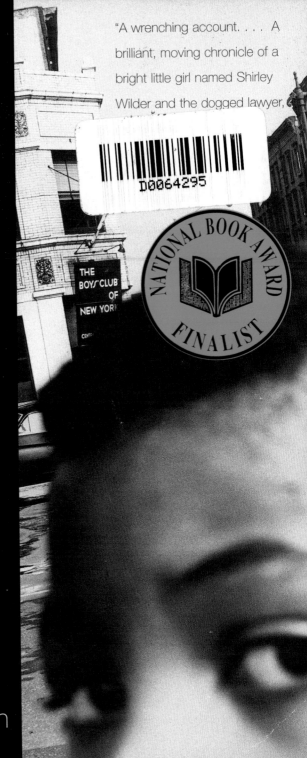

"A wrenching account. . . . A brilliant, moving chronicle of a bright little girl named Shirley Wilder and the dogged lawyer,

D0064295

THE BOYS' CLUB OF NEW YORK

NATIONAL BOOK AWARD FINALIST

Acclaim for Nina Bernstein's

THE LOST CHILDREN OF WILDER

"[Bernstein's] account—gripping, capricious, and humane—is reminiscent of a Dickens novel."　　　　　　　　　—*The New Yorker*

"One of those rare nonfiction books that is quite likely to stay with [its] readers forever."　　　　　　　　　—*St. Louis Post-Dispatch*

"Bernstein is a terrific, dogged reporter. . . . At times, the profusion of detail lifts Bernstein's writing to a kind of poetry."　　—*Chicago Tribune*

"An impressive feat. . . . Bernstein has performed a valuable public service, recording an important chapter in New York City's social history."
　　　　　　　　　—*Newsday*

"A remarkable feat of reporting and storytelling. . . . A disturbing and riveting narrative that should be required reading for anyone who professes concern for children."
　　　　　　　　　—Alex Kotlowitz, author of *There Are No Children Here*

"A compelling, panoramic drama . . . a satisfying read that enlightens, unsettles, and nudges us toward introspection—a book that is, in the best sense, provocative."　　　　　　　　　—*Elle*

"These are painful stories, and Bernstein tells them with care and understanding."　　　　　　　　　—*The Boston Globe*

"Bernstein's success is the thoroughness and nuance with which she chronicles the endless loop of child welfare reform, and the lives of the successive generations of children who tumble through each repeating cycle."
　　　　　　　　　—*The Washington Post*

"*The Lost Children of Wilder* is such a compelling and troubling book that you may be tempted to put it aside only long enough to hug your kids."
—*New York Law Journal*

"Combine[s] prodigious reporting with literary perceptiveness about human motives."
—*The Christian Science Monitor*

"Journalism of the highest order, a truth-telling work that has the eloquence to change the national debate on child welfare. Bernstein manages this powerful indictment, leveled in many directions, through a story that is as rich in detail and as human as a novel."
—*Youth Today*

"Bernstein's mini-portraits of lawyers, judges, social workers, private-sector providers, elected and appointed officials are empathetic but unsparing."
—*The Atlanta Journal-Constitution*

"In the spirit of journalists such as Alex Kotlowitz and Ron Suskind, [Bernstein] brings the story to life by focusing on one family ravaged by the system."
—*Brill's Content*

"This viscerally powerful history of institutionalized child abuse and the criminalization of poverty, of civil rights and social change, is compelling and essential reading."
—*Publishers Weekly* (starred review)

"A human saga of broken homes, broken children, and broken laws."
—*Richmond Times-Dispatch*

Nina Bernstein

THE LOST CHILDREN
OF WILDER

Nina Bernstein is a reporter for *The New York Times*. In 1994 her *New York Newsday* series about *Wilder* won Columbia University School of Journalism's Mike Berger Award, and she was awarded an Alicia Patterson Foundation fellowship to continue her research into foster care. In 1995 she received the George Polk Award for distinguished metropolitan coverage. She lives in New York City.

THE LOST CHILDREN OF

WILDER

The Epic Struggle to Change Foster Care

NINA BERNSTEIN

VINTAGE BOOKS
A DIVISION OF RANDOM HOUSE, INC.
NEW YORK

FIRST VINTAGE BOOKS EDITION, FEBRUARY 2002

The Library of Congress has cataloged the Pantheon edition as follows:
Bernstein, Nina.
The lost children of Wilder / Nina Bernstein.
p.   cm
Includes index.
ISBN 0-679-43979-X
1. Foster children—New York (State)—New York.   2. Foster children—
Legal status, laws, etc.—New York (State)—New York.   3. Child welfare—
New York (State)—New York.   4. Wilder, Shirley—Trials, litigation, etc.
1. Title.
HV885.N5 B46 2001
362.73'3'097471—dc21   00-057456

Vintage ISBN: 0-679-75834-8

Author photograph © Suzanne DeChillo
Book design by M. Kristin Bearse

www.vintagebooks.com

Printed in the United States of America
10 9 8 7 6 5 4

To my parents

to Andreas

and for everyone's children

CONTENTS

A case can act as a midwife to change. You can't read the social forces in advance. Society changes in relation to the case. You cannot foresee the outcome.

—PAUL CHEVIGNY

INTRODUCTION

EARLY IN 1990, researching a newspaper article on New York City foster care, I spent a morning with a stack of court documents from a long-standing lawsuit known as *Wilder*. The lawsuit, citing the First Amendment's separation of church and state and the Fourteenth Amendment's guarantee of equal protection, had challenged New York City's 150-year-old foster-care system in 1973 for giving private, mostly religious agencies control of publicly financed foster-care beds. The Catholic and Jewish charities that dominated the field were by law allowed to give preference to their own kind. Black, Protestant children had to wait or do without. The system did poorly by all children, the suit charged, because it placed them according to creed and convenience, not according to their needs.

In the marble and mahogany splendor of Manhattan's federal courthouse in the 1990s, lawyers often likened the *Wilder* case to *Jarndyce and Jarndyce,* the suit in Dickens's *Bleak House* that dragged on for so long that people forgot what it meant. *Wilder*'s course paralleled a national trajectory from great optimism to great skepticism about the possibility of righting social wrongs through the courts. Yet *Wilder* had engaged the passions of three generations of social reformers even as it fell short of helping three generations of children in foster care.

Halfway through the legal papers, I found, tucked in a paragraph of the fourth amended complaint, a fact that I could not forget: Shirley Wilder, the named plaintiff, had given birth to a son and placed him in foster care in 1974. I wanted to know what had happened to that baby, and to understand why.

THE TWO-HUNDRED-YEAR HISTORY of American child welfare is littered with programs once hailed as reforms and later decried as harmful or ineffective, only to emerge again in the guise of new solutions to past failures. Why do these problems seem so intractable, so often only redefined, rather than remedied, by changed laws and new philosophies?

The answers, I believe, are mirrored in the *Wilder* lawsuit. They lie in the child welfare system's place as a political battleground for abiding national conflicts over race, religion, gender, and inequality. They are found in the unacknowledged contradictions between policies that punish the "undeserving poor" and pledges to help all needy children. And during twenty-six years of *Wilder* litigation, the lost children of *Wilder* grew up with the consequences.

SHIRLEY WILDER WAS HERSELF a motherless child of twelve when she fled from an abusive home into the net of the child welfare system. She was thirteen when, in 1973, the New York Civil Liberties Union filed the class-action lawsuit that would make her name a routine entry on the federal court docket. She was fourteen and still in the system's charge when she gave birth to the child she couldn't keep.

Shirley Wilder had disappeared, I was told when I tried to find her, and her son was one of thousands of anonymous children growing up behind the veil of confidentiality that hides the foster-care system from public scrutiny. For three years I followed other stories to other places, but every so often I checked back to see whether Shirley Wilder had resurfaced. In the spring of 1993, she did.

"Find out about my son," she begged, a slim, impulsive woman in cutoffs and T-shirt, living like an interloper amid the plastic slipcovers and graduation photos of another family's East Harlem apartment. She was thirty-three then, her parental rights long gone. But she was still haunted by the memory of the baby she had left to the system, and by the federal court case that her own suffering had set in motion a year before he was born. The system, she had said once in a deposition, was "winter, all year round"; she never meant to leave her own child in that cold.

HISTORICAL AMNESIA HAS SHIELDED US from a full understanding of our child welfare dilemma. For three generations, "child welfare" has been a category that has covered child abuse, child neglect, foster care, and adoption, but not "welfare," or Aid to Families with Dependent Children. In public opinion and public policy, the universe of child welfare is peopled by deviant parents and unlucky children from families of all income groups, while "welfare" is a program for poor folks. This division tends to downplay the reality that children in foster care and at risk of entering foster care are overwhelmingly the children of the poor.

During long periods of American history, the relationship between poverty and family breakup was unambiguous: with no public relief, parents too poor to support their children had to put them into orphanages or up for indenture or adoption. The old and familiar conviction underlying such policies, that parents who cannot rear their children without public aid are almost by definition unfit to bring up the next generation, still holds sway in this age of welfare reform.

The effort to sever the destiny of needy children from the fate of their unworthy parents repeatedly slams against unyielding truths of child development: the need for intensive human attachment, the traumatic effect of childhood separations, the rapid transformation of yesterday's children into today's childbearers. It defies hard economic realities, too, like the fact that even mediocre substitute care for children (whether in foster home or institution) costs much more than family subsidies, and that adoption, which is ideally both cost-effective and humane, is also governed by unforgiving laws of supply and demand.

There has long been an iron rule in American social welfare policy: conditions must be worse for the dependent poor than for anyone who works. The seldom-acknowledged corollary is that the subsidized care of other people's children must be undesirable enough, or scarce enough, to play a role in this system of deterrence. In the late nineteenth century, charity reformer Josephine Shaw Lowell expressed this view when she insisted that the "honest laborer" should not see the children of the drunkard "enjoy advantages which his own may not hope for." Annie Fields, another nineteenth-century American reformer, argued that men would struggle to support their families only if they found "the room cold and the table bare," and not if they believed their children would be generously cared for by charity. In periods of widening inequality like theirs and like our own, the result of this invisible law becomes so harsh for children that it is difficult to reconcile it with the rhetoric of benevolence. Yet the stronger the desire to discipline society—and growing inequality demands stricter social discipline—the stronger the appeal of schemes that promise to rescue poor children by removing them from their failing families. Only with the passage of the Aid to Dependent Children provisions of the Social Security Act in 1935 did the number of children in out-of-home care decline dramatically, to stay down during more than two decades of narrowing income gaps. The placement rate rose again after 1961, when new rules allowed federal money to follow the poorest children into private, nonprofit foster care of every kind.

By the 1990s, a different kind of child welfare rhetoric had gathered momentum across the nation. Its byword was "tough love," calling for personal responsibility for adults and modern-day orphanages for unadoptable children whose parents failed the test. It envisioned little role for government in child welfare beyond contracting with the private sector; it harked back to a time when churches and charity did the rest, and poor children were said to be the better for it. This vision was remarkably similar to what was known a hundred years ago as the New York system, whereby state wards were placed in private, mostly religiously affiliated agencies at public expense, on the assumption that charitable bodies could be trusted to spend money in the best interest of children. Nowhere did that basic structure take hold so completely and last so long as in New York. It was the very system that *Wilder* tried to transform.

The meaning of *Wilder* is inscribed in the lives of its protagonists, in their burden of history, in their struggle against the past. This book is a quest to understand what went wrong—in one family's entanglement in the foster-care system, and in recurrent crusades to make American child welfare fulfill its promise of benevolence.

PART ONE

1972—1974

ONE

THREE DAYS BEFORE CHRISTMAS 1972, SHIRLEY WILDER, a young black girl with nowhere to go and a need to keep running, stood before a Manhattan Family Court judge who had spent her long career battling for the rights and needs of poor children.

Judge Justine Wise Polier wore no robes, and her desk was a simple table set before grimy windows in a low-ceilinged room. She needed none of the trappings of power to radiate authority. A tall woman who always wore heels, Polier had spent nearly four decades on the juvenile-court bench and was soon to retire. Her piercing intellect, relentless energy, and uncanny command of case records still kept the young lawyers who appeared before her in awe.

Polier came by her regal bearing naturally, born into a family that counted its unbroken lineage of rabbis back nineteen generations. Her father, Stephen Wise, had been the last and greatest of them, a preacher of social justice and leader of American Reform Judaism whose eloquence could fill Carnegie Hall and sometimes sway Congress. Her mother, from a German Jewish family so proud it saw her marriage to Wise as a mésalliance, had Eleanor Roosevelt as an ally in her lifelong crusade for child welfare.

Polier was a child of the Progressive era, embodying an American tradition of social reform that stretched from the settlement-house movement before the turn of the century to Lyndon Johnson's War on Poverty. As a college student in the 1920s, she had worked undercover in a New Jersey textile mill to expose brutal working conditions, defying the inspectors who caught and threatened to arrest her and later championing a strike. ("If you're going to get into that kind of trouble," said her delighted father, who counted a mill owner as one of the most important members of his synagogue, "you had better go to law school.") Assigned to the juvenile-court bench as New York's first woman judge in 1935, she was surprised to find neglect and discrimination in an institution conceived by the Progressives as an oasis of individualized justice. In her own courtroom, despite caseloads that "demanded a speedy disposition of the living poor not unlike the disposition of the dead during a plague," Polier had tried to challenge the power of public officials and private charities to place or exclude children according to creed, color, and bureaucratic convenience. She had joined citizens' groups to press for more services for children brought to court as neglected, delinquent, or PINS—"persons in need of supervision," in the catchall phrase that included runaways for all reasons. And through her husband Shad Polier, a civil-rights lawyer who won early prominence as part of the defense team in the landmark Scottsboro case, she had forged the state's first statute on termination of parental rights, in an effort to free for adoption children held for years in foster care.

Yet on December 22, 1972, all Polier had to offer Shirley Wilder was commitment to the state training school at Hudson, New York, a harsh reformatory for delinquents. In the foster-care system that had evolved in New York City over more than a century, 90 percent of all foster beds were controlled by private agencies that could pick and choose among the children the city tried to place. State law let the leading Catholic and Jewish charities select their own kind, leaving behind a growing pool of black, Protestant children like Shirley.

The thick file on Polier's desk told a story of loss and rejection. Shirley's mother had died of tuberculosis when Shirley was four. The ailing grandmother who took charge of the child and her baby sister in a Harlem project died when Shirley was eleven. Sent to live with her father, Shirley had been made to feel unwanted by a stepmother who beat and berated her. She had run away and returned to beg forgiveness several times before her father brought her to court, in December 1971, asking that she be "put away." The judge and a psychologist determined that she needed residential treatment to work through deep feelings of abandonment. But over the next ten months, as Shirley ran or was shunted among relatives, shelters, and the jail-like juvenile detention center, every voluntary agency that was approached turned her down. Most claimed she needed more therapy or more structure than they could offer; some just rejected her as "unsuitable."

The file hinted at mysteries in her background, at a burden of family secrets so heavy it warped her childhood. She had been born before her parents were married and was never given the last name of her father, James Adam All. She was a Wilder, just like her mother—and just as bad, her stepmother and paternal relatives never tired of telling Shirley and anyone else who would listen. They had all tried to steer Shirley right, they complained to caseworkers, but almost from infancy she had been following in her mother's path.

Shirley was the eighteenth child summoned to Polier's court that day. She waited outside the closed door at first while Carol Sherman, the Legal Aid lawyer who served as her law guardian, made a last-ditch plea on her behalf. Twelve times that year the matter of Shirley had come to court. Twelve times the judge had been informed that there was no agency willing to take the child. But Sherman, a Long Island pharmacist's daughter who had lost her own mother at fifteen, wasn't ready to give up.

"There was already something special about Shirley," Sherman would later recall. "She had a real charm—there was almost a delight to her. She was very young, but she was bright. Shirley had a real strength and resilience that I admired. I wanted so much for her to be in a good place. I really didn't want the judge to send her to Hudson. I wanted to keep trying."

Sherman, a small, slender woman two years out of Harvard Law School, rose to face the judge. She summarized the record. She noted that Shirley's father had stopped visiting her in detention. She quoted the most recent psychological finding: Shirley was an unhappy child suffering neglect and deprivation who needed therapy and direction. And then she began citing recent Appellate Division cases that declared the state training school not a proper place for PINS children, offering up the litany of children's names and initials like a prayer: *In the matter of Arlene H.* . . . *Janet P.* . . . *Ilione I.* . . . *Stanley M.* . . . *Edward S.* . . . *Richard S.* . . . Stumbling now, she began to read an opinion handed down by the Supreme Court of Erie County, Pennsylvania, in a related class-action suit barely three months before. Polier stopped her; she knew the opinion already.

But the young lawyer plunged on with a detailed report on the lack of services at the state training school: it had only one part-time psychiatrist-consultant for 125 residents, and no individual therapy. "The training school is not a proper place for this child, who is here on one PINS for running away and has been deprived and neglected," she declared at last, her voice trembling.

Sherman knew Polier cared about this girl, though Shirley was one of many. Again and again over the past months, the judge had asked in the lull between other cases, off the record, "Have you found anything for Shirley?"

Polier herself had been a rebellious child, testing the tolerance of a mother and father she later characterized as "among the first of progressive parents." At ten, left in Germany with strict and condescending maternal relatives while her parents toured Palestine, she had used her pocket money to cable them, threatening to run away if they didn't rescue her immediately. They quickly wired instructions for Justine's German governess to bring her to meet them in Naples.

But that was all long ago. In the dingy courtroom, silhouetted by pale winter light, the sixty-nine-year-old judge shook her head. "This child has been studied repeatedly by various agencies," she said. "She has been rejected by Edmund [Edwin] Gould Services, Lakeside, Saint Germaine's, Hillside, Wayside, Green Chimneys, Edmund [Edwin] Gould Residence"—and five more that went unnamed—"and this court knows of no voluntary facility that will accept this child.

"In the opinion of this court, this child represents one of a class of cases where treatment services are indicated for children who are emotionally disturbed . . . and for whom voluntary agencies will not accept responsibility. The court finds it necessary to place this child in the Division for Youth, which will mean undoubtedly Hudson. . . . There is no appropriate place."

Polier later would call it a "miserable decision." She never agonized over her defeats, but neither was she capable of giving up. She had already chosen her new line of assault in the matter of Shirley Wilder. Hadn't the time come, she asked Sherman on the record, for the law guardians of New York County to follow the Erie County, Pennsylvania, example and sue the state on behalf of children like Shirley? Such a suit could force the government to provide needed therapy at the state training school.

Only then, after checking with Sherman that the girl knew the probable outcome of the hearing, did Polier ask for Shirley to be brought in.

A year had passed since James Adam All first took his runaway daughter to court. Polier had seen Shirley then as a small, attractive twelve-year-old with a resilient spirit and a mischievous smile. In a later court appearance, after her father stopped his detention visits, the judge heard Shirley ask in a near whisper, "Is my father here?" The answer was no, and the child hardened her face in a show of indifference. Now she had a look of defiance mixed with fear, and an adolescent body straining at drab, ill-fitting detention clothes.

"I have spoken to your law guardian, Shirley," the judge said, "and I am sorry I could not get you into a smaller residence. At this point I know you can't be home, and I'm going to have you at the Division for Youth, where you will go to one of two schools. We are going to ask them to give you as much as they can. Is there anything you would like to say?"

The girl moved close to Sherman and whispered urgently in her ear.

"Your Honor," the lawyer said, "Shirley has requested that I ask the court if she can go home for Christmas Day."

"No," Polier replied. "But if she wants us to notify her aunt or her father and they will visit her, I shall be very happy to do so."

Another whisper. "She said, yes," Sherman said.

"Have you spoken to your father?" Polier's voice was gentle. Shirley nodded, saying nothing.

"All right," the judge said, closing the file. "That's all."

IT WAS, OF COURSE, only the beginning.

TWO

SHIRLEY SPENT CHRISTMAS 1972 WITHOUT VISITORS, BE-hind the high wall that surrounded the Manida Shelter for Delinquent Children, the girls' detention center in the South Bronx.

Manida's basement dining room and dimly lit fourteen-bed dormitories had not been renovated since the main building was constructed as a monastery in 1904. There were plumbing leaks throughout; wet, falling plaster; and such chronic flooding that whenever it rained hard, the children had to wade through several inches of dirty water to get to their meals. A 1970 fire had destroyed two dormitories; girls were now packed into the seven that remained. Lack of hot or cold water often made showering impossible. No running games were allowed in the "gym," a dilapidated basement room with two large poles in the center that restricted movement; the girls spent most of their time crowded into a small day room in the flickering light of a television set.

For at least ten years Manida had been on record as "unsuitable for the detention care of children." A year before Shirley's original detention there, an appellate-court commission had urged that it be closed. The commission's report called the conditions deplorable, unsanitary, dangerous, and directly linked to the widespread incidence of homosexual activity, both forced and consensual. In a class-action lawsuit filed in 1971, the Legal Aid Society added allegations of physical abuse and psychological humiliation by staff to the general picture of decay. Two months before Christmas 1972, a U.S. District Court had ruled that conditions at Manida were so hazardous and unhealthy that they amounted to cruel and unusual punishment, in violation of the Constitution's Eighth Amendment. But Manida would not be shut down until August 1973, months after Shirley left on a bus bound for Hudson, 110 miles away.

The road to the Hudson institution cut through woods of sumac, poplar, and locust and climbed up to the remnants of a massive stone and iron gate. Behind an eight-foot fence, on a 168-acre bluff overlooking the Hudson River Valley between the Catskills and the Berkshire Mountains, stood the redbrick buildings of the State Training School for Girls. "It has the appearance of a school campus," the institution's superintendent, Tom Tunney, had written in 1968, "with spreading trees bordering three quadrangles where the cottages are located." The fourteen "cottages"—imposing two-story brick buildings that housed twenty-five to thirty girls each—had barely changed since the oldest ones were built in the 1880s.

On January 9, 1973, six weeks after her thirteenth birthday, Shirley entered her assigned cottage and found herself back in the gloom of a small-scale Manida. Peeling paint, cracked plaster, and gaping holes marked the walls. The kitchen and dining room for the twenty-five cottage residents were in a dingy basement that doubled as a common room. At 8:30 P.M., Shirley and the others were shut into their individual bedrooms. In the dark hours before the 6:30 A.M. wake-up call, sleep was broken by the sound of urgent knocking, as girls who had to use the toilet tried to draw the staff's attention. The long list of rules tacked inside each door included "Never leave your room without first getting permission of the staff on duty. (Knock on door.)"

There were thirty-three other basic rules on the list, some broad, some oddly specific: "Do not be disrespectful to any staff"; "Do not talk unnecessarily after prayers are said"; "Do not use profanity at any time"; "Do not talk or yell out of your window at any time to anybody"; "Do not go upstairs, downstairs, basement, outdoors, or to another girl's door without first getting permission from the staff on duty." There were eleven rules especially for the morning, including "Do not wash personals in A.M., only when they are stained." There were rules for the dining room, including "Ask the staff's permission to get up for seconds." And if you broke the rules, there were rules for punishment: "No talking when serving room confinement—rule of silence."

Shirley was "a youngster hungry for affection," a Manida caseworker had reported to one of the private agencies that rejected her. At Hudson the basic diet was regulation and escalating punishment, larded with the rhetoric of home, school, and hospital.

But there was a counterpoint to the institution's world of oppressive regulation: a pervasive shadow society run by the inmates themselves. It had its own code of conduct, its own language and customs, its own rewards and sanctions. As a newcomer, Shirley was assessed by "hard daddies" and "trust-to-be-butches" with such nicknames as Smokey, Butchy Boy, and Torch. She was eyed by "jive-time fems" and "trust-to-be-fems" known by names like Heatwave, Little Heart, and Tenderness. Theirs was a world of teenage courtship rituals, of secret notes full of song titles, number codes, and acronyms like "H.O.L.L.A.N.D." (Hope our love lasts and never dies)," "SWMTK" (Sealed with my tongue kiss), and "T.H.A.W." (True husband and wife). It turned the institution's conventions to its own use, producing "marriage" and "divorce" certificates in typing class, dropping Bibles during chapel service to signal a sub rosa "wedding," punishing "squealers" by setting them up for staff discipline. It was a society of elaborate kinship ties, of extended "families" complete with aunts, uncles, and cousins who were expected to share scarce commodities with their family members and to fight to avenge them. And it was a society that borrowed gendered brutality from the adult world: a "daddy" had the right to beat up a "mom" and to have more than one sex partner; a "mom" was expected to be faithful and deferent or suffer the consequences. The competition for partners was fierce, and any newcomer was fair game.

They called it "the racket."

SOME OF THE HARSHEST and pettiest-seeming rules at Hudson—no talking between girls from different cottages, for example—were part of the institution's undeclared war against the racket, but they seemed only to strengthen its hold. References to lesbian-centered make-believe families at girls' reform schools date back to 1913. The year before Shirley arrived at Hudson, in a survey of the inmates published in a book by a sociologist named Rose Giallombardo, 87 percent acknowledged that they belonged to such groups. Giallombardo described the homosexual relationships at the center of the racket as voluntary, but she conceded that homosexual attacks sometimes occurred, "usually involving adolescent inmates who have expressed an unwillingness to participate in homosexuality."

New staff members like Joann Concra, who was twenty-one when she came to work at the training school in the late 1960s after a sheltered Catholic upbringing, were shocked at first by these sexual assaults. "They'd use broom handles on the girls. A girl would confide, 'Yeah, I got it last night in the bathroom.' You'd say, 'Tell the supervisor.' And the answer would be, 'I can't now. I'm in too deep.' I never wanted to ask too much because I didn't want to get involved. I used to tell my mother. She'd say, 'Well, just do what you're supposed to do and mind your business.' "

Concra's duties included helping out in the office of the institution's longtime resident dentist, R. Mary Wend, and she asked her what she should do. Wend was an older woman of frugal ingenuity and worldly knowledge; she had tried to straighten inmates' teeth with bamboo braces of her own design, and she had written a master's thesis on the history of prostitution in the city of Hudson.

"Honey, these things go on here," Wend replied. "You have your choice. If you want to work here, you have to learn to get used to it and not let it bother you. If it really bothers you, you have to move on."

Concra stayed. She was working somewhere on the Hudson grounds the day the racket came after Shirley Wilder.

THEY CORNERED HER IN HER ROOM on the second floor of the cottage after supper. "We're going to get you," Shirley heard one say. "We're going to initiate you." They were big girls, older than she was, a dozen of them. Seven held her down. Some pinioned her arms and legs. Some pulled at her clothes. She saw the stick and suddenly understood. They were trying to thrust it between her legs, inside her.

Sexual brutality was not new to Shirley. She had twice been raped at the age of nine—the year, she once told a social worker, when she finally understood that her mother was dead and would never return to rescue her. Since then the line between consent and force had often blurred for her. One man's seduction remained the secret violation of her childhood, a wound that never healed; yet she had also courted couplings with big boys that turned so rough and painful that she fought to stop them.

Shirley had always been a fighter. She had scrapped in school and with her cousins, vying with the strongest boys instead of hanging back to watch. She had fought with an elementary school teacher who grabbed her in class, flailing wildly with clenched fists until the teacher let her go. She had even battled the home attendant who came to tend her sick grandmother, as though by fighting off the intruder she could beat back death itself. Now she fought her hardest, writhing, bucking, screaming for help.

In retrospect it all seemed to happen at once—the attack, the fight, and her own punishment. "Oh, man, the way they treated me! They took broken glass and cut my arm because I wouldn't go to bed with one of them. But the staff put me in the hole because I started fighting. The dark room—no windows, no screens, sleep on the cold floor."

"The hole" was a section of the institution's old hospital building where girls were kept in isolation cells for days at a time. Staff stripped Shirley of her clothes and dressed her in pajamas with Velcro fastenings so she couldn't use metal snaps or buttons to harm herself. Then she was locked in a bare room with padded walls. Every ten minutes, a staff person would peer through a peephole at her. That was part of Joann Concra's job. She was to record any unusual behavior, "like sitting in a corner and rocking or holding the knees."

"Individuals who are not familiar with the day-to-day operation of institutions for juvenile delinquents naively assume that the staff in so-called treatment institutions dispose of situations involving rule infractions by sitting down with the inmates to talk it out," Giallombardo, the sociologist, wrote after studying Hudson and two similar girls' reform schools in the West and Midwest between 1968 and 1973. "This is simply not so. At all three institutions, the initial response of the staff was always punitive segregation."

One housemother, Mattie Harris, had encountered the inextricable escalation of protection and punishment on her very first midnight shift, in 1964, in a scenario that came to seem unremarkable over her long career at Hudson: a girl locked in her room for breaking a minor rule smashed her window and used a piece of broken glass to cut her arms; maintenance men were called to remove the remaining glass, cover over the window frame with a sheet, and take out the furniture. The girl was "taught a lesson" by being left to serve out an extended confinement in cold and darkness. Protective measures were thus part of an entrenched spiral of humiliation, revolt, and further deprivation. Indeed, by cutting Shirley's arm with glass in imitation of self-mutilation, the girls in the racket had ensured that her punishment would be more severe.

At Hudson, reasons for solitary confinement included what Concra called "weird behavior"—fighting, running away, or speaking of suicide. "Perhaps someone got a sad letter from home and was threatening to kill themselves—your mother dies, you're thirteen years old, you're locked away, that can be pretty traumatic," Concra would explain. "As your behavior would get better, you could get a mattress. It was like, 'It's seven o'clock now, you want to sleep on a mattress, you calm yourself down. You're hollering, you're cold—you stop hollering, we'll give you a blanket.' Then, say, like three days had passed and she cooperated and she's starting to come around, she's starting to act like a human: 'Maybe we'll let you have sheets.' "

Sometimes confinement backfired. The girls who were remembered years later by the Hudson staff included the inmate who hanged herself in the hole with a sheet and the one who broke out and hitchhiked all the way to New York City in her pajamas and bedroom slippers. Still, there were up to twenty rooms set aside for solitary confinement and at times all were occupied. Some girls were tranquilized because they screamed and beat their head against the walls; the staff had standing orders for such medication. Once a day, a doctor checked each girl for self-inflicted wounds. Twice a week a psychiatrist stopped by. "The social worker might say, 'I think Friday she'll be ready, and we'll monitor her over the weekend," Concra remembered. "Finally, when she's healed and cleansed herself, she's ready to mix back with the population."

Some girls never made it back from the hole; they were transferred instead to the Brookwood Annex, a maximum-security facility in nearby Claverack for the most "difficult" girls in the State Training School system. At Brookwood, where inmates could be as young as seven, solitary confinement had been used as a treatment for eighty-one individual girls for a total of 369 days during April, May, and June of 1971, according to court depositions.

Despite protracted litigation and legislation to curtail its use, the solitary confinement of children in five-by-eight-foot cells had proved extraordinarily hard to stop in state training schools. Several years after a federal judge limited the length of "time-outs" in such "quiet rooms" to twenty-four consecutive hours, "two employees of a state training school emerged to reveal that the school had invented the practice of confinement for twenty-three hours, release for one hour, and confinement for another twenty-three hours in order to avoid the court's restrictions."*

When Shirley came to Hudson, 83 percent of her fellow inmates were "persons in need of supervision," meaning truants, runaways, and throwaways; only 17 percent had been committed as juvenile delinquents for acts that would have been crimes if perpetrated by adults. Many, like Shirley, were there by default because no private agency or relative would take them. Many had been sexually abused at home. Even the serious delinquents often had started out as sexual victims and runaways. One redheaded girl committed for murder, for example, had run away at fourteen after being sexually abused by her father and her uncle. Hitchhiking across the country, she had stabbed and killed a truck driver who didn't want to pay her for sexual favors. She was glad she was pregnant, she said, and hoped to care for her baby when she got out, " 'to give it all the love I didn't have in my lifetime.' "

SHIRLEY WANTED TO FIGHT THE RACKET, but she realized that at Hudson, fighting brought only cold, darkness, and isolation. When she was returned to her cottage from the hole, she resolved to run away.

*Ira Glasser, et al., *Doing Good: The Limits of Benevolence* (New York: Pantheon Books, 1979), p. 149.

THREE

THERE WAS STILL SNOW ON THE GROUND THE DAY SHIRLEY Wilder and another girl followed a dirt road at the upper end of the grounds into the woods, hunting for a way out. The road soon vanished among the drifts and wet black tree trunks. Moving through the shadows of a grove of cedars, they suddenly found themselves in a clearing at the edge of a steep, wooded ravine.

It was a small cemetery. The old gravestones had been so tilted by spring frosts and winter thaws that they looked almost scattered. There were no dates on the weathered markers, and no epitaphs——only girls' names, fading from bare limestone.

Lizzie French. Nellie McGovern. Anna Schabesberger. Julia Coon. Mary O'Brien. Louella Roarack. Lydia Althouser. Jennie Fuller. Barbara Decker. Anne Withey. Helen Peer.

Shirley remembered the stories she had heard from a housemother and some of the girls. They said a secret graveyard lay hidden in the woods on the Hudson grounds. Years ago, dead babies born to inmates were buried there, and bad girls, too——girls caught trying to escape who later died inside the institution. Other bodies were sent home to their folks for burial, but even after death, runaways were punished. This was their solitary confinement: a cold, dark grave lost in the woods forever.

Shirley began to tremble, and the other girl cried out in fright. They turned and ran away as fast as they could.

At the other end of the Hudson grounds they climbed over the fence together and slid down a slope into a stubble of cattails and frozen loosestrife. For hours they stumbled through the big swamp that bordered the institution, looking for a road out. Pockets of ice cracked underfoot and gave way to marshy ground. They fell and scrambled upright again, foul-smelling muck soaking their shoes and clothes. Running, trudging, running again, they couldn't escape the icy wind that whipped in off the river. They clutched at stiff weeds with raw fingers to keep from slipping. Shirley's feet swelled, and her ears went numb with cold.

They were lost, lost in the vast wetland that had once been the South Bay.

WHALING SHIPS WERE MOORED HERE in another century. The first ones carried the town's founders, prosperous whalers from Nantucket and Martha's Vineyard who came seeking a safer harbor in the revolutionary world of 1783. The Proprieters, as later generations would call them, sailed up the Hudson with all their goods lashed to the decks of their ships, even their disassembled houses. In later years, tugboats idled in the South Bay after guiding great shipping vessels to the deep-water wharves on Hudson's Front Street. In the 1840s, when impoverished tenant farmers rebelled against their vassalage under Hudson Valley landowners, troopships sailed here, too, bringing soldiers to crush the revolt.

Then the railroad arrived. The New York-to-Albany line was laid on causeways right across the mouth of the South Bay, cutting it off from the river in 1851. An iron factory spewed its wastes into the stranded bay. The bay became a putrid swamp. And on a promontory above this swamp, the House of Refuge for Women was built. The word *Refuge* was misleading: from the moment the stone and wrought iron gates of the institution first swung open on May 7, 1887, solitary confinement was the preferred mode of treatment.

"Though I have been very much impeded by the newness of the institution in my desire to enforce rigorous discipline," Sarah V. Coon, the first superintendent, reported in November 1888, "still so far as it has been possible in our overcrowded prison, I have tried to isolate each girl, upon her arrival, from the older inmates. . . . Sometimes, upon detecting a developing tendency to misbehave, I still keep her in solitary confinement until I see a change in this respect. . . . Besides solitary confinement, confinement in dark cells, with disciplinary diet and handcuffs, is in vogue."

Shirley, scrambling through the marsh in the slanting winter light of 1973, was one in a long line of girls who had tried to escape this form of education. Most were quickly apprehended. The very first inmate committed to the institution after it was dubbed the New York State Training School for Girls in 1904 was a thirteen-year-old named Rose Conte who ran away at four o'clock that July day and was caught by nine P.M.

A few got away. "TWENTY-FIVE DOLLARS REWARD," announced the *Hudson Gazette* on November 14, 1895. "Saturday last a reward of $25 was offered for the return of Catharine Burns, who escaped from the House of Refuge for Women in this city on the night of October 23. The woman is described as "23 years of age, 5 feet 7½ inches tall, very dark hair, large, dark blue eyes, strongly marked dark eyebrows, pale complexion, well proportioned and rather striking in appearance."

Catharine Burns was never found. Perhaps she melted into one of the lost colonies of runaways that people the legends of the Hudson River Valley. But to Shirley, a city child lost in a tangle of scrub oak and swamp hickory, the wilderness held no promise of refuge. At last, through thickening woods and gathering dusk, she saw the lights of a house and ran to it.

A fire was blazing in the grate. A woman was at home. When she answered the door, Shirley begged her for help. Would she please call a taxi to take them to the city? The woman agreed and invited the two shivering girls inside to warm themselves at her hearth. They were so grateful. They were still huddled there, holding their hands out to the flames, when the Hudson security guard walked in to take them back.

SHIRLEY SPENT THREE DAYS in solitary confinement as punishment for running away. When she emerged from isolation, she was transferred into the new Behavior Modification Unit in Cottage E.

Cottage E was the last building in the far quadrangle, the closest to the woods that hid the old cemetery. Beyond the graves, blocked from view by trees, stood the superintendent's house. It was a mansion, really, built in the Federal style when the rolling grounds were still a rich man's estate. Embellished in the mid-nineteenth century, it boasted an Italianate tower, octagonal halls with big bay windows, and a stone veranda with a commanding view over the trees to the mountains.

One after another the institution's superintendents had lived there. Tom Tunney, arriving with his wife and four children in 1965, was the last. The state provided the residence free of charge and supplied a staff to match: a uniformed chauffeur, maintenance men to tend the temperamental furnace, a gardener, a cook, and a full-time housekeeper. Traditionally, ten girls worked under the housekeeper's direction. They kept the marble fireplaces clean and dusted the grand circular staircase; they washed and ironed the family laundry in the basement; they peeled and chopped and scoured in the kitchen. Some served at table, answering the summons of a peremptory bell. The girls were not paid, of course. This was "vocational training."

Gale Smith, Tunney's right-hand man, knew it was typical throughout the training-school system. "There were always kids who worked in the superintendent's home. It was patterned after the old system of county sheriffs who had control in their bailiwick and prison inmates working for them. It was all part of English tradition. Some of the training schools had a tailor who would actually tend to the family's needs. Most of them managed their own storehouse, and the superintendent's house got the choice cuts from the meat. They were little fiefdoms."

For Tunney, a white liberal who had spent the summer of 1964 in Mississippi agitating for Negro civil rights, what came to mind was not England but the antebellum South. His first week at the institution he said to his wife, "My God, Patty, I've got a plantation here to run."

By then, most of the girls at Hudson were black. Perhaps 35 percent of the staff was, too; many came from black families that had lived for generations in the town of Hudson. Tunney's first proclamation put a halt to the unpaid labor of inmates in the mansion. When he learned that many staff members were taking girls to their own homes to do laundry and cleaning under the guise of "vocational training," he decreed that the inmates would have to be paid two dollars an hour. "Suddenly not too many people wanted to take the girls," he would remember.

But the institution itself remained dependent on the inmates' unpaid work. Not only were society's narrowest expectations for young women embodied in the vocational-education courses—homemaking, cooking, and beauty culture topped the list—but all "vocational assignments" had to be fitted into the maintenance needs of the institution. There were, for example, no janitors at Hudson because the girls did all the cleaning—in the academic school, the chapel, and the administration building as well as the cottages. They also did the laundry, including linens for several other state facilities, on equipment rated "altogether obsolete" by inspectors. To accommodate the workload, many of the girls went to school only in the morning or the afternoon, or two to three days a week. No girl's room had a desk, no cottage a space for study; the school's sparsely supplied library was open to inmates for forty minutes, once a week. Most inmates would be at a serious disadvantage when they returned to their community schools. The irony was that many had been committed to Hudson as truants.

In 1972, after Tunney's own children went off to college, he moved out of the big house into a more modest farmhouse on the grounds. In 1973, when Shirley Wilder arrived at Hudson, the superintendent's mansion stood unused and overgrown, like the old cemetery below it.

Tunney thought he had broken with his predecessors. A Korean War air force veteran turned registered Socialist and student of Buddhism, he saw himself as a radical reformer unafraid of controversy. "When I came here there were 350 kids and the place was a mess," he would say. "My idea was to close it down. I wanted to close them all down."

In his first years at Hudson, Tunney did close Cottage A, the punishment cottage that had operated since the 1920s; but then he built isolation cells into the old hospital building instead. Few if any of his supporters knew the institution's history well enough to appreciate the irony: the hospital, remodeled several times, had started out as the prison building at the House of Refuge. Its prison cells had been superseded at the turn of the century by a "guard-house . . . where girls may be put into solitary confinement." The guardhouse in turn had been replaced by a disciplinary cottage—Cottage A. Now the site of punishment had come full circle.

The hospital cells were backed up, of course, by the Brookwood Annex. "Annex units of this type are common in several states and they are in every sense disciplinary cottages 'away from home,' " Giallombardo, the sociologist, noted in 1973. "Held as a threat to any inmate who resists outward conformity to institutional rules, the units provide the same function as would a maximum security cottage located on the grounds. In addition, its location elsewhere makes it possible to present a public image of the institution that is less than the whole truth, if not altogether false."

Mindful of the harshness of Brookwood's regime, Tunney decided to create an experimental alternative—a behavior-modification unit. It was to be an enlightened version of the annex, a state-of-the-art application of B. F. Skinner's work to the treatment of juvenile delinquency. Instead, it would become another place of punishment reverberating with echoes of a forgotten past.

LIKE TUNNEY, JOSEPHINE SHAW LOWELL, the nineteenth-century social reformer whose tough-minded campaign first established the Hudson House of Refuge for Women, saw herself as a radical. She came from a distinguished family of abolitionists. Her brother, Robert Gould Shaw, had died leading the first Negro regiment in the Civil War; her father had organized the Freedmen's Bureau; and she began her lifelong charitable work by inspecting black schools in the South and raising relief funds for freed slaves. Appalled by conditions in New York's poorhouses and jails, where the Irish had predominated since the great migration of the Irish Famine, she fought for policies that she thought would eliminate poverty, not just cope with its consequences. She became a leader among the new "scientific" social reformers who focused on family patterns as the primary source of poverty and social disorder, and on the role they believed indiscriminate charity played in perpetuating those patterns.

Nineteenth-century ideology had cast the "true woman" as the guardian of social morality, and her home as a haven from the marketplace, where the next generation would learn industriousness and Christian virtue. But by the 1870s, fears about the formation of a permanent class of paupers and criminals had turned the cult of true womanhood on its head: the "fallen woman" was seen as the progenitor of idle and vicious generations that drained the resources of the republic and threatened its stability.

"One of the most important and most dangerous causes of the increase of crime, pauperism and insanity, is the unrestrained liberty allowed to vagrant and degraded women," Lowell told New York's state legislature in 1879, in arguing for the creation of a reformatory for women under the management of women. "There are two distinct and separate objects to be aimed at in dealing with these women: To reform them if possible, but if that cannot be done, at least to cut off the line of hereditary pauperism, crime and insanity, now transmitted mainly through them."

The hybrid reformatories that Lowell envisioned for female offenders and young mothers of illegitimate children were to provide a kind of reprogramming in "true womanhood" through an institutional replication of family life, isolated from the outer world. When the state finally opened the House of Refuge in 1887, "as an experiment," it embodied most of Lowell's plan and all its contradictions.

The targets, typically convicted of prostitution or vagrancy, had been subject in the past to terms of ten days to half a year in jail or the county poorhouse. Now they were sentenced to Hudson for five years, with earlier release only at the discretion of their keepers. In the shadow of the ninety-six-cell prison building where inmates spent at least the first two months, cottages housing fifteen to twenty young women were "fitted up as nearly as possible like an average family home for the purpose of teaching inmates all manner of domestic work." They were at times allowed to talk to each other in "a low, pleasant voice," but only under the eyes of the supervisor, "who checks any boisterousness or unladylike manner," as Coon, the first superintendent, reported. Even unhappiness was cause for reproof. A complicated point scale was used to grade inmate behavior, backed by a system of surveillance, denunciation, and self-confession for such small faults as tilting a chair or sitting on a bed. "So much attention is given to these minute points that a girl, it is considered, can not attain 100 as an average at any time." Room confinement on bread and water was standard punishment for breaking rules designed as much to ensure the smooth functioning of the institution as to remake a "bad" girl into a "respectable" woman.

But the results were often disappointing, to judge from the oversized parole ledgers stacked and forgotten in the basement of a Hudson administration building. To be sure, sometimes a young girl or woman was reported to be "doing well" after discharge—married, employed as a servant by a "respectable" family, or living with her parents. But most entries were less sanguine. "Dora Miller . . . did well for a few months, then went back to an evil life," reads the entry on a Jewish girl born in Berlin who "had worked in a collar shop" before spending three years at the institution for disorderly conduct. "Went to pieces immediately after final discharge and now acting disgracefully in Troy," is the report on Mamie King, who had spent five full years at Hudson.

The institution itself rapidly declined. The site on the bluff above the river had seemed so healthful to the founders when they chose it. But by 1899, in its twelfth annual report, the board of managers called the need for sewerage urgent, "the dungeons . . . damp and cold," "the ceilings in the main building and in the cottages . . . poor, many of them having already fallen and others in danger of falling hourly." Later reports complained of harmful overcrowding, girls sleeping in corridors, and a nearby cement works that emitted "noxious gases and blinding clouds of dust which have harassed the residents of this institution for some years." Again and again the board begged the state legislature for funds "to bring the Institution up to the real purposes of a Reformatory."

Meanwhile, the ledgers filled with names and numbers, and sometimes, in the woods, another grave was dug.

Here lay Anna Louise Schabesberger, five months old, who died on May 7, 1892, the fifth anniversary of the day the House of Refuge's gates opened. Here, too, lay Anna Schabesberger, the baby's twenty-one-year-old unwed mother, who died giving birth to her namesake. She was inmate number 338, a German immigrant and domestic servant committed from Yonkers for petit larceny soon after she became pregnant by an unnamed man.

Here lay Nellie McGovern, a New York City child of Irish immigrants, who was eighteen and said to be married when she died at Hudson in the winter of 1894, suffering from syphilis and childbirth fever. A child named Michael McGovern died four months later at Mt. Loretto, Staten Island, a Catholic orphanage also known as the Mission of the Immaculate Virgin.

Mary O'Brien: sent to the House of Refuge at sixteen as a "common prostitute," she died of tuberculosis after two years there, on September 26, 1894, her occupation listed as "domestic" on her death certificate.

Lizzie French. She was only fourteen and reported to be in good health when she was sent behind the high board fence to be reformed; she had been working in a caramel shop in Troy, New York, and was committed for petit larceny three weeks before Christmas 1892. She died of tuberculosis when she was seventeen.

Julia Coon: an unwed housekeeper, half German, half Irish; she died at twenty in June of 1893 in childbirth, two months after her commitment as a "disorderly person." There is no record of what happened to her baby or who its father was.

Helen Peer: she died at twenty-one in the spring of 1896, suffering from syphilis and "chronic diarrhea"—probably typhus contracted after three years in the unsewered House of Refuge, where the only drinking water came from the polluted Hudson. A collarmaker by trade, she had been convicted of being a vagrant in Glens Falls, New York, after the bitter depression winter of 1893.

By then, reformer Josephine Shaw Lowell had come to see low wages and unemployment, not family patterns and charity, as the primary causes of pauperism. She began to support organized labor and binding arbitration; she raised money for striking garment workers; she founded a consumers' league to boycott stores that underpaid and overworked salesgirls. But the Hudson "experiment" she had launched continued.

AS PART OF TUNNEY'S behavior modification unit (BMU) in Cottage E, Shirley Wilder became the subject of a system of grading and scrutiny. In the BMU, nothing came free except a bare bed and food on a tray in room confinement. Tokens were charged each day for the privilege of eating in the dining room, having a lamp in one's room, having window curtains.

"They would earn so many tokens for going through the day without a problem, and they would lose tokens if they would have a problem—act out, throw food, have an argument with another person," Betty Williams, one of the BMU housemothers, would recall. "Some kids just got worse. They got so deep in the hole, they just didn't care.

"We did some modification of the whole twenty-five kids at the end. It was too many kids. At most you'd have three staff to do that. It's not enough to deal with normal kids, whatever normal is."

Shirley hated the BMU. "The counselors would hit you like you were a man," she said. "We had to mop the corridors and the bathroom on hands and knees with a rag. We was nobodies."

To Gale Smith, head of programs for Tunney, the problem was that the staff was too warm. In order to run this kind of operation, he felt, staff had to be extremely objective, almost cold and detached. "On our staff we had some of the most nurturing, caring ladies you can imagine."

There were other hindrances. During the early 1970s every major newspaper in the United States, including the *New York Times,* published exposés of conditions in the juvenile penal system. Class-action lawsuits and investigative commissions around the country criticized state institutions for internal abuses ranging from sexual violence and solitary confinement to the punitive use of psychotropic drugs. The bad publicity led New York to create the short-lived post of state ombudsman for children. Tunney found that ombudsman interference frustrated the behavior-modification system. "The ombudsman would come in and say, 'You can't deprive kids of going into the dining room.' The big thing was children's rights."

Even as he clashed with the ombudsman, though, Tunney increasingly caught himself wondering if he was doing harm rather than good: "We just don't know enough to help, and we get desperate in our efforts to help, and we do damage in our efforts to help."

IT WAS SO HARD TO CHANGE even a small detail of institutional life. Toilet paper, for instance. Girls were given a roll of toilet paper once a month, or else the staff doled out four sheets of paper each as the girls lined up to go to the bathroom. As far as staff members were concerned, there was no choice. They had only so much toilet paper, so they devised ways to make it last. The underlying problem turned out to be that the training schools ordered toilet paper in bulk based upon the needs of boys. Tunney and Smith spent months figuring this out and writing memos to change it. But the hardest part came *after* they succeeded in increasing Hudson's toilet-paper allocation.

"We had a hell of a time convincing the staff to put toilet-paper holders in the bathrooms," Smith would recall. "They said the kids would waste toilet paper, they would shine their shoes with it, plug the toilet with it. It took a long time to convince them that there was almost an endless supply of toilet paper in the world."

Everything was in this toilet-paper anecdote: the humiliation of everyday life for young girls in the institution, the system's ingrained sexism, the power of bureaucratic inertia, the niggardly budget, the staff that actually preferred the power of administering scarcity to the loss of control entailed by abundance. No small victory against such entrenched forces could be considered permanent.

Reform was in the eye of the beholder, anyway. The pattern in social welfare seemed to be for one generation's hard-won program to be attacked for its abuses and dismantled by a later generation—only to resurface again as a promising innovation in the next era of reform.

An earlier reformer, Gloria McFarland, the institution's psychologist in the 1950s and early 1960s, had particularly hated the baby nursery that still existed at the Hudson of the 1950s. It was her task to screen infants born to Hudson inmates for any signs of retardation that would make them unadoptable. In the unit in the Hudson infirmary where they waited for placement in foster care or adoptive homes, babies languished. "Weeks would pass," McFarland would recall. "The babies got marasmus—they were depressed because the girls didn't pay any attention to them."

Marasmus is a wasting-away of the flesh with no organic cause, a failure to thrive in the absence of love that can be as fatal for a baby as meningitis or pneumonia. Examining skinny, listless infants in their cribs, McFarland was haunted by the thought of the overgrown cemetery and the dead babies said to be buried there. She fought to have the nursery closed, and eventually she succeeded.

With the nursery gone, the state stopped committing pregnant girls to Hudson. Then Tunney and Smith arrived and decried the lack of services for Hudson girls who turned up pregnant. Private maternity programs refused to take them, and some were in the streets without prenatal care. So Tunney and Smith created a special unit for them in one of the cottages. But the girls couldn't keep their babies. Eventually, new reformers began to push for the opening of institutional nurseries as a means of rehabilitating young women and preserving families.

At heart, Tunney believed all institutions were harmful. His career had started at a mental hospital in Arizona and included a maximum-security prison in Wisconsin and the girls' reformatory in that state. "One problem is that institutions begin to deal with problems that were not even problems before the child went to the institution," he would explain. "Everybody knows whether your shirttail should be in or out and your hair combed and whether you should swear. Nobody knows how to deal with a girl's sexual promiscuity. So you set up rules around shirttails and swearing and the things you know, and then you start to get children punished for breaking those rules. And you can sit there and see that it isn't doing a damn bit of good."

He could not really defend the practice of isolating children in distress, for example. Staff should hold or stay with a girl in danger of hurting herself, he said, but he had never had enough staff to do that. Still, he kept trying. Tunney had what he called a "Buddhist perspective on things": "In the beginning I felt, 'What I'm doing isn't very important, but it's very important that I do it. Whatever's in front of you, do as well as you can.' In my middle years, I felt, 'What I'm doing is not very important, and it's not very important that I do it, but there's nothing else I can do'—not with a sense of futility, but with the feeling that once in a while you could be helped by one of your clients or patients, and we're in this thing together, and how much I'm learning, understanding, and growing. I despaired of ever trying to make it prettier, but I tried to make myself as pretty as possible."

A month before Shirley Wilder arrived, an internal report by the State Division for Youth had declared Tunney's institution "both obsolescent as a child-caring facility and obsolete as a physical plant." But though its budget had been cut back by a third, the report cautioned, the training school remained one of the biggest employers in Hudson: "To close the school, cancel the payroll and eliminate a large customer of local goods and services would damage the economy of this depressed city, and, for that reason, could be a politically difficult matter to accomplish. This aspect has deterred construction of a replacement training school closer to New York City."

It was an unusually candid admission of how political and economic interests vested in the status quo outweighed changes in professional wisdom about what children needed. There was a special irony in the economic benefit Hudson had reaped for nearly a century from its reformatory for young prostitutes and other sexually misbehaving females: the town had simultaneously cashed in on a flourishing, nationally notorious red-light district. In the earliest days, the town founders had tolerated bawdy houses and grogshops because they catered to the transient sailors and wagon drivers who served the inland port. In the 1920s and 1930s, "Legs" Diamond was one of the bootlegging gangsters whose steamboat patronage boosted Hudson's reputation as a center of vice. The thriving brothels that lined Diamond Street near the deep-water wharves became a valued part of the local economy. A state crackdown in 1950 ended the era of openly organized prostitution, but decades later retired merchants were still regretting its demise.

And in the end Tom Tunney, who had arrived with the dream of closing the training school, joined local businessmen in lobbying to keep it open.

FOUR

I T WAS ONE OF THE FIRST WARM DAYS OF MAY, AND AT THE wheel of her brand-new blue Volkswagen Beetle, Marcia Robinson Lowry was exhilarated.

Less than three months had passed since the New York Civil Liberties Union had hired her to create a children's rights project. Already she was on the verge of launching a class-action lawsuit that would challenge New York City's whole foster-care system as unconstitutional. Now, on this sparkling day in 1973, she and her colleague Risa Dickstein were driving to Hudson to sign up the perfect lead plaintiff.

Among all the Legal Aid clients Lowry had considered as candidates, this child suggested by Carol Sherman stood out. In some records the girl's name appeared as Shirley All rather than Shirley Wilder, and Lowry was reveling in the brave title she could slap on her suit against city, state, and every private foster-care agency in New York: *All* against *Sugarman*.

It was the kind of showy gesture she loved, a defiant flourish to cap her anger. Not that she was particularly angry at Jule Sugarman, the city's well-meaning but ineffectual human-resources commissioner under Mayor John Lindsay. Sugarman, as she saw it, was merely the titular head of a grotesquely dysfunctional system in which private agencies, not government, called the shots. But her anger was real, surging like gas to the throttle every time she remembered kids she had represented and been unable to help.

Pamela was the first. A neglected thirteen-year-old born to a teenager in foster-care, she had been in a fight in Callagy Hall, one of the city's squalid temporary shelters for children, and had been relegated to the still grimmer Manida. Lowry, assigned the case early in her first stint as a lawyer for a poverty program, was sure Pamela could be helped at Hawthorne–Cedar Knolls School, a respected residential treatment program in leafy Westchester County. So she persuaded her troubled "kid client" to accept placement there—only to have the girl be rejected by the agency.

Seasoned family-court practitioners took such rejections for granted; they knew the odds were stacked against black Protestant kids' making it into Hawthorne, which was run by the Jewish Board of Guardians, or into similar programs affiliated with Catholic Charities. But to Lowry, a granddaughter of Jewish immigrants who was fresh from a civil-liberties fellowship at New York University Law School, it came as a revelation and a personal affront.

"I couldn't get her in anyplace, despite over two years of personal involvement," Lowry later told a reporter for the caseworkers' union newspaper. "She wasn't psychotic or brain-damaged, and I knew there were Catholic and Jewish kids with the same problems who were getting good care. It made me sick."

At the time, Lowry was working for Community Action for Legal Services (CALS), part of an effort funded by the federal Office of Economic Opportunity (OEO) to send young lawyers into poor communities to advocate for the powerless. But battling the child welfare system over a two-year period left Lowry feeling powerless herself. The day Pamela, by then fifteen, turned up pregnant and wanting an abortion, Lowry was almost relieved. "I thought, 'Great, I can really help her.' "

Roe v. *Wade* had just legalized abortion. Pamela, kicked out by her mother with only the clothes on her back, had been sleeping on rooftops and was now nearing the end of her second trimester—the margin of what the U.S. Supreme Court decision allowed. Lowry arranged for a necessary sonogram, made an appointment at one of the best private abortion clinics on Manhattan's Upper East Side, and, replacing Pamela's tatters with clothes from her own closet, accompanied her to the abortion clinic. "I wasn't functioning as her lawyer—I was trying to be her savior," she would say later.

Days after the abortion, the teenager showed up in the middle of the night at Lowry's brownstone apartment in Brooklyn's Cobble Hill, brought by a kind taxi driver who had found her wandering through the neighborhood, lost and feverish. She had a massive uterine infection. Lowry took Pamela back to the private clinic and sat in a waiting room full of nervous patients, listening to her screams as she underwent a painful pelvic exam. The doctor was furious: Pamela's infection was the result of her having had sex immediately after the operation. Soon afterward, Pamela disappeared.

"I had a rescue fantasy," Lowry realized. "There was too much already missing that I couldn't address. You underestimate the depth of the problem. You can't intervene for a little while and think that everything will be better."

If personal intervention didn't seem to work, neither did test-case litigation. In New York State Supreme Court, where Lowry filed a series of suits accusing the city of neglecting her child clients, there was no limit on adjournments, and judges passed through on a two-week rotation. Lowry watched an emotionally fragile girl named Francine sink closer to despair each time the city postponed her case: "There were sixteen or seventeen adjournments. I couldn't get the judge to pay any attention. I said, 'If this kid goes into Callagy Hall, something terrible will happen, she won't withstand it.' And sure enough, she tried to kill herself." The only saving grace was the embarrassment of city officials when a reporter for the *New York Post* wrote an article about it.

One day Lowry found herself on the verge of punching out an attorney for the city on the courthouse steps. Confronting each other in front of the majestic facade at 60 Centre Street, they must have seemed unlikely sparring partners, this fierce, strong-featured young woman with long, dark hair that perpetually rebelled against a would-be Joan Baez look, and the balding assistant city corporation counsel, older, skinny, Jewish, who kept saying in placating tones, "You know, I'm not a bad guy." Suddenly Lowry was yelling at him, "Don't come close to me, I'm going to swing at you!" And meaning it.

Not long after that standoff, Barbara Blum, the charismatic new administrator of the city's child welfare services, invited Lowry behind enemy lines. Blum presided over what was then called Special Services for Children, a division of the Human Resources Administration superagency of which Sugarman was chief. Blum had been impressed with Lowry during settlement discussions for one of her CALS lawsuits against the city. They agreed that a key problem was the lack of good city services for troubled teenagers like Lowry's clients. "I need people like you inside government to help me fix it," Blum told her. "You can do more from within."

It was the right pitch at the right time. Lowry knew she was way overextended emotionally: she even dreamed about the kids. Worst of all, she wasn't making a difference. In 1972, Lowry left CALS to become Blum's special assistant for program development.

For a long time Lowry had been telling friends that the city's foster-care scheme was unconstitutional. Surely the city's blind reliance on religious agencies violated the First Amendment's separation of church and state. Surely, in practice, the system trampled black, Protestant children's Fourteenth Amendment guarantees to equal protection and due process. Even on their face, state statutes that required the use of religious agencies to fulfill a public mandate seemed constitutionally indefensible. Her usual companions might debate the particular line of case law she was casting that night, but basically, they would agree. The man in her life then, Carl Weisbrod, had been defending poor parents in family court as a lawyer with Mobilization for Youth (MFY) when Lowry met him at a storefront MFY office; at twenty-seven, still boyish and freckle-faced, he had become a city housing official dealing with homeless families. Her best friend was an MFY social worker.

As Blum's special assistant, Lowry learned firsthand how little power the city actually wielded over the cobbled-together scheme it was financing. The great black migration from the South had drastically changed the demographics of need in New York City; 52.7 percent of the city's twenty-eight thousand wards were black. But the Catholic and Jewish agencies that consumed most of the public dollars available for foster care retained a nineteenth-century mandate to favor their own kind. Only 25 percent of the children in Catholic agencies were black, and only 23 percent of those at Jewish-affiliated agencies. To Lowry, the numbers illustrated a wider wrong: the city had delegated the public good wholesale to a collection of sectarian agencies with a license to discriminate.

Her city job was to jump-start new programs for hard-to-place adolescents. Old hands admired Lowry's rapid success in launching a small group-home program for disturbed teens in conjunction with Bellevue Hospital; she herself thought it took forever to get off the ground. Other projects bogged down in what she considered "endless bullshit meetings"; one program was stillborn when Blum bowed to community opposition over the site. Within a year, Lowry was convinced there was only one way to fix this system: dismantle it. Then the NYCLU's Ira Glasser offered her the chance to do just that.

Glasser, a sports aficionado, was notorious for conducting job interviews on the basketball court, judging the content of a lawyer's character by the nature of his game. "I don't play basketball," Lowry volunteered when she met him, "but I do have bad knees." Glasser loved the line and recognized in Lowry a player who wasn't afraid of high jumps or hard landings.

Glasser himself had more or less stumbled into children's rights after being contacted by students suspended from high school for Vietnam war protests. He became the ACLU architect of the student rights movement and soon led the civil-liberties charge into other enclaves whose inhabitants lacked the protection of the Bill of Rights: mental hospitals, asylums for the retarded, prisons, and juvenile reformatories.

One day a horrified family-court judge came to Glasser to tell the story of Nettie Lollis, a thirteen-year-old PINS girl she'd committed to the state training school. The judge had made a surprise visit upstate and found Nettie Lollis in solitary confinement—because she'd argued with a matron over cosmetics. "My God, I'm sending these kids here!" the guilt-ridden judge exclaimed. When the NYCLU's federal lawsuit for Nettie Lollis was met with outraged cries of confidentiality from the state, Glasser smelled blood. To him closed doors suggested not protection but hidden abuse. He began to think of juvenile rights as suitable terrain for the NYCLU's next special project.

Just then, a report from a family-court committee crossed his desk. It was called "Juvenile Justice Confounded," and it offered a detailed and sweeping indictment of a system where dozens of ground-breaking lawsuits could conceivably take root. The report's author was Judge Justine Wise Polier.

Marcia Lowry had encountered Polier while working for the city, at what she had dreaded as another "bullshit meeting"—a gathering of family-court personnel and city social-services officials to discuss that perennially hot topic, disturbed, aggressive adolescents. Polier came as a shock to Lowry: tough in the details, uncompromising at the core, with a presence that made her seem larger than life. "This is unacceptable," the judge had said, and the phrase reverberated.

The 1972 Polier report read like a road map to potential legal challenges. Its study of 395 cases of children placed by the court was framed by a trenchant discussion of the "right to treatment" concept then developing in case law. It quoted a spate of recent decisions holding that involuntary civil confinement without appropriate treatment could be attacked as cruel and unusual punishment. It documented systemic racial discrimination in child placement and denounced it as "malign neglect." And it warned of a day when due process would require trial judges to release disturbed children into the streets regardless of risk, rather than deprive them of liberty without treatment.

Under New York's Family Court Act, treatment was the legal justification for taking troubled children into custody when they were found delinquent or "in need of supervision." But treatment was being systematically denied to those children who needed it most, the study showed: acting-out adolescents, seriously disturbed children, children with uncooperative families, and black and Puerto Rican children. Polier's report revealed a stark double standard: all but 22 percent of the white children had been accepted by the treatment-rich voluntary agencies, which received as much as $24,000 a year in public funds for each child's care. But 73 percent of the minority children went to public shelters or to state training schools with a median per capita cost of $10,000 and no treatment.

Most novel was the section on voluntary foster-care agencies. The study discovered that private, publicly funded agencies had become increasingly selective since the early 1960s, insisting on higher IQ levels than in the past, demanding younger and easier children with intact families, and altering their policies in other ways that effectively excluded the neediest children—and most of the black and Hispanic ones. The report also described a stunning failure of oversight by the government offices that paid the bills: officials couldn't answer basic questions about agencies' total budgets, staffing, or even the number of children served each year.

When Glasser asked Lowry to direct the new Children's Rights Project, Risa Dickstein was already on board, hired as the project's number-two lawyer before the number one had been selected—a managerial mistake Glasser would never repeat. He was enchanted with Dickstein, he told others: she was bright, she was funny, and she had pizzazz.

No one would describe Marcia Lowry's energy as "pizzazz." Glasser himself likened her to a laser beam. Her headlong purposefulness was tempered a bit by dry, self-deprecating humor and depth of feeling, but it gave short shrift to social niceties. She could be brusque without knowing it, as heedlessly intimidating to junior staff as the huge, good-hearted Doberman she often brought to the office.

Risa Dickstein, in contrast, had the approachability of a woman used to being the cute one in the family; her intensity and political savvy were part of a vivacious personality that telegraphed charm. Where she was acutely tuned to other people's reactions and skilled at playing them to her purpose, Marcia Lowry sometimes seemed almost tone-deaf. Early on, Glasser wrote a memo misspelling her name as "Marsha." Another woman might have let it pass to save her boss embarrassment, in the knowledge that he would catch the mistake himself soon enough. Lowry fired back a memo: "If we're going to work together, you're going to have to spell my name right."

It was as though, having skipped a grade early in childhood, she had coped with an inevitable sense of social awkwardness by dismissing the importance of such things, and never developed an ear for the nuance of human interchange in the politics of everyday life. She was always surprised when others reacted to her with hurt or anger, whether it was to one of her lawsuits or to an unsparingly blunt phrase at a social gathering.

Yet she and Risa seemed to fall into instant friendship. In no time Risa had found Marcia and Carl a new apartment in Greenwich Village, three blocks from where she and her husband, Paul Dickstein, lived. The two women would walk the six blocks to work together, to the NYCLU's offices near Union Square; at lunch, over cartons of congealing take-out and open law books, they would swap nuggets from the cases they were prospecting; often they and their partners reassembled as a foursome for a late dinner or a movie, trading barbed gossip and moral indignation.

DRIVING UP THE TACONIC PARKWAY with the windows open to the smell of a greening world, Marcia Lowry and Risa Dickstein were happy. There was hard work ahead: the legal complaint still had to be written, and conflicts over strategy ironed out between Legal Aid and the NYCLU. But the outcome was not in doubt. "It was the seventies, and we were very young," Risa Dickstein would recall. "We were cocky and we were smart, but we really didn't believe the system wouldn't just say, 'Oh! OK.' Because we had right on our side."

As the little blue car turned up the winding road to the training school, and its stone and iron gate loomed into view, they fell silent. Inside the institution, their high spirits flagged. Like so many juvenile facilities, Hudson looked like a camp from the outside and was unmistakably a prison within.

They met Shirley in the gloomy half-basement rec room of a dilapidated brick building. Dickstein persuaded an official to let them take her for a walk in the sunshine. Shirley figured the staff had warned them against her. "They told Marcia Lowry I was a rebellion child, very angry. I said, 'Won't you go live for two weeks in the BMU, and you'll see why I was that way.' "

To Dickstein, Shirley seemed very excited that two older girls—that was the way she seemed to view them—would come up to see her and listen to her. "Test-case plaintiffs don't realize they're not really your client. They don't realize you can't protect them. She had a lot of complaints about sexual abuse at the facility, and she used a name for it that I was not familiar with at the time: 'the racket.' "

As they walked along the pebbled pathways of the grounds, Shirley told them about trying to escape and getting lost in the swamp. Describing how she had naively waited by the fire for a taxi, she laughed at herself. "She had the most beautiful smile, this smile that lit up her face," Lowry would tell people later. "She was pretty and she was funny. She had this great sense of humor. She said, 'I gotta do my time.' Her expectations were so low."

The two lawyers tried to raise them. "We told her she should be in a program where she could learn and have a normal life and get married and have children and not just be tossed through the system like a number," Dickstein would recall. "We went out of our way to explain to her that she should not be denied a place in a program paid for by the public just because of her religion."

To Risa Dickstein, Shirley seemed the perfect example of a child who could have been salvaged by a more equitable system. "She was so open-eyed and so glistening. She was like those poster kids in the United Colors of Benetton. She wouldn't have needed that much—a foster home, even a group home. The thing was, she was so lost.

"We went up there in a spirit of great lightheartedness and left very depressed."

But in Lowry's briefcase, scrawled on a piece of memo paper and signed in a back-slanting, childish hand, was the consent needed to launch the lawsuit. Because Shirley had insisted on using her own last name, not her father's, it would be known as *Wilder*.

TWICE MORE THAT SPRING Shirley Wilder tried to flee. Once, after a week in solitary for fighting with an older girl, she made it out, reached a main road, and managed to thumb her way home. But her father turned her in and had her sent back to Hudson.

Alone in the empty room where she was confined in punishment, she broke the window with her fist and carved her own flesh with broken glass. It was as though by inflicting pain on her body from the outside she could stop the pressure of the growing pain within, as though the swell of loneliness would seep out of her like blood.

FIVE

F OR MARCIA LOWRY, THE *WILDER* LAWSUIT MARKED THE CON-
vergence of historical forces that had crisscrossed her life from
childhood.

Born Marcia Robinson in 1941, she was the grandchild of a Jewish
housepainter from eastern Europe who identified with the socialism of
labor leader Eugene Debs rather than the noblesse oblige of Rabbi Stephen
Wise. For years, Lowry kept a tattered poster quoting Debs on the wall of
her legal office, amid yellowing children's drawings: *While there is a lower
class / I am in it, / While there is a criminal element / I am of it / and / while there is a
soul in prison / I am not free.*

Her father, Arthur, had dropped out of school during the Depression
and moved his young family from Brooklyn to Miami, where he joined his
widowed father-in-law as a tailor. Growing up in the South in such a family, Marcia knew at an early age that segregation was wrong. Not long
after she had learned to read the signs on Miami buses ordering Colored
Seat from the Rear, her father's sister Miriam, visiting from New York,
took Marcia, Marcia's younger sister, and her own small daughter on a
bus trip; she chose seats in the back. "This very properly attired woman
came up to my aunt when we got off to transfer," Lowry would recall.
"She told her, 'You must be from the North. We're very fortunate in this
part of the country. We can separate ourselves from the coloreds.' And
there on this street corner in Miami, with three kids listening openmouthed, my aunt held her responsible for the whole history of segregation in the South." After the woman marched off in a huff, Aunt Miriam
told the children it was important to do what she had done: "You must
confront this kind of thing. You cannot let it pass."

The lesson stuck, despite parents who wondered why Marcia always had to be the troublemaker. As editor of the student newspaper at all-white Miami Senior High School, where Jewish girls weren't allowed to join service clubs or be cheerleaders, she wrote about discrimination and campaigned for joint sports programs with black high schools. At the end of her senior year, the paper's faculty adviser, upset at the dissension such coverage had caused, told Marcia she would never let another Jew be editor of the paper. Lowry had adored the woman, who had helped her win a journalism scholarship to Northwestern University's summer school after her junior year. Anti-Semitism wasn't new to Marcia—she had been called a kike by neighbors as a child, and at Northwestern, where she had won the summer program's top award, the dean of admissions had informed her coldly of the school's 7 percent Jewish quota—but this was different. This hurt. And it underlined what she had believed as a child: "It was Us against Them, and Us was the Jews and Them was everybody else."

At Northwestern, where she was admitted to the journalism school on scholarship, Marcia felt no kinship with the Jewish minority, however. She was a misfit on the conservative rich kids' campus, so alienated by the superficial chitchat at a Jewish sorority party, and so hating the "idea of sorting yourself out by groups," that she dropped out of rush. "The dean of women called me and said, 'You're going to ruin your life.'"

She spent her junior year at the London School of Economics and returned to Evanston with an impatience to graduate to the real world. In the early spring of 1962, when a handsome young Freedom Rider came through on a fund-raising speaking tour, her image as a rebel made her the obvious choice to be his campus guide.

John Lowry was one of the young northern whites who had answered CORE's call for volunteers to ride with blacks on the segregated interstate bus lines of the Deep South, braving mob violence and Mississippi jails. The only white man in a group that went on to Monroe, North Carolina, to picket the courthouse at the invitation of a local black radical, he ended up in the midst of a small riot and was charged with kidnaping.

"When I met him, he was out on bail," Marcia would say when she told the story. "Oh, he was so handsome! He was very intense. He was from New York. And he cared passionately about this stuff. He just dazzled me." Four days later she called her parents and announced her engagement to an indicted felon. The wedding was held in a Miami synagogue that summer. They were both twenty-one.

John Lowry's mother had died when he was small, and for a couple of years he and his brother had been in foster care through the Jewish Child Care Association. Their father, a hotel manager, eventually took them back, but he died, too, when John was eighteen. When Marcia married John, his foster-care past seemed to her just part of the romance of his different background. He was Jewish, too—though her mother never quite believed that—but exotic in every other way.

He hadn't finished college when they married. Tall, dark, lean, and handsome, he worked days as a model and took night courses at Queens College. Marcia held a series of jobs writing public-relations copy; she had worked as a reporter for the *Miami Herald* every summer throughout college, but it was hard for a woman to get a good journalism job in New York in the early 1960s. With growing anxiety, the couple waited for John's case to come to trial as the civil-rights movement surged on— through "Bull" Connor's police dogs and fire hoses, through Alabama governor George Wallace's unsuccessful "stand in the schoolhouse door," through the fatal shooting of Medgar Evers in Jackson, Mississippi, and the deaths of four little girls in the bombing of a Baptist church in Birmingham.

One night at a party they met Andy Goodman, a twenty-one-year-old fellow student at Queens College. They talked about Mississippi and its legendary state prison farm at Parchman, where John Lowry and other arrested Freedom Riders had been transferred in the dead of night, fearing for their lives and singing freedom songs: "*O-o-h, freedom, o-o-o-o-h, free-dom, before I'd be a slave, I'd be buried in my grave. . . .*" Goodman wanted to hear John's experiences because he was heading to Mississippi himself for the Freedom Summer of 1964. He was to die there, executed in the night by Klansmen on a lonely road along with twenty-one-year-old James Chaney, a black CORE volunteer, and twenty-four-year-old Michael Schwerner, a white social worker from New York. Before their bodies were discovered under an earthen dam on a farm near Philadelphia, Mississippi, John Lowry was summoned to stand trial.

THE CHAOTIC EVENTS underlying Lowry's indictment two and a half years earlier had inflamed the town of Monroe, North Carolina, a Ku Klux Klan stronghold about thirty miles southeast of Charlotte. Robert

F. Williams, a local militant known for a publication he called *Negroes with Guns,* had invited the Freedom Riders to town on their release from Parchman Prison in August 1961. John Lowry was one of sixteen Freedom Riders who answered Williams's invitation and joined local blacks in walking a peaceful picket line outside the county courthouse. They were sprayed with insecticide, pelted with Coca-Cola bottles, and shot at from passing cars during a week of mounting tension. Finally, on the afternoon of Sunday, August 27, 1961, a crowd of white men charged the picketers, and John Lowry, the only white demonstrator, was one of the few not beaten and jailed in the ensuing melee. He ran to the black part of town, where he found a crowd fearful of Klan attack surrounding the car of a rural white couple. Some in the crowd ordered the couple out of their car, and Lowry drove the Ford sedan the few feet from the middle of the street to the curb. Then he left, returning to the house where he was lodging. He was not present for the event's escalation: the white couple were taken into Williams's house and tied up, and a call was made to the sheriff demanding the release of the jailed demonstrators in exchange for the pair. A few hours later, the husband and wife were untied and sent home, and Williams fled to Cuba with his family. John Lowry was among four others charged with kidnaping.

The trial unfolded in a surreal atmosphere. The courthouse, topped with a giant neon cross, was packed with white men in overalls, and the town square seemed to glint with gun barrels. Dick Scupi, a young CORE lawyer, had gone down a week ahead of the others to file motions challenging the racially segregated jury pool; the locals who had been spitting in his soup and pouring ketchup on his head at the nearby diner were by now spoiling for better sport. Celebrated trial attorney William Kunstler gave the Lowrys little comfort. He spread out the manuscript of his next book on the defense table and became absorbed in his own words while witnesses testified; when the time came for cross-examination, he would turn to Scupi and inquire, "What should I ask the guy?" The defense contingent had been staying at the home of a local black doctor, whose closet safe held the bail money collected in anticipation of Lowry's inevitable conviction. But shortly before the verdict was due, men with guns came to the house and seized the cash.

The jury was out. The banks were closed. John Lowry was afraid he was going to be beaten up in jail, and so was Marcia. When the verdict came back guilty, Bill Kunstler asked for current bail to be continued, but the court refused. Marcia Lowry started to cry.

As her husband was marched to the back in handcuffs, she ran after him, and he cried out, "Get me out of here, get me bail!"

Years later, she could not tell the story without choking up again, back in the skin of her twenty-three-year-old self.

"I started to lose it. The courtroom was packed, and everybody was staring at me. And Berta Green, this wonderful motherly woman from New York who had helped raise money for the case, ran up to me and said, 'Don't give them the satisfaction, don't let them see this.' And that was enough, I got it under control. I called my parents, and they made bail. They borrowed the money, I don't know how."

THERE HAD NEVER BEEN much money in the family, even after her father earned an accounting degree at night and quit tailoring, which he hated. Her parents had originally moved to Miami to help raise her mother's little sister, who was fourteen when their mother died. Marcia's parents were both children of eastern European Jews, immigrants from parts of Russia, Poland, and Romania with shifting political borders and steady persecution. Her father's family put more faith in the Workman's Circle than in the synagogue; her mother's family was Orthodox, and her mother persisted in keeping kosher.

Marcia Lowry would speak of herself as a "difficult child to raise." Like many women in her generation, growing up, she rejected her mother. ("God, what a miserable person I was to her! As my mother said, the happiest day of her life was the day I went to college.") Only later did she come to realize how much there was in her mother to admire. But even when she and her parents railed at each other, she knew she could count on their support—whether it was the four thousand dollars' bail for her husband or a loan for law-school tuition when she left journalism. "I always knew I could pick up the phone in the middle of the night," she said, "and they would always be there."

Perhaps that was why it wrenched her so to see John Lowry stand alone and frightened in a courtroom, with no one but herself to be his family, and the overwhelming sense that she had failed him.

Eventually his conviction was overturned on appeal—thanks to the racially based jury exclusions Scupi had documented—but by then John Lowry's life had been permanently constricted. "He was a convicted felon—he couldn't get a good job," Marcia would explain. "He tried to make it as a model; my aunt got him a job as a bank teller . . . the FBI had a tap on our phone." After the trial John Lowry's political passion seemed spent, while Marcia's would be stoked at every turn.

Working on the women's section of the *Long Island Press,* a mediocre evening paper of declining circulation, she noticed that women journalists doing the same type of work as men had a separate job classification and lower salary, and in 1966 she led a proto-feminist revolt. The Newspaper Guild promised to support the protest, and she rallied female colleagues in her apartment with her favorite record, the Almanac Singers belting out such union classics as "Which Side Are You On?" Then the managing editor called her in and offered to make her an editor if she would shut up about the others. When she demurred, he transferred her to the city desk with no assignment, in effect consigning her to answer phones.

The paper's managers were bad people out to break the union, she declared, in an echo of her grandfather, the Socialist housepainter who spoke in vehement Yiddish of the days when strikers were shot dead in the streets. But the head of the guild had lost interest. "You're not going to win this fight," he told her. "I'll get a settlement for you. You should leave." She gave up on journalism and enrolled in the last entering night-school class of NYU Law School.

It was the beginning of the end of her marriage. Her life and John's diverged too much when she went to law school. They had simply married too young. By 1969, she was divorced and living on her own with a Doberman named Duke and an aging English Scottie, on a seedy Upper West Side block where she had to sprint to keep ahead of the muggers.

ASSEMBLING A CAST OF PLAINTIFFS for her lawsuit was harder than Marcia Lowry anticipated. At least 90 percent of children brought to family court were represented by the Legal Aid Society under its contract with the state. Legal Aid and the NYCLU were supposedly natural allies, but from the start Lowry found the attorney in charge of Legal Aid's juvenile-rights division, Charles Schinitsky, maddeningly reluctant to give her access to "his" kids for use in her lawsuit. At first she thought it was all a question of turf. Schinitsky had established a juvenile right to counsel in New York five years before the 1967 U.S. Supreme Court ruling In re *Gault* extended to children most of the same constitutional due-process rights guaranteed to adults. Lowry wasn't the only outsider to complain that Schinitsky sometimes acted as though he held a patent on children's issues. Later, Lowry suspected that Schinitsky might have understood right away what she failed to see herself: this particular lawsuit threatened to ignite a political explosion in his own backyard.

The Legal Aid Society was the country's oldest and largest legal-services organization. It had been founded in 1876 as Der Deutsche-Rechtsschutz Verein, under the auspices of the German Society, by a group of public-spirited merchants and lawyers eager to provide legal assistance to impoverished immigrants. Most of the legal matters handled by the society in its earliest days were civil cases—property disputes, landlord-tenant conflicts, consumer and credit problems, and family-law controversies. The founders' purpose was not only to help the poor, but "to deflect them from anarchy, socialism, and bolshevism." Vice President Theodore Roosevelt embraced the legal-aid movement as a "necessary bulwark against 'chaos' and 'violent revolution'" such as France had experienced in the Commune.

Legal Aid was weighed down by a century-long tradition of noblesse oblige, a blue-chip board, and a daily role in the system. Its day-to-day work in the trenches was both a strength and a weakness. At best, it kept the society's systemic litigation timely and relevant to the real problems of poor people. At worst, it made the society's lawyers reluctant accomplices in an unjust system, less willing to strike out for bold and sweeping change.

"Legal Aid was afraid to sue the charitable institutions," Martin Guggenheim, who was head of special litigation for Legal Aid at the time, would assert later. "That wasn't its history; it attacked the state, not the private sector. It's a tricky matter, because the Legal Aid board was made up of the same people who ran these agencies. Conflict was written all over this case from the very beginning."

But Guggenheim welcomed Lowry's project with enthusiasm, and he interceded for her with Schinitsky: "To me, anybody who was going to change things was a friend, period, and we should cooperate. Those were heady days. We were winning left and right. And I saw this case as an impressive effort, because it was bigger than what Legal Aid was trying to do. It was a step above the focus Schinitsky had. I said, 'I'll do whatever I can to help.' And Marcia said, 'Do you have any clients?' "

He had Tommy Edwards, a boy whose fate evoked his lasting fury. "The fucking system put him in a mental hospital because they couldn't find a bed. They absolutely would have found a place for him if he'd been a nice Jewish boy. Tommy Edwards was a young boy getting old very quickly by juvenile-court standards, lurking between fourteen and sixteen. There was no foster home for him, no Pleasantville kind of place where I placed my white clients." Pleasantville was a cottage-plan residential treatment center run by the Jewish Child Care Association in Westchester County, and one of a dozen agencies that rejected Tommy.

"He ended up at the Kings County Hospital mental ward. When I went there, I was just shaking in my boots at what this young kid was being exposed to—older men, mental illness. This was not a mentally ill kid at all. The system could do nothing for him but fuck him up. In my own mind he was a victim of racial and religious discrimination."

Tommy Edwards's history reflected how porous were the family-court categories "neglected," "dependent," "PINS," and "delinquent," and how new traumas inflicted on already damaged children could become the basis for denying them better care. Tommy came to the attention of the city at thirteen, after he was accused of a purse snatching. Investigating his home, caseworkers discovered an apartment without food, pervaded by urine and filth. The delinquency petition was withdrawn, and he was sent to Jennings Hall, a crowded, understaffed city shelter notorious as a place where weaker children were robbed and abused by bigger ones. In short order Tommy was raped by an older youth there. Evaluated as a mildly retarded boy who did well in school but needed therapy, he was briefly accepted to fill a vacancy at Lincoln Hall, a Catholic residential treatment center upstate. But the agency sent him back to Jennings Hall within ten days, supposedly because he had discussed running away and was suspected of having sickle-cell anemia. Like Lowry, Guggenheim was convinced that the agency would not have rejected Tommy after such a short time or on such grounds had he been white or Catholic.

Finally Tommy grew so desperate at the Jennings shelter that he tried to jump from its roof, and was sent to the mental ward of Kings County

Hospital. That began a new cycle of shuttling between mental hospitals, where doctors said he didn't belong, and Jennings, the predatory place he feared most.

Lowry felt Tommy Edwards's story had the most pathos. But Shirley's offered the best documented history of rejection by voluntary agencies, and a transcript ringing with Judge Polier's condemnation of the whole system. Shirley would be the lead plaintiff. Carol Sherman would continue to represent the child in family court. Later Sherman would serve as co-counsel on behalf of Legal Aid in the lawsuit as a whole. Besides Shirley and Tommy, Lowry chose four more plaintiffs, all black.

Lowry and Dickstein drafted their complaint in Bermuda during an off-season weekend getaway in late May 1973, brushing beach sand from the papers. Day's end would find them cutting and pasting on the floor of the rooms in their cheap pink hotel.

WHEN LOWRY FILED the complaint in federal court on the afternoon of June 14, 1973, it was a sweeping document that named as defendants six state and city officials and seventy-seven voluntary agencies and their directors. It asked the court to declare unconstitutional the entire statutory basis for the provision of child welfare services to New York City children.

The suit charged that the legal scaffolding created by the New York state constitution, New York statutes, and the administration of these laws was in violation of the First Amendment separation of church and state. The structure itself resulted in a child-care system permeated by religious and racial discrimination, in violation of the Fourteenth Amendment's guarantee of equal protection. It was a system in which those children most in need of care were denied adequate services and instead were sent to institutions where they were subjected to cruel and unusual punishment, in violation of the Eighth Amendment.

About 85 percent of the twenty-eight thousand children then in care outside their homes were placed in residences run by the so-called voluntary child-care agencies, most organized along religious lines and all privately operated but largely publicly funded, the suit said. It contended that public funding of sectarian agencies that excluded children of other faiths or gave preference to children of their own faith was in violation of the First Amendment's proscription against laws either establishing religion or prohibiting the free exercise of religion.

The cases of the six plaintiffs put flesh on the damning statistics. Of all children in care, the suit said, 52 percent were black. But in Jewish agencies, only 23 percent were black; in Catholic agencies, only 25 percent; by contrast, in Protestant agencies, 86 percent, and in city-operated shelters, 84 percent. The suit asked the court to enjoin the government from funding voluntary child-care agencies that discriminated on the basis of religion and/or race; to prohibit government agencies from referring children for placement on the basis of religion and/or race; and to ban the placement of children in "injuriously inadequate programs" and "injuriously inappropriate institutions," such as New York's state training schools, following their rejection by voluntary agencies for constitutionally unacceptable reasons.

The suit asked for unspecified money damages for the six named plaintiffs; the class they claimed to represent was defined in the lawsuit as more than ten thousand children who were not white, not Jewish or Catholic, and were in need of foster-care services.

In effect, the class-action lawsuit demanded nothing less than the wholesale replacement of a set of political, religious, and social arrangements that had been in place for a hundred years.

THERE WAS PANDEMONIUM when the papers were served on June 29 at the offices of the city's Special Services for Children, where only months before Lowry had enjoyed the privilege of an office down the hall from Barbara Blum. Outrage, fear, and a deep sense of betrayal overwhelmed general agreement with the substance of the suit.

Alarm focused first on the money damages demanded of the named defendants. All were being sued not only in their official capacities but "as individuals." Lowry had used that tactic merely as a legal device to assure the right to take depositions from the named officials, but no one in Special Services knew that. The list named eighty-four individual defendants starting with Sugarman and Blum, and included twenty-four nuns, two rabbis, and five other clergymen. As they were served, they telephoned Joseph Gavrin, director of COVCCA, the Council of Voluntary Child Caring Agencies, the umbrella group for all the private organizations.

Gavrin came running to Blum's office in high dudgeon. He had been barraged with calls from people frightened of losing their homes and savings.

"It scared everybody, that nonsense that people would be personally liable," Karin Ericksen Perez, an assistant to Blum, would remember later. "These were not wealthy people. It was like a cheap shot."

Barbara Blum herself was no career bureaucrat but rather an outsider who had discovered the inadequacies of children's services as the mother of an autistic son and as a citizen activist. She had accepted Mayor John Lindsay's invitation to head the city's child welfare system in 1971 after a series of scandals, with the explicit mission of improving services for the "hard-to-place" children packed in New York City's juvenile shelters. Used to inspiring unusual devotion and loyalty from her staff, she now felt personally betrayed by the young lawyer she had taken behind the scenes as her protégé.

Many members of Blum's staff felt the same way. They saw the lawsuit as Lowry's bid for personal glory and profoundly resented the way it ran roughshod over Blum's efforts. The depths of defensiveness and anger that *Wilder* stirred in those first days became an intensely personalized, longlasting grudge against Marcia Lowry, held by many in city government who had once considered her an ally.

In the agencies, the sense of outrage was no less personal. People who saw themselves as good, generous, and dedicated to the unfortunate felt as though Lowry had publicly proclaimed them the venal Bull Connors of the child welfare system. The nonsectarian and Protestant agencies, even those with a nearly all black clientèle, were also on the roster of defendants. From Lowry's standpoint, the racial breakdown merely underlined the system's de facto segregation. Her legal position was that any participant in such a system was aiding and abetting discrimination. Her personal view was that most directors at these agencies wouldn't publicly break ranks with their colleagues in the more powerful sectarian organizations unless they felt the heat themselves.

Board members were bewildered. As news of the lawsuit spread, waves of indignant phone calls also poured in to Gerald Bodell, a lawyer who represented a variety of Catholic and Jewish agencies as well as some old-line institutions with timeworn Protestant origins. The executive director of Greer, A Children's Community, a cottage-plan child-care agency sited in the wealthy environs of Millbank, New York, couldn't get over his astonishment.

"His board of directors," Bodell would recall, "were very shocked that they were charged with deliberate discrimination. A lot of these people give their time and think they're doing a wonderful thing taking care of these children. They said, 'We'll fight it tooth and nail.' "

Bodell's Catholic clients saw the lawsuit as an attack on their very existence, part of a vicious ACLU effort to secularize all the agencies. Within his Jewish client agencies, the sense of grievance was all the more intense because directors and trustees could point to the support they had given the fledgling ACLU back in the 1930s, and because Lowry, Dickstein, and Glasser were Jews. The NYCLU's Children's Rights Project itself had been launched with "Jewish money"—grants from foundations associated with such wealthy and liberal Jewish families as the Buttenwiesers, the Loebs, and the Guggenheims. David Roth, then associate director of the JCCA (Jewish Child Care Association), described a sense of hurt that revived turn-of-the-century resentments between assimilated German Jews and the observant Russian Jewish immigrants whom they were overly eager to Americanize. He added, "Many of us felt wounded and upset that Marcia Lowry was just given free rein, money on a continuous basis, to really attack the sectarian nature of child care."

Risa Dickstein, who had grown up in an Orthodox Jewish family, was pressured by her rabbi and her parents not to sue the Jewish agencies. Charitable Jews had to protect each other first, they told her: "If we don't, no one will." Even within more secular circles of the Jewish charitable establishment, many were appalled by the lawsuit. "I have spoken to a number of attorneys who have read the brief and they are in agreement that it is a good brief and might quite possibly lead to a verdict for the plaintiffs," Leonard Block, a top official with the Federation of Jewish Philanthropies and a member of the state Board of Social Welfare, wrote to the Children's Defense Fund that summer. "I can imagine nothing more harmful to the children in foster care than to have this occur. . . . To force the other institutions into a 70 to 80 percent nonwhite position would radically change the character of the institutions, and to the extent that the additional children were more severely disturbed, would completely change the program, and most probably the value of the institutions, and quite possibly [their] motivation and inner drive. We also run the risk, which is quite substantial, of loss of the private support which has been important not only in the financing but also in the character, drive and thrust of the institution."

The federation was particularly vulnerable to the lawsuit's line of attack. The basis of its fund-raising appeals was that it financed services for Jews. If the *Wilder* plaintiffs succeeded in ruling out agency preference for Jewish children, the impact on donations could be disastrous. In fact, the number of Jewish children in residential foster care was very small by this time, only a sliver of the need that had driven the creation of such programs near the turn of the century, when impoverished Jewish immigrants filled the Lower East Side. As the percentage of non-Jewish children at Hawthorne, Pleasantville, and other Jewish-sponsored institutions rose, board members and donors began to ask, "Why, since we're a Jewish agency, should we be doing this?" The most pragmatic answer was that while the federation's contributions were tiny in comparison to public funding for these agencies, the federation got considerable fund-raising mileage out of listing Jewish child-care services among its beneficiaries. A trial that publicized how few Jewish children actually benefited from federation subsidies would be undesirable even if the plaintiffs lost.

Worse, federation executives believed, the legal principle that could be established by the case if the plaintiffs won threatened a much larger and more costly part of the federation's government-subsidized activities: nursing homes for the Jewish elderly. This view shaped the decision to oppose the lawsuit vigorously not only by hiring a law firm for Jewish defendant agencies but also by entering the fray with an amicus brief in strong opposition.

Controversy over *Wilder* erupted at a divisive board meeting of the Legal Aid Society that summer. Several board members who also served on the boards of defendant agencies were upset that Legal Aid had joined the Civil Liberties Union in bringing the lawsuit without first consulting the board. Other board members retorted that achieving consensus on such a lawsuit was not the board's proper function, and raised the embarrassing specter of conflict of interest. One member, Leonard Sand, was caught in a particularly awkward position: he and his law firm had been asked to represent both the Jewish Federation and its member agencies in *Wilder*. He put the question to the meeting: Could he, a board member for one of the plaintiffs, represent defendants? The answer was yes— another sign, perhaps, that the power structure *Wilder* challenged was more far-reaching and entrenched than Lowry understood at the time.

Not until August 2, the day of the first court appearance in the case, did Lowry and Dickstein finally grasp the magnitude of what they had taken on. Every agency director, every trustee, every social-service specialist from city and state—each with at least one lawyer, it seemed—packed one of the largest courtrooms in the U.S. Courthouse, Southern District of New York. Ruddy, silver-haired partners from the city's most prominent law firms watched over flocks of pale-faced nuns. In-house lawyers whispered to outside counsel over the balding heads of prominent donors. Envoys from the attorney general's office jostled delegates from the city corporation counsel, and Barbara Blum disciples squeezed in beside rabbis and Episcopal priests. The clamor of their voices surged through the courtroom like a roaring sea.

At the plaintiffs' table, the two women sat alone.

The courtroom scene became an indelible memory, a war story to tell younger colleagues in later years: the two of them all by themselves, the growing throng of lawyers, clergy, and public officials on the other side, and the feeling that suddenly gripped them both: Oh my God, what have we done?

SIX

JUSTINE WISE POLIER WAS DELIGHTED AT WHAT MARCIA Lowry had done. *Wilder,* filed half a year after Polier's official retirement, seemed no less than a validation of her thirty-eight-year struggle against religious and racial discrimination in child welfare, and a redemption of her failures.

From the very beginning of her career as a judge, she considered the system's sectarian structure the overriding obstacle to meeting children's needs. She was still Justine Wise Tulin when Mayor Fiorello La Guardia appointed her in 1935 to what was then called Domestic Relations Court. A young widow with a small son, she was confronted daily during the Depression by the desperation of single mothers who lacked the money, parental support, and education that had seen her through the illness of her husband, Yale Law School professor Leo Tulin, and the aftermath of his death from leukemia in 1932.

"How was your first week on the bench?" her father asked in a letter from Europe, where he had been working on behalf of refugees from Hitler and Jewish settlers in Palestine on the day of his daughter's judicial investiture. "Another saddening job for you. This time you are going to be up against the 'religious interests' and their tenth rate representatives."

He had been right, as usual. One of the first legal documents presented to guide her as a new judge was the New York City Welfare Department's version of a state charities law, requiring placement of children "under the control of persons of the same religious faith when practicable." Any deviation from strict religious allocation was to be explained by the presiding judge in the minutes of the court hearing. Polier quickly learned that the city accorded the three "established" religions a virtual property right to children, regardless of what was best for them or what their own parents wanted.

She would remember some of those children all her life. There was Anne, whose Catholic mother had chosen to place her in a nonsectarian agency, paying for her care while she worked. When the mother lost her job, she sought aid from the Welfare Department to keep Anne where she had placed her, explaining that the girl was doing well and that she didn't want her uprooted and moved to a Catholic institution. But a city welfare official reprimanded Polier for approving the placement and submitted the case to Catholic Charities under an unwritten agreement to clear all placements "out of religion." When the judge refused to change her decision, the city held up reimbursement to the nonsectarian agency for all the children in its care, including Anne. "It was never clear whether the City's punitive action was intended to punish the mother, to warn me against such action in the future, or to deter nonsectarian agencies from accepting non-Protestant children," Polier wrote decades later.

What she called her "first baptism by religious fire" came in 1936, when four neglected children of a mixed marriage were brought before her for placement. The Catholic mother and Muslim father had been married by a Protestant minister. "During one of their many quarrels," Polier wrote later, "the mother had the oldest boy baptized in the Catholic Church without the knowledge of the father. When a daughter was born, the father retaliated by having her initiated into Islam against the mother's wishes. Having thus punished each other, neither parent had done anything about the religion of the next two children. None of the four children had received any religious education. The case was brought by Catholic and Protestant institutions to whom the children had been allocated [after their mother fell ill]. Religious baptism became the central issue."

The oldest boy, a tall and swarthy fifteen-year-old, had run away three times from the Catholic institution, insisting he wanted to be a Muslim like his father. The thirteen-year-old girl, blond and blue-eyed like her mother, said she feared her father and wanted to be Catholic. Because of the father's violent objections to a Catholic placement, the three younger children were in a Protestant institution, but the father was threatening to blow up the church to which they were being sent. After a full investigation, Polier came to a Solomonic decision. The older boy would be placed, as he wished, with a caring paternal uncle who was Muslim. The three younger children would be kept together and placed in a Protestant foster home where they were to receive no religious instruction. The mother would be permitted to take her older daughter with her to the Catholic church, while the father could take the younger children to Muslim services.

The judge wrote a detailed opinion, In re *Vardinakis,* holding that infant baptism did not make a child the property of any church, and that no interests were entitled to consideration except those of parents and children. The outraged response was captured by a sensational headline in the *Brooklyn Tablet,* a tabloid published by the Brooklyn Diocese: DAUGHTER OF RABBI WISE GIVES CHILD OF CHRIST TO THE BLACK BEARDED PROPHET OF MOHAMMED. Later a Catholic judge telephoned Polier at home to say that Patrick Cardinal Hayes was deeply troubled by her decision.

Few judges were willing to challenge a sectarian system so embedded in the city's ethnic power arrangements. It was an era when even probation officers were assigned according to religion and expected to insist on religious observance by their juvenile charges. One of Polier's colleagues declared at a judicial meeting that no judge who did not accept the divinity of Christ was fit to preside over the case of a Catholic child. Other judges at the meeting disagreed, but to Polier this view, antithetical as it was to the First Amendment's separation of church and state, flowed almost logically from the vested parochialism of the city's child welfare policies.

Nothing could have been more discordant with Polier's own religious upbringing, by a mother who had flirted with the secularism of Felix Adler's Ethical Culture Society and a father who preached an ecumenical social gospel rooted in the idea of a common public good. Rabbi Wise had turned down the pulpit of Temple Emanuel, the most prestigious synagogue in the city, rather than agree to submit his sermons to the censorship of its board of trustees. He had attacked the city's machine politics and patronage as corrupt, helping to oust "Gentleman Jimmy" Walker from the mayoralty and preparing the way for La Guardia's reformist administration. Although Wise became the nation's foremost voice of Zionism in the thirties and forties, before the rise of Hitler he was more likely to be found preaching against the Ku Klux Klan in Topeka, Kansas, or rallying strikers in Passaic, New Jersey, than advancing anything so narrowly definable as "Jewish interests."

"I have tried to repay my debt to America in part," Wise wrote to his son in 1925, on the fiftieth anniversary of his arrival from Hungary as a sixteen-month-old. "Anything you and Justine will in the future do is to be a further installment of my indebtedness to America." More than Judaism, her parents had transmitted an allegiance to their ideal of America—inclusive, just, tolerant, and transcendent of all differences—and more than any religious ritual, they had inculcated a duty to try to make that America real. "You and I were born and wedded to protest unfairness," Rabbi Wise once wrote to his wife, Louise Waterman Wise. They expected no less from their children.

Racial injustice was the original and abiding sin that blighted that vision of America, and combating it was practically a sacred trust that linked Justine's generation with the nineteenth-century heroes of abolition, woman suffrage, and social reform. The connection was not just intellectual: her father had been a cofounder of the NAACP in 1909 and of the American Civil Liberties Union in 1920. To her, there could be no greater indictment of the sectarian spoils system that she encountered in child welfare than its routine exclusion of children of color. Her own compliance with the unjust treatment "imposed by law, tradition and institutional practices" became the nightmare of her job as a judge, "lightened only by the rescue of a few children and by efforts (after court hours) to help change systems that treated black children as inferior."

The black population of New York City had doubled between 1920 and 1930, to more than 5 percent. The Depression further spurred migration of large black families from the impoverished South, where sharecropping was a kind of starvation-level serfdom. The newcomers were submerged in the misery of the city's worst slums. "To an even greater degree than the poorest white citizens," Polier wrote in 1941, "they and their children were thus exposed to the crowding, dirt, sub-standard housing, disease and criminality that abound in the worst areas of large cities. In addition they were subjected to high rentals, limited job opportunities and various other forms of segregation from which there was no escape. They entered a complex industrial society for which they were poorly equipped, where their labor was exploited, where few of their own race were in a position to aid them, and where all too few members of the white race were concerned with what befell them."

The black rate of infant mortality was sixty per thousand, almost double the white rate; maternal mortality was triple that of whites, and the rate of death from tuberculosis five times greater. Between 1927 and 1939, as the number of white children annually brought before the children's court declined more than 31 percent, the number of black children rose by 147 percent. But the established charities, organized around white ethnic poverty for more than a century, added few if any services for black children. The little they did do was steeped in unselfconscious racism, like the grudging agreement by one sectarian agency to accept a small black child for foster-home placement, "but only on the condition that the mother, of darker complexion, would not visit the child who would 'pass.' " When Polier refused to agree to such a condition for care, agency representatives were outraged.

The stunted public sector, long forbidden by statute to compete with the institutional offerings of the religious agencies, provided only temporary shelters—the "black holes" of the system, Polier called them—and reformatories for delinquents. Although one thousand dependent children had been placed in foster homes by the New York City Welfare Department before World War I, that program was shut down under political pressure after sectarian groups attacked it as an invasion of their domain. In 1939, twenty-three of twenty-seven Protestant agencies took only white children. The few private agencies that did accept black children repeatedly suspended their intake because they were full. In practical terms, this meant that needy black children often had to be labeled juvenile criminals to qualify for any out-of-home placement. Shirley Wilder was only one among many children sent to state reformatories over the years for lack of alternatives.

"In 1936, when a ten-year-old boy ran away from a miserable home situation to sleep on rooftops and beg food for survival, he was charged with juvenile delinquency," Polier recalled fifty years later. "Probation advised that the Juvenile Court could do nothing for him until he committed a felony or became twelve and could be sent to the State School for delinquents. I took twenty such cases to Mayor La Guardia. Shocked by the exclusion of young, black children from care, the Mayor called the Episcopal Bishop of New York, who turned for help to the Protestant

Episcopal Mission Society. They agreed to set up a summer camp for black youngsters."

Polier, eager to keep the place open all year long, enlisted the help of philanthropic foundations to replace the broken-down furnace and furnish other improvements. It became the Wiltwyck School for Boys, the first agency in the East to accept neglected and delinquent black boys between the ages of eight and twelve without regard to religion. But how marginal such an enterprise remained to any recognized Protestant goal became clear in 1942, when the Mission Society decided to abandon its role at Wiltwyck to concentrate on preparing chaplains for the armed services. Only a drive by Polier, support from Eleanor Roosevelt, a loan by black singer Marian Anderson, and a new interracial, nondenominational board saved one of the city's only residential resources for neglected black children.

In 1940, the New York Archdiocese had redistributed black Catholic children cared for in two segregated institutions to the twenty-three Catholic agencies that previously had accepted only white children. Since most blacks were Protestants, and there were almost no black Jews, the directors of Catholic and Jewish agencies could smugly stand back and fault the Protestants for not taking care of their own. In fact, the old-line Protestant agencies had never really accepted the sectarian scheme championed by Catholic and Jewish immigrants. Most Protestant agencies dated back to a time when "public" essentially meant white Anglo-Saxon Protestant, and when social uplift for the poor was heavily laced with proselytizing by an upper middle class confident in the superiority of "American" Christianity over foreign "popery" and "Old World super-stition." Other ethnic groups, understandably distrustful of the Protestant establishment's brand of "nondenominational" charity to all, fought back with their own institutions as soon as possible. The sectarian division of public funds was a reflection of their hard-won gains in urban political and economic power, and of the decline of the old Protestant establishment. Only under pressure from the city to conform to the Catholic and Jewish model was the Federation of Protestant Welfare Agencies formed, and for years it remained uncertain and divided over its mission.

In 1942 Polier worked for passage of a municipal ordinance drafted by her second husband, Shad Polier, which would prohibit city reimbursement to any charitable institution refusing a "reasonable proportion of inmates from any racial group because of race or color." But it was amended with a large sectarian escape clause—"provided that no institutions be required to accept persons from any race or group other than those who belong to its own religious faith." Jewish and Catholic agencies were therefore virtually exempt from its provisions.

In response to the ordinance, nine Protestant agencies refused outright to take children of color, forgoing public funds and expelling their 626 public charges, all white children. Others officially agreed to the terms, only to make endless excuses for rejecting referrals. Of ten agencies that had not taken a black child before the ordinance, three had yet to take their first such child three years later, and the other seven had accepted only one hundred black children all told. The law eventually became a basis for quotas and tokenism. In the 1950s the director of Children's Village told Polier there was a " 'threshold of tolerance, and if we accept more than 20 percent of Negro children, it is too much.' "

Even as she fought to open charitable institutions to black children, Polier had few illusions about such places. The woman who had capped her undergraduate education at Bryn Mawr, Radcliffe, and Barnard with undercover work in a textile mill was not content to send children to places she had never seen; as a young judge she had insisted, over private agency resistance, on her right to make unannounced visits.

The hierarchy of charity was captured for Polier in the memory of one cavernous institution with three sets of dishes: good ones for the benefactors who visited occasionally, a second, simpler set for staff, and an assortment of chipped remainders for the children. "The ghostly air of the place became heavy," she wrote later, "as the director pointed to children and spoke of their problems as though the children were not alive and were not listening."

Polier herself still listened with the ear of the child she had been in 1916, when her mother first took her to visit the huge Jewish orphanage in Manhattan. Shocked to learn that no agency placed Jewish children in adoptive homes, though Protestants and Catholics had adoption services, Louise Wise had determined to fill the breach. Mother and daughter were ushered into the director's office and received with formal courtesy— until Louise Wise presented a list she had obtained of children legally free to be adopted.

"When a little girl of about five or six wandered into the office, my mother asked in a whisper whether she was free for adoption. A rough, loud answer came, 'You want even a common little thief?' My only other recollection of that visit is of walking from the director's office into a large room, where small children surrounded us and begged, 'Will you be my mommy?' From that day on for months, my father never knew whether his bed would be occupied by a child my mother brought home until she could find an adoptive family."

Polier remembered how she helped to bathe one little girl who had arrived in a shabby dress, watching "her carrot-colored hair turn to gold" as it dried clean. The child was dressed in a Liberty frock and taken downstairs to meet her prospective parents in the same parlor where Justine and her brother, James, had so often thrown themselves at their father, squealing with gleeful terror as the rabbi tumbled to the rug with them in a rolling embrace, "like a great bear pawing his cubs."

Over the years, as Polier watched a procession of abandoned children be denied any chance at adoption, how many times had those pictures played in her memory? Her own family had expanded by ties of love. "My dear, we've got one of each kind," Shad once told her, meaning Steve, who was her son by her first marriage; Jonathan, who was their son; and Trudy, who joined the family as a nine-year-old refugee from Nazi Germany and became their daughter in all but blood.

What had Polier not done to try to change a system that condemned so many children to grow up outside any family circle, just because of their skin shade or the religion listed on their birth certificate?

She had lobbied at city hall for the creation of public programs that would serve the children rejected by the voluntary agencies—and heard her proposal denounced as "Communistic and totalitarian" by an emissary of the Catholic Church. She had garnered foundation support for demonstration projects that proved good black homes could be recruited—but the evidence failed to change major agency practices. She had deployed her husband, Shad, as her secret weapon to draft new state laws, including one that allowed the termination of parental rights for "permanent neglect." It passed over the opposition of sectarian agencies proclaiming the "natural rights" of birth parents, even to children they had not visited for years. But the same agencies ignored the law or used it for their own purposes, making some children legally free only to keep them in institutions and boarding homes year after year.

The city had long acquiesced in a system that treated children like property; its foundling-rotation system was the perfect example. In the 1930s, the Catholics were given all the foundlings discovered from noon to midnight, the Protestants all those found from midnight to noon. Polier's mother, president of what was then called the Child Adoption Committee of the Free Synagogue, objected to the scheme's disregard of Jews, who then made up a third of the city's population. With a nod to Father Coughlin if not to the Third Reich, the commissioner replied that he would regard it as "wrong to make any child a Jew who was not a Jew." The two-way split of unidentified babies continued until the 1950s, when another commissioner tried to put rules for it in writing, and Polier renewed her late mother's protest, adding First Amendment objections of her own. By then Polier was serving as president of the adoption agency, renamed Louise Wise Services in its founder's memory. It was a measure of how far the Jewish community had risen in the city's power structure that the other two religious groups immediately agreed on a three-way division of city foundlings.

As Louise Wise Services received its share of black foundlings, Polier seized the opportunity to make the agency one of the first in the country to extend adoption services to nonwhite children. To the perturbation of the Jewish Federation, the agency's board became nonsectarian and interracial. But for Polier, the rotation itself remained an emblem of the sectarianism she loathed, and when a new commissioner of public welfare took office in 1959, she called publicly for its abolition. Foundlings should go to the best adoptive home available, regardless of religion; anything else was wrong and unconstitutional. (The rotation continued into the 1960s, until it was stopped by Mitchell Ginsberg, commissioner under Mayor John Lindsay.)

Judge Polier's fury and frustration at the city's child welfare structure crystallized seven years before *Wilder,* in an opinion she rendered in the case of a child she called Ellen Bonez. Abandoned by her mother at nine months of age, Ellen had been allocated to New York Foundling, a large Catholic agency. After four years in custody, the child still had not been placed in an adoptive home, nor had any legal steps been taken to free her for adoption. The problem with this "appealing, attractive, alert child," an agency representative told Polier when she pressed for an explanation, was "her darker skin coloring."

Polier tried to enlist the assistance of three nonsectarian adoption services with a track record of recruiting nonwhite adoptive families (including Louise Wise Services); later she discovered that New York Foundling had sabotaged this effort, telling each agency privately that its help was not needed.

"During this entire period the Public Welfare District for New York City had remained silent and uncooperative," Polier wrote in her 1966 opinion In re *Bonez*. "Its lack of responsiveness, together with the resistance to adoptive placement by the agency having custody, has resulted in this superior, attractive child being placed in a shelter, a congregate institution and three successive foster homes." Ellen's case, the judge noted, "is typical of the tragic history of many children now dragging out their lives on public subsidy in a succession of boarding homes without becoming part of a family."

She blamed "the supremacy of the voluntary and sectarian agencies in the child care field" and the state and city's failure to demand accountability. "Non-white children have suffered most because of the failure of the public services to provide or secure adequate services," she wrote. "The City Public Welfare District has . . . not been willing to exercise its responsibility to remove children from the no-child's land of temporary, interim care, congregate care, so long as a private agency would physically accept a child. . . . This court is, in practice, made entirely dependent on the decisions of the private agency and is treated as a rubber stamp that is used only to secure continuing tax subsidies."

Refusing to be a rubber stamp, Polier removed Ellen Bonez from the indignant Catholic agency and placed her with Spence-Chapin, a nonsectarian adoption service that within twenty-four hours had the child in a preadoptive home where she was later adopted. But Ellen was only one child; the system remained fundamentally unchanged.

In Polier's eyes, *Wilder* had all the makings of a landmark, of a child welfare version of *Brown* v. *Board of Education*—an impression only strengthened later when Lowry recruited renowned black social scientist Kenneth B. Clark as an expert witness and then as a taxpayer plaintiff, some twenty years after Clark's doll tests had helped persuade the U.S. Supreme Court in *Brown* that segregation damaged children psychologically.

Polier's rejoicing over this lawsuit could not be dampened by the fact that Louise Wise Services was among its defendants. She was to argue the suit's merits until the Jewish philanthropic federation asked her to resign as its representative on the city's Human Resources Advisory Committee. She was to advocate its cause so fiercely that her fellow trustees of the

American Jewish Congress, founded by her father, reluctantly agreed to remain neutral on the case, rather than file an amicus brief in support of the defendants. She was eventually to be deposed as a star witness in *Wilder,* marshaling her own life's work—and her own shortcomings—in its behalf.

"The case is only symbolic of the hundreds of various cases where courts are not doing justice," she would testify. "We have a daily emasculation of the legislative intent as well as the rights of children.

"Over and over again I was forced to recognize that if this child had been white, the child never would have stayed in a shelter, never have stayed in detention that long, and would not have been rejected by all these agencies. I say this on the basis of my experience over the years."

SEVEN

S HIRLEY, STILL THREE MONTHS SHY OF HER FOURTEENTH
birthday, was as tall and shapely as a grown woman when she stood
beside Carol Sherman in family court again on August 9, 1973. Her cell
door had been unlocked by a test case brought by the New York Legal Aid
Society on behalf of another child, *In the matter of Ellery C.*

On July 2, the New York Court of Appeals had ruled that a juvenile
adjudged to be a "person in need of supervision" (PINS) could not be confined in a state training school along with juveniles convicted of committing criminal acts. This spelled the beginning of the end for the girls'
training school at Hudson, which would close two years later. Justine
Wise Polier had retired from the bench, but another judge formally
vacated Shirley's commitment in light of *Ellery C.*, and ordered her placed
in a "suitable foster home" run by the state Division for Youth.

Again, Shirley was confined while she waited for placement—this
time not in Manida, which had just been closed, but in a cramped section
of Spofford, the boys' jail. Years later, passing Spofford in a car, Shirley
would speak of the sexual couplings that took place there in an under-
ground tunnel, where staff members rewarded inmate enforcers with
access to the girls they chose.

Spofford had a long history of brutality and scandal. After a child died
there in 1966, a Bronx grand jury had issued a report saying that it was
rife with beatings, aggressive homosexuality, and wretched medical care.
Witnesses at a state legislative hearing testified that both Spofford and
Manida were run like concentration camps, with the most brutal inmates
serving like staff; a legislative report called conditions "shocking and
inhumane."

Yet the establishment of Spofford and Manida had been spurred by scandals in the detention centers that preceded them, shelters run by the private Society for the Prevention of Cruelty to Children (SPCC) with public money and no oversight. Justine Wise Polier had helped expose the SPCC shelters as cruel and incompetent in the 1930s, when on impromptu visits she saw terrorized children being fed watery soup under a rule of silence while the motley patronage staff—a former undertaker, a real estate man, a shipping clerk—ate a lavish meal in a separate dining room at taxpayer expense. In 1943, a riot at the shelter on Fifth Avenue had prompted a formal investigation, again headed by Polier. It found crowding so severe that the children, aged two to sixteen, slept three to a bed; their feet were encased in rags instead of shoes, the better to polish the waxed floors of the shelter, an old mansion facing the conservatory gardens of Central Park. The children's only recreation was a few minutes in a caged-in rooftop playground; punishment was confinement in a dark basement cell.

Shirley's stay at Spofford was short. By the end of August she was placed on probation in a state-run foster home on East 222d Street in the Bronx—actually a group home for seven to nine girls on probation or parole from Hudson, operated by a married couple. Within weeks, she ran away.

AGAIN AND AGAIN, over the years, Shirley would run away. Sometimes there were clear reasons to run; sometimes there were none that other people could understand. Sometimes it seemed anything at all would set her in motion, the way a colt might shy from its own shadow or a bird take flight at a flicker in the underbrush. At other times her escapes seemed part of a headlong rush to escape destruction.

"She is guarded, highly suspicious of the intentions of others and wary of anticipated attacks," a psychiatrist, Norman Pelner, would write in a 1974 evaluation of Shirley that typified the way systemic brutalities could become symptoms of individual disturbance. "It is evident that she devotes considerable energy to ways of protecting herself from what she sees as danger and malevolence in the outside world. . . . Shirley described how on one occasion, she had to stay up all night with a weapon in her hand because she was convinced that an alleged lesbian she had argued with during the day would attack her in her sleep. Another time, she explained that she ran away from her group home after an altercation with a girl she accused of being jealous because Shirley feared that if she stayed she would either lose all control and become homicidal or would be the victim of this girl's revenge at night."

In the logic of a system more comfortable with psychological interpretation than with its own realities, Shirley's experiences with the racket came to be seen as symptoms of delusion. The diagnosis: "Personality disorder, paranoid personality in type."

Shirley had a simpler explanation. "When I came out of Hudson I was more aggressive," she would say. "I learned how to fight."

The other teenagers housed in the basement of the Bronx group home were also veterans of the Hudson racket, and Shirley quickly clashed with them. At first the foster mother, Mrs. B., was especially kind to Shirley, and the other girls resented Shirley for it. Mrs. B. even telephoned Shirley's father and stepmother and tried to intervene with them on her behalf. But when they refused to talk to her, Mrs. B. seemed to give up. Mrs. B.'s husband used what Shirley called "foul language" with the girls, and Mrs. B.'s son tried to fondle her. And when Shirley asked Mrs. B. about birth control, Mrs. B. told her she didn't need it because she was too young to think about sex.

When Shirley walked back to the group home from Junior High School 142, where she was enrolled in eighth grade, men whispered hoarse, honeyed come-ons as she passed them on the sidewalk. There was no sexual act they could suggest that she did not know already.

"I learned about sex from home," she would say later. "I was a wild child, which wasn't my fault."

But to hear her aunt Carrie talk, it had always been her fault, or the fault of the bad blood she'd inherited from her mother, Helen Wilder.

EVEN THOSE WHO SPOKE ILL of Helen Wilder said that she was beautiful. Not a single photograph survives—her husband, Jay, destroyed them all in a drunken rage after she died—but she still dances through the memories of those who knew her. They conjure up the image of a tall, slim, vibrant woman in a tight red dress, her straightened hair upswept to show her graceful neck, her high heels swinging lightly from one hand as she runs down the stairs barefoot and slips out an open door: Helen Wilder, sneaking out on death to party one more time.

Jay and Helen had met in Charleston, South Carolina, when it was swollen with struggling back-country families like their own, driven off the land by hardscrabble poverty and the mechanization of cotton. Jay's father, who died in 1941 when Jay was seven, had so little education that he introduced a variation of the family name, Auld, by misspelling it as All. Jay, who used both versions, was not yet nine when his older half brothers joined the military, and during the Korean War he lied about his age to enlist in the air force. It was after he came home with a dishonorable discharge that he fell in love with Helen Wilder. As Carrie Powell saw it, he should have known from the start that Helen was trouble. When they were dating, a married, older man tried to run Jay down in the street out of jealousy, and Jay had to dive over the car to avoid being hit. He left Charleston for New York but soon sent for Helen to join him.

It was 1954, and they were all of twenty-one. To be a young South Carolinian in Harlem in those years must have been heady. There were house parties to go to every weekend, with plenty of liquor and rock and roll to lift a week's worth of wet laundry and squirmy babies from a young woman's mind or break up the rhythm of the assembly line in a young man's body. At first Jay and Helen went to parties together, but Jay's jealousy gave him no peace, and the couple had violent fights. "Jay didn't want her to go out, so she had to sneak," Ruth Simmons, a sister-in-law, would remember of the dances that she and Helen went to together. "When she came home, that's when the fight would start. He would go after her with his fists. She would fight back, now, but she would get the worst end of it."

Shirley Ann Wilder was born into this violent relationship on November 25, 1959. Her parents were married a little over a year later, on February 1, 1961, by the pastor of the Mount Sinai Baptist Church. Three months after the wedding, Virgie was born. At a time when illegitimacy still carried a stigma, those three months made a big difference. Virgie, Jay, and Helen were joined together as Alls, and Shirley was set apart by a name that seemed to flaunt her mother's reckless past. For all her disapproval of Helen, even Carrie Powell acknowledged Shirley's unmistakable resemblance to Jay: she was her father's child. But two babies didn't end Helen's dancing days, or her defiance of Jay's possessiveness. She was still too young, it seemed, to spend every waking hour in a small fifth-floor apartment on West 129th Street caring for two little children. Sometimes she took the dimes Jay had counted out for the laundry, did the wash without soap powder, and went to a party with what she'd saved.

"She would work hard, cleaning the house, keeping the kids while he was at work," Ruth Simmons insists. "But he never said, 'OK, now you can go out with your friends.' If she'd wait on him, she couldn't go out. So she'd leave somebody baby-sitting before he come home." Waiting for her return, Jay would drink and seethe. Afraid to face his fists, Helen would stay away still longer. "He'd be so mad at her that he take the spite out on the children. Shirley used to cry a lot because she missed her mommy. Shirley loved her momma."

In Carrie Powell's version, the blame was exclusively Helen's, but Jay's heavy drinking and detachment from parenting came through as well: "All of my other brothers put diapers on their children. Jay wasn't the type for that. The children would be wet. He would never put diapers on the young ones. The kids, they'd be hungry, no milk."

Carrie Powell believed that Jay had good reason to be jealous, that Helen was flagrantly unfaithful. At three or four, Shirley saw her mother having sex with strange men while her father was away at work—or so her aunt Carrie said: "Prostitution. Helen used to prostitute. She was just no good." But even after Ruth Simmons became a churchgoing woman whose drinking days were done, she would defend Helen: "You can't say that she was no good—just a person that's young and like to have a good time. She wasn't running behind men. She loved Jay, she cared about her kids, but that was just in her, to have a good time."

Mary Auld, the wife of Jay's younger brother Earl, took the most balanced view: "There was blame on both sides. They would drink each other to death, then fight, then make up so you couldn't separate them. They had this love-hate relationship, remind you of a TV movie, and the kids curling in the bed trying not to make a sound."

No social-service agency intervened in the domestic violence of the All household. Child placement, not preventive services, drove the budgets of the private agencies, and since they made few if any places for black children, their limited family-counseling programs were devoted to their own ethnic and religious clientele. Public social services were largely tied to public assistance, which the Alls weren't receiving; public assistance in the early 1960s went to less than half the families poor enough to be eligible for aid.

Beyond such structural reasons, there was a kind of societal shrug about drunken violence among poor black migrants from the South, a disdainful view that nothing better could be expected from these "primitive" people. Racism no doubt gave a special shape to these attitudes, but they were remarkably similar to the views that prosperous white native Protestants had about foreign immigrant families a century earlier, when Irish Catholics, for example, were categorized by many charity reformers as an inferior "race" congenitally given to drunken family brawls amid squalor. Moreover, acknowledgment of male violence was at an all-time low in Helen's day, as the psychiatric influence on social work and the decline of feminism's first wave led caseworkers to blame family conflict on the wife's maladjustment to her proper sexual role in the nuclear family.

When Helen fell ill and went to the hospital, the children were not allowed to visit. She had "some of everything," including cancer and tuberculosis. Ruth Simmons came to say good-bye. Instead of a red dress, a white sheet clung to Helen's body, and she was so painfully thin that her bones looked sharp, her skin ashen. Jay, a burly, laconic man with the look of a bull in his slightly wall-eyed gaze, was pacing beside her bed in a kind of frenzy, as though this had been the nightmare behind all those nights of rage, the real abandonment that made the threatened loss of love such torment.

Helen knew she was dying. "Jay," she told him as Ruth Simmons listened, "take care of my kids."

Jay said nothing, as though to say yes might be to let her leave him.

Mary Auld bought a little blue dress for Shirley to wear at her mother's funeral. The child wasn't five yet, but she was big for her age and sturdy, the opposite of her sister, Virgie, small and frail at three. "He wasn't doing nothing for 'em," Mary Auld said of their father. "They needed some kind of security. They couldn't live the life he was living. He was drinking hard."

Shirley's grandmother Elvira Auld stepped in. Despite arthritis, clouded vision, and the sag and ache of a body that had borne thirteen children, outlived five, and buried two husbands, she still seemed strong.

"She was a very proud lady," a daughter-in-law would remember. "She dressed very stately and churchgoing." At sixty-five, she was eligible only for the lowest of Social Security survivor's benefits, no pension in her own right. Officially taking over the children's care, she told welfare workers her son was an alcoholic and that she did not know his whereabouts. It may have been true at the time; certainly it was necessary to obtain the minimal welfare check needed to feed and clothe two little girls.

To Carrie Powell, it seemed as though Shirley's small body began to exude the sexual heat that Helen's had lost to death. "From a little kid, she was built," Carrie Powell would tell others of Shirley, her voice deepening with disapproval. "She'd do all kinds of nasty dance, shaking her behind."

Official records on Shirley began in June of 1968, when she was eight. A pediatrician referred her to Mount Sinai Hospital's child psychiatry clinic for behavior problems. Her grandmother reported that the child cut and tore her clothes, hit her sister, and was reluctant to go to school. A clinic doctor prescribed medication for manageability, apparently without probing for the causes of the child's distress. In later years Shirley would say she had been gripped by fear that her ailing grandmother was about to die. The prospect of being left behind was so devastating, she recalled, that she once considered jumping from the window of the fifth-floor apartment to her own death.

It was about then that a male cousin of fourteen, known in the family for being "really mean," had sex with Shirley in a backyard garage in the Bronx while the grown-ups were all inside the house. Shirley's little sister, Virgie, heard them. "Virgie, if you tell, I'll beat you up," Shirley threatened the frightened seven-year-old. The teenaged cousin didn't have to say anything.

"I know it wasn't no rape," Aunt Carrie would declare when Virgie finally told her about the incident twenty-five years later. "She GIVE it to him. Shirley was just a monster and the biggest liar God ever created."

After all, hadn't the girl played a dirty trick on her ailing grandmother about that same time? "She fooled Mama that her period is on. She put iodine on Kotex and throw it out the window. Pinky—that's what we call Shirley in the family—Pinky was so wicked she would take her clothes and cut 'em up and throw 'em in the incinerator, throw her clothes right down the garbage chute."

To different eyes, these acts might resonate with unspoken pain. Iodine on Kotex hurled from a fifth floor window seems like a child's attempt to heal a secret wound and to proclaim the unspeakable failure of such healing; clothing torn and cast into the trash must surely be the oldest human symbol of grief and loss. But Shirley's aunt Carrie saw wickedness, saw Helen Wilder come back to taunt them all again through her first-born daughter.

"I was bad, but my grandma was always there for me," Shirley would say. "When my grandmother died, that's when the trouble started."

Shirley learned early on that to be like Helen was to provoke the desires of men. The first time she ran away from home was soon after her beloved grandmother died, when relatives moved in and she was molested by the husband of a pregnant cousin. Shipped off to her father's place, she found a stepmother so jealous that she would push James All's daughters out of his lap to sit there herself. It was a time of such change and torment that Shirley no longer had the feeling of belonging to her own body. At eleven, she met big boys for stairwell sex after school, according to her sister, who was as scared and sickly as Shirley was wild and strong. "She'd meet these boys in the hallway and have sex, and I had to stay there with her because she was my older sister and we both had to take the bus together," Virgie, always the good sister, would recall with disgust years later. Yet the only incident vivid in Virgie's memory sounds to an outsider's ears more like a rape than an assignation: "There was one time when the boy was hurting her and she was trying to get him off her, and we were both beating him, trying to get him off, but he was too big."

When Liz, her common-law stepmother, took Shirley back to Mount Sinai's child psychiatric clinic complaining of her rebelliousness and behavior problems at school, Shirley said nothing about sex. "Shirley, a friendly child, appeared somewhat younger [than her age]," the psychiatrist wrote. "She related easily without shyness, talking in a superficial way about school, daily routines. She was somewhat tangential in her speech, was coherent, fully oriented, memory seemed intact with no overt anxiety. Stelazine 2 mg b.i.d. was begun with reported change in manageability."

Stelazine is a psychotropic tranquilizer—sleeping pills, Shirley called them. They did nothing to stop her stepmother from drinking herself vicious, nothing to reverse the metamorphosis of her own body into something disruptive and dangerous. In 1971, on April 1, her grand-mother's birthday, Shirley sat alone in her room at her father's apartment trying intensely to remember good times past. Suddenly she heard her grandmother's voice calling her and saw visions of her grandmother on the wall. Grandma told her she loved her, told her to be good, exactly as she often had when she was alive. Several times that spring and summer Shirley isolated herself in her room and talked to her grandmother, seeking consolation. One psychiatrist would later liken it to a child's conception of an imaginary companion, or to pseudo-hallucinations brought on by traumatic loss.

Then one day shortly before her twelfth birthday, Shirley acquired a boyfriend. They met at Sam's Soul News, a sundries store on 125th Street and Lexington Avenue run by his uncle. Peanut, they called him, because he had been small as a child, but he was fifteen when they met, his wiry body already turning muscular, and he combined sweet talk with a kind of pugnacious nonchalance toward the world that made her feel safe at his side.

Lingering at Sam's one November afternoon, she bantered with Peanut in the dusk, running one finger over the boxes of Good & Plenty, laughing at his boasts and wishing she never had to go home. When it was late enough that going home meant a beating for sure, he asked her over to his mother's place. She didn't return home for three days; four days later she left again, and stayed away nearly two weeks.

Peanut's mother was too drunk to mind her presence very much. There was a changing cast of male cousins and lodgers who looked and leered, but that only underlined that she was Peanut's girl. They slept together on whatever bed or couch was empty, or on a blanket on the floor. There wasn't much furniture: Peanut's mother had been burned out of their apartment the year before, in one of the tens of thousands of fires that raged through New York's poorer neighborhoods in those years, fueled by building abandonment and arson-for-hire.

Shirley told Peanut's folks she was sixteen. When his older sister, Brenda, found out that she was only twelve, Brenda made her wash dishes and sweep the house, spanking her once for leaving the work undone. Brenda herself was no more than sixteen at the time, but she already had her boyfriend's heroin habit and a baby son who had been sent down south to relatives when he was born addicted, too.

Shirley went back home two days before the anniversary of her grandmother's death, on December 20, 1971, and wove a story about having stayed with different girlfriends and having tried to get a job.

"Shirley was not able to explain or give an account for the two episodes [of truancy]," Vanderschraaf, the psychiatrist, reported. "She was disoriented for some time, lacked insight and judgment. She was irrelevant, ambivalent, bizarre, showed magical thinking. . . . Did not want to go home for fear of punishment, though worried about them and therefore could not think. Thought that her sister became sick because she was away and this was proven by the fact that she recovered when she returned. She had nightmares in which her parents got killed. . . . Stayed with other girls, being hidden in their rooms, or escaped questioning when the mother was not present. Did not go to school, slowly moved to addresses closer to home and finally had her father called up to get her 'so he would cool off and not beat me up, instead he bought me many nice things.' She admitted to see her grandmother (deceased) who spoke to her many times recently.

"The plan was formulated to medicate Shirley immediately, consider inpatient treatment and or/immediate referral for long term placement."

The psychiatrist sent Shirley and her father to family court to file a PINS petition so the court could order the placement—an order needed in part to guarantee financial coverage. Also needed was a formal diagnosis. The reverberations of the one Vanderschraaf chose would be felt long after the diagnosis itself had been discarded: *childhood schizophrenia.*

Shirley promptly ran again, this time taking her clothes and staying away seven weeks. Later, locked in Manida, she boasted to peers about sexual experiences with her boyfriend, trying hard, a Manida caseworker noted, to act older than her chronological age and to gain some standing in the group. But she was transparently immature, the caseworker added—extremely playful and hungry for affection. During her detention, emissaries from Linden Hills, a residential treatment center run by the Jewish Board of Guardians, found her "fairly responsive and soft-spoken" but "able to talk rather openly about her sexual behavior, which seems to be her way of meeting dependency needs."

SHIRLEY'S FLIGHT FROM SEXUAL ABUSE into sexual delinquency might seem contradictory, but it repeated a pattern of behavior known to caseworkers for more than a century. Linda Gordon, the historian who analyzed social-service case records in Boston going back to 1880, could have been writing about Shirley instead of Irish, Polish, and Italian girls long dead when she described how many had learned from familial sexual abuse "not only to expect little consideration from those closest to them, but also that sex was their best means of gaining rewards or even acceptance." In a double-edged rebellion, many took to the streets, accepted "badness" as part of their identities, and developed survival skills to match.

In Gordon's reading of the case records, sexually delinquent girls were attempting to regain some autonomy: "The girls who remained trapped in their homes, victims of domestic incest, were more passive and fatalistic than the delinquents who were using their sexuality—the only resource they 'owned'—to manipulate others and accumulate some personal power."

Today, when it is commonplace to link early sexual activity to a modern breakdown in community standards, it may seem startling that Shirley's predecessors were just as young or younger. As with these "tainted" children in the old case records, Shirley's bid for autonomy had made it more likely that she would be judged unsalvageable. At Manida, Shirley was successfully treated for trichomoniasis, a common vaginal infection; Linden Hill's report mistakenly transformed that into treatment for gonorrhea and syphilis, and noted meaningfully that Shirley had once managed to survive for seven weeks on the run. The interviewers' conclusion: her problems were "characterological" and made her "atypical" of their population. Another agency rejected her as "more mature" than its own girls. These code words seemed to echo the fears of their Victorian predecessors: a child who had lost her sexual innocence, whatever the circumstances, was irrevocably polluted and contagious to others, especially if she belonged to a race or ethnic group suspected of heightened sexuality.

By the time she ran down the sidewalk from the state-run foster home on September 12, 1973, Shirley had spent most of two years confined with strangers in dreary places where the only safety came from isolation, and isolation was too hard to bear. Now she ran to the cracked sidewalks of her childhood, where the pockmarked stoops seemed to sag under their human weight on a warm evening. There would be old friends to take her in, teenagers with mothers too stoned or weary to care if they hung out half the night. Maybe somebody's brother or cousin would drive up in a big old Buick, and they'd all pile in, thighs sticking to the plastic upholstery, shrieking with laughter when the sharp turns sent them careening into each other, whooping out the open windows into the rush of cool night air, with the radio blaring and the city glittering at them through the girders of the George Washington Bridge.

She was picked up in Jersey City by the police on September 17, 1973, riding in a stolen car with older teenagers.

"Shirley indicated that she was aware of the seriousness of such behavior, and wanted another chance in the foster home," a state Division for Youth worker reported. "This opportunity was granted and Shirley made attempts to stabilize herself. However, on 10/16/73, Shirley left the foster home going to the corner store and has not returned to this date, 11/2/73."

The state worker notified Shirley's stepmother and told her to take the girl back to court if she showed up at her father's apartment. "It is recommended that the court arrange for Shirley to be placed in a more secure setting, as foster care has proven unsatisfactory in meeting the needs of this youngster."

With that, and a brief cover letter to New York County Family Court, the state washed its hands of Shirley Wilder, not quite fourteen. "We regret that we are unable to do further planning for Shirley. She has been un-cooperative in that she has run away from the home on several occasions, and her present whereabouts are unknown."

When Shirley Wilder came to official notice again, two months later, she was pregnant.

EIGHT

FOR CHILD-CARE AGENCIES AND RELIGIOUS ORGANIZATIONS, *Wilder* precipitated a crisis played out in the summer and fall of 1973 in passionate membership meetings, anguished position papers, and back-door power moves. Two weeks after *Wilder* was filed, two Supreme Court decisions struck down New York legislation that provided a variety of public funds to parochial schools. The decisions only heightened consternation over the potency of Lowry's First Amendment argument.

One of the big three soon broke ranks: the Federation of Protestant Welfare Agencies, a 240-member umbrella group, declared late in October 1973 that the city's child welfare system "in its structure and its operation does result in religious and racial discrimination and inadequate care and service for a substantial number of children." It voted to file an amicus curiae or friend-of-the-court brief supporting the plaintiffs. This stance was ardently opposed by ten agencies out of the twenty-nine in the Protestant federation named as defendants.

"[*Wilder*] is a grave confrontation for all the religious faith groups," the dissenters wrote in a memorandum to the Protestant federation, warning of a "financial catastrophe of major import" if the suit was successful, of a "total withdrawal of public tax support from all [religious] child-care agencies in the city of New York," of the wholesale demise of philanthropic institutions. They argued bitterly that the planned amicus curiae brief would undermine their position as defendants, possibly jeopardize insurance coverage for legal costs, and "unjustly characterize the voluntary child caring agencies defending the suit as unlawfully practicing racial discrimination and visiting cruel and unusual punishment upon the foster children whom we serve in institutions." ("Or do not serve!" Polier added in a fierce scrawl on her copy of their paper.)

But the *New York Times* article reporting the Protestant federation's support for *Wilder* quoted only the praise from James Dumpson, a past commissioner of public welfare and dean of the Fordham School of Social Services, who said the action "took courage, even risk" and rekindled his faith in people's willingness to stand behind their values. Later, before an angry overflow crowd at a public forum sponsored by the National Association of Social Workers, Dumpson, a black Catholic, dismissed the dire predictions as unwarranted and urged "that human equity, the Judeo-Christian concept of charity . . . the rights of all children . . . take precedence over institutional interests."

People who were used to occupying the moral high ground now found themselves outflanked. It was particularly galling to some in the Jewish and Catholic camps, who considered the Protestant agencies the most vulnerable to charges of deliberate racial discrimination and the least threatened by an uncontrolled influx of children not "their own." The Protestant agencies had less to lose, it could be argued, because Protestant charitable contributions had already dwindled to insignificance with the exodus of white Protestants to the suburbs and the eclipse of WASPs in the New York political economy; and the agencies' programs were already 86 percent black. By those measures, the Jewish agencies had the most to lose, with the smallest percentage of black children (23 percent), the most significant private donations, and the highest average per capita expenditure, at $34.21 per day, compared to $19.32 in Protestant and nonsectarian agencies and $21.60 in their Catholic counterparts.

If institutional self-interest added to the outrage of those early months, so did deep personal convictions that the lawsuit represented destruction of the best, most socially valuable care for needy children. As *Wilder* opponents saw it, the answer for "hard-to-place" black children was further expansion of the religious sector, not its dismantlement; the lawsuit itself could not "create a single additional facility, nor hasten the placement of a single child," the leaders of Catholic Charities and the Jewish Child Care Association of New York argued in a joint statement. "The child care system under attack in this suit has deep roots," they wrote, "antedating by far the colonization of this country. Both Christianity and Judaism have a long tradition of concern for the ill, the neglected and the aged, a tradition brought to this country by the earliest settlers."

This Jewish-Catholic alliance over a First Amendment controversy was an extraordinary departure from a long history of polarization between the two communities on church-state issues. Only a decade earlier the New York Board of Rabbis had hailed a U.S. Supreme Court decision outlawing official prayers in New York schools; Cardinal Spellman had declared himself "shocked and frightened" by the same ruling. The indigenous political tradition of New York City's Jews was both secular and socialist. As Nathan Glazer and Daniel Patrick Moynihan detailed in *Beyond the Melting Pot,* it had clashed repeatedly with Irish Catholic conservatism at least since the days when the *American Hebrew* newspaper celebrated the Bolshevik revolution as the overthrow of dictatorship while the *Catholic World* denounced it as the overthrow of civilization. It was no fluke that this long-standing gulf was bridged by *Wilder,* a case that in effect championed blacks at the expense of white ethnics. Reaction to *Wilder* began a new script in city politics—one that Ed Koch would later use in his mayoral campaign to build a winning coalition.

The packed *Wilder* forum at which Dumpson spoke on the evening of November 29 quickly turned into an even more emotional free-for-all. Dumpson had come to the event, held at the Hunter College School of Social Work, bearing a powerful thirteen-page paper that cited chapter and verse of past failures to fix the system's inequities. "Only a court mandate will bring systems change in foster care in this city," he declared. He almost felt sorry for Joseph Gavrin, the executive director of the New York State Council of Voluntary Child Caring Agencies, who had come to speak in response armed only with a handful of disheveled notes and was having difficulty articulating his defense.

Gavrin said he was not going to play the "numbers game," then dismissed the suit's claim to represent a class of ten thousand black Protestant children. In fact, he said, the class probably consisted of only a few hundred multihandicapped children who needed placements. The suit's allegations were just allegations at this point, he stressed, and the court might not adopt the Civil Liberties Union's position in the end. As reasonable professionals, they would all do better to find those few hundred children the care they needed and stop beating each other up over the inadequacies of their system.

The lawsuit imperiled the slow, natural development that had been changing child care over the last dozen years, Gavrin asserted. He blamed lack of funds, not racial discrimination, for inadequate care and warned that public services could not be the answer. In the current climate of government cutbacks, it was difficult to keep even minimum services functioning in the public sector, never mind quality services. Agencies were indeed selective on the basis of religion, but not on the basis of race, he said. "At that, the entire room moaned," reported Joan E. FitzGerald, a staff member from the Children's Defense Fund who was in the audience taking notes.

The panel of nine experts seated on the stage behind Gavrin included Marcia Lowry, and it was heavily weighted in favor of the lawsuit. One expert, Charles King, deputy director of the New York State Division for Youth, responded viscerally to Gavrin, saying he was sick to death of hearing such nonsense. Given a fair chance, he protested, public services could be damn good. Another expert, Patricia Morisey, who was black and a professor at the Fordham University Graduate School of Social Services, answered Gavrin with tears in her eyes, saying, "Sometimes I feel like a motherless child."

Emotions on the other side were just as raw. Standing up and speaking in a piercing voice, a Catholic nun in the audience proclaimed that as a defendant and a social worker she was deeply shocked and offended that the National Association of Social Workers had forwarded requests to workers in various agencies asking them to cite instances of discrimination for use in the case by the NYCLU.

With no articulate spokesman for their side on the panel, the many *Wilder* opponents in the audience began to focus their mounting frustration on Lowry. The crowd's hostility reminded her of the South: "People were firing questions, they were shouting over each other, 'Where do you get your funding? Where do you get your funding?' And it seemed the answer was Russia—it was implicit in the question."

In the eyes of Joan FitzGerald, a veteran of thirty-two years in child welfare work who shared Judge Polier's views of the system, Lowry's response to the question was not worthy of a standard-bearer for a reform movement that had been theirs long before it was hers.

"Lowry didn't move an inch from her usual slouch," FitzGerald wrote to Polier, likening Lowry to a sullen teenager. "She merely looked straight forward—not even at her questioner—and said, 'That is the business of no one in this room.' There was a general rustle of papers and shifting about and then a murmur started. The people on the panel with her leaned over and obviously suggested that she go to the mike and try to be a bit more civil. She got up and when she got to the podium, she stared straight into space. . . . She fiddled and faddled and finally said that the source of the ACLU funds was a matter of public record and that the Union would be 'glad to send you that information. I suggest that you write directly to them for it.' "

The meeting went downhill after that. Agency directors in the audience who opposed the class action spoke out bitterly against it. One asked what Lowry's real purpose was in filing the suit. When Lowry made no move to reply, the moderator, Carol Parry, said she felt that was an unfair question and wouldn't submit Ms. Lowry to the indignity of answering it.

"If Marcia Lowry won't speak to that point, I will," said Dumpson, taking the mike. "I want to see the end of this system of child care because it's not responsive to children's needs and because it causes them tremendous suffering."

From the back of the room, a woman from the Jewish Board of Guardians protested in a voice choked with feeling that the sectarian agencies were doing all they could in a rough situation. "The general tone was hurt indignation," FitzGerald wrote. "Something along the lines of, 'We're doing the best we can so why don't you bullies leave us alone.' "

In the jumble of comments that followed, another exchange stood out. A woman from the Columbia School of Social Work called for careful reflection and consideration. "I do think we've been carefully considering for a while now," said a black social worker sitting behind FitzGerald, and her friend responded, "These people ain't gonna do nothing, honey."

"I felt sick," FitzGerald wrote. "And mad as all hell at Lowry."

All that lingered in Lowry's memory was the crowd's anger and the blank she drew as she tried to summon up the names of funding sources for the Children's Rights Project. The only one she was able to remember and cite that evening was the Carol Buttenwieser-Loeb Foundation. The words seemed to infuriate the audience all the more.

IN THE WORLD of high-powered philanthropy, Buttenwieser was a name to conjure with. Helen Loeb's marriage to Ben Buttenwieser had joined two great Jewish banking fortunes in the 1920s; Carol was the daughter who had died young. Ben Buttenwieser was cut from the cloth of the New York rich, but Helen had reveled in the role of political radical. Older civil-rights lawyers recalled her as a spitfire who threw fancy cocktail parties in her Fifth Avenue mansion and came down the staircase barefoot, and who had invited Alger Hiss to be her houseguest during his trial. By the 1960s, Helen Buttenwieser was sitting on the board of the Civil Liberties Union, but she had also become a distinguished lawyer specializing in children's issues, and many of her clients were voluntary child-care agencies. One of these was the Jewish Child Care Association, a *Wilder* defendant.

Peter Buttenwieser was his mother's boy—a champion of civil liberties, racial justice, and educational reform—but his brother Lawrence was their father's son, a real estate mogul who didn't quite like the Civil Liberties Union and who presided over the Federation of Jewish Philanthropies. *Wilder* shook every fault line that ran through the family.

Three days before the Hunter forum, Lawrence Buttenwieser had run an executive-committee meeting of the federation that was in effect a showdown over whether this powerful umbrella group would weigh in against the *Wilder* plaintiffs with an amicus brief. Overriding the eloquent arguments of Justine Wise Polier, the federation entered the *Wilder* lawsuit on the side of the defendants.

Wilder opened fault lines in other organizations, too. In the pages of the Jesuit publication *America,* Brenda G. McGowan and Edward L. Delaney criticized the official Catholic opposition to *Wilder* as evidence of a "pre–Vatican II worldview" and of political power arrangements that "may have done much to corrupt the church's primary mission as a servant church, dedicated to every human person, black or white, rich or poor, Catholic or non-Catholic."

At the American Jewish Congress, where support for the separation of church and state had been an article of faith, some members argued that a successful *Wilder* suit would threaten the very survival of the Jewish community and, specifically, its old-age homes. As Lowry saw it after being queried at one of the meetings, "The real embarrassment for them was that they had been very, very strong against support for parochial schools, including Jewish parochial schools, but they saw the Yeshiva-schools people as crazy, whereas the homes for the aged [housed] their parents, so they were terribly threatened. Their problem was how to weave some consistent intellectual line through all this. It was quite Talmudic."

There was nothing subtle in some of the battles waged for amicus briefs that summer, and nothing obscure about the conflicts of interest they highlighted. Among the members of the New York State Board of Social Welfare, which was supposed to oversee and regulate the voluntary child-care sector, was Leonard Block, a top official with the Jewish philanthropic federation who used his financial clout to try to neutralize *Wilder*'s potential allies. Hearing that the fledgling Children's Defense Fund was considering filing an amicus brief in the case, Block dangled the possibility of new funding for it "through a foundation with which I am very intimately connected and with which I have a great deal of influence." Nevertheless, the Children's Defense Fund produced a pro-*Wilder* brief drafted by Polier.

The behind-the-scenes conflicts over *Wilder* culminated in January of 1974. Newly inaugurated Mayor Abe Beame asked Dumpson to be his commissioner of human resources and social services, only to withdraw the invitation under pressure from Catholic and Jewish welfare agencies furious over Dumpson's support for the lawsuit, the *New York Times* reported. The *New York Post* ran a story that hit the Beame administration and quoted Kenneth B. Clark's denunciation of the agencies for "short-sighted vindictiveness." Three days later the *New York Times* published a stinging editorial headlined "Religious Veto?"

"The objections to the Dumpson appointment registered at City Hall by some Roman Catholic and Jewish agencies represent an indefensible intrusion on the selection process," the *Times* asserted. "These objections are based on Dean Dumpson's open endorsement of a court suit challenging the present religion-based method of assigning troubled children to child-care agencies. It is to the credit of Mr. Dumpson, himself a Catholic, that he wants to institute a fairer system. The Beame administration, after first pulling back the job offer in response to the anti-Dumpson pressure, is now said to be reconsidering. The decision ought to be easy if Mr. Dumpson is still willing to accept."

Dumpson always took pleasure in relating the sequel: "After the editorial the mayor called me and said yes, he did want me to be commissioner. Then the agencies invited me to a breakfast, and a federation official told me, 'You must understand, we love you—it was all a mistake.' "

As his deputy in charge of Special Services for Children, Dumpson named Carol Parry, who had helped steer a pro-*Wilder* amicus brief through the board of the National Association of Social Workers. "I thought Marcia was absolutely right, and I wanted to change things," Parry would recall. "The lawsuit motivated me to take that job. That was my whole reason for going into government. I was trying very hard to do from the inside what Marcia was trying to do from the outside."

THERE WERE OTHERS who saw themselves as Lowry's collaborators. To many in a younger generation of social workers and parent activists shaped by the civil-rights movement, *Wilder* was an electrifying link between their own everyday struggles and a broader push for systemic change.

For Judy Schaffer, the moment of truth came when she scanned the thick sheaf of discovery papers that Marcia Lowry had mailed to her Westchester home. Schaffer was the executive director of the Council on Adoptable Children, an organization founded by adoptive parents battling private-agency policies that denied foster children a chance at permanent families. Her own introduction to the issue had come in 1970, when she and her husband, middle-class liberals who had campaigned for Robert Kennedy, decided it would be selfish to give birth to a child as long as there were children already born who needed parents. Schaffer called the four agencies listed under "Adoption" in the Yellow Pages, asking about a child between two and six. There were no such children available, she was told coldly, and besides, unless she was infertile, agency rules made her ineligible to adopt. Eventually the couple managed to adopt a so-called hard-to-place child from another state—a seven-week-old, healthy, mixed-race baby girl. Only then did they learn that nearly twenty-nine thousand children were hidden away in New York City foster homes, half of whom had not seen a family member in five years and most of whom would at eighteen be discharged to "independent living"—that is, discharged to the streets.

With a kind of missionary zeal, the Schaffers and a handful of similar adoptive parents banded together to challenge a system that locked children like their own into what they called the "limbo of foster care." They recruited thirty new families every week—including numerous middle-class blacks—who were willing to adopt older and/or biracial children. But most of the agencies continued to stonewall their inquiries. Efforts to find out how many children in agency care were potentially adoptable were flatly rebuffed: "When you questioned anything, they said, 'We're charitable; we don't have to tell you anything. We're accountable only to our board of directors.' " The agencies cultivated a perception that their work was financed primarily through charitable contributions and endowments left by early philanthropists, but they were exempt from the state's charitable-reporting requirements, and their budgets were secret.

Now, in the *Wilder* discovery papers that Schaffer read with triumphant indignation, the secret was out. In cold, hard figures it was revealed that most of the voluntary agencies relied on public taxpayers for 85 to 95 percent of everything they spent. And here were the names, addresses, and affiliations of every trustee. To Schaffer, "it was like a burst of sunshine."

With righteous glee she published the information in a council newsletter mailed out to several thousand people. "I thought it was very important for people to know the voluntaries were not independent, that they were in fact public entities. Advocates began to feel we had the right to demand changes."

Unlike mainly working-class foster parents and poor birth parents, adoption advocates were a constituency with political connections and media savvy. And in New York City they challenged a key assumption— the assumption that children then in foster care, at considerable public expense, needed to be there. If many children were in foster care unnecessarily, if the same system that had turned away Shirley Wilder was warehousing adoptable toddlers, it only strengthened the case for a fairer redistribution of foster-care resources and underlined the need for greater public control.

Within days of mailing out the *Wilder* data, Schaffer received an angry telephone call from COVCCA's Joseph Gavrin. "He said, 'How dare you, that was our privacy.' He was really miffed at me. They genuinely believed they were private and had independent rights."

And no wonder: remembering the list of trustees, Schaffer would marvel at their collective clout. "It was Sullivan, Cromwell and Paul, Weiss. It was the churches and the top white-shoe law firms and the major blue-chip corporations. It was the permanent government. I don't know how Marcia ever was able to do anything. She was fighting against the most powerful, wealthy people in New York, and they had God on their side."

Lowry thought she had the law on hers. Her constitutional case was so strong that she expected the courts to be openly receptive. Instead she met undisguised judicial hostility and found herself wandering in a legal wilderness of avoidance and delay.

"*Wilder* varied between being very demoralizing and very exciting," she said once. "It made you feel like a real rebel: I was making people with real power very nervous. That was intoxicating. But I wasn't getting anywhere."

NINE

EFORE CHRISTMAS OF 1973, CARRIE POWELL BEGAN GET-
ting telephone calls from people she knew. They said her niece
Shirley—"Pinky"—was on the street, living from house to house, sleeping on floors: " 'Pinky is hungry, begging for food.' "

Carrie Powell contacted her brother Earl, who had a car, and they
drove around looking for her. They expected little help from Shirley's
father, who had been laid off from his job in a downtown belt factory. Half
the time he wouldn't even answer the phone. "I would ask Jay, 'Why
didn't you answer the phone?' And he'd say, 'Because they're calling me
about Shirley, and I'm tired.' "

But prodded by his siblings, Jay finally took the subway down to family
court. It was a place he hated. A few times during the long effort to
have his daughter sent away somewhere, he had obeyed a summons to
court, only to leave before her case was called. Shirley's probation officer
couldn't understand such behavior. But Charles Schinitsky, the chief
lawyer in Legal Aid's juvenile division, no doubt could.

"Fifty thousand cases of the most sensitive kind are called before the
city's family courts each year," Schinitsky told a reporter in the mid-
1970s. "The courts are overcrowded, the waiting rooms are terrible
places, each case involves a minimum of three to four people, not counting lawyers and court personnel, and they sit there all day with no notification of when their cases will be called. In many cases jobs have been
lost. Two to three million people in this city have passed through these
courts, more than a hundred thousand last year, and every one of them
has left with a terrible impression of the law, of the judges."

This time Jay couldn't even find Shirley's law guardian, Carol Sherman, who had been transferred to the headquarters of Legal Aid's juvenile division in Brooklyn Heights that month. He waited for guidance amid the press of doleful families sweating in their winter coats, letting the din of wailing babies and surly adolescents wash over him. Finally, at around five, he trudged out the door and took the subway home again, having accomplished nothing.

Eventually Carrie Powell learned that a Mrs. Betty Washington had called Jay demanding Shirley's birth certificate in order to add the girl to her own welfare grant. Carrie Powell might be quick to condemn other people's children, as her older sister complained, or too set in her thinking about bad blood, as her sister-in-law said, but her sense of family duty ran strong. She took the subway to Intervale Avenue in the Bronx and climbed five malodorous flights to Mrs. Washington's apartment to check out the situation. Her voice filled with indignation when she described the scene she found.

"Everybody walking in and out, look like they on drugs. The kids, the bigger ones, looked like stone bums. I mean, they were in stone RAGS. The little kids running around NAKED. The house were cold; they had no heat. Not a chair to sit on, and filthy, filthy, filthy.

"That lady was drunk. That lady, she cursed me out. I have nothing against people on welfare. When I had an operation I was on welfare. But you can live on welfare and can live a decent life."

On January 14, 1974, Carrie Powell phoned in a complaint to the office that most people still called BCW—the city's Bureau of Children Welfare, which had been renamed Special Services for Children.

The resulting "child abuse or maltreatment report" was one of 11,836, involving 21,854 children, made to city child-protective workers that year, and it automatically triggered a seven-day preliminary investigation of Shirley Wilder's need for protection.

"Pinky has run away from a foster home—has 'always been a problem,' [it] is said her case is closed," the protective caseworker in the Manhattan field office scrawled on a state form after listening to Carrie Powell's account. "Father refuses to cooperate to have person who presently cares for child appointed guardian for child by providing birth certificate, etc. This woman is on [public assistance] herself. PA [paternal aunt] hasn't enough room for child. 'Pinky' is fearful of being sent back to a home and is said to pick up extension phone if she suspects a change coming on and would run away again. PA is reluctant to discuss alcoholism problem of father and his paramour. Child not in school."

In the section titled "Nature or Evidence of Abuse or Maltreatment," two boxes were checked: Acute Alcoholism and Inadequate Supervision.* The same girl who had been written off to the streets three months earlier by one part of the system—the state's Division for Families and Youth—was suddenly entitled to emergency attention under the rules of another part of the system, the state Department of Social Services.

Shirley might reasonably have been the subject of a child-protective investigation much earlier. Staff at Bellevue Psychiatric Hospital, where she had been evaluated for two weeks as a twelve-year-old by order of the family court, reported early in February 1972, "We do feel return home, even while awaiting placement, is not in her best interests, as she states she has been beaten by her stepmother and has a history of running away from home. It appears her running away is related to her home situation." The Mount Sinai psychiatrist noted about the same time that Shirley's father had been described as an alcoholic by his own mother. And a juvenile probation officer at Manida recorded Shirley's complaint that her stepmother "drinks seven days a week."

Yet Shirley's situation had never before been defined as a case of suspected child abuse or maltreatment. The child psychiatrists saw a need for psychiatric treatment and medication; the juvenile detention center staff saw a need for correction. In a juvenile lockup, repentance is the proper path to rehabilitation; in a children's psychiatric clinic, adjustment to family and school life is the mark of mental health. For abused children in these settings, the double bind can be fierce. They are considered more deviant if they're strong enough not to blame themselves for the abuse they've suffered; they're considered sicker if they rebel, rather than adjust to being victims.

---

* The law's definition of a maltreated child includes one "whose physical, mental or emotional condition has been impaired or is in danger of becoming impaired as a result of the failure of his parent or other persons legally responsible for his care to exercise a minimum degree of care . . . (3) by the infliction of excessive corporal punishment; . . . (5) or by using alcoholic beverages to the extent that he loses self-control of his actions" (abstract sections from Article 6 Title 6 Soc. Serv. Law, Section 412, 2. [3] and [5].

But in the two years since Shirley had entered the child welfare system, another concept of intervention had come into its own: child-protective services.

The concept of child abuse itself was rediscovered in the early 1960s by pediatrician researchers who developed the notion of the "battered-child syndrome." State legislators around the country, seizing the opportunity for no-cost rectitude, passed mandatory reporting statutes with extraordinary speed. Child abuse was deliberately popularized as a classless phenomenon long after many researchers linked its incidence to chronic problems of poverty. In 1971, President Richard Nixon won public approval for his veto of comprehensive child-development services for poor children living at home. Emphasizing classlessness was a conscious political strategy to separate child abuse from antipoverty programs, which had become increasingly unpopular. "Not even Richard Nixon is in favor of child abuse!" Senator Walter Mondale declared in sponsoring the Child Abuse Prevention and Treatment Act (CAPTA) in 1973.

Congressional hearings, some held in New York City, helped spur passage of a 1973 New York state law requiring counties to have special child-protective units and setting up a toll-free twenty-four-hour telephone hotline. In January 1974—the same month Shirley's aunt complained to the city about her plight—Mondale's bill was signed into law, and local child-protective services became a gateway to some of the $86 million in federal grants earmarked for child abuse. Capturing such new funding streams was all the more important because the Nixon administration had cut and capped previously open-ended social-service spending.

Child abuse itself was not new, of course. Even its dramatization as a special social problem was the reprise of an old theme. In 1874, exactly a century earlier, New York City had been scandalized by newspaper accounts of little Mary Ellen, chained to a bed and beaten daily with a rawhide whip by the woman usually described as her stepmother but more accurately termed her foster mother. Mary Ellen, supposedly the illegitimate daughter of the woman's first husband, had been "indentured" to her at eighteen months by the New York Board of Charities. The case inspired the formation of the New York Society for the Prevention of Cruelty to Children (SPCC), the first of 250 child-protective associations to spring up across the country by 1900.

Founded by prominent Protestant lawyers from the same "scientific charity" movement that inspired Josephine Shaw Lowell to create Hudson, New York's SPCC had enormous power over poor, mostly immigrant families. Extreme, even bizarre cases of physical abuse were highlighted, but the bulk of SPCC intervention involved cases of neglect that often were hard to untangle from the effects of immigration and of poverty itself.*

Although the society was a private corporation, it had police powers to remove children and prosecute parents, and New York state law made interference with the work of its designated child-protective agents a misdemeanor. It even refused to allow an inspection of its shelters by the state Board of Charities. It built a formidable partnership with large private children's institutions, all publicly subsidized under the same contract system that *Wilder* would later challenge. By 1890, the New York SPCC "practically controlled the lives of an average number of about fifteen thousand children, and an average annual expenditure for their support of more than one and one half million dollars," Homer Folks wrote in 1902. "Its influence has done more to strengthen and perpetuate the subsidy or contract system . . . than any other one factor. By a vigorous enforcement of the laws authorizing the commitment of vagrant, begging, and various other categories of exposed children, they have . . . become the feeders of institutions."

The SPCCs were built on the dominant belief that breaking up poor families was the most efficient way to prevent pauperism, but the spectacle of massive unemployment during the industrial collapses of the 1890s persuaded many charity reformers that individuals were virtually helpless in the face of business cycles, and that private charity was inadequate to cope with the consequences. By the first White House Conference on Children in 1909, a very different consensus had emerged: no child should be removed from his own home for poverty alone. The SPCCs were overshadowed by the mothers' pension movement that followed. Especially between 1910 and 1920, the movement swept the country with arguments for local and state programs to provide cash aid to

---

* One small example, cited by Linda Gordon in *Heroes of Their Own Lives:* when Italian immigration swelled, SPCC workers—Anglo-Saxon Protestants all—condemned garlic as a dangerous aphrodisiac; mothers who persisted in cooking with the herb were considered neglectful of their daughters' morals.

"deserving" poor single mothers raising children, usually highlighting the plight of widows forced to put their dependent children in institutions (at great public expense), to send the children to work, or to leave them neglected by going to work themselves. In practice only a tiny fraction of potentially eligible families received aid, and the stipends were paltry and available only after a humiliating investigation. The poor, almost by definition, continued to be suspected of a failure to be thrifty, and critics warned that public aid even to the most self-sacrificing widow was potentially dangerous: it would "encourage men's irresponsibility, diminishing their need to save."

But as the urban poor became less foreign—literally, since World War I and the restrictive immigration laws of 1924 virtually halted the flow to Ellis Island—the image of the American child endangered by alien parents receded further from the public imagination. It was a new kind of immigration, the Great Migration of southern blacks to northern cities, that helped set the scene for the rediscovery of child abuse. Like the immigrants fleeing the Irish Famine in the nineteenth century, the black migrants lived in transition between a rural culture in which a large family was an economic advantage (indeed, the only form of insurance against death and disaster) and an urban society in which it meant having too many "dependents"—prima facie evidence of irresponsibility in the eyes of the middle class. Again, public focus soon shifted from trying to reform the alien adult poor to trying to save the next generation.

Shirley's case itself illustrates how different aspects of family violence—child abuse, child neglect, wife-beating, incest—are emphasized or covered up at different times, periodically "discovered" anew in an ebb-and-flow pattern of public concern that demonstrates the understanding of the problem is a political and historical construction.

THE INVESTIGATION of Shirley's 1974 case fell to Thomas Hirschmann, a child-protective caseworker at Special Services for Children. He spent several days interviewing the protagonists and filled a dozen closely typed pages with a vividly detailed narrative of his contacts.

He had to start from scratch. The family-court files on Shirley, the Manida and Spofford reports, the story of her childhood repeatedly told in psychiatric and psychological evaluations and probation reports—none of this was available to him, though he did discover a glancing reference to an earlier investigation of neglect that had been closed in March of 1968, apparently after Carrie Powell agreed to help the girls' ailing grandmother with their care. Although Shirley was the lead plaintiff in the most controversial lawsuit then pending against the child welfare departments of the city and state, her name meant nothing to him. But Carrie Powell had provided him with the telephone number of another paternal aunt, Margaret Moody, and when he called he learned that Shirley had temporarily taken refuge with her.

It wasn't the first time. In December 1971, after Shirley's father first took her to court, a judge had placed her in this aunt's home temporarily; a week later Shirley had run away. Summoned back to account for her niece's disappearance, the high-strung woman had been soured permanently on family court.

But Hirschmann was impressed that the second-floor apartment in the Bronx occupied by the aunt and her husband, a skilled laborer who worked in Paterson, New Jersey, was "spacious, attractive and quite clean," and located in a three-story frame dwelling that they owned; they rented out apartments on the other floors. He was disconcerted, though, to find that the front door was unlocked, and nonplussed when Mrs. Moody stayed on the telephone for half an hour after he arrived.

"Therefore, we interviewed Shirley Ann Wilder, alone," he wrote in the faintly disapproving royal "we" in which he couched most of his report. "Shirley Ann Wilder goes under the nick-name of 'Pinky.' Pinky is a fourteen-year-old Black girl, who appears at least twenty-one years of age. She is quite tall, and [has] large proportions."

She was very nervous, he noted. When he asked about the scars on her arms, she told him about her ordeal at Hudson and its Brookwood Annex, and at times she covered her face with her hands. "Pinky told us that she wants to reside with her father, Mr. James Adams [sic] All, of 135 E. 125 Street Manhattan, but she was not able to because his common-law wife, Elizabeth Booker, whom Pinky referred to repeatedly as a step-mother, did not want her in the household. . . . The step-mother reportedly feels that Pinky interferes whenever she is there." This, of course, had been the problem from the beginning.

Eventually Margaret Moody joined the caseworker and Shirley. She was so agitated, Hirschmann found her "not too coherent at times"; he later decided that the forty-six-year-old woman was "very neurotic."

"She said in a very loud, emotional charged voice that she thinks Pinky is mentally disturbed, because all she likes to do is eat and sleep," Hirschmann wrote. What they didn't know was that "Pinky" was then about two months pregnant, a time when craving for sleep and food can be overpowering.

Mrs. Moody went on to declare that she was unwilling to care for her niece on a long-term basis and "requested vehemently that we not involve her in any further problems concerning Pinky, especially any problems that would require her going to court."

"Why do you get into fights with so many people?" Hirschmann asked Shirley.

" 'Because I don't like their attitudes,' she replied.

" 'If you don't change your attitude, you are not going to live to age twenty-five, at least you are not going to live here anymore,' " her aunt shouted in exasperation before stomping off to the kitchen to finish the laundry. "Pinky gonna hit the road as soon as her clothes dry," she told the caseworker.

When Hirschmann saw Shirley again a few days later, it was at Carrie Powell's place on Fifth Avenue and 112th Street, the same three-bedroom apartment that had been Shirley's grandmother's before she died. "The building is in terrible condition," he wrote, "with broken doors, broken locks, and graffiti-splattered walls. But Ms. Powell's apt. shows good evidence of good housekeeping."

Carrie Powell was then working as a day-care mother licensed by the Human Resources Administration, the same city superagency that employed Hirschmann in the Special Services for Children division. She cared for the maximum six children of working mothers at a hundred dollars a month each, and said she had been afraid that if she kept Shirley, regulations would force her to give up one of the day-care children. Reassured on that point by Shirley's law guardian, she said she was now willing to take the girl. Shirley would have to sleep on the living-room couch, however, and help with household chores. The caseworker recorded her other conditions without comment: psychiatric help and a good medical checkup for Shirley and at least two hundred dollars to buy her clothes suitable for school and for attending the family's Baptist church, Prince of Peace, at 145th Street and Eighth Avenue.

Carrie Powell told Hirschmann about Shirley's childhood, explaining why she had sent the girls to live with their father after their grandmother's death. "Pinky started showing off the day Mama died, fighting my daughter like they were men," she would say in later years. "I said to Jay, 'I'm not going to put my kids out for yours.' I said, 'If Liz loves you, she'll take the kids.' I didn't have to give Jay those kids, but I couldn't take it no more with Pinky. I couldn't put up with Pinky another second. She eat like a pig. She didn't want to take a bath. Throwing panties out the window!"

But Pinky was older now and should be easier to handle, she told Hirschmann. "Nobody is going to give you love like your family," she added. He wrote it down.

Then he brought up the question of virginity.

" 'Tell Mr. Hirschmann how you were raped twice at the age of nine!' " Powell urged Shirley in a loud, excited voice.

"Pinky confirmed this to be true. She is currently having sexual relations with her boyfriend and is taking no birth control of any kind. Ms. Powell said she would take care of Pinky and check up on her all the time, and said that she needs money for Pinky as soon as possible."

Years later Carrie Powell would deny any knowledge of rapes, would deny that such a conversation had ever taken place with Hirschmann. "Shirley was a big liar from day one," she would say. "That girl would look Jesus Christ in the eye and lie."

The mention of birth control—the first in a record replete with references to Shirley's sexual experience—was too little, too late. "I watched her just like I watch my children," Powell said. "I expected her period to come. Last part of the month I told her, 'Pinky, your period hasn't come on.' She look at me and laugh. 'Pinky, are you pregnant?' She just laugh."

FROM THE RECTITUDE of Carrie Powell's home, Hirschmann traveled to the squalor of Betty Washington's.

"Ms. Washington lives in a run down tenement that qualifies as the archtype of a slum dwelling," he wrote, his disgust frequently getting the better of his spelling and syntax. "The apt. is in a total state of disrepair, shows no evidence of housekeeping whatsoever. All of the furniture in this apt. is broken with sofas that have protruding springs, beds that are settleing to the floor. There is only one blue light bulb dangling from the ceiling. The premises are filthy, and all of the posessions in the apt., without being demeaning, can be described as junk and disray. When we arrived, Ms. Washington was intoxicated. During the interview, she dranked out of the bottle of cheap scotch. We also think that Ms. Washington was high on some form of narcotic drug. It was very difficult to conduct the interview, because of Ms. Washington's behavior, and the presence of other people in the apt. Also present during the interview were Prentis Smith, 8/20/56, who described himself as Pinky's boyfriend, whom he met several years ago at Sam's Soul News at 125th and Lexington Ave. There was a gentleman lying on a bed, in what appeared to be a drunken stupor, and another gentleman sitting in what is called the living room. This man had an unusual gold cross around his neck, described himself as a Hebrew minister, but we later learned, in speaking separately to Prentis Smith, that he is a voodoo priest, who lifts spells, lifts curses which have been implanted on people. He makes a good income from this business according to Prentis Smith.

"Ms. Washington described that Pinky was in her house for a period of time, recently. She said she had to force Pinky out of the house when Pinky was shown, was seen by the cousin, Mr. Michael Saey, to be in a provocative position about to have sex with Pinky."

(Curiously, Hirschmann made Pinky both the subject and object of this hopelessly convoluted clause. Was Saey a witness or an actor? It may be a case of bad syntax revealing conventional bias: the provocative fourteen-year-old runaway, not the adult man, was responsible for any sexual act that took place between them.)

"In a round about way, through relatives, Ms. Washington was also informed that Pinky was pregnant," Hirschmann continued. "Ms. Washington said she does not want Pinky in the house. However, before leaving the apt., Ms. Washington changed her mind completely and said that she would be most willing to take Pinky in if BCW would keep an eye on her. Ms. Washington, who was totally obnoxious, by the time we left, actually demanded money from us 'to tide her over until the next welfare check.' "

Ms. Washington's daughter, Brenda Smith, had herself been the subject of a BCW protective case in the Bronx field office, Hirschmann learned. "According to Ms. Washington, she is now in Memphis, Tenn., being over eighteen and not under supervision as a 'junkie' anymore."

Hirschmann found his interview with Shirley's seventeen-year-old boyfriend no more reassuring.

"Prentis, also known as Peanut, said that he plans to go to training school or go into the U.S. Army. He has a criminal record. He told us that in 1970 that his family was burned out of their apt. He said that a man was designated to hold the furniture for them until the family was relocated. This furniture was reportedly stolen by this man, so Peanut stole $4 from the man in retaliation. He was in jail for awhile for this offense. In another situation, Peanut claims an intoxicated man 'stomped on his sister and beat her up.' " His response had led to a case pending against him in Bronx Criminal Court, he told Hirschmann; if it wasn't dismissed, he said, he would skip town. Peanut thus "in a nonchalantly manner seemed to justify his retaliation with people who had done him wrong.

"We feel that this environment is totally unsuitable for Shirley Ann Wilder for visiting purposes, let alone on a residential basis," the caseworker concluded. As to its suitability for the other children in the household, including Prentis's four younger half-brothers, ages five to twelve, he had no comment. Presumably they would have to wait for their own complaints before they would be candidates for a child-maltreatment investigation.

HIRSCHMANN HAD BEEN TOLD that Shirley's father was a nonfunctioning parent and an alcoholic, but he found him rather a sympathetic figure, introverted but cooperative. Again, housekeeping was the touchstone. The three-room apartment on 125th Street was very clean and neat, Hirschmann reported. "The furnishings are worn, and somewhat frayed, indicating that the family's financial resources are limited. However, the apartment shows some pride. There is only one bedroom, which is occupied by Mr. Auld [sic] and his common-law wife. The daughter, Virgie, sleeps on a convertible couch in the living room." Clearly, though he did not say so, there was no place for Shirley in this household.

"Mr. All, who was very congenial and polite to us, gave us the detailed background information concerning his relationship with his daughter, his daughter's inability to get along with people in various foster homes and his inability to control her behavior, which he repeatedly described as 'wild.' " Taking Shirley to family court had been a last resort, he said, and had brought him no help for his daughter whatsoever. "He feels that the Law Guardian [Carol Sherman] has 'only screwed things up.' "

Jay All told Hirschmann he was opposed to his daughter's remaining at his sister's house, that "because she is now older she will be more trouble" and would probably run away again. "He stressed . . . that he would like her placed in a group residence."

All described his other daughter, Virgie, twelve, as "no problem," and Hirschmann himself was very favorably impressed with her. "She is a very lively youngster, and appeared to relate extremely well to her father, at least based upon our limited impression."

A few years later, when Virgie was fifteen, her father would throw her out because she had become a Jehovah's Witness. As an adult, Virgie would summarize her childhood this way: "I had a stepmother who used to beat the tar out of me for no reason and a father who was drunk all the time."

THERE WAS NO BASIS for a finding of neglect, Hirschmann determined. Who would be guilty of such neglect, after all? It was the state that had last had custody of Shirley, and it had closed its books on her when she was on the street or in the "archtype slum" where her boyfriend's mother lived. As long as she stayed with Carrie Powell now, the problem seemed resolved, except for the financial arrangements. Powell was eligible for public assistance for her niece, but she could not leave her day-care charges to apply for it in person.

It was Carol Sherman who took Shirley to Planned Parenthood's Margaret Sanger Clinic in early February 1974, confirming that she was pregnant.

Hirschmann wrote: "Mrs. Powell is adamant against abortion for Pinky's child. Mrs. Powell is afraid of possible complications. She will not sign for abortion and reportedly neither will the natural father of Pinky, Mr. Adam [sic] All. He is apparently leaving responsibility of Pinky's care to Mrs. Powell. Mrs. Powell said that 'Somebody will take the baby when the time comes' referring that a relative will assume the responsibility. Mrs. Powell is also opposed to maternity shelter for Pinky. The girl herself stated that she doesn't want abortion or maternity shelter, but wishes to remain in Mrs. Powell's home. Pinky has been told not to see her boyfriend at residence of Mrs. Washington. Mrs. Powell . . . concluded by stating that Pinky is too young for sex."

Hirschmann referred Powell to another department for consideration as her niece's foster parent, which would bring her a higher stipend than public assistance and obviate the need for an all-day wait at a welfare office. But by the time the documents wound their way to the right unit, Carrie Powell had changed her mind. Shirley had run back to her boyfriend's apartment, and her aunt had her arrested and returned to Spofford. The family court placed her in a maternity shelter to await the birth of her baby.

"Shirley needs planning for the baby as well as for herself," a case-worker there wrote. "She has no outside resources to turn to."

TEN

IN THE SPRING OF HER PREGNANCY, SHIRLEY'S FLIGHTS BECAME ever more frantic, as though her changing body left her no peace from the longing to escape.

She ran to her father's house, fruitlessly begging him to take her back home; she ran back to Peanut's in the Bronx; one night she slept on the floor next to his bed while he lay in it with another girl. She stayed with two sisters whose mother had recently died; they were eighteen and sixteen and worked in a nearby after-hours club, as barmaids or as prostitutes, depending on whom you believed. She would sporadically telephone her new probation officer, Gloria Trexler, and return to Inwood House, a voluntary (private, nonprofit) maternity shelter on Manhattan's Upper East Side.

Trexler was no ordinary probation officer. She was part of an experimental program at Manhattan Family Court, based on a diagnosis-and-treatment model used in California. Specially trained and carrying very small caseloads, six social workers offered intensive counseling to a dozen teenagers each, all of them already rejected for placement by at least one agency. The caseworkers were on call twenty-four hours a day; Trexler had given Shirley her home phone number, and Shirley made use of it when she was on the run. Once when Shirley called in the middle of the night, Gloria Trexler drove from her home in Brooklyn to a street in the South Bronx, where Shirley was waiting for her in the rain.

Like Judge Polier, Carol Sherman, and Marcia Lowry, the probation officer responded to Shirley's combination of resilience and vulnerability. The program required a lengthy, taped interview of each child and an evaluation taking into account the child's self-perception as well as the staff's view of her; this was supposed to result in a sophisticated treatment plan based on classification of the child by maturity level. The eight-page report Trexler prepared on Shirley is an extraordinarily sensitive portrait, rich in insights about the family script that had set her up for failure and the strengths she had developed nonetheless.

"Her mother's 'Ghost' seems to haunt the All family," Trexler wrote. "Paternal relatives and stepmother seem always to be reminding Shirley she is 'just like your mother.' Unfortunately the reasons they give are that her mother would stay out, drink and fight. For Shirley this woman she barely remembers is very much alive in her fears. Shirley also compares herself with her father who is quiet and withdrawn and tends to flee his problems either physically or through drink. (Shirley wishes he would stop drinking and worries when he doesn't come home.) . . .

"Shirley sees herself as fairly autonomous, unafraid, not asking anybody to do things for her in order to avoid obligation which leads to trouble. While never really happy, she does not really need help, at least never in the present. She is similar to her father in that both have quick tempers. When hurt or sad she gets off to herself, not talking to anyone. She [believes she] has changed in that she no longer fights a lot when angry like she used to. . . . Shirley feels she is mature in that she doesn't act rowdy, doesn't argue back at people, doesn't care what people say, doesn't do things just because [a] friend does. She is unique—her own woman—autonomous."

Trexler's own view was quite different.

"Shirley is a very deeply troubled and disturbed youngster. She has little control and must run from stressful situations. She seems to seek relationships, but keeps her distance emotionally for fear of being ripped off by people. . . . Our relationship is now at a stage of tentative trust pursuant to further behavioral testing on Shirley's part. The record indicates that Shirley began to form a relationship with one foster mother, too, but then Shirley talked for a whole week about her grandmother's death and absconded. (Is she afraid in her neurotic subconscious that she may cause people to die and thus flee[s] for fear of doing it again?)

"One thing is clear, Shirley is not sure where she belongs and she cannot stay anyplace long enough to give anyone a chance to help. The record indicates a preoccupation with sex and seductive behavior when Shirley was twelve. Anyway, her sexual problems must exacerbate her already numerous childhood emotional difficulties.

"And curiously, Shirley is a strong kid with a rigid value system, positive standards, a sense of right and wrong and a determination not to be fully taken over or done in by her numerous difficulties. She has not become involved in criminal activity nor has drink or drug-taking gotten to her like so many teenagers around her. She possesses strength in spite of her serious emotional difficulties."

The pregnancy—six months along by the time Trexler typed up her completed report in May—was so threatening to Shirley's effort to be autonomous that she sometimes talked to Trexler as though it didn't exist. "Someday, if I have a baby," she prefaced one remark, when she was three and a half months pregnant. "When I was little I was wishing I was pregnant," she said on another occasion. "Now I'm not so sure."

Most of their counseling sessions centered on Shirley's longing to be accepted back home by her father. Trexler promised to talk to him about it.

"Her father, when he brought her to court, it seemed as though he was coming to dump her someplace because he didn't want to have to be bothered with whatever problems were going on for Shirley," Trexler later testified. "There had been numerous efforts to get him involved. He would never cooperate. And he would tell us—I mean court workers, social workers, the whole gamut—'I don't want her. I don't want the kid at home.' "

But he wouldn't tell Shirley that directly. Every time she called or turned up, he evaded her plea with vague promises. Trexler recalled, "He would tell Shirley, 'I want you home, I will make arrangements. I will move to a bigger apartment, move to a different place.' And then when it would come down to the wire, he never wanted her."

This time, All told Trexler emphatically that he would never take his daughter back. The caseworker had to break the news of his decision to Shirley, who began to cry as though she would never stop.

"Shirley cried in my arms," Trexler wrote in her report afterward. "She was so needy herself, and was able to say that being pregnant just complicated her life more. We tried to help Shirley see that her father's own personal problems got in his way of meeting her needs. We also assured her that we would stick by her and help her work out some of her difficulties."

In Shirley's case, "relationship is the only real vehicle for treatment," Trexler concluded in her report. "The goal is to get her to the point that she feels, 'Maybe if I'm O.K. with someone else, I'm O.K. enough to look at myself.' It will take a long time, exorbitant patience, and a willingness on the part of authorities to let her work through her difficulties, remaining 'there' when she runs and returns. Closeness and expression of emotion are the same as loss of control for Shirley, and loss of control is most fearful of all. Her running seems an effort to avoid that fear."

Trexler considered Shirley's situation desperate. Her baby was due at the beginning of August; the maternity shelter would let her stay for up to two weeks after the baby's birth. Beyond that, there was no place for her to live. The question was not what kind of place Shirley needed, but what place would accept her.

Trexler had handled hundreds of juvenile cases during seven years as a regular probation officer in Brooklyn's family court, and she knew the dilemma only too well. She might be sensitive to the nuances of Shirley's story, but on paper, Shirley was commonplace.

"Shirley was average," she would testify later in a deposition for the *Wilder* suit. "Shirley, in fact, her case was so ordinary, so typical of PINS cases, of PINS girls especially, the running away, the problems that she had, are so typical of PINS cases that—I mean it is almost boring to read her case record because you have read it so many times, in so many kids. This kind of kid didn't have anything outstanding about her. She ran away, which is what most PINS girls do. She didn't have an inordinately high IQ. Although she initially wanted placement, eventually she got to the point where she recognized she wasn't going to get placement, and eventually it began to be OK. Without a black Protestant child having something really interesting about his case—I guess that's what it boils down to—it is very difficult to get a placement for them."

The agencies' reasons for rejection were a familiar and useless litany. Needs more therapy. Needs less therapy. Needs more structure. Needs less structure. Insufficient motivation for placement. Parent not sufficiently cooperative. Would not benefit from our program.

These statements meant simply that a child wasn't wanted, wasn't appealing enough or special enough to overcome the built-in bias against a non-Jewish, non-Catholic, nonwhite kid. That was the conclusion Trexler had reached five years earlier, after working to place a girl she called by her initials, C.H., when she later recounted her case in a court deposition.

Trexler had referred the black, Protestant Brooklyn girl to the Jewish agencies' joint planning board for placement at Hawthorne in 1968. Months passed with no word. At last a social worker from the board explained, off the record, that Hawthorne had a quota of 60 percent Jewish children and 40 percent non-Jewish; there was a delay in acting on the case because the facility presently housed 46 percent non-Jewish children. Eventually, in March 1969, the teenager was granted a preplacement interview on campus. C.H., accompanied by her mother and her grandmother, traveled up to Westchester with Trexler for the interview. There were half a dozen people assembled in the room from various departments: social workers, a psychiatrist, school personnel. "The girl was very forthright in telling the reasons why she felt that she needed placement," Trexler would testify. "Finally, the man from the school said, 'Well, we already have too many C.H.'s here. You do not have the emotional controls to make use of our program. We have too many C.H.'s already.' "

THE DAY AFTER SHIRLEY sobbed in Gloria Trexler's arms, she ran from the maternity shelter again. She was seven months pregnant now; she had no money, not even bus fare, but she just kept walking north. Soon she left the hosed-down sidewalks of the Upper East Side, the uniformed doormen and the yellow taxis. The cool green islands that coursed up the center of Park Avenue gave way abruptly at Ninety-sixth Street to elevated train tracks. Grimy stone and iron broke out of the street and thrust subterranean ugliness against the sky. Old cars lay abandoned in the underpasses beneath the tracks. Trash eddied in the gutters. When a train roared overhead, the smell of stale urine rose from the darkness. Shirley's legs ached, but she kept walking.

It was twilight when she reached Peanut's neighborhood in the South Bronx, eighty blocks from Inwood House, but it was still light enough to see the smoky haze from last night's fires. Loose-limbed young men lounged outside the bodegas, tipping brown paper bags to their lips. Men older than her father played cards to Spanish music crackling from a radio wedged in an open widow. The smell of frying peppers and onions slipped into the air. It was almost suppertime. Soon the little girls jumping double-Dutch jump rope would scatter for home. They were chanting old counting-out rhymes that Shirley knew from Harlem: "Engine, engine number nine, going down Chicago line, if the train should jump the tracks, will I get my money back?"

Shirley was breathing hard; she could feel the smoke in her throat. Then the pain started, a new kind of pain that gripped her belly until she thought she might die right there in the street.

FOUR DAYS LATER, on June 4, 1974, at 9:04 P.M., Shirley Wilder, fourteen, gave birth to a baby boy at New York Hospital. He was premature but healthy, weighing five pounds, three ounces. She named him Lamont Lyn (Smith) Wilder.

PART TWO

1974–1981

ONE

HER FATHER NEVER CAME TO SEE HER IN THE HOSPITAL. No relatives visited. Two days after Lamont was born, while Shirley was giving him a bottle in the hospital nursery, three caseworkers met in the sitting room outside to discuss what to do with the fourteen-year-old mother and her child. They were a little like the three Fates in the earliest versions of that classic myth, weaving the newborn infant a swaddling band embroidered with his clan and family marks and assigning his destined place in society. Who would raise Lamont, where would he grow up, what chances would shape his childhood—such questions threaded through every decision they made now.

The presence of the three women—Joan Hessel from the city's Special Services for Children, part of the Human Resources Administration; Gloria Trexler from Manhattan Family Court; and a Mrs. DeHaas from the Inwood House maternity shelter—suggested the fragmentation of the placement process itself. Three separate entities, at least, would be involved in the decision to place Lamont. The city, specifically the commissioner of social services (who doubled as head of the Human Resources Administration), took legal custody of any child who was placed in publicly financed care. Private agencies like Inwood House supplied 90 percent of actual placements, from temporary foster homes to would-be adoptive families. And family court was the ultimate arbiter, issuing or denying the legal orders necessary to transfer and extend custody or effect an adoption.

But Gloria Trexler's presence also reflected the fact that Shirley was herself a child in public custody, under the jurisdiction of the family court. At first Trexler had hoped that Shirley and the baby could be placed in a foster home together, but administrators at the maternity shelter said she was too young for any of the existing mother-child programs. Trexler was the only one of the three women who actually knew Shirley. Shirley's original caseworker at the maternity shelter had left at the end of May, after referring the case to the city and enlisting Joan Hessel's help in planning for a baby then due in August. Mrs. DeHaas had inherited the file only days before Lamont's birth on June 4.

The three women quickly agreed that Shirley should sign commitment papers, formally turning the baby over to the city for placement in foster care. At fourteen, she could not provide a home for the baby herself, and at the moment she had no other home to take him to. If Hessel was to arrange publicly subsidized care for the baby through an agency, even if only for a few weeks while other plans were made, he had to be in city custody.

Ideally, the baby's voluntary placement was supposed to give the young mother a chance to pull her life together while the child received proper care. Because the placement was voluntary, it ostensibly honored the emphasis in religion and custom on the primacy of a parent's tie to her biological child, a tie that the state could not unilaterally sever by law at this point anyway. Yet mother and child would be separated in fact, presumably rescuing both from the worst consequences of the ill-timed birth—and strengthening the state's hand if a permanent separation was warranted later. Supervised visits were allowed but limited by virtually all agencies to once a month, during office hours.

Trexler agreed to talk to Shirley about signing the papers. She also urged that the baby's father be involved, and Joan Hessel, the city caseworker, assured her that he would be contacted about signing paternity forms at Fort Dix, where he was said to be stationed.

"Shirley joined us a few minutes later," Hessel wrote in the city social-service record. "She is a pleasant-looking girl, with big brown eyes, dark complexion and a warm smile. Shirley admitted that she would rather not place the baby in foster care but that she hadn't spoken to anyone about caring for the baby and she understood that it was necessary at this time. She did express some concern about only being able to visit the baby once a month and Mrs. T[rexler] asked if we could request a placement where visiting is more frequent and flexible. I told them I did not know which agency the baby would be referred to but that I would specify their request in my referral."

After Trexler and DeHaas excused themselves to see other clients, Hessel went over the commitment forms with Shirley, reading them aloud to her and showing her where to sign. Hessel was responsible for placing only the baby, not Shirley, who was Trexler's responsibility. This was a voluntary temporary placement of three months' duration, but it could be extended if necessary, and the fine print included the line "I understand that when the reason for placement no longer exists, I should ask for the child's return and that the Commissioner will return the child, provided that the Commissioner is satisfied that I am able to care for the child." The sentence quietly shifted the burden of proof from the state to the parent: the signer now had to prove parental fitness to get her child back, though to take a child away against a parent's wishes in the first place the state would have had to prove parental *unfitness*. Few mothers encouraged to sign such voluntary placement forms understood how hard it might be to satisfy the social-services commissioner of their parental ability when they wanted to retrieve their child. Nor was it really the commissioner who had to be satisfied, but rather the personnel of whatever private foster-care agency was caring for the child—and being paid a daily rate from public funds for each child it kept in care.

"While the child is in placement, it is my right and responsibility to visit the child regularly and to actively participate in planning until the child can have the benefit of a permanent home, either with me or in an alternative setting," the form stated. "Under the laws of the State of New York if, for a period of six successive months, I do not keep in contact with the child, my failure to do so may be considered abandonment. In addition, if, for a period of one year, I have not made efforts to plan for the child, my failure to do so may be considered permanent neglect under the law. If either of the foregoing should occur, Court action may be taken to terminate my parental rights."

The social-service laws invoked by this section had been drafted and redrafted by Shad Polier in an effort to allow adoption without the consent of parents for children left emotionally adrift in custodial care. The original 1959 legislation had been sponsored by the Citizens' Committee for Children of New York—where Shad Polier was counsel and Justine Wise Polier a founding member—in response to a study reporting the diminished likelihood of a child's return to the natural parents with each passing year in placement. Courts generally had been reluctant to find abandonment. According to the original statute, a finding of permanent neglect required both a failure to maintain contact with the child for more than a year and a failure to plan for the child's future, despite the physical and financial ability to do so. But many agencies still balked at using it to pursue termination of parental rights. Amendments later shortened the time span from a year to six months in an effort to make termination easier. The form Shirley signed in quadruplicate had been revised only seven months earlier to reflect the most recent changes. Her signature also waived notice of the family-court proceeding that would formally transfer Lamont's care and custody, acknowledged her responsibility for care and support of the child, and committed her to "make appropriate payments toward such care and maintenance to the Department of Social Services as soon as I am able to do so."

Finally, there was Form M-309, titled "Religious Designation of Child(ren)." This, too, had been revised to conform with legislative changes drafted by Shad Polier. Polier's 1970 amendment to the Family Court Act was meant to give parents a way to opt out of the religious-allocation system Judge Polier so despised. The written intention of the parents, not an automatic classification, was to control the role religion played in the assignment of a child to a particular agency. The form offered the parent the choice of checking off a box requesting that the child be placed "in the best available placement without regard to religion," or of filling in a blank with the name of the religion in which the child should be placed "if practicable and consistent with the child's best interests." In theory, Protestant parents who checked the box waived the right to a Protestant placement if a Jewish, Catholic, or nonsectarian program was superior for their child's needs. But few parents understood what the box meant, and in fact it did nothing to enhance the chances of a child's acceptance. Although the lawsuit filed in Shirley Wilder's name fundamentally challenged the whole sectarian structure of the foster-care system, Shirley herself now chose a religious placement for her son, writing in the words *Baptist-Protestant*. At the bottom of each form she signed her name. No father's signature was required for a child born out of wedlock.

"Shirley said that she understood and had no questions," Hessel wrote.

"I felt it had been a long morning for Shirley and therefore didn't get into any other areas. I did say that I would want to meet with her boyfriend and with her after her discharge from the hospital."

What the three caseworkers hadn't discussed with one another, and what Hessel did not mention to Shirley now, was an option they might have considered seriously had mother and baby been white: the baby's immediate surrender for adoption. Adoption services for black babies were still notably scarce. Through the 1960s, adoption agencies had nationally handled only 5 percent of black babies born out of wedlock, compared to 75 percent of white babies born to unmarried mothers, about half of whom actually surrendered their child for adoption in the end. This racial discrepancy was commonly attributed to the greater reluctance of black women to give up their children and the supposedly lesser stigma of illegitimacy in the black community. But in the mid-1960s, when Louise Wise Services integrated its maternity homes and consciously offered black and white unwed mothers the same options in a "pro-surrender culture," almost as many black as Jewish women chose to relinquish their infants for adoption. Louise Wise was the exception that proved the rule: black mothers were rarely given that choice.

Separated from other child-care services, adoption agencies traditionally were even more aloof than foster-care agencies from the needs of nonwhite children and families. Historically, many adoption agencies had developed in the early twentieth century as elite services catering to well-to-do white couples who wanted children, not as vehicles to serve children without families. But demand by an expanding white middle class soon outstripped the supply of babies considered "adoptable." By the mid-1960s, even before the legalization of abortion further reduced the supply, adoption agencies had an estimated 182 adoption applicants for every 100 available white babies. By 1974, it was not uncommon for dozens of adoptive applicants to be herded together at the same orientation meeting and informed that they were all competing for the same one or two babies. Agencies whose culture was so shaped by exclusion had a hard time shifting gears to recruit "good enough" black families for babies of color waiting fruitlessly for adoptive homes.

Concerted efforts to find more black adoptive families and foster homes began as early as the 1950s. An estimated two thousand black and Puerto Rican children in New York were eligible for adoption and waiting in 1955, when a program called Adopt-a-Child was started. But more than half of the families recruited either dropped out or were rejected out of hand by the agencies. Indeed, several agencies used the additional black applicants referred by the demonstration project as a way to be more selective in placing the same tiny number of black children, rather than as a means to secure adoptive homes for a greater number. Rules varied from agency to agency, but among the exclusionary standards the project had to contend with were arbitrary age limits, a ban on working mothers, and requirements for a separate room for the child and a well-maintained neighborhood. Some of the black caseworkers employed at traditional adoption agencies were among the most hostile to the project's goals, complaining that it was "lowering standards" for black children. Nevertheless, over the project's five-year life span, total adoptions of black children by participating agencies more than doubled, from 115 children in 1954 to 237 in 1959, when the project's grant expired.

In 1959 a deputy mayor escorted Justine Wise Polier home from a meeting and informed her that the city was planning to reopen a ward of a defunct tuberculosis hospital on Long Island for the care of hundreds of black and Hispanic babies waiting on hospital wards for foster homes. Polier spent a sleepless night thinking about the high rates of infant death and deterioration in such settings and came up with an idea: the city should pay approved AFDC mothers to board an infant, simultaneously improving each family's economic condition, giving the mother useful work, and saving babies from institutional neglect.

Polier promptly went to the state commissioner of public welfare with her scheme. "If your city would do anything so reasonable," he told her, "I think you would find us very receptive here in Albany." That same afternoon, after court, she took the proposal to the city's commissioner of public welfare, James Dumpson. Dumpson, then at the start of his 1959–65 stint in that job under Mayor Robert Wagner, was shocked at first. He invoked a social-work principle still strong at the time: no foster child should be placed in a home where financial support was necessary.

"Then you should close up all the sectarian agencies," Polier retorted.

"Gee, you're tough!" Dumpson answered, laughing at her reference to the private agencies' reliance on public subsidies.

Dumpson launched the project over private agency opposition, even traveling to Washington to secure waivers from the Department of Health, Education and Welfare so foster-care stipends wouldn't be deducted from the foster mothers' welfare grants. It was the city's first overtly public foster-care program. As a political compromise to mollify the Jewish and Catholic agencies and to win the mayor's support, Dumpson agreed that only infants rejected by private agencies would be placed in the public program. Predictably, more than 90 percent were children of color. Furthermore, the homes were only licensed to provide emergency care for ninety days. In effect, the program accepted the premise that these largely black and Puerto Rican homes were good enough to take care of babies briefly but not long-term, good enough for the private sector's rejects but not for "better" babies—those more in demand because of their desired skin shade and religious designation.

Like so many child welfare innovations born of crisis, the program had unintended consequences. Care in the ninety-day emergency temporary homes often stretched into years as the systemic shortfall of regular placements for children of color continued unresolved. In 1971, after the state legislature mandated a family-court review of each child in foster care—a measure designed to capture maximum federal funding (Section 392 of the Social Services Law)—the city sent caseworkers to pull hundreds of uncomprehending three- and four-year-old children out of the inadequately licensed homes where they had lived all their lives.

By then, babies of color had become part of a new category called "hard to place," which included older white children and children with physical or mental handicaps. The city had opened its own Division of Adoption Services for "hard-to-place" children in 1957. Like Louise Wise, Spence-Chapin (Protestant) and New York Foundling (Catholic) had opened their adoption programs to children of color in the 1960s, but few other agencies followed suit. Those who remembered the Adopt-a-Child project only considered it evidence that recruitment couldn't produce enough good adoptive homes to meet the needs of black children. In the 1970s, members of Judy Schaffer's Council on Adoptable Children complained of the same agency attitudes that had stymied their predecessors twenty years earlier. The council used advertisements in the *Amsterdam News*, on television, and in church newsletters to gradually recruit a thousand families, half of them black and all of them interested in adopting hard-to-place children regardless of race; but very few families were successful in obtaining agency approval. "They find some agencies pursue a hard line, taking the position that if anyone applies for a hard-to-place child, there must be something wrong with them," Polier reported in late October 1973, after meeting with frustrated representatives of the group.

The bottom line was that adoption by a stranger still seemed like an impossibly long shot for any black baby.

AFTER SECURING SHIRLEY'S SIGNATURE and sending her back to her hospital room, Joan Hessel, the city caseworker, went to look at this baby in his plastic isolette in the first-floor nursery. She copied the information from his chart into the social-service record:

> Birth weight: 5 lbs. 5 oz.
> No apgar score recorded
> No congenital defects
> Not yet circumcised
> Heart rate low and extremities jittery

But on the form referring the baby to Allocation, the unit of the city's Special Services for Children that actually parceled children out to foster-care agencies, Hessel recorded a more significant piece of information: "Lamont Wilder is a medium dark complected child with a full head of black hair."

A child's skin shade was an essential component in placement decisions; a "medium dark" complexion would limit the range of possibilities, just as the label "LIR"—"light interracial"—would open doors. Justine Wise Polier had protested such racial typing in 1962, when a black probation officer objected to the detailed racial information required about black and Puerto Rican children before Allocation would accept them for emergency or temporary placement. Polier noted, "Allocation workers must know the exact shade or coloring of a child: light, brown, dark or black, and if the hair is coarse or straight. [They] ask, 'Does the child have Negroid features?' " She lobbied then–Commissioner of Social Services Mitchell Ginsberg to order the practice stopped, and in 1969 Ginsberg complied. But two years later, during her last year on the bench, Polier walked into her chambers and overheard a worker say into the telephone, "Yes, he is Negro, but he is a beautiful little boy. No, I can't say he is light-skinned. He is dark-skinned, but he is a beautiful little boy."

Seizing the phone, Polier demanded to know why skin-shade questions were being asked about a two-year-old child in need of temporary care. "I am following regular procedure," replied the startled Allocation worker on the other end.

When pressed, workers would insist that they needed the information because the voluntary agencies required it before accepting or rejecting a child. Agency staffers in turn contended that skin shade was an issue for foster parents and their neighbors. Some foster-care workers said that matching skin shade was a legitimate way of easing a child's adjustment to a new environment; others saw it as a pernicious form of racial steering that fulfilled the old saying "If you're white, you're all right/If you're brown, stick around/ if you're black, stand back."

Since Lamont's mother was only fourteen, it took no special foresight to recognize that unless he was placed with a relative, he was likely to spend several years in foster care. The longer children stayed in care, the more moves they were likely to experience. Research on childhood attachment and the trauma of separation had been marshaled to argue that the instability of such a life was psychologically devastating—often worse for a child than the conditions foster care was supposed to cure in the first place.

A passionate debate around these issues had broken out in the popular press the year before Lamont's birth with the publication of *Beyond the Best Interests of the Child,* a book by Albert Solnit, Anna Freud, and Joseph Goldstein. Stressing "the need of every child for an unbroken continuity of affectionate and stimulating relationships with an adult," the book argued that child placement law and practice should ensure a child's bond with at least one "psychological parent," should recognize that an absent birth parent rapidly became a stranger, and should treat all placements other than brief temporary care as permanent. While agreeing that "foster-care drift" was bad, critics protested that the authors underestimated the resilience of children, ignored the importance of blood ties, and sought measures that would drastically tip the scale against any birth parent seeking to reclaim a child from foster care. Both sides reflected a consensus that had emerged by the early 1970s: the purpose of the child welfare system was to repair families quickly or find new ones, not to rear children in substitute care.

Such studies and debates had not changed the way caseworkers like

Hessel understood their real choices, however. Unless a grandmother or aunt was willing to take over the baby's care, Shirley's extreme youth was the best argument for extended foster care, not a reason for her to relinquish the child to the uncertain prospect of adoption. Shirley was considered too young to comprehend what it meant to surrender parental rights, too young to be judged permanently inadequate as a mother.

"At this point there are no known possibilities for placement with the family but they have not all been explored," Hessel wrote on the Allocation referral form. "It has been requested that the baby be placed in an agency with the most flexible and frequent visiting schedule. Discharge date for baby still unknown as there have been respiratory complications."

Carol Sherman, still Shirley's law guardian in family court, called Hessel a few days after the meeting to check on plans for the baby. The caseworker told her that Allocation was still looking for an appropriate placement. "Ms. Sherman was very upset about the fact that Shirley would have limited visiting privileges and could not go every week as well as on Saturdays," Hessel wrote. "I suggested that the agencies felt that it was in the best interest of the child to have visits on a regulated basis and that most agencies did not have Saturday visiting. Sherman told me that Saturday would be the only day that the alleged father could see the baby."

Hessel called Prentis Smith's mother, Betty Washington, to offer her Lamont. Betty Washington was the same woman another city caseworker had described only five months earlier as drunken, obnoxious, possibly high on drugs, living on public assistance with an assortment of shady characters in a filthy slum apartment unsuitable even for visits by Shirley. But case files were typically chaotic, bulging assemblages of outdated information that could take hours just to sort chronologically, if they could be located at all, and Hessel apparently never read the narrative written by the other caseworker, Tom Hirschmann.

Lamont was now two weeks old and still in the hospital. Betty Washington told Hessel that she could not care for the baby, nor could she see herself caring for Shirley and the baby together. At the present time her own daughter and *her* child were living with her. The daughter was Brenda, whose use of heroin at fifteen had showed up in her firstborn's blood. That was another matter of record buried in some other part of the child welfare bureaucracy.

Hessel talked to Carrie Powell, Shirley's paternal aunt, later the same day. "She said that she had a friend from church who lives in New Rochelle who said she might be able to help out. Mrs. Powell said that she did not feel that she could care for the baby and it would make her feel better if someone she knows has him. She said she would be able to assist them. Mrs. Powell went on to say that Shirley certainly couldn't care for the baby, that she has the mind of a child, that she's just running all the time. As far as she was concerned Shirley doesn't want things any better. Mrs. Powell knew that Mr. Smith wanted to marry Shirley and that she did not want to marry him. That brought her to Mrs. Washington who she told me should not have the baby either, as she is an alcoholic. Mrs. Powell ended by telling me that if Shirley surrendered the baby, she knew a pastor who would take him, but only under those circumstances."

Hessel had not discussed surrender with Shirley and did not ask for the name of the pastor, but she took the name and telephone number of the friend in New Rochelle, Eva Evans. She had to call several times before she reached Mrs. Evans. Meanwhile, she learned that Allocation had referred Lamont's case to Speedwell, a Protestant foster-care agency, and that a Speedwell caseworker named Mrs. Hobby had located a possible placement. "She said that they had an LTC [long-term-care] home, possible adoptive home for Lamont Wilder," Hessel noted. At Speedwell, adoption was very rare indeed, but it was true that long-term foster homes sometimes became adoptive homes. Hessel told the Speedwell caseworker that the baby had originally been referred for temporary care and that adoption had not been discussed with the mother. By now Shirley Wilder was on the run again and could not be reached. Discharged from the hospital on a Saturday morning, Shirley had left Inwood House the same night, returning briefly on Monday before vanishing. In respecting the mother's wishes as far as she knew them, Hessel was also discouraging Speedwell from assigning Lamont to its most stable kind of home—a home with the potential to become permanent in the statistically likely case that Shirley proved unwilling or unable to retrieve her son from foster care.

At the same time, it would have been hard to find an agency in the city with a worse track record than Speedwell's. The city received annual reports about each of the 550 children in Speedwell's care. Year after year, all but a handful remained in care, neither returning to their birth families nor being placed in adoptive homes. In a city foster-care system that kept children for an average of 5.2 years, Speedwell's children stayed 9.7 years. Speedwell children also experienced a high rate of disruption, an average of more than two transfers per child, not counting the original entry into care. A third of Speedwell children deteriorated while they were in the agency's custody and began manifesting such symptoms as severe anxiety, constant nightmares, bedwetting, and severe hyperactivity. Speedwell's statistical profile would not be formally compiled and made public for another two or three years, but the information had been accumulating for at least ten years in the city's files. Only a few children were discharged from Speedwell in any given year. Of these, as many were discharged to themselves because they had turned eighteen as were returned to their parents; as many were passed on to other agencies or institutions as were sent to relatives or adopted. The child who escaped the fate foretold by these numbers would be beating extraordinary odds. But no foster child's odds were much better at the time. Only one foster child in five was likely to return home, and a quarter were expected to "age out" without ever finding a permanent home.

Hessel did not ask for more information about the foster parents the Speedwell caseworker had picked out for Lamont. Instead, in keeping with the wishes of Shirley's aunt, who seemed the most concerned and stable member of the family, Hessel seriously pursued the home in New Rochelle where Eva Evans, Carrie Powell's church friend, was caring for ten mentally ill adults and three mentally retarded children under a special license from the Westchester County Department of Social Services.

"She told me that the children were seven, eight, and twenty-one, explaining that the twenty-one-year-old was limited. I asked her if she thought she could handle the additional work involved in caring for a baby. She seemed hesitant, but finally responded in the affirmative. She was quick to point up that this would have to be approved by her worker," Hessel recorded.

Shirley and Carol Sherman had both made a point of asking for more frequent visits, which placement with a friend of the family might have allowed. But Eva Evans "did say that she would want the visits regulated [and] that she got no indication from Mrs. Powell that she would want to be actively involved. Mrs. Evans also said that she understood that the mother did not have any interest in the baby and is not a responsible person."

Hessel pressed Mrs. Evans again to take the baby. "She said that she really wanted to get approval from Ms. Mancini, her social worker, before making a final decision."

Hessel called Mancini herself. "Ms. Mancini spoke very highly of Mrs. Evans, stating that she was very special. She felt that she was a capable woman, but that everyone should limit themselves at some point. Ms. Mancini told me that the people Mrs. Evans cared for came from Harlem Valley State Hospital"—here Hessel paused in her typing and went back to X-out the word *Hospital*—"which is a home for the mentally ill. The ones she had in her house were not considered a danger to themselves or anyone else, but they were limited and did have problems.

"She then spoke of a very concrete problem, that being that Mrs. Evans' home was specially licensed for retarded children, and that besides there being no room, when there is, they really should use it for a mentally retarded child, otherwise she will lose her special license. We did not get into the specifics of how this could be arranged if it was felt a good plan."

There were more conversations back and forth, and it emerged that Mrs. Evans "really did not want the responsibility of a baby, that she thought it would be too confining for her," but she didn't want her friend Mrs. Powell to know this was her reason for refusing to take her newborn great-nephew. Hessel finally called Mrs. Evans one last time to offer absolution. "I told her that she had to make a decision that would be good for all those she already cares for as well as for herself and that she should not feel badly about her decision."

Checking with the hospital on June 27, Hessel was told that Lamont was medically ready for discharge. No family member or friend was willing to care for the baby, as far as she and Trexler had been able to determine, so he would go to Speedwell after all.

Speedwell's intake day was Wednesday, and the next Wednesday was July 3. Hessel was instructed to bring the baby to the ninth floor of the agency, at 3 West Twenty-ninth Street, between nine-thirty and ten that morning. But an unspecified problem at the agency delayed the transfer for another week. On July 9, the day before the second placement date, a Speedwell caseworker sought yet another week-long postponement, "indicating that there were some problems at their end right now and that in her words they didn't know what they were doing." Hessel spoke with someone in the medical intake division and was assured that placement could occur as scheduled.

On July 10, Speedwell certified Alicia and Frantz Fils-Aime as new foster parents. The same day, they were told to pick up Lamont Wilder. They already had their plane tickets to Puerto Rico for a vacation with Alicia's family, and when they left on July 15, they took Lamont, along with their own four-year-old son, Henri. Their five-week trip turned into an interagency controversy. A casework supervisor at Speedwell sought the city's official approval for the vacation after the fact; approval was indignantly refused. "I explained that Miss Hessel, the BCW worker for Lamont, had no knowledge of the plan for the child to accompany the foster parents to Puerto Rico," a supervisor named E. Norris wrote into the record. "I expressed concern that we were not informed of the foster parents' plan to take vacation prior to placing the infant in this home as we would have asked for another home. We feel this created many unnecessary changes for this infant to adjust to in a very short period of time. I pointed out that it was especially unwise in this situation for the child to go on a trip without BCW approval or that of the mother, in that we may be asked to bring the child into court."

The Speedwell supervisor, who was new to the job, responded that the agency couldn't have contacted the mother about the trip because it had only the most limited information about her. The placement had been made on an emergency basis. It was now September 5, and the three-month commitment was about to expire, but Speedwell still had not received a long-term-care referral from the city.

Later a Speedwell caseworker called to defend herself. She had telephoned Special Services for Children before the foster parents took the child to Puerto Rico and had had a hard time finding the person responsible for the Wilder case. She had finally talked to a Mr. Hirschmann, who "advised her that he did not know the mother's whereabouts. He spoke to his supervisor and gave approval for the foster parents to take the baby on the trip."

The city supervisor then explained that there were two cases: the maternal grandparent's, with Shirley as the child, was Hirshmann's; the baby, with Shirley as the parent, was Hessel's.

This was the new world of foster care that Lamont inhabited: at once haphazard and inflexible. Foster care existed in a zone of constant friction between private and public bureaucracies, between social work and courts of law, and the gears of accountability were better attuned to catch an unapproved vacation than a houseful of schizophrenics or the ongoing purgatory of foster care without end. Lamont's placement, like so many, had threaded past lost options and narrow escapes to bind him to a family that would never be his own. It had been selected not through some conscious weighing of alternatives informed by law and social policy, but in a kind of paroxysm of bureaucratic improvisation. It could have been better. It could have been worse.

TWO

AT ABOUT SIX O CLOCK IN THE EVENING ON FRIDAY, SEP-
tember 7, Gloria Trexler got a call at home from Shirley's stepmother. "Shirley is here," Liz Booker said. "What do we do?"

"Hold her," Trexler ordered.

Shirley had spent part of the summer living with her girlfriends in the
Bronx while Trexler, her probation officer, tried to arrange a placement
for her at an agency called Abbott House; it had a new group home for
disturbed teenagers operated in conjunction with Bellevue Hospital—
the very program Marcia Lowry had helped start when she was working
for the city. Shirley had been remanded to Spofford by family court after
missing appointments with the probation officer to visit the agency's
main offices in Irvington, New York, but on August 20 she had been
paroled to her law guardian, Carol Sherman, for a day trip to Abbott
House. They stopped on the way to pick up Shirley's clothes at her girlfriends' apartment, and before Sherman knew what was happening,
Shirley had bolted out the door and down the street. She had been calling
home ever since, asking to speak to her father, wanting to be taken back
into the family. Now she planned to wait until he came home to ask him
again face to face.

Trexler telephoned the police precinct. Neither she nor the stepmother had a copy of the warrant issued by family court, and without it,
the cops were unwilling at first to pick up the runaway. The probation
officer eventually prevailed upon them to call Central Files to verify the
warrant's existence. When the police finally arrived at the Alls', it was
past midnight. Shirley was still there, but her father, who had come home

a few minutes earlier, refused to let them take her away. When Trexler got him on the telephone, he said he didn't want Shirley to spend the weekend in Spofford. As soon as the police left, however, he threw her out of the house.

The Alls' apartment was on the first landing, and the stairs outside their door went right into the street. Shirley stood on the bottom step for a while, not knowing what to do. It was a warm Friday night on the seedy end of Harlem's main drag, about the time of night when the first bar fights start spilling out to the sidewalk and the hookers emerge from the train underpass to hoot and cheer them on.

Upstairs, her stepmother was still talking to Trexler on the telephone. Liz was very angry at Shirley's father, Jay. Every so often she put down the receiver to relay the probation officer's critical comments and to add her own. At last Shirley's little sister, Virgie, picked up the telephone.

"Shirley's still downstairs," she said.

"Go ask her to come to the telephone and talk to me."

Virgie ran down the stairs and brought Shirley back up to the phone.

"Shirley, you know I have a warrant for you," Trexler told her.

"Yes."

"Shirley, what I want you to do now is to turn yourself in."

"All right," she said. "I'm ready to go back."

Liz accompanied Shirley to the precinct at 1:00 A.M. At daybreak she was back in Spofford. Trexler felt a corner had been turned, that the night's events had forced Shirley to see that her father's rejection was final.

Soon afterward, Holy Cross Campus of Pope Pius the XII, a Catholic residential treatment center in Rhinecliff, New York, agreed to accept Shirley on a ninety-day trial placement. Trexler was delighted. In her experience, Holy Cross didn't tend to see children in terms of psychiatric diagnoses; it provided therapy when needed, but the emphasis wasn't on the child's gaining insight through psychotherapy, which would be of little help to Shirley, she thought. Opened as a drug program in 1971, Holy Cross had shown a willingness to take troubled black and Hispanic teenagers from New York City when many other residential centers still seemed determined to hold out for the white ethnic children they had served in the past. And Shirley, who knew someone who had gone to Holy Cross, preferred it to Abbott House.

"Shirley's wisdom in this situation exceeds our own," Trexler wrote the Holy Cross intake director. "An open group residence in the city is not appropriate for Shirley at this time. She knows the opportunity to deal with problems by running is greater here. Naturally, we recognize that the opportunity exists for her anywhere, but it is lessened by lack of immediate availability of 'safe havens.' "

The strength of Holy Cross's location, a hundred miles up the Hudson, was also its greatest drawback when it came to Shirley's chance to build a relationship with her child, Trexler realized. Carol Sherman was especially worried about the bureaucratic obstacles to that bond. She wanted Shirley at least to be able to call the baby's caseworkers at Speedwell and the city's child welfare office whenever she wanted, to find out how the baby was doing. But besides having a probation officer and a law guardian, Shirley now had a social worker at Spofford involved in her case, too, and she disapproved of such unregulated calls.

"It would get out of control with the other girls," the Spofford social worker, Mrs. Brown, told Trexler when the two of them met with Joan Hessel to discuss the case. She meant that the detention routine would be disrupted if other girls at Spofford who had children in foster care began to demand the privilege of calling to ask about them whenever they pleased. Normal procedure required Shirley to go through her social worker, Mrs. Brown, to contact the baby's caseworker. Besides, it was Carol Sherman, the law guardian, not Shirley, who kept expressing concern about the baby, the Spofford social worker complained. Shirley hardly even mentioned the baby on her own.

Trexler told them that Shirley had expressed a great deal of guilt about not wanting to have the responsibility of the baby now. If she went upstate, it was important that she be able to find out how the baby was doing. After some negotiation, it was decided that for now Shirley could call Speedwell once a week, but that if she wanted to speak with Joan Hessel, who had supervisory and planning responsibility for the baby, she would have to go through Mrs. Brown.

"While all this was going on I pointed up the fact that everyone wants to protect Shirley's rights to the baby for the future, but that with three or four concerned people asking Shirley if she's called about the baby, we are never going to get any estimation of Shirley's own desires and motivation," Hessel wrote in her running case narrative. "It was already agreed upon that she is feeling guilty at the present time, and I suggested that if a worker mentions the baby once a week, it will be at those times that she will follow through on it. I told Mrs. Trexler that Shirley has to understand that at the present time there was no alternative for the baby and there were no programs available for her and the baby so LTC [long-term care] seemed inevitable. She also had to understand that no one was going to keep after her, and that if she had an interest in the baby, she should express it. When she is in placement, I said there should be a way of her coming to N.Y.C. and having monthly visits if they are requested. It is only when Shirley's feelings about the baby are expressed, or not expressed[,] without coercion that the situation can be dealt with realistically."

To Hessel, motherhood was a test that Shirley had to pass or fail on the system's terms; coaching her would be cheating. Meeting alone with Shirley, Hessel watched for tears when she told the young mother that her baby would have to remain in foster care "until an appropriate plan could be worked out," which might mean twelve months or more. "There was no physical reaction that I was able to see," she reported. "I tried to impress upon Shirley the fact that she did have rights to her child . . . however it would be her responsibility to initiate calls and visits, and that no one would be keeping after her. . . . Shirley did not seem to be too connected to our conversation and she had this faraway look on her face."

Shirley had not seen the baby since her discharge from the hospital. She asked if she could use the telephone to call Speedwell right then, but Hessel told her she would have to make arrangements with Mrs. Brown to use the phone. Shirley asked about the baby, but Hessel had no answers. "She seemed confused about why I didn't know too much about the baby and I explained that the worker at Speedwell is the one who works with the baby and the foster mother and knows all about his progress. I on the other hand really just work with her, and I would have to call the foster-care worker to find out any information on Lamont.

"I then asked Shirley about the baby's father. She told me she hadn't seen him or heard from him in a while and that they were not going together anymore. I asked her if she still wanted the baby to have his name and she told me it would be all right. She said I could contact him regarding paternity if I wanted to, and that she thinks he should still be at Ft. Dix."

Eventually Hessel and Shirley went looking for Mrs. Brown, and Shirley again asked if she could use the phone to call the baby's worker at Speedwell. Yes, tomorrow, Mrs. Brown said, and she sent Shirley away.

PREPARING A PACKET OF INFORMATION on Shirley for Holy Cross, Trexler enclosed the psychiatric and psychological evaluations prepared by Abbott House. "Shirley is a depressed, frightened, insecure adolescent who is afraid of coming in touch with her own feelings," the psychologist had written. "She is not believed to be psychotic. . . . Shirley shows much early childhood deprivation. Lack of this basic love and nurturance leaves Shirley feeling frail, insecure and distrustful. Her self-doubt becomes projected onto others, and only after they have proved their strength to her repeatedly will she allow herself to open up to them. This closeness usually takes the form of dependence. In more clean-cut and reality-oriented inter-personal relationships, she can however be unusually independent and mature for her age.

"Despite her very poor self-image, Shirley shows a healthy need and concern for other people. This need is a major strength which enables her to return, both emotionally and physically, when she runs away. Behind her fears and hiding is a girl who is still asking for help.

"Shirley shows normal heterosexual interests. She sees boys as more assertive and capable than women. She does not project herself as a sexually acting-out girl but rather somewhat impulsive." The diagnosis: "Runaway reaction of adolescence."

Trexler ended her letter to Holy Cross with her own assessment: "Shirley is a strong young lady, despite her propensity to flee. She has never been involved with delinquent activity. Though some of her friends were known to use drugs or alcohol, she has not succumbed. She wants assistance, and historically has learned it is hard to trust (people die or reject, for her). Our goal for Shirley is the goal which Holy Cross states is its own: 'New ways to handle stress and accept responsibility.' "

One major issue remained to be resolved: birth control for Shirley. Trexler had talked with the teenager about it, with her stepmother and with the social worker at Spofford, who arranged for Shirley to see a nurse there. Everyone agreed that Shirley needed contraception, and Shirley was willing to get an IUD. But the intrauterine device could be inserted only during her menses, and she had not yet started menstruating again after childbirth. The fitting would have to wait.

ON OCTOBER 16, 1974, Trexler took Shirley up to Holy Cross. A nun met them at the Rhinecliff train station. She was Sister Dorothy Gallant, Shirley's new social worker, a small woman in a modified brown habit with a sweet, high voice and the broad vowels of the small Massachusetts mill town where she had grown up. She drove them through a forest of towering trees to Holy Cross Campus.

It had once been part of Levi Morton's thousand-acre estate on the Hudson River. Morton was a self-made merchant banker of the Gilded Age who flourished in Republican politics. The estate had served to certify his accession to a superior class, since the same Social Darwinism that condemned excessive relief for the poor glorified the spoils of the wealthy as evidence of their evolutionary entitlement. Morton left most of the estate to his daughter Helen, who converted to Catholicism after her marriage to a French viscount and passed the property to the Catholic Archdiocese of New York. Between 1946 and 1970, it had been the site of an ambitious Catholic military academy meant to evoke a junior West Point for three hundred cadets. Then the Vietnam war abruptly ended the appeal that military schooling held for prosperous Catholic families, and Cardinal Farley Military Academy went bankrupt. It had been reincarnated in 1971 as a residential treatment program for the rising number of adolescents entering city foster care—with public funding to cover at least 90 percent of the archdiocese's costs. The arrangement typified the tradition of mutual dependence of the foster-care system and the Catholic Church, without resolving any of its growing contradictions. More and more of the children in need of placement were black non-Catholics, and the system's ostensible purpose now was to quickly repair and reunite families—a goal not notably served by a separation of a hundred miles.

When Sister Dorothy turned in to the main entrance of Holy Cross Campus, Shirley saw a white statue of the Madonna, an expanse of green lawn, and large brick dorms set on a hill. There were one hundred residents aged thirteen to seventeen, about equally divided between boys and girls. The girls lived two to a room in Spellman Hall, a large brick building with a huge metal cross affixed to its three-story facade. The cadets' rose garden was no more, and the chandeliers in the dining room had been replaced with fluorescent lights. But there were still tennis courts, a swimming pool in the gym, and white marble statues of saints lining the walk to the chapel.

Gloria Trexler and Sister Dorothy accompanied Shirley through the admission procedures, which included a physical examination by a nurse. Later Trexler would relate her conversation with the nurse and the nun in a court deposition. "I explained to Sister Dorothy that [Shirley] had had a baby, and that we felt that there was a need, especially this being a coeducational facility, for contraceptives in Shirley's case. Sister Dorothy agreed. We discussed it briefly with the nurse and . . . the understanding was that when [Shirley] had her menses at Holy Cross, that arrangements would be made for her to see a doctor and to have an IUD emplaced."

TO TREXLER, THE NUN'S ACCEPTANCE of contraception in Shirley's case only underlined that no one could fail to see the need. If she became pregnant while at Holy Cross, she would have to leave. Perhaps the program could eventually help her change her sexual behavior, but what was imperative in the meantime was to ensure that she didn't get pregnant again. Trexler left Holy Cross believing the issue had been resolved. In fact, it had only been referred by Sister Dorothy to Shirley's treatment team, and from the team to Father Richard LaMorte, the priest who chaired the institution's sex committee.

"The PO [probation officer] who was influential in having Shirley placed at Holy Cross has advised that Shirley be able to take these precautions as soon as possible as both the PO and her intake material indicate that Shirley is a very sexually active and aggressive child," the chair of the treatment team, Maureen Murphy, wrote in a memo detailing Sister Dorothy's inquiry about "the possibility for securing an IUD birth control device for Shirley Wilder."

When Trexler and Carol Sherman visited Shirley at Holy Cross more than three weeks later, they were told that contraception had been ruled out. "I was informed that the archdiocese had said no child in a Catholic institution may have birth control, and if they do have it emplaced at point of admission, they must either remove it or leave the agency," Trexler later testified in a deposition. She had talked about the issue with

Sister Dorothy; with Larry Pixley, the agency's director of social work; with Ed Dohrenwend, the director of Holy Cross Campus; and with Dr. Steve Gold, Holy Cross's clinical psychologist. "All of them were in agreement that for this child, birth control was indicated. However, they were obviously not in a position to be able to do anything about it. By that time, Shirley already had a boyfriend."

The boyfriend, a linebacker-sized resident named Arthur Johnson, was mentioned in reports prepared by Holy Cross staff—reports also noting that Shirley had told staff she would probably see her baby's father again on home visits and would likely become reinvolved with him sexually. She had renewed her request for an IUD or birth-control pills.

"This request has been denied," Pixley, the treatment team leader, reported, "because Pius XII School, Holy Cross Campus, as a member agency of the Department of Child Care of the Archdiocese of New York, has a policy which prohibits the use of Birth Control. Furthermore, Shirley needs to develop the kinds of controls around sexual behavior which will help her avoid relationships which can give her difficulties such as she has just experienced with the birth of her baby. Shirley has been informed that this kind of behavior is not acceptable and we will be carefully monitoring it to help her in coping with it. At this time, her goals will be to avoid sexual activity. Shirley has indicated a great interest in counseling on sex and Sister Dorothy will proceed to develop her relationship with Shirley in this area." Sister Dorothy was also designated as Shirley's therapist and directed to begin therapy sessions immediately.

Sister Dorothy was an unlikely sex counselor. Born in 1938, she had entered the novitiate of the Felician Sisters when she was seventeen, after a very sheltered, small-town childhood as the youngest of three daughters in a devout Catholic family. Her parents worked in the mill, like most people in Webster, one of the first Polish immigrant communities in Massachusetts. For fun the family went mushroom- or berry-picking together, or for walks to look at the autumn leaves. Once in a blue moon they went into the city, which meant Worcester, a town of 160,000. When she first saw people begging there, "it just hurt my heart," Sister Dorothy would say later. Like many sensitive and idealistic Catholic girls in the 1950s, she found that a religious vocation answered all the inchoate longings of her adolescence. "I loved God and I loved people and I wanted to express my life in some dedicated way—and I followed where it led me."

It had led to her novitiate at Our Lady of Angels convent in Enfield,

Connecticut, and then to Brooklyn, New York, where she taught parochial school. In 1969, her order had sponsored her study of social work. While earning a master's degree at Fordham, she served as housemother for twenty-two blind, disabled children between the ages of four and twenty-one in an institution in the Bronx. When she received her degree, in 1971, she went to the after-care program of Wiltwyck School for Boys as a family liaison worker. She worked out of a Harlem office at 125th and Lexington—just down the street, in fact, from Sam's Soul News and Shirley's father. In 1973, after a boy in her caseload was murdered by a rival gang, Sister Dorothy moved upstate to live in an experimental Christian community in Kingston, seeking the spiritual growth that she hoped would sustain her in a life of fellowship with the poor. She now commuted to Holy Cross across the Kingston-Rhinecliff Bridge, which spans the Hudson River. She had been in her job there only a little over a year when Shirley arrived.

Like the reformatory at Hudson, Holy Cross used a system of phases and levels of increasing privilege, and it was the first time Sister Dorothy had worked within a behavior-modification model. It was also her first experience in a drug program; at the time, she considered marijuana a heavy drug. As for sex—well, she kept a *Sex Encyclopedia* in her office.

WHEN TREXLER LEARNED that Shirley had been denied birth control, she notified Pius XII officials of her intention to seek a court hearing on the matter and asked for a written explanation of the agency's position. "Holy Cross is an excellent institution which offers Shirley the kind of care which she has needed for so long," she wrote the director of the campus, Ed Dohrenwend. "As you can well appreciate, we do not wish to do anything which will jeopardize Shirley's placement as she is doing so well at Holy Cross. However, we do feel strongly from a casework position [that] birth control is imperative for this girl."

The director forwarded the letter to Donna Santasiero, assistant to Monsignor Robert Arpie, the director of child care at Catholic Charities, along with a memo that noted: "We have verbally informed Shirley's probation officer and attorney that we are not able to provide Shirley with birth control because this is a Catholic agency and the Archdiocese of New York does not permit birth control. As per our talk, will you take it from here and respond to the probation officer."

But there was no response, and Trexler's many telephone calls to Santasiero were not returned.

Meanwhile, the nurse and Sister Dorothy met with Shirley to explain the rhythm method of birth control. Since sex outside marriage remained as proscribed as ever by the Catholic Church, teaching rhythm to an unwed mother of fourteen with no impulse control and a new boyfriend was neither sound theology nor effective social work; it was a form of desperation.

In late November, about the time of her fifteenth birthday, Shirley saw a doctor on campus who said she might be pregnant again. She ran away the next day, before a test could confirm the doctor's suspicion. Trexler was certain that if Shirley had not been pregnant when she left Holy Cross, she would be when she surfaced again. To everyone's relief, however, when Shirley returned voluntarily to Holy Cross six weeks later, a pregnancy test was negative. But the condoms she secretly brought back with her to campus were soon discovered and confiscated in one of the periodic "shakedowns" of the girls' rooms. Shirley couldn't understand the reasoning behind the denial of birth-control devices and talked to the nurse about it several times.

"She tried to explain to me why I couldn't have it," Shirley would testify later in a deposition. "She said, 'Because this is a Catholic place and Catholic people do not believe in birth controls.' So I told her, 'I'm a black Protestant, I don't go by your laws.' She said, 'That doesn't mean nothing. You are on our grounds.' "

Of course sexual intercourse was against the rules, but that hadn't prevented Sister Dorothy and the nurse from explaining how Shirley could time intercourse to coincide with her infertile periods. Shirley had no trouble drawing the conclusion that condoms and other birth-control devices were contraband because the rules of Catholicism were being imposed on non-Catholics like her.

Shirley's placement at Holy Cross was officially a ninety-day remand by the family court, and it was about to expire when she returned there on January 16. Her case as a "person in need of supervision" came up on the court calendar three days later. Trexler told the judge, Harold Felix, that access to birth control was going to be an issue in the effort to turn Shirley's remand into a regular twelve-month placement. It was a constitutional question, Judge Felix declared, not appropriate for a family-court ruling, but he wasted no time in adding that he was not in favor of issuing birth control because it would give children license to have sex. Still, he asked for a copy of Trexler's letter to Holy Cross and said he would call the archdiocese about the matter. Trexler's administrators told her to do nothing else until she heard back from Judge Felix, who had extended Shirley's remand for another sixty days.

A month went by. On February 21, 1975, the judge told Trexler informally that he had spoken with an attorney at Catholic Charities. "And then the judge wondered aloud if we should not 'find another placement for Shirley and save Holy Cross the embarrassment' of the birth-control issue." Coupled with a reiteration that there was nothing family court could do, that was his only suggestion. The matter was quietly dropped. In March, with Holy Cross in agreement, the court formally placed Shirley there for twelve months.

THREE

ALICIA FILS-AIME KEPT THE TINY AQUA-BLUE SLEEPER THAT Lamont was wearing the day she brought him home, July 10, 1974. It was still big on him the first week, its fleecy folds drooping around him. But after their five-week trip to Puerto Rico that summer, he was too big for it. He seemed to fatten on the balmy ocean air, rocked in the arms of "Mama Negra," the stout, dark-hued grandmother in Alicia's light-skinned Puerto Rican family, who held him on the balcony and cooed over his big dark eyes and halo of fuzzy hair.

By November, when a caseworker instructed Alicia to bring Lamont downtown to the Speedwell agency for his first visit with his teenaged mother, he was five months old, and his weight had more than tripled. He was a beautiful baby, so good-natured that he sometimes paused in the sucking of his bottle just to smile milkily up at Alicia. Henri, her four-year-old son, did not seem jealous. As a parent, Alicia exuded calm; she was unhurried and deliberate in her care of both children, with a tender gravity that was affectionate but self-contained. Lamont slept in a white crib in Henri's room, and sometimes before they went to sleep Alicia would hear the baby babbling and Henri's murmuring reply.

When she had applied to be a foster parent, she explained that she was unable to have another child after Henri and wanted to share their warm family life with children who lacked such a home. On most levels, it was true. She had kept her mother's tradition of setting housework to song, and Spanish refrains soared over the vacuum cleaner in the family's four-room apartment. They lived in a secure, well-kept housing project in an integrated section of the northeast Bronx. Her husband, Frantz, a shipping clerk, was a good provider who was always bringing her little gifts. Saturdays they took Henri to watch the softball games in the park, often picnicking with nieces and cousins from the extended family on both sides. Sundays found them at the Mount Eden Spanish Evangelical Baptist Church, where Alicia taught Sunday school and was active in the women's group that went on Bible retreats and organized the church's volunteer fix-up crews.

Family and church had always been at the center of her life. She was the oldest of four sisters raised alone by their mother in a small town in northern Puerto Rico. Their father was not in the picture, and their mother was a woman too proud to beg for support. To earn a living, her mother did ironing and laundry for people in the neighborhood, ran their errands, cleaned for them. It was a poor community, and when her clients couldn't afford to pay her in money, they would offer a meal for the children instead. Alicia remembered this not as a humiliation but as part of the communal spirit in which she grew up. The family was originally Catholic, but when Alicia was still a child, a neighbor started taking her and then her sisters along to the Baptist church. Eventually even their mother was baptized there. After Alicia graduated from high school, she came to New York City to baby-sit for the children of an uncle, a chef who had married an Irish girl. She met Frantz soon afterward, in an evening English class for immigrants.

He was five years older, five foot seven and strongly built, with golden skin and a dark mustache that made many New Yorkers assume he was Hispanic. But he was Haitian, born into the light-skinned mulatto elite that had long dominated that impoverished black republic. He had grown up as one of nine children in a family of property owners of a class that typically sent its children to be educated in France. His adolescence had been a time of political turmoil, marked by the rise and fall of several provisional presidents. In 1957, when Frantz was nineteen, "Papa Doc" Duvalier had been elected in a plebiscite on a promise to end the reign of the light-skinned wealthy and to put political and economic power into the hands of the black masses. Some of Frantz's older siblings left right away, others when they saw power flow to Papa Doc's terror thugs, the Tontons Macoute. By 1964, when Duvalier had himself elected president for life, the exodus of the Fils-Aime family was almost complete.

Frantz and Alicia dated for three years before they married. He joined her Baptist church, to the consternation of his Roman Catholic family, and Alicia quit her job filing at the midtown headquarters of the Diner's Club credit-card company when her supervisors wouldn't give her time off for a honeymoon. She planned to get pregnant right away, but it didn't happen for five years. Meanwhile, she went to work as a teacher's assistant in a junior high school, studied French with phonograph records so she and Frantz could converse in his native tongue, and painted and plastered on the church's volunteer work crews. She quit work again when she was pregnant with Henri.

But within a marriage that appeared both traditional and contented, there were strains. Alicia had a fierce need for autonomy, a craving for her own space that Frantz could never understand, let alone accept. When he was home, he wanted to be with her every minute. She felt besieged and invaded by his need for constant physical closeness, all the more so because she knew he experienced her reserve as a personal rejection. So she sought acceptable escape from the intensity of his presence. Besides her women's retreats, she went out to dinner with her own friends every Friday night. Teaching Sunday-school classes was more than a religious commitment; it was a way of guaranteeing herself breathing room on weekends. Perhaps on some unconscious level, she saw taking in a foster child as a way to add another buffer zone to her marriage.

ON THE DAY OF SHIRLEY'S FIRST VISIT, in November, Alicia found it strange to bring Lamont to a caseworker at the Speedwell office and just leave him there. She walked around aimlessly for most of the two and a half hours set aside for his young mother to touch and hold him. Alicia felt great compassion for this teenager she had never seen, and she accepted the idea that Lamont would go to live with her when she had grown up enough to assume his care. But it seemed sad that Shirley would miss so much of his growing up.

"Shirley didn't seem to know how to act initially and appeared to be somewhat awkward in handling the baby," Sister Dorothy wrote after the first visit. "Later, she warmed up, became more relaxed and seemingly comfortable. She kissed him a few times and focused a good deal of attention on his external features. The baby did not cry during the visit. At times, Shirley gave me the impression that she couldn't believe that she really had a baby.

"Mrs. Spector, the baby's worker, met with us but focused most of the attention on Shirley's adjustment to Holy Cross. Because this was Shirley's first visit with the baby and because she could have been filled with a lot of feelings which she was unable to surface, Mrs. Spector thought it best that we didn't begin getting into the area of Shirley's future plans regarding Lamont. Surfacely [sic], Shirley separated from the baby quite easily at the end of the visit. On the return trip to Holy Cross, Shirley did make mention of an aunt who reportedly said she would take care of Lamont when he was a year old. She spoke of herself getting a job after Holy Cross and caring for the baby."

The supervised visits were supposed to be monthly, but because Shirley went AWOL for six weeks, the next was not scheduled until February 13. Alicia was ill that day and called Speedwell to cancel the appointment.

Sister Dorothy and Shirley already had traveled down from Rhinecliff and were waiting at Speedwell. Even the baby's caseworker, Mrs. Spector, was not there, and another worker told them she might be leaving the agency. "Shirley was angry and her first response was to express her desire to remove the baby from Speedwell," the nun wrote later. Shirley asked that Brenda Smith, the sister of the baby's father, be considered as a foster parent instead. She gave Speedwell Brenda's address in the Bronx. Had the agency ever pursued the matter, Brenda's history of heroin addiction and relationship with a drug-dealing boyfriend might have emerged. But Brenda had no telephone, and the suggestion went nowhere.

During his first year, Shirley visited her son four times. It was on Lamont's first birthday that Alicia and Shirley first saw each other. The meeting was an accident, strained at the start. Lamont's caseworker was late. This was the third worker to be assigned to the case; they kept leaving the agency. Alicia was sitting in the waiting room at Speedwell with Lamont and Henri when Sister Dorothy and Shirley walked in. For a long time the nun and the teenager waited on the other side of the room, Shirley looking on as Alicia held Lamont and kept him amused with toys.

"Shirley had not met the foster mother prior to this and was surprised that she is Spanish and not Black," Sister Dorothy wrote later that day. "The foster mother and I talked and after awhile made a decision to let Shirley hold the baby before the worker came. The foster mother appears to be very serene and sensitive. Her interest in Lamont is obvious. Her five-year-old son played with Lamont and Lamont seemed quite content and comfortable with his foster family."

It was Alicia who carried Lamont over to Shirley and put him in her lap. "Shirley is your mother," she told the one-year-old. "She has beautiful eyes like you."

Shirley and Alicia would see each other only one other time, at a visit on August 28, 1975, but Alicia often repeated those words to Lamont. It was not to say that she herself was not his mother, only that he had another mother, too, a mother with big eyes and smooth dark skin like his own.

Shirley responded to Alicia's gesture in the waiting room with a new feeling of warmth toward this light-skinned stranger who was mothering her son. Later she gave the Speedwell caseworker a note to pass on to Alicia, thanking her for taking good care of Lamont. Alicia was touched as much by the careful handwriting on the little slip of paper as by the words. Before each visit, she felt proud that Shirley would see how well Lamont was developing, how responsive and bright he was, how adorable.

TO SISTER DOROTHY, the visits with Lamont were like stepping stones toward Shirley's maturity, simultaneously a form of treatment, a test of progress, and a reward for good behavior. On one occasion the nun canceled a session scheduled by the baby's caseworker because Shirley had spent a Sunday AWOL the week before. "Dorothy is Shirley's therapist and would like to have her feel that she is responsible for her actions and that her actions will affect her time spent with the baby," the treatment team's memo explained.

In her written account of each visit, Sister Dorothy approvingly remarked any signs of maternal behavior in Shirley. "Shirley continues to appear more comfortable with Lamont though still somewhat stiff," the nun wrote after the girl's visit with her eleven-month-old son, who babbled with enthusiasm, clapped his hands responsively, and had doubled his teeth from two to four in three weeks. "Shirley fed Lamont and was especially motherly during this process. It is interesting to note the difference in Shirley's behavior at Holy Cross and during the visits with the baby. The immaturity which characterizes her behavior at the Cross disappears and she presents herself as a responsible and rather mature fifteen-year-old. Shirley is moving in the direction of keeping the baby in foster care until she can assume caring responsibilities for him. No pressure is being applied in terms of the amount of time Lamont will need to be in foster care before she is ready to care for him. Shirley's decision may change as time progresses."

IF NEITHER SISTER DOROTHY nor the succession of Speedwell case-workers pressed Shirley about her plans, it was in part because their social-work tradition treated motherhood as the best bridge to female rehabilitation. It had not always been so. In the days of the Women's House of Refuge, sexual transgression in girls was considered a sign of hereditary mental incapacity for which the only treatment was the enforced chastity of institutionalization. Girls too "feeble-minded" to defend their virtue were to be locked up both for their own protection and for the protection of society from their presumably defective offspring. But after World War I, the more sympathetic attitudes of several women leaders in social work gained dominance. At a conference on illegitimacy and female delin-quency held in 1921, psychologist Marion E. Kenworthy articulated the centrality of childbearing:

"We must not lose sight of the fact that in the pregnancy itself we may find a potent factor for good. . . . If through our efforts we furnish this mother with an unstigmatized opportunity to remain with her child, to assume the responsibility of its care, to have a normal outlet for the pent up love craving, we will discover that much of the libido (the hunger) finds a normal outlet through the sublimational channels of mother love."

The child-saving zeal that seized and united social reformers at the turn of the century cast the child not as the victim of a degraded family that should be broken up, but rather as the agent of adult redemption. The reasons for this shift are complex, but efforts to enshrine children and to elevate the moral importance of maternal feelings seem to have been spurred in part by male anxiety over signs of female emancipation, in-cluding the woman suffrage movement, low marriage rates among college-educated women, rising rates of divorce, and falling birth rates among the "fittest."

Through the 1950s, the rise of psychiatry and family-conflict theories of deviant juvenile behavior provided another gloss on the idea that acceptance of motherhood could transform an uncontrollable adolescent into a good woman—or at least a "well-adjusted" one. It was an approach that concorded particularly well with Catholicism. Pope Pius XII had declared in 1945 that every woman was called upon to be a mother in a physical or spiritual sense, and therefore women should not be employed outside the home. Catholic churchmen took the lead in exalting maternity during the postwar American effort to return women to the hearth. As the Virgin Birth had overcome Original Sin embodied in Eve, so motherhood could be seen as overcoming the dangerous sexuality of the female transgressor.

According to these complementary lines of thought, Lamont's presence in Shirley's life held the promise of her redemption; his loss would represent the risk of her unrestrained descent into promiscuity. Although Shirley had expressed nothing but regret and ambivalence about motherhood, Sister Dorothy expected her to grow into the role as she matured and learned self-discipline.

"Shirley is beginning to make some behavioral changes which she recognizes in herself and feels positive about," the nun wrote after the birthday visit. "Before, she seemed to be burdened by guilt for being a 'bad mother.' Now, she seems to see herself as doing that which is best for Lamont as she is preparing herself to be a 'good mother' to him. . . . I find during our visits to the baby she is more available to looking at the future. The reality of her responsibilities and need to mature is reinforced."

It suited Sister Dorothy's patient personality to wait through Shirley's uncertainty rather than push for a decision the girl might later regret. But the city child welfare office had a different timetable. On the anniversary of Lamont's placement, there was paperwork required for an extension of the placement, and unanswered questions were suddenly considered pressing. The forms called for some assessment of Shirley's progress toward the goal of assuming responsibility for her child. Legally, Shirley's father was responsible for contributing toward the cost of her care, unless he could be recertified as financially unable to do so. Likewise, Lamont's father was financially responsible for his son's support, but no one had ever gone after him. Shirley had never even been asked to sign an allegation of paternity.

Sister Dorothy was unavailable when the city caseworker, Joan Hessel, contacted Holy Cross about having Shirley sign paternity papers, but a colleague demurred on her behalf: "Sister felt it unwise for Shirley to become reinvolved with the alleged father."

Joan Hessel countered that Shirley would have no contact with the alleged father—her signature on a form was all that was necessary for city workers to do the rest. The Holy Cross counselor wasn't swayed. Sister Dorothy was worried that Shirley might want to see Lamont's father again if she knew he was going to be contacted. Although it had been a long time since their breakup, Sister Dorothy suspected that Shirley harbored a fantasy of resuming their relationship.

Hessel was impatient with this tiptoeing around a fifteen-year-old's daydreams. Shouldn't Shirley's fantasy be confronted and dealt with rather than ignored? she asked. Later, in her notes, she recorded other arguments: "I explained that whatever their relationship is, the baby does have some rights to know who his parents are, and Mr. Smith does have some responsibility in helping to support his son. I also explained that in Mr. Smith's acknowledging paternity, it gave the baby certain rights that he otherwise would not have." Official documents had continued to list Smith's last known address as Fort Dix, New Jersey. If he was indeed in the service, his son would be eligible for a range of military dependent benefits as well as Social Security entitlements and inheritance rights.

On September 4, 1975, the nun put her objections in writing at the request of Hessel's supervisor. Sister Dorothy sent a copy of her letter to Carol Sherman, who had promised to research Shirley's legal rights in the matter. Keeping the man who had impregnated Shirley out of the picture might be consistent with a religious and cultural construction of maternity as a chance to redeem sexual sin, but there was a secular argument to be made, too. As a Legal Aid lawyer supportive of individual rights against state coercion, Sherman was also sympathetic to the idea that the girl should not be required to sign. Like so many issues raised in the city's foster-care files, however, the question was neither pursued nor resolved; it was dropped. Joan Hessel had already left the city child welfare office when Sister Dorothy's written objection to a paternity action reached the case file. The next caseworker let the nun's letter be the last word on the issue, and backed away, as well, from the effort to contact Shirley's family for a yearly reevaluation of its financial resources. The Holy Cross family liaison worker, Iris Hudis, had vigorously complained that the city's pressure was jeopardizing the good casework relationship she had just started to establish with the family to ease the tensions between parents and child. In fact, the parents were under severe financial stress, she claimed, both unemployed and on Medicaid.

Holy Cross was astonishingly tenacious in maintaining hope of a reconciliation between Shirley and her family, despite evidence that this not only was unlikely but probably destructive. Iris Hudis's first interview with Shirley's stepmother, in December 1974, left her with the impression that "there was perhaps an incestuous relationship between Shirley and her father." As the treatment team later summarized Hudis's oral report, "She felt that Mr. Auld sees Shirley as his deceased wife. It is possible that he is rejecting Shirley now to try and put some distance between them because of this transferrence and also because he finds Shirley sexually threatening. The possibility of this kind of relationship with her father should be explored as a therapy issue." Iris Hudis, who had great difficulty even maintaining contact with Shirley's family, continued to report in 1975 that "Mr. Auld and Shirley appear to have unresolved oedipal feelings toward one another," and that "Mrs. Auld . . . is jealous" and "has a lot invested in Shirley not doing well as this keeps her from becoming reinvolved with her father." A year after Shirley started at Holy Cross, another treatment-team memo confided, "At a family conference with Shirley and her father the workers noted a mutual seductiveness that made the conference extremely difficult." Nevertheless, the team called for more such discussions to determine whether Shirley could go home after her discharge from the institution.

Months after Hudis's incest memo, Sister Dorothy was still linking the prospect of Shirley's father's acceptance to her improved behavior. Like Lamont, Shirley's father was to be a tool in her rehabilitation. Some of the specific behaviors she was urged to change in order to qualify for the privilege of home visits were "her swearing, her jumping on the bandwagon when there are problems in the cottage, etc." Turning Shirley into a good girl seemed inextricably linked to making her a good daughter—regardless of what kind of parents she had.

At one point, in early March 1975, Shirley's lack of progress made her treatment team question whether she should be kept on at Holy Cross. She was then still on the lowest rung of the Holy Cross "phase-level system," which was based on a behavior-modification scheme of points awarded for "appropriate" actions in school, therapy, and living quarters. She was friendly and social in her "cottage"—a floor of the dorm where she lived with fourteen other girls—and had no problems with aggression or drugs, they agreed. But she was easily distracted by boys in her remedial classes, where she was reading at a fifth- or sixth-grade level after missing almost two years of school on the run or in detention. She often cut class with her boyfriend, Arthur Johnson, or sneaked out to the boys' unit at night to be with him.

"It is believed Shirley continues to have sexual relations with her boyfriend," the treatment team reported at the March 4, 1975, meeting. "They are involved in a mutually dependent relationship which takes on aggressive tones. Shirley is constantly complaining about him beating on her, yet she has made no attempt to terminate the relationship. It is also believed that she has continued to have homosexual relationships, although these seem to be within normal limits of adolescent homosexual behavior. Shirley has hinted that it consists mostly of mutual masturbation." In therapy sessions, Sister Dorothy had tried to get Shirley to talk about the deaths of her mother and grandmother, but Shirley either changed the subject or left the office.

At Sister Dorothy's urging, it was decided to have Shirley tested by a psychologist the following week. Meanwhile, however, "Shirley was invited into the meeting and was given a very strong message about her recent behavior"—specifically her relationship with her boyfriend—"and how she would have to become more appropriate in this so it did not affect her school work and progress in the cottage and phase level system. Shirley seemed quite shaken by this confrontation and indicated that she did desire to stay here and would make an effort to show some improvement."

Six days later, the results of the tests by the psychologist, Daniel Pienaar, were startling. Based on a diagnostic interview and her responses to Rorschach tests, T.A.T. cards, and a Bender test, he reported that she was a psychotic child suffering from visual and auditory hallucinations linked to her grandmother's death. There were indications, he said, that she wanted to be hurt by males and to hurt females, and her response to one card suggested to him that she might act out some of her hostility on her child. "He felt she was suicidal, prone to injury and pain but not to death," Sister Dorothy wrote in a summary for family court when Holy Cross asked for a twelve-month extension of Shirley's placement. "Shirley has a poor identity and needs frequent bodily confirmation of herself. Her sexuality is subservient to this and she can be homosexual, heterosexual, or self-stimulative." Plans included an intensive course of therapy and "setting clearer limits on Shirley in both the cottage living situation and in the school."

Under the new intensive-treatment plan, Pienaar joined the nun in Shirley's therapy sessions for five weeks, introducing a method designed to help the fifteen-year-old "define her physical boundaries" through a therapist's nurturing presence, frequent body contact, and relaxation exercises. The technique was based on the work of Austin Des Lauriers, a psychologist who had theorized that childhood schizophrenia reflected an inability to differentiate between self and others, which could be remedied through simple physical interactions and a therapist's almost maternal affirmation of the patient's identity. In 1962 Des Lauriers had published a monograph describing the method's clinical success with seven patients, aged eleven to seventeen, who were living on the children's ward of the state mental hospital in Topeka when he was its chief psychologist.

Des Lauriers's own career reflected how dramatically fashions in diagnosis and treatment could change. In the 1940s, he had worked on a Bellevue Hospital research project directed by Lauretta Bender, which used electroshock treatment (ECT) on children aged four to eleven who had been diagnosed as schizophrenic. Bender was also the author of one of the psychological tests Pienaar administered to Shirley. As early as 1951 there were skeptics who reviewed Bender's tests and interpretations and concluded that under such criteria, "no child would be entirely safe from the diagnosis of schizophrenia." By 1955 the methods of treatment in vogue for such children included insulin and metrazol shock, ECT, and even prefrontal lobotomy, the last advocated by doctors "with a view to terminating the fantasy life and reducing the expenditure of emotional energy upon the self." By the late 1960s, however, the diagnosis of schizophrenia in children, like lobotomy, had fallen into serious disrepute; many children previously diagnosed as schizophrenic were found to be autistic instead, while others were said to be suffering from various disturbed reactions to childhood that were often outgrown. Yet mental-health professionals educated or influenced by an earlier generation kept the diagnosis alive, even as they adopted different modes of intervention.

Whether or not the Des Lauriers body-contact exercises helped, Shirley did grow more attached to Sister Dorothy over time. "She was more like an aunt than a nun," Shirley would say later. "She always had little treats for me. I never got a visit [from family], so that was my visit. I remember one day I was being so bad, Sister Dorothy told me, 'I've been getting phone calls about you all day. Come to my office.' I was really worried—'I'm in trouble with Sister Dorothy!' She had a lunch there waiting for me, with chocolate candy. She said, 'Just sit and relax.' That made my day, because everybody was having a visit, and I didn't. She understood what was wrong with me."

But when Shirley finally followed the rules long enough to earn the privilege of home visits, in the fall of 1975, her family still didn't want her. On November 11, two weeks before her sixteenth birthday, she ran away to Arthur Johnson's grandmother's in New York City instead. Before Arthur left on his approved furlough that day, he was given a return ticket to Rhinecliff, good for a ride in either direction, and he secretly passed it to Shirley. She ran all the way to the Rhinecliff station to make the 7:45 train he was taking; it had already started moving when she jumped aboard. Through Thanksgiving and Christmas and the anniversary of her grandmother's death, she and Arthur lived together at his grandmother's in the Bronx. They quarreled, and often he hit her. She went back to Holy Cross on December 28.

"The AWOL seems to have convinced her that marriage is not appropriate at this stage of her life," a treatment-team memo observed.

By the time she saw Lamont again, on January 27, 1976, more than three months had passed between visits, and he had grown a good deal. He was more subdued than during past sessions. Shirley felt strange with him and uncomfortable in front of his caseworker. She had hoped that her father would be present at this visit to see his nineteen-month-old grandson for the first time, but he didn't come. Her father wasn't psychologically ready, Iris Hudis told her, but he hadn't closed off the possibility of seeing Lamont at some point in the future. Toward the end of the allotted time, when Alicia arrived to pick up Lamont, Shirley felt a surge of resentment and depression. On the train ride back to Holy Cross she told Sister Dorothy about her negative feelings toward her son's foster mother.

"Shirley seems to be struggling with ambivalent feelings about having a baby and the responsibility involved; having her baby in foster care and what other people, i.e., her father and friends at Holy Cross, expect of her in terms of being a mother; her own desire to be free and not tied down," Sister Dorothy wrote. "She can relate to some of the above but needs to deal with the feelings as well as the realities involved in future planning."

The nun asked Shirley to write out her feelings about the visit. The words are on lined paper, the i's dotted with perfect circles, with a child's flourish under the signature to mark the end:

> I was really happy to see how tall Lamont has grown, but I was a little up set because I don't want him in the foster home any longer. I want Lamont to live with my aunt Carrie. It's really hard and uncomfortable with Mrs. Redmen [Redmond, the baby's worker] and for what reason I don't know I can't injoy the visits. I never told Sister Dorothy that before because I always cover it up. but any other than that the visit was nice
>
> —SHIRLEY A. WILDER

Like all their train trips, this one seemed to Sister Dorothy valuable for building a therapeutic relationship with her skittish client. The nun sometimes brought along word games, books, and puzzles for the two-hour journey, but often she and Shirley just gazed out the windows of the train when they weren't talking. It was surely one of the most beautiful train rides in America. The tracks ran right beside the east bank of the Hudson River, past landscapes that the Indians called "the mountains-of-the-sky" and views defined by nineteenth-century painters as sublime.

"What are you thinking?" the nun would ask.

"Being with my family. Water's peaceful. It always puts you in a daze."

The Hudson has been termed a drowned river. Rising seawater flooded its old course thousands of years ago, when the last glacier melted. Sea anemones still grow under the George Washington Bridge, and sixty miles upstream, the water is salty. The ocean tides run all the way up to the Federal Lock and Dam at Troy, New York, not far from the Canadian border. The Mahican Indians of Henry Hudson's day called the river Muhheakunnuk, meaning "great waters constantly in motion." But in some ways that motion is deceptive. Over long stretches, for every eight miles that the current and ebb tide carry a fallen tree branch downriver, the flood tide pushes it back up as much as seven miles.

So Shirley traveled up and down the river, neither severing her ties to her son nor moving much closer to his life. There were times when she talked of studying to be a nurse and making a home for him. There were months when she didn't see him at all because she was on the run. He was still two months shy of his second birthday on what would turn out to be her last visit, April 7, 1976.

"She assumed the mother role in feeding him, combing his hair, taking pictures of him, hugging, carrying him, etc.," Sister Dorothy wrote. "Shirley appeared quite pensive during intermittent periods. Prior to the visit, she had spoken of her complicated and ambivalent feelings regarding keeping the baby in foster care or surrendering the baby. Shirley has feelings for Lamont but also feels that he is a burden to her. She feels guilty feeling this, as these feelings are contrary to what a good mother should be feeling according to her. This is an area Shirley is looking at seriously now. As she works on defining plans for her August discharge from Holy Cross and her future, it has become clear to her that she needs to reach a decision regarding her baby."

In a meeting with the baby's caseworker and Carol Sherman, Sister Dorothy and Iris Hudis told Shirley that family conferences with her father were needed to discuss whether she could return home after her Holy Cross placement expired in August. Shirley spoke of feeling hurt that her father had been so unresponsive to Hudis's efforts to involve him in her treatment. "Shirley has a classic 'symbiotic relationship' with her father. She wants to return home to live with him on one hand, yet, realistically she knows that none of the conflict areas with her father and stepmother have been worked out," Sister Dorothy wrote.

Three days later, on April 10, 1976, Shirley went AWOL again. This time she did not come back.

FOUR

ONE CHASE MANHATTAN PLAZA STANDS ON A RAISED PLAZA in the financial district of Manhattan, a sheer eight hundred feet of aluminum and glass aloof from the street life around it. It was a fitting site for the offices of Davis, Polk & Wardwell, the august Wall Street firm that had taken the lead in the agencies' defense against *Wilder*. Even in its historic claim to the archdiocese's legal business, Davis, Polk stood aloof from the ethnic life of the city's streets: one of the firm's impeccably WASP partners had converted to Catholicism early in the century, so at a time when the socially elite firm wouldn't have dreamed of naming an Irish Catholic partner, it became the advocate of choice for the Catholic Church in New York.

From the start, Marcia Lowry thought, the lawyers of Davis, Polk had made no secret of their disdain for the young women of the Civil Liberties Union. Their conference rooms had the ambience of a very exclusive men's club: cigars were smoked, and servants padded about discreetly replenishing drinks and replacing ashtrays. Occasionally the pin-striped formality might be punctuated by a manly guffaw or the flash of cuff links as one attorney clapped another on the back over some shared joke. As though not to be outdone, Robinson, Silverman, Pearce, Aronsohn & Berman, the white-shoe firm that represented the Jewish Board of Guardians, often sent over attorneys in triplicate. The *Wilder* gatherings were like convocations. Just walking into the room meant drawing the collective gaze of a dozen men who seemed to think you should be wearing an apron.

In the early days, being treated as an interloper here had been part of the thrill of the case for Lowry, a kind of confirmation that she was doing battle for the weak. In their own strategy sessions in the NYCLU's shabby warren of offices near Union Square, she and her colleagues were like conspirators from a counterculture. They took turns going to the deli and collected change for coffee. A baby in a red snowsuit used to toddle through their discussions—that was the son of Eli Gilbert, the wizard of statistics recruited to help prove racial discrimination by the numbers. Damon, her own Doberman, would amble by, stopping to prick his ears and utter a bark or two if their internal arguments grew too heated.

"I only have one question," Eli Gilbert threw in once, kidding on the square. "Is it good for the Jews?"

"Yes, Eli," she replied after they stopped laughing, "it's good for the Jews; it's good for everybody."

The line became a running gag as the Jewish establishment grew more vocal and more outraged at *Wilder*. That was the irony, that they were all Jews who had taken the teachings of their parents' faith beyond the mitzvah box and the New Deal.

Gilbert himself, for example, was a man of her own age whose parents, union people traumatized by McCarthyism, had sent him to Queens College with the admonition "Don't sign any petitions." He liked to say he was the kind of guy who basically believed the Jewish Federation could do no wrong. But he had been introduced to the concept of social conscience in an undergraduate contemporary-civilization course, and he had never looked back. For him, Marcia's certainty was like a moral guidepost. He had so much confidence in her and in the case that when he started as a consultant he asked if the CLU had appointed a *Wilder* historian to record what was bound to be a landmark case. She took it as a joke and laughed; he was serious. It made them all feel very close, this sense that they were doing something big and important together.

But Marcia Lowry had not filed *Wilder* to make friends or nourish esprit de corps. Whenever friendship conflicted with the demands of the case, friendship lost. First and hardest had been the firing of Risa Dickstein. It had been a terrible blow to discover that Risa, so savvy and funny and full of fashion advice for a Miami girl confronting Wall Street, just didn't produce written work strong enough or fast enough to win the legal war they had to wage. Lowry agonized over the problem for weeks; then she went to Ira Glasser, and he did the deed. Risa Dickstein never stopped being hurt and bitter about it. She blamed Lowry's ego. "Marcia's very driven," she would warn lawyers considering a job with the Children's Rights Project. "If she decides you're in her way, she'll drive over you."

Peter Bienstock, seven years younger than Lowry and only a year out of law school, had been next. They'd worked wonderfully together: he was so attuned to detail that colleagues teased him about his proofreading envelopes; she was a prolific writer who could produce a well-argued legal brief almost as fast as she could type, as long as she left blanks for the supporting citations to be added later. But Bienstock had simply blown up at her one day in 1976, criticizing her legal strategy, claiming he was not receiving the respect and scope he deserved, impetuously giving notice. The rift had come at a particularly bad time. It wasn't that Lowry's personal life was in tumult, though it was; it wasn't that she had drawn the wrath of most of the legal-services community in another of her lawsuits against the city, though she'd been stung by some of the more personal attacks. No, the real problem in the timing of Bienstock's angry departure was *Wilder: Wilder* was on the verge of trial. When Bienstock's replacement, Steven Shapiro, asked to take a month's vacation before starting his job with Lowry in the summer of 1976, she refused his request. They needed him, she explained, to help prepare for the imminent *Wilder* trial.

But now here it was the end of 1977 and there was still no trial. Shapiro's lost vacation had become another standing joke.

Was there some shortcut she'd missed? She didn't think so. True, she had started out knowing little about how to structure and litigate a civil-liberties case of *Wilder*'s scope and factual complexity. But as Ira Glasser liked to point out, at the time nobody else knew how to go about it, either. They were all learning as they went along, drawing inspiration from the NAACP Legal Defense Fund school-desegregation cases that culminated in *Brown* v. *Board of Education*. They were pioneers, girding themselves against the contempt of buttoned-down lawyers with an overriding sense of purpose and confidence in the power of the law.

After starting out with an almost naive respect for the judiciary, Lowry had learned that the courts could be as clubby as the conference rooms of Davis, Polk & Wardwell. Her awe for the transcendent role of judges made her uncomfortable even attempting small talk with them while waiting for an elevator. It was a shock to discover how political they could be.

First was Federal District Court Judge Harold Tyler, whose mother-in-law sat on the board of one of the defendant agencies. Tyler and Richard Nolan, the tall, craggy senior attorney for Davis, Polk, outdid each other in demonstrating that they considered the case a silly waste of time. Even clearing the initial legal hurdle—securing a finding that her lawsuit was substantial and not frivolous—was a procedural ordeal. Hers was not a radical legal analysis, she thought, yet she constantly had the sense of being treated like—there was no other phrase for it—a radical *girl*.

Then one day the hostile courtroom tone abruptly changed: on December 17, 1974, the *New York Times* ran an editorial giving full support to the lawsuit. Judge Tyler commented on the editorial and treated the case as though it were respectable for the first time. He called the parties into his chambers and said, "You know, there may be problems here." He encouraged settlement.

The settlement talks were hopeless, of course; mainly the meetings served to exacerbate conflict between the plaintiffs' two sets of lawyers. Legal Aid's Charles Schinitsky was eager to resolve this lawsuit that so appalled his board members. Lowry hewed to an uncompromising line that was alien to the whole accommodationist culture of Legal Aid. Carol Sherman, Schinitsky's representative on the case, was caught in between. "But Marcia," she would object plaintively in strategy sessions, "but Marcia, he'll yell at us!" "He" might be the magistrate, the judge, or Schinitsky himself; it didn't matter. Being yelled at was not a deterrent to Marcia Lowry.

The real problem was what the judges *didn't* say and didn't do. Tyler convened a three-judge court to consider the constitutional questions posed by the case, as was then required by federal law. But over objections from both Lowry and the lawyers from Davis, Polk, the three-judge court decided to limit arguments to whether the child-care statutes were unconstitutional on their face, rather than as applied, and to consider only facts agreed to by both sides. Those limitations, announced by the panel on June 4, 1974—the day Lamont Wilder was born—ignored the heart of the case: whether, as applied, the statutes resulted in unconstitutional religious and racial discrimination. On November 18, 1974, seventeen months after the case was first filed, the panel ruled that the laws were not unconstitutional on their face. How the laws worked in practice was left unresolved, pending the development of facts through discovery and, if necessary, a trial.

Tyler left the bench for the number-two position in the U.S. Justice Department in the spring of 1975 without either denying or signing an order crucial to the case: the certification of the plaintiff children as a class. Without such an order, Shirley Wilder and the other plaintiffs remained individuals, not legally recognized representatives of what Lowry claimed was a class of ten thousand homeless children deprived of equal protection by the system because they were not white and neither Catholic nor Jewish. Although she had moved for class certification just six weeks after filing suit, Tyler had held the motion in abeyance for almost two years, leaving her nothing to appeal. Then he said he would sign a certification order, and departed for Washington without doing so.

The more damning the facts that emerged through discovery, the more uneasy judges seemed to be about *Wilder*. And some of the depositions were humdingers. Sister Cecilia Schneider, the nun who directed New York Foundling, testified that throughout the 1960s, whenever there was some doubt about the racial origins of one of the babies in the institution's nursery, nuns would carry the child over to the Museum of Natural History to be examined and classified by its resident anthropologist. Those determined to have Negro blood were less likely to be adopted, of course, and some waited out their babyhood in an institutional nursery.

In another deposition, Gloria Trexler, Shirley Wilder's probation officer, related a textbook case of discrimination from the more recent past. Two fifteen-year-old boys had been referred to her for placement on the same day. One was a white, Jewish delinquent who didn't want to be placed. The other was a black PINS boy whose mother was terminally ill and who longed to join his unusually cute little brother at Pleasantville, the cottage school run by the Jewish Child Care Association. The white delinquent was actively recruited by the Jewish agencies despite his hostility; the black boy's case was ignored for months despite Trexler's best efforts. A series of patently false excuses was proffered by Pleasantville officials as to why the black teenager was not suitable for their facility. When Trexler persisted, they grudgingly summoned the boy and his dying mother on short notice to an interview at Pleasantville, only to reject him weeks later "due to his age and lack of a suitable peer group"—

the same phony reasons offered half a year earlier and dropped when it was pointed out that several even older teenagers were residents at Pleasantville. As it happened, the boy's official rejection came down the same day the three-judge panel ruled that New York's religion-matching statute was not unconstitutional on its face.

Eli Gilbert had the numbers to drive home the anecdotes. Jewish agencies had almost twice as many beds as they could fill with Jewish kids, but the "surplus" went disproportionately to non-Jewish whites. Eli could show that the preference wasn't just white-Jewish, it was white-anything. As for Gloria Trexler's testimony on how the Catholic Archdiocese had barred Shirley Wilder from getting contraceptives—well, you couldn't ask for a more compelling demonstration of the violation of the establishment clause, Lowry thought. It had opened a powerful new vein of legal argument.

Yet for Lowry the high point of the depositions had not been some juicy anecdote or statistical revelation, but an intellectual and moral duel that seemed to cut to the heart of the case. It had taken place in this very building in late February 1976, in one of the fancy Davis, Polk conference rooms reached by an inner stairway and lined with oil portraits of self-satisfied-looking dead white men. The witness was George Silcott, the big, black director of the Wiltwyck School for Boys. His opponent was Leonard Sand, a trim, almost dapper man who represented the Jewish Board of Guardians for Robinson, Silver, and who took as much pride in his liberal credentials as in his considerable skill as a litigator.

In a sense, the boys at Wiltwyck stood for everything the religious agencies feared. They were the kids who had been rejected elsewhere because they were deemed too aggressive, too deprived, or just too different to suit programs designed for emotionally disturbed Jewish children or troubled Catholic youngsters. Leonard Sand didn't say that, of course, but he worked to elicit an acknowledgment that even Wiltwyck screened out some children as unsuitable. Wasn't it reasonable, he asked, to remove a disruptive child who didn't fit the mainstream of a program, so the program could continue to deliver optimum service to the greatest number of children?

Silcott didn't bite. Wiltwyck, he said, had deliberately changed a policy that used to result in its sending ten to fifteen youngsters a year away to state hospitals because they were too difficult to handle. Instead, the board had increased staff accountability and committed the institution to resolving the kids' problems rather than passing them on. And no, that did not mean sacrificing the good of the many for the few. In the real world, it was terribly frightening for the children who remained to see the staff give up on a child by sending him away.

George is so smart—he sees right through Leonard, Carol Sherman scrawled on the legal pad she and Lowry were sharing.

Was Wiltwyck School a segregated facility? Yes, Silcott said. And he described the role of the central referral agencies controlled by the religious federations, their "creaming off" of children for the sectarian agencies, their use of arbitrary criteria to rule out the placement of others. "It is the absence of randomization that creates the segregated quality of our facility," he said. He defined randomization as a "process of placing children in agencies on a first-come basis in the relevant facility for meeting their needs, so that vacant bed number one is available for the next child who can use that service." Under randomization, all agencies would be responsible for supporting the religious identities and practices of all children in their care, and each agency would better reflect the system as a whole.

This was exactly what the Jewish agencies feared. With Jewish children making up only 4 percent of the total pool, complete randomization, Sand noted, would mean programs for fifty children that served no more than two who were Jewish.

"Is the sole objective which you seek to accomplish by this process, what you describe as randomization, integration of the child-care system?" the lawyer demanded.

Randomization is becoming this suit's busing, Lowry wrote to Sherman. *Is integration a bad word?*

Silcott was already two steps ahead of her. "Integration of the child-care system?" he echoed in polite rebuke. "I am talking about equal and appropriate services to all children."

Sand tried another tack. Suppose there was a massive infusion of resources into the child-care system. No child neglected, no child waiting, all treatment needs met, but with religion given the same weight that the present, inadequate system gives it. "Would you have a quarrel with such a system?"

"Of course," Silcott shot back. "That is precisely what we have, isn't it? Don't we have a system that has a lot of money infused in it?"

Although momentarily nonplussed, Sand persisted. "We have been told, and I don't think there is too much controversy about it, that the present system does not have adequate facilities to meet the needs of all children. I am supposing a system in which there is no child who is in need of placement . . . whose needs are not being met."

"So what you are saying is what?" Silcott retorted, very calm, very dark, his eyes twinkling now. "*Plessy* v. *Ferguson*, separate but equal?"

Oh, touché, Lowry exulted inwardly, *touché! Plessy* v. *Ferguson,* the notorious 1896 Supreme Court decision used to justify legal segregation for sixty years. *Plessy* v. *Ferguson,* bulwark of state-enforced racial discrimination, upholding "separate but equal" railroad cars and with them the whole structure of oppression—separate water fountains, separate lunch counters, separate schools—until Chief Justice Earl Warren, speaking for a unanimous Supreme Court in *Brown* v. *Board of Education,* announced the end of the line for Jim Crow: ". . . in the field of public education the doctrine of 'separate but equal' has no place. Separate educational facilities are inherently unequal."

Why do we have to try Brown *again?* Sherman scrawled.

I have known all along we were going to, Lowry wrote back.

To her ears, Sand's response was like an admission of defeat. "I am trying very hard not to deal in legal concepts," he said testily, "because I don't want to argue law. I want to talk about child care."

Sand was grim-faced when he finally called a halt to the deposition at nearly two o'clock in the afternoon. For four hours he had probed and pushed, using the best arguments the sectarian system could muster; and Silcott had not only stood firm, he had parried and thrust to such devastating effect that in an aside to Sherman, Lowry quipped that he should be their only witness, and perhaps argue the case, too.

As the meeting broke up, Silcott paused to take note of the large bust that dominated the conference room where they had sparred. It was the head of John W. Davis, leader of the giant law firm for thirty-four years, the most accomplished and admired appellate lawyer of his day, who, at the age of eighty, had argued the defense of segregation in *Brown* v. *Board of Education* in his last appearance before the U.S. Supreme Court. "There is no reason assigned here," Davis had declared as the voice of South Carolina's racial order, "why this Court or any other should reverse the findings of ninety years."

Lowry would always relish the memory of George Silcott, the big brown bear of a man who led an institution founded by Eleanor Roosevelt and Justine Wise Polier, smiling as he glanced from the bust of John W. Davis to Leonard Sand and back again. He had forced Sand to stand for Davis, a peerless corporation lawyer and gentleman racist who had gone down to defeat arguing on the wrong side of history.

BUT THE STRONGER the *Wilder* case grew, the more of a hot potato it was. Its second judge, Inzer Wyatt, openly loathed it. He telephoned Harold Tyler in Washington to berate him for dropping it in his lap. He regularly screamed at Lowry during hearings.

"You're saying these agencies discriminate and they're religious and you want to get your clients IN them?" he yelled in high-pitched incredulity during one tirade, before breaking off to demand suddenly, "Have you ever read the novels of Anthony Trollope?"

"No," the startled Lowry replied, groping for a connection, "but I've read Jane Austen."

Wyatt proceeded to give her a lecture on church-state relations as depicted in Trollope's novel *The Cathedral.*

Early in 1977, Judge Wyatt went into semiretirement in Alabama without ruling on the class-certification issue. Nor did he rule on a later defense motion to dismiss the whole case on the ground that since no class had ever been certified, Shirley Wilder's age—eighteen—made her claim moot.

Both sides were told that the case had been reassigned to a Judge Gerard Goettel. Not so, Goettel informed Lowry when she wrote to him. Another six months passed before the case was bounced to Judge Robert Ward.

After her experiences with Harold Tyler and Inzer Wyatt, Lowry had been very happy to draw Ward as a judge in November 1977. Research on his past decisions revealed him to be stricter on the establishment-clause separation of church and state than any other judge in the district. But Lowry's first appearance before Ward was terrifying.

It was on a Friday afternoon soon after he learned that he had been stuck with the *Wilder* case. Obviously angry, he told the lawyers assembled in his court that the case was too old. He was a judge, he declared; he moved cases to trial; and the trial in this case was going to start promptly on Monday. The plaintiffs would get one day to put on testimony, and the defendants one day, with a third day for rebuttal. And that would be it. "We'll be finished by Wednesday," he bellowed. Appalled, Lowry sprang up to protest: he couldn't do this; it was unfair, it was prejudicial to the plaintiffs. And all the while she was thinking, Oh my God, can I reach Eli Gilbert? It's Friday afternoon; I don't even know where he is. She began looking over her shoulder at the clock to see if she had time to appeal Ward's decision to the Second Circuit before the end of the day. Then suddenly the judge suggested an alternative: withdraw the case without prejudice and refile it. Later it dawned on her that Ward's threat of an immediate trial had never been serious; this was what he'd wanted all along, in order to cut the aging legal knots Tyler and Wyatt had left behind.

So here she was, in December 1977, back at the beginning again. There would have to be an amended complaint, new discovery, more depositions. Finally, she thought, there would be a trial. But first there was the glass skyscraper at One Chase Manhattan Plaza, where her enemies at Davis, Polk were waiting to wrangle over the terms of *Wilder*'s reincarnation.

FIVE

Although Wilder was stalled in the courts, in many ways it had been driving city policy. When Carol Parry took charge of the city's Special Services for Children in 1974, she brought with her a blueprint for change shaped by Marcia Lowry's lawsuit. Yet she had been in office no more than four months when Lowry sued her.

The federal class action, known as *OFFER* after the Organization of Foster Families for Equality and Reform, demanded that the city provide due-process hearings for foster parents faced with the removal of children who had lived in their care for a year or more. Parry considered herself a civil libertarian, but she resented this Lowry lawsuit as an irrelevance, a failure of perspective.

Special Services for Children, one part of the welfare superagency now headed for the second time by James Dumpson, the commissioner of human resources and social services, was a cumbersome and overwhelmed bureaucracy. It had about twenty-three hundred employees and several operating subdivisions, including an Office of Field Operations that administered five field offices (one in each of the city's boroughs) and an Office of Direct Care Services that managed the city's own children's shelters and foster boarding homes. The field offices were responsible for investigating all allegations of child abuse and neglect funneled to them through the state's "Central Registry," better known as the child-abuse hotline; caseworkers in the field were also supposed to provide or arrange services for troubled families, decide on admissions to foster care, and recommend placements to another large subdivision called Allocations and Inter-Agency Relations. Many of the staff worked in rooms the size of football fields, where the desks of caseworkers were aligned so closely that their edges touched, their surfaces stacked high with manila folders bearing children's names.

"Under the system, the workers make decisions about children they have never met, place children in institutions they have never visited, and approve services to children without means of verifying their delivery," Linda Schleicher, a former caseworker, recalled.

Overseeing everything from a distance was the New York State Department of Social Services, which was responsible for establishing regulations and setting reimbursement rates for foster care. It licensed foster-care agencies and monitored the performance of the city and other local districts in all child welfare matters. Almost half the cost of foster care was covered by the federal government; the state and city shared the rest.

Parry was in her early thirties when Mayor Beame appointed her. Her first job in city administration had been as head of the Agency for Child Development, where she helped to open city day-care centers and Head Start programs. Far from assuming that a government program had to be inferior to what was offered by the old-line charities, she believed that progressive public programs could set the standard for good and innovative care.

She was convinced that the only way to deal with the voluntary agencies was to shift the balance of power away from them. The problem was fiscal as well as political. The city had placed twenty-six thousand out of some twenty-nine thousand children at the agencies without written contracts, and the agencies simply billed the city comptroller's office for each day a child was in care, absorbing more than 86 percent of the budget for Special Services for Children in the process. As long as the private sector had nearly all the kids and nearly all the money, the city agency was helpless to change the overall shape and direction of the system. Private agencies had been allowed to define their own service boundaries instead of filling publicly defined needs within a comprehensive plan.

"The tail is wagging the dog here," Parry told people.

The battle lines were drawn early. One of Parry's first official actions was to issue a new policy: each agency was now to be under contract to serve all the children the city referred as long as the agency had vacancies, unless it could prove that a given child did not fit the terms of its contract.

Parry was denounced by agency directors as a dictator, a saboteur of quality programs. But she was not afraid of confrontation. She knew that Barbara Blum, her predecessor, had been legendary for her ability to forge consensus. But Parry thought Blum had a tendency to compromise too much. Not only were the voluntaries opposed to being told which kids to take, they also balked at the development of public programs that might compete with their near monopoly of child welfare dollars. At some point, Parry felt, you just had to say, "That's it. This is the way it's going to be."

Bitter negotiations with the COVCCA, the umbrella group that functioned like the agencies' cartel, were to be the hallmark of Parry's four years in office. Twice, angry delegations went to Mayor Beame to try to have her curbed or forced out. But the agencies were rebuffed at city hall. Their political leverage had suddenly weakened. Jim Dumpson, having won his post in the teeth of their opposition, owed them nothing. Nor could they drive a wedge between him and Parry, who saw eye-to-eye with him on the need for what Dumpson called an equal partnership between the public and voluntary sectors. Parry was quick to build her own constituency for change among Legal Services attorneys, family-court judges, foster-parent organizations, and a series of legislative committees and good-government groups that focused intensely on children during the 1970s and kept issuing reports condemning the existing system.

But paradoxically, Parry's real salvation was the city's disastrous economic state. "I pretty much could do what I wanted," she would say later. "The city administration wasn't worrying about being reelected. They were worried about living through the fiscal crisis."

Caught in back-to-back recessions (1969–72 and 1973–75), New York City had increased spending more rapidly than revenues under Mayor Lindsay and in the first years of the Beame administration, bridging the gap with short-term loans. By 1975 the threat that the city might default on its debts triggered a frantic restructuring of municipal spending to meet the demands of the bankers and bondholders who controlled its fate.

Foster care itself was one of the few areas that did not experience major cutbacks. Some critics said this was a testament to the private agencies' extraordinary and enduring political clout. But others noted that as New York teetered on the edge of bankruptcy, the electoral power represented by the Jewish and Catholic organizations was attenuated, if not eclipsed, by the power of those watching the bottom line. The agencies' insistence that their services were a bargain, since the public funds they received were supplemented by donations, seemed increasingly irrelevent. Millions of public dollars were being wasted by private agencies on unnecessary and often harmful foster care, report after report declared. Children needed permanent families, not limbo, a steady drumbeat of studies argued, seizing on the politically winning convergence of what was humane and what saved money. With astonishing speed, media treatment of the religious foster-care agencies shifted in the mid-1970s from Christmas features about charitable nuns caring for little outcasts to exposés about arrogant agencies holding children hostage to greed. The result was that in a time of massive cutbacks in public spending, Dumpson and Parry were able to add public foster-care institutions and programs that their predecessors had been unable to establish when city government was at its most expansive.

But the fiscal crisis cut both ways. Facing its own budget deficits in 1974, the state's Department of Mental Hygiene abruptly began emptying out children's wards in state psychiatric hopitals and institutions for the mentally disabled, with no plans for what to do with the inmates. Most were poor minority kids with no responsible parents in the picture. Eighty percent were from New York City, to which the state now suddenly passed responsibility for their care. Some children had been born severely handicapped or suffered traumatic injuries; Parry even found herself scrambling to find foster care for children on life-support systems who had been dumped into city hospitals. But many of the most troublesome cases were the damaged byproducts of the foster-care system itself, children who had languished in institutional nurseries as babies and then bounced through abusive foster homes and feral shelters, "acting out" more and more until they reached the end of the line: the back ward of some state institution. The withdrawal of such repositories left Parry desperate for placements of last resort. At great expense, she ended up sending children all over the country, to profit-making facilities in fifteen other states.

She was not alone. By the mid-1970s, most state and county placement agencies were exporting children. It amounted to a grotesque but hugely profitable interstate commerce. All but five of the fifty states were involved in the trade; twenty-seven received children from the same states to which they sent their own, a Children's Defense Fund investigation eventually discovered. In certain states, particularly Texas and Florida, lax regulation fostered a boom in entrepreneurs willing to take any child from anywhere for the right price. Only a third of the states shipping kids ever sent caseworkers to check on them, Children's Defense Fund investigators found. A series of journalistic exposés and legislative investigative committees in Texas, Illinois, and Louisiana revealed many of these places to be understaffed, ill-equipped warehouses. "Children have become economic pawns in private attempts to gain wealth or governmental attempts to save money," a Texas legislative committee reported in the midseventies. An unwritten axiom seemed to drive this cruel exercise: the further away from his own family a child was placed, the more public money became available to pay for his care.

One of the first class-action lawsuits Marcia Lowry had ever filed demanded prompt placement for children discharged from mental institutions; the strict deadlines set by its settlement were among the factors compelling Parry to make out-of-state placements. But by 1977, Lowry ruefully sued the city on behalf of the children sent out of state. To settle that lawsuit, the city ultimately had to bring them all back.

During her four years as head of Special Services for Children, Parry was sued dozens of times. An event once rare enough to send Barbara Blum's office into a panic had become almost routine by 1978; Parry used to joke about the "case of the day." In part, the proliferation reflected a surge in the number of public-interest lawyers; they still accounted for only one out of five hundred lawyers nationwide, but their ranks had increased fourteenfold since 1968. Foundation and federal-government support for public-interest litigation had grown in the aftermath of political activism by minorities, consumers, and the poor, and as decisions by the U.S. Supreme Court under Earl Warren confirmed the role of litigation in changing public policy. The ingredient usually missing in such legal challenges, as far as Parry was concerned, was a remedy. In the real world, things happened because people compromised, she always argued, not because some judge issued an order.

Even in retrospect, Parry would see no alternative to her out-of-state placements. She didn't have the luxury of putting child placement on hold while she tried to change things.

"It's a hell of a lot more difficult trying to run that place than when you're a lawyer outside on the side of the angels," Parry told Lowry, who belonged to the same social circle of contemporaries, all of them in public-service careers launched in the orbit of the Lindsay administration. "It's the attitude of a lot of lawyers: We'll just tell you to change and you'll change—wave a magic wand. If you had to run this place, you'd see things differently. The doors open every day."

It was what the doors opened on that haunted Parry. One night she showed up unannounced at Jennings Hall, the city shelter in Brooklyn for boys aged five to eighteen. It was like something out of Dickens, she thought: rows and rows of beds, the child-care staff numb, the kids all mixed together, some very tough. The whole place was taut with the threat of violence—scabby walls, encrusted linoleum, the ominous smell of rancid sweat. A very scary place. She felt nervous there as an adult; years later, the thought of being a child there could still make her shudder.

Parry was determined to shut down the city's six children's shelters. But even as she succeeded in closing five, the last one, the Children's Center in Manhattan, grew progressively worse. It became the sole repository for the city's most unplaceable children, and increasingly, these were teenagers. Parry wrote in a 1977 progress report that a child welfare system designed to deal with younger and relatively untroubled children had been unprepared to cope with a dramatic rise in the number of adolescents entering care, and she cited the figures: from eighty-three hundred teenage entrants in 1970 to twelve thousand in 1974 to fifteen thousand in 1977.

But the history of the Children's Center itself contradicted the notion that the system as a whole had functioned better when the children needing care were younger. In the early 1960s, the old building on Fifth Avenue and 104th Street, formerly run by the Society for the Prevention of Cruelty to Children, had housed as many as 614 children between the ages of two and sixteen in space licensed for 323, with cribs and cots in corridors and schoolrooms turned into dormitories. These were among the two thousand city children then waiting for foster care, more than half of them black or Puerto Rican. During a strike by city welfare staff in 1964, private agencies were persuaded to take 202 children from the center on a temporary basis, thus revealing that they had plenty of vacancies. This was the first time in fifteen years that the Children's Center was under capacity. But when the strike was over, the voluntary agencies sent most of the children back to the shelter again: they were children of the wrong kind, of the wrong religion, of the wrong color. A decade later, like the repressed returning, the system's discarded children were back in the Children's Center, grown into frightening adolescents with no homes.

Spofford was bursting at the seams with them, too. The state's Division for Youth had no funding to keep up with the surge in commitments, so children as young as nine piled up at Spofford for months waiting for an opening in a reformatory. One night when Parry had fallen into an exhausted sleep, the relentless ringing of the telephone woke her. It was some reporter asking if she knew that a kid had just jumped off the roof at Spofford.

Why the hell was he calling her about this? What was she supposed to do about it at two in the morning? It was as though she had suddenly assumed personal responsibility for everything that went wrong in a system that had never been right. No matter how bad the mess when you took the job, she thought, the news media gave you about five minutes' grace before blaming you for everything you hadn't fixed. No matter what your track record as an advocate had been, Legal Aid, Legal Services, and the Civil Liberties Union would frame the system's most long-standing, complex problems as violations of constitutional rights taking place this minute, on your watch. And in truth, Parry needed class-action lawsuits and news-media scandals as political leverage to force the changes she herself sought. But she couldn't help but be ground down and chewed up publicly in the process. No one could last very long in such a position—and everyone knew that, including the rank and file of the bureaucracy, who had watched so many other commissioners come and go.

The *New York Times* published an exposé of violence and abuse at the Children's Center shelter in 1975, and in 1977 Legal Aid sued Parry in U.S. District Court under the Civil Rights Act, seeking the center's immediate closure on the ground that its conditions represented cruel and unusual punishment. "Youngsters held at the center are repeatedly subjected to violent assaults, rapes, fights and beatings with sticks, knives, chains, glass and other weapons," the suit charged. It also cited forced homosexuality and rampant use of alcohol and marijuana.

"I think it's an awful place, and I want it closed," Parry said in response at a press conference. "But we want it closed in an orderly fashion. Right now, there is no place for the children to go." The account ran on an inside page in the *New York Times* the following day, next to a piece about the cutoff of public funds to forty-nine city day-care centers, many of them started by Parry in her first job in city administration. It was easy to dismantle the good, it seemed; shutting down the bad took longer. Still, the lawsuit helped in the final push, and the Children's Center closed its doors that year.

Parry succeeded in replacing the shelters with a network of small city diagnostic centers and group homes, the beginnings of a public institutional structure that she hoped could compete with the private sector. Both she and Dumpson were well aware that by expanding the public sector while the voluntary agencies still gave preference to children of their own kind, they were in danger of creating an even more segregated system. As a black man, Dumpson was prepared to run that risk: nobody was going to accuse him of being a racist, he figured. His great hope, however, was that *Wilder* would eventually result in a breakthrough that would force the private agencies to accept responsibility for all children, and strengthen the city's control over placement.

They both learned the perils of trying to ride waves of media attention to fix agency problems. Even when you won, you lost, though sometimes it was worth the price.

"Big Money, Little Victims," a six-part series in the *New York Daily News* that blasted the city's foster-care system, hurt the agencies much more than it did the Parry and Dumpson administration. Appearing the week of May 13, 1975, as the private agencies fought fiercely against tougher city contracts, it amounted to a public-relations coup for Parry. The series painted an overwhelmingly negative picture of the agencies, charging that they pleaded poverty in order to reap private donations while hoarding blue-chip stock portfolios; diverted public money meant for their charges' food and clothing; and denied children the chance to escape foster homes where many were being abused, neglected, and sexually molested. In the *News* series, the conflict over city contracts came across not as a bid by the city to seize control of agency intake, but rather as the agencies' self-interested resistance to demands for an accountability that was long overdue. The series even contrasted the private sector's poor performance on adoption with the city's success.

Speedwell Services for Children had only four adoptions in 1974 out of 577 children, the story pointed out. Greer Children's Community showed no adoptions at all that year out of the 326 children in its care; the Cardinal McCloskey School and Home had five adoptions out of 495 children; and St. Vincent's Hall, a Catholic agency in Brooklyn with 725 children, had only one. The *News* cited—and knocked down—the claim by COVCCA's Joe Gavrin that the agencies were trying to rehabilitate these children's parents: "Some of the parents they claim they're rehabilitating haven't been heard from in years," one quoted caseworker scoffed. Parry herself told the *News* that efforts to rehabilitate natural parents were "almost nonexistent in some agencies," and that the vast majority of the others were "doing a very poor job" of it.

Although Dumpson and Parry provided some of the series's ammunition, they couldn't help but feel the heat of its findings. One story in the series, headlined "Child-Care Horrors Abound, but City Sees No Evil," declared, "New York City is turning its back on the thousands of children it is dumping into the laps of private child-care agencies each year by assuming a hands-off policy toward the physical and emotional abuse, the neglect and even torture that many of these children experience in agency-approved foster homes." Parry responded publicly that understaffing left her powerless, and that if she could assign one person to each agency, she could double the number of adoptions each year—a $700,000 investment of manpower that could reap $4 million in foster-care savings.

This, it seemed, was the other side of the equation that had produced the Children's Center: if you cracked down on the agencies that were hoarding "adoptable" children, you could open up beds and resources for the shelter kids.

For Parry, that was the right battle. She resented being forced by Lowry into the wrong one, through *OFFER,* Lowry's lawsuit over foster-children transfers. Sure, there were kids who were moved when they shouldn't be. But that had to do with the poor qualifications of caseworkers, their lack of training, the lack of government commitment to fund adequate casework, the spotty quality of family-court judges—problems a new layer of hearings would do nothing to resolve, she believed.

"If [Lowry] had brought a lawsuit forcing us to hire trained caseworkers, I would have kissed the ground," Parry would say later. But hearings?

It was as though Lowry were going out of her way to become her adversary. "She could have gotten more by working with me. It wasn't necessary for us to become enemies. She knew where my heart was. I felt she should have had more faith in me. She chose not to."

Dumpson resigned two and a half years into his tenure to return to his professorship at Fordham University. The city budget director's weekly demands for more cuts left him no leeway for self-respect, he said, adding that he had not taken the job as HRA commissioner to preside over the dismantling of the system.

Parry hung on. In her 1977 report, "A Time of Transition: Child Welfare in New York," she warned that more than half of the children in foster care were not being moved toward permanent homes. She called for aggressive monitoring of early planning for children placed in foster care, and a reimbursement system that could be linked to agency performance. As though to illustrate that the city meant business, she cited the termination of one private agency's city contract.

Privately, Parry confessed that the agency in question should have been cut off years earlier. Only when the state suspended its license to operate was the city emboldened to pull the plug. "It was a horrible place," she said. "It was terribly run. A weak administrative staff, very poor service. The only reason it had been kept alive as long as it had been was because it was minority-run."

The agency was Speedwell Services for Children. Officially, it went out of business on September 1, 1976. On that day, Lamont Wilder was one of several hundred children whose names and records were transferred en masse from Speedwell's filing cabinets to the filing cabinets of another Protestant foster-care agency around the corner.

SIX

IN THE EVENING, WHEN FRANTZ FILS-AIME RETURNED FROM work, Lamont was always the first one to the door. "Daddy, Daddy!" he would call, trotting out, a little pigeon-toed, with his arms open for a hug.

He had always been a sunny child. "Coat-on!" he would crow when he was just learning to talk, reaching for the jacket that signaled the start of an expedition to an outside world where he invariably won smiles from strangers. He was smart, too, quick to learn everything Alicia taught him, from a simple grace recited before meals to the trick for releasing and catching the advertising fliers he found fastened to the front doorknob every afternoon when he and Alicia brought Henri home from kindergarten.

Henri was reserved and quiet compared to his foster brother. In looks, Henri was unmistakeably the Fils-Aimes' son, with Frantz's light-golden skin and long face and Alicia's narrow-bridged nose. But Lamont, who looked like no one in their family, was a child after their own hearts.

One warm April day, Alicia wrote a poem about him. With the first letter of each line, she spelled out his full name.

> Lips always smiling
> arms reaching out
> many beautiful memories
> out of such a tiny boy
> never complaining
> truly you are a real joy

whenever I see you
in your face there is love.
lessons you taught me
dear, dear Lamont
every thought you bring
reaches deep in my soul

When she was finished, she dated it—"April 28, 1976"—and placed it carefully in the drawer atop the tiny turquoise sleeper.

"LAMONT IS A HAPPY, well developed, friendly and normal baby. He is responsive to everyone and gets warm response in return," his last Speedwell caseworker wrote that spring in a brief update for the city that listed the agency goal for the boy as "continued care." When Speedwell stopped sending out foster-care checks in the final chaotic months before its demise, some foster parents joined together to sue the agency for the money they were owed; a few even tried to return their foster children. Frantz and Alicia let the money go. They spent more on Lamont than the stipend provided for his care, anyway. If they had waited for the quarterly clothing allowances from the agency, he never would have have been properly dressed for Easter or Christmas, and his shoes would have been perpetually too tight. Not that they didn't need the $204 a month they began to receive from the Sheltering Arms Children's Service, which took over Lamont's case and their foster home in the fall of 1976; prices were soaring, and Frantz's clerk's salary wasn't keeping up.

The new Sheltering Arms caseworker, Gertrude Kihara, was effusive about Lamont's charm and his obvious contentment in the Fils-Aimes' home. But she hinted that things could not just continue this way. She spoke of a need for "permanency planning" for Lamont. Too much time had passed without a visit from Shirley. Either Shirley had to establish a relationship with her son and a concrete plan to retrieve him, or she had to give him up for adoption. Kihara, a slim young Japanese-American woman with long hair, was going to do her best to find Shirley to ask her to surrender her parental rights voluntarily.

Alicia had never understood why Shirley and her baby son hadn't been placed in one foster home from the start so they could grow up together.

Now she tried to put the prospect of losing Lamont out of her mind, without giving herself over to the other possibility hinted at by Kihara, that they might be able to adopt him themselves. For years foster parents had been barred from adopting their foster children in most agencies; one heard of exceptions, but one also heard of foster parents who had tried to adopt a longtime foster child only to forfeit the child to another foster home because the agency claimed they had become "too attached." The more cynical critics said it was all about money: agencies didn't want to lose their stable of foster parents through adoption, or halt the flow of public money for the children's care, since they kept more than fifty cents out of every dollar they received from the city for foster care. Many foster parents felt they couldn't afford to adopt anyway. Without the foster-care stipend, how would they stretch their modest household income to pay for the child's expenses? Although adoption subsidies had been introduced in 1968 to cover just such situations, a city study in 1971 revealed that agencies rarely told foster parents about this possibility, which would eliminate the agency's role even as it cut the public's cost in half. Generally, it seemed, the more desirable a child, the more affluent the families considered to adopt him. And in Alicia's eyes, Lamont was a child anyone would want.

"Lamont has an exuberant personality," Kihara wrote in an annual report to the city when the boy was not yet three. "He is always talking, and verbalizes tremendously for his age, both in Spanish and English. He 'reads' stories by remembering them and can identify many objects. He is very active, amuses himself constantly, calling the attention of adults present to his activity frequently. He is typically aggressive in his play. He is a very responsive and attractive youngster, who converses and retains information easily.

"Lamont is very well adjusted to the foster family, the foster extended family, and the neighbors. He obeys the foster parents directly, and discipline is very calm and controlled. Lamont displays sibling rivalry toward Henri, foster parents' son, but he treats Henri's possessions carefully and enjoys playing with him. This worker has met the Fils-Aime neighbors, all of whom expressed positive feelings toward Lamont. He interacts very well with them. Lamont attends a family service program at a nearby elementary school where his foster mother volunteers. Thus he is in contact with other children and elementary learning experiences."

This winning child had not been contacted by his teenaged birth mother since the previous April, technically longer than the six months necessary to constitute abandonment. By now there was strong public pressure on private agencies to try to free such foster children for adoption. Only one foster child in five was likely to return home, a study by the nonprofit Foundation for Child Development found in 1976, and unless the system was changed, 26 percent were destined to grow up entirely in foster care. But Speedwell had failed to document any efforts to find Shirley and involve her in planning for Lamont after her final AWOL from Holy Cross, so the legal case had to be made from scratch.

All during the winter and spring of 1977 Kihara pursued what were called "diligent efforts" to contact Shirley. The phrase came from the language in Social Services Law Section 384 about what steps were required before an agency could obtain termination of parental rights for abandonment or permanent neglect. The caseworker kept a careful record of the telephone calls she made and the letters she wrote in her endeavor to locate Shirley: Sister Dorothy, Carol Sherman, the Aulds/Alls, Shirley's aunt Margaret Moody. No one had Shirley's address, but Margaret Moody said she sometimes saw her and would tell her to get in touch with Kihara. Word spread through the family, and one day Carrie Powell called the agency to request weekend visits with Lamont, the great-nephew she'd never seen. Kihara recorded two unsuccessful attempts to call Carrie Powell back, and never heard from her again. Likewise, a man identifying himself as Prentis Smith phoned the agency once, on January 31, 1977, and requested a visit with his two-and-a-half-year-old son. But when Kihara called back to confirm the arrangements, he was unknown at the telephone number he had given.

The certified letters worked no better. Shirley signed the receipt for a letter addressed to her at her aunt Margaret Moody's house in late January 1977, but she neither kept nor canceled the appointment it set for her. The same pattern was repeated in February and March, when letters were sent to a Harlem apartment she supposedly shared with a girlfriend. On April 1, Kihara dispatched another letter formally notifying Shirley of her plan to go to court to seek termination of her parental rights unless she contacted the agency by April 11. April 11 passed with no word from Shirley. But at the end of the month, the notification letter was returned marked "unclaimed."

"Natural mother is a teenager who has been unamenable to supervision in the past. She has no plans which include Lamont but fails to follow up contacts concerning surrender arrangements," Kihara wrote in the annual reauthorization request to the city, checking off "adoption" as the new goal for Lamont. "We discussed our intentions to go to court with the foster mother. She regrets the natural mother does not show interest in Lamont, of whom she is proud. She must discuss the possibility of his being free with her family."

In May, Kihara visited the apartment at 127 East 125th Street that had been Shirley's last known address, and handed the notification letter to a young girl who said that Shirley no longer lived there, but she could pass on the word for her to contact the agency.

Three days later, Shirley finally called.

"I want Lamont back," she told Kihara.

Lamont was turning three. Shirley hadn't seen him in over a year, and before that only for brief supervised visits. She had signed Lamont voluntarily into care in 1974. At the time, agencies had had almost total discretion to refuse to return children; mothers who objected had to file suit in court. But under a 1975 amendment to state law, designed to keep children from disappearing into foster care, Shirley now had a right to take Lamont back within twenty days of requesting his return in writing, unless the agency filed a petition in court charging neglect or abuse. Kihara told Shirley how important it was that she visit her child again and build a relationship with him before seeking his return. She inquired about Shirley's circumstances. Shirley, not yet eighteen, insisted that she did live at the 125th Street address and that she was receiving public assistance. She agreed to call back before the end of the week to learn the name of the caseworker who would be assigned to work with her.

She didn't call.

A FEW WEEKS LATER, City Comptroller Harrison Goldin issued an audit report titled "The Children Are Waiting: The Failure to Achieve Permanent Homes for Foster Children in New York City." It was an unsparing indictment of private foster-care agencies, based on a random sample of cases from five such agencies: Brooklyn Catholic Guardian, Angel Guardian, Louise Wise, Edwin Gould, and Speedwell. Speedwell, studied before it went out of business, was the worst, but none of the five agencies provided biological parents with the services they needed for a child's return, nor did any promptly free abandoned children for adoption, recruit adoptive parents, or try to interest relatives in taking children permanently. Goldin estimated that the city had spent $206 million unnecessarily for 10,977 children who had lingered in care for six years or more when they could have been adopted. Of children not legally free for adoption, eleven thousand like Lamont, had not been visited by a parent in more than a year.

Lamont himself was luckier than most. He had stayed in one foster home almost since birth, defying all the odds. Speedwell had the second-highest average in placements-per-child among audited agencies—a mean between two and three placements for each of the 553 children in its care in 1975. Unsurprisingly, it also claimed a high proportion of children whose emotional health and social adjustment had deteriorated.

If an agency caseworker elected to move Lamont to another foster home, Alicia would have no legal standing to challenge the decision, nor did Lamont have any legally recognized interest in staying with the Fils-Aimes. Traditionally, no matter how long children had stayed with a foster parent, they could be moved at will.

Just before Lamont's birth, as it happened, Marcia Lowry had filed suit in federal court challenging this state of affairs—the very lawsuit Carol Parry so resented. Lowry hadn't planned it as a major case. She never anticipated the bitter opposition it would generate. She had simply responded to one foster mother's determination and anguish.

MADELEINE SMITH was a middle-aged black woman whose new caseworker had decided she was too disabled by arthritis to keep Danielle and Eric Gandy, a brother and sister who had been in her care since they were two and four years old. Before coming to live with her on the second floor of an old rowhouse in Queens, the children had been shuttled through a series of institutions and foster homes from birth; after three and a half years with Mrs. Smith, they considered her their "Ma," and she loved them. Desperate to stop the private agency, Catholic Guardian Society, from moving them to another foster home, Mrs. Smith began calling Marcia Lowry's office for help.

"We don't take individual cases, but refer her to Legal Services," Lowry told her secretary.

But Legal Services was no help, and Mrs. Smith kept calling. One day she told Lowry's secretary, "I've gone to court and I've asked for an adjournment so I can get a lawyer, but the agency has told me they're going to take the children this week, and I'm just frantic."

The secretary, Susan Kaiser, knew that Lowry respected her good judgment. Walking into an office knee-deep in *Wilder* interrogatories, she advised Lowry, "You really have to do something." And Lowry finally spoke with Mrs. Smith herself.

"That was the critical moment," David L. Chambers and Michael S. Wald wrote in a detailed analysis of the case included in the book *In the Interest of Children*. "We too have met Mrs. Smith. It seems quite unlikely that anyone could speak to this powerful, loving woman and say 'no.' . . . When she spoke to Lowry, she was absolutely determined to keep 'her babies.' The question for Lowry was not whether to help, but how."

First she tried direct intervention. The head of Catholic Guardian explained politely that he had to support his workers. "How long will it take Mrs. Smith to work through her feelings about this so she can turn over the children?" he asked Lowry. She told him it would take about four days to help Mrs. Smith work through her feelings, and promptly went home to prepare a lawsuit.

Lowry believed that the decision to move the Gandy children was wrong, arbitrary, and all too typical of foster-care agencies. She and Carl Weisbrod, the MFY lawyer who was then the man in her life, brainstormed for a legal theory. He pointed to *Goldberg* v. *Kelly,* a 1970 U.S. Supreme Court decision holding that before a state could terminate benefits to a recipient of public assistance, it must offer the recipient an adequate opportunity to be heard. A few days later Lowry named Mrs. Smith and the Gandy children as plaintiffs in a class action on behalf of all foster parents whose foster children had been with them for at least a year, and on behalf of all such foster children. The federal lawsuit sought a full hearing before the children were removed, regardless of whether the state proposed to place them in another foster home or institution or return them to their birth parents.

Lowry quickly won a temporary restraining order against the removal of the Gandy children. The agency soon abandoned plans to move them, and eventually they were adopted by Mrs. Smith. Her gratitude toward Lowry was effusive. The suit also resulted in the city's "voluntary" redrafting of its rules, providing for a formal hearing by a city hearing officer before children were transferred from one foster placement to another against their current foster parents' wishes.

But the lawsuit that came to be known as *OFFER* also dragged Lowry into a major legal battle that turned much of the city's legal-services community against her. In the eyes of many poverty lawyers—her natural allies—Lowry was a traitor for arming foster parents against the already disadvantaged biological parents who were those lawyers' clients. Leading what became a kind of crusade against *OFFER* was Louise Gans, who held the very same job at Community Action for Legal Services (CALS) that Lowry herself had used to begin battling for children's rights.

For Gans and many of her colleagues, the true road to children's rights lay in defending poor parents against the state's abuses of power. Gans believed that poor families were routinely misled and mistreated by foster-care agencies—their children unnecessarily removed, their visits curtailed, and reunification wrongfully discouraged. More passionately than most, she felt that legal reform efforts should concentrate on changing the state's treatment of biological parents. Yet here, instead, was CLU litigation that risked establishing some kind of constitutional right for foster parents—another weapon agencies could use against poor families. It didn't help, from her perspective, that in an attempt to broaden the class action, Lowry had enlisted the Organization of Foster Families for Equality and Reform (OFFER) and added two white families. Most controversial were the Lhotans, a Long Island couple, and their four foster daughters, the Wallace sisters, who were resisting return to their own unwed mother. Issues of class and race figured in Gans's distress: as she saw it, foster care often served as a way for middle-class social workers to shift the children of the poor—mostly black and Puerto Rican—into middle-class homes. Yet for the poor, foster care was often the only resource available in a crisis; unlike the well-off, they couldn't hire babysitters and psychiatrists or send troublesome children to boarding school. Patricia Wallace, for example, had turned to foster care in 1970, when she was suffering from postpartum depression, alone and on welfare with six young children.

There were personal and historical dimensions to the intensity of Gans's commitment to protecting the parent-child bond. Born into a Jewish family in Germany in 1933, she had eventually been sent, along with her mother, to a concentration camp. Both survived, but her greatest terror in those years was that she and her mother would be separated; her greatest longing was to see her father again. She did, after six years of separation. The moment of reunion had remained an emotional touchstone during the difficult years of family adjustment.

Seven years older than Lowry, Gans had graduated from law school in 1959, a female rarity, motivated not by a desire to change society but by an allegiance to law as opposed to lawlessness, law as a means of protecting human rights. She married late and was past forty when she gave birth to a son. She had just returned to work full-time when she learned about Marcia Lowry's foster-parent case from an article in the New York Post.

The meeting she sought with Lowry quickly became a confrontation. Gans, a short, matronly woman, told a surprised Lowry that she intended to file a cross-complaint on behalf of a class of biological parents, and tried to persuade her that she had brought the wrong case. In reply, Lowry told Gans to stay out of her lawsuit; both biological and foster parents were victims of high-handed agencies, and a hearing was just a minimal way to protect the children at stake. Neither woman would retreat.

Gans and other Legal Services people felt embattled. Their clients had terrible problems, and their staff and resources were always inadequate to help. By their standards, the CLU was rich. That made it all the more galling that with a million lawsuits to chose from, Lowry should bring one that in their view threatened to make things worse instead of better. "Both sides felt like they had high morality on their sides," Ira Glasser would recall. "It got quite accusatory. They accused us of ratifying the worst intrusions of the state and we accused them of duplicating the worst intrusions of the state by repeating them on the kid. They wanted to use the child as an exclusionary rule to punish the government for screwing up, saying, 'Now you have to give this child back to make the parent whole, even though it's ten years later.' But what about the kid?"

As the litigation went on, the rift took on the intensity of the worst kind of family fight. One poverty lawyer ran for the NYCLU board of directors on the sole platform of having Marcia Lowry fired; others ostentatiously crossed the room to avoid her at social events. At a bar association forum, Danny Greenberg, then director of Legal Services and a former colleague of Weisbrod's at MFY, attacked the lawsuit and Lowry in a way that sent the usually unflappable Glasser into a rage.

Greenberg, a big, bushy-haired man easily picked out of a courtroom crowd as the "lawyer who looks like a bear in a suit," cornered Glasser in the hall. "My God, Ira," he said, "think of the class issues in this. You think of yourself as a Brooklyn Dodger fan, a supporter of the underdog. Only a Yankee fan could bring a lawsuit like this! The Yankees would love this lawsuit."

For Glasser, it was as though the grand coalition of the 1960s were coming apart under the pressure of the child welfare system's Dickensian reality. For Greenberg, the Civil Liberties Union was to blame: "My God," he said to himself, "the CLU is taking the half dozen of us who are progressive and splintering us into half a dozen camps!"

The division was made complete when the court ruled that Lowry could not represent both the children and the foster parents in her case and appointed Helen Buttenwieser to speak for the children instead. Buttenwieser, a longtime NYCLU board member, had also represented and advised private child welfare agencies for decades. As she had already told Glasser and Lowry, she was strongly opposed to their position—though not because she agreed with Gans. Unlike both Gans and Lowry, she had faith in the judgment of agency caseworkers and believed that hearings at best were unnecessary and at worst would delay needed transfers. Also, she was alarmed by the implications of constitutional rights for foster parents: in the Progressive tradition, she disapproved of any adult rights in relation to children, feeling that the children's needs should be paramount.

In the spring of 1976, a three-judge panel gave Lowry more than she'd ever asked for. Foster parents did not have a right to a hearing, the judges ruled, but foster children did—and not just if their foster parents asked for it, but before every single transfer, whether to another foster placement or to a biological parent. That would mean an estimated forty-two hundred hearings a year, compared with the mere fourteen that had been requested in the nine months since New York City's revised regulations had gone into effect. "I don't care what it takes," Carol Parry declared, "we're going to beat this one." Like the city and the state, Gans and Buttenwieser appealed to the U.S. Supreme Court, which agreed to hear the case on the merits.

The case vividly illustrated the difficulty of determining who really should speak for children. As Glasser saw it, the adversary system had exposed the presumed unity between the poor mother and her child as a fiction. But here was Buttenwieser, who had never even spoken to the seven plaintiff children, arguing on their behalf that hearings were not in their interest. Greenberg, who helped draft Gans's complaint, was appalled to find himself in the position of asserting that children had no rights of their own; his greatest fear was that the Burger Court would seize this as an opportunity to overrule *Gault*, the Warren Court's landmark decision granting due-process rights to juveniles.

Lowry knew she wasn't going to win: the Supreme Court obviously had not taken the case in order to affirm it. The question was how badly she would lose. For her, the most personally painful aspect of defeat was already past. The Wallace sisters—Cheryl, thirteen; Patty, twelve; Catherine, ten; and Cynthia, nine—had begged her to help them stay with the Lhotans, their foster parents of five and a half years. The girls said that they considered their birth mother, Patricia Wallace, a stranger, that she had hardly ever visited them, that when they lived with her there were days when they ate flowers and leaves from bushes because they were so hungry. But Lowry had already lost that custody battle a year before. A Nassau County justice had sent the girls back to their mother and ordered the Lhotans never to see them again.

"How can they do this?" one of the sisters had cried. "Isn't there some law to stop them?" Two of the girls, placed in an interim foster home, had run away to dramatize their wish to return to the Lhotans'. Before turning themselves in, they'd sent a reporter a handwritten statement pleading for assistance from "lawyers and judges and anyone who can make it possible for kids to have a choice."

Lowry remembered sitting alone on the small terrace of her apartment on Twelfth Street on the afternoon that she realized she had failed them. She had felt devastated, as powerless as the girls were themselves. It was her empathy with the kids that drove her crazy, she thought. She felt no bond with Mrs. Lhotan, a policeman's wife who turned the girls' bedrooms into little shrines of dust ruffles and pink poodles and who disapproved of their mother because she had borne four daughters out of wedlock. Lowry wondered if she might not have won the custody case if she had attacked Patricia Wallace in court on the ground of conventional morality—for hanging out in bars and having illegitimate kids. But she hadn't had the stomach for that. She wanted to win on the right issue: over time, this mother had forfeited her relationship with these children. Sure, the system should have worked to help Wallace keep her family together in the first place, instead of swallowing the children into years of foster care. And Lowry herself had brought a separate class-action lawsuit, *Black* v. *Beame,* to try to force the city to provide such preventive services to families in trouble. But if someone had to be hurt years later, she believed, it should be an adult, not a child.

Gans's answer was in her reply brief: "An essential characteristic of the fundamentally protected rights of parents to the care and custody of their children must be freedom from the power of others to compete for those rights because they too love the children or even love them more. . . . Measurement of the private emotions of parents and children toward one another would be the ultimate invasion of privacy. It would be dangerous for government to have such power."

The brief included a footnote referring to a breeding program run by the Nazis. The Nazis embodied the ultimate abuse of state power, the ultimate contempt for family ties. And yet the experts in Lowry's corner— Joseph Goldstein, Anna Freud, and Albert J. Solnit, authors of *Beyond the Best Interests of the Child*—would have ratified the forced dismemberment of Jewish families. Who could fail to empathize with the Jewish parents of Holland, who returned from concentration camps at the end of World War II to reclaim the children they had hidden with Christian neighbors? Yet many of these children had become psychologically attached to their foster families and estranged from their own flesh and blood. And unlike the Dutch courts, Goldstein, Freud, and Solnit wrote, they would have denied those parents custody. For Gans, there could be no more compelling evidence that Lowry's side was the wrong one.

Gans, Buttenwieser, and Maria Marcus, an appellate lawyer for the state, all argued against the district court's decision. Lowry stood alone to defend it before the nine Supreme Court justices. Even her bitterest adversaries found her performance impressive. Some of the justices went after her hard, their questioning harsh if not hostile during the forty-five minutes allotted to her side. But she never lost her composure or the line of her argument. To her astonishment, she even enjoyed it.

IN JUNE 1977, the month Lamont turned three, the Supreme Court issued its decision, unanimously reversing the judgment of the district court.

All v. *Lowry?* Not quite. Two justices had joined Justice Stewart in his concurring opinion, dismissing the foster relationship as a figment without a valid "liberty interest" protected by the Constitution. Had that been the majority view, Lowry would have lost badly indeed. But the majority opinion, written by Justice Brennan and joined by five others, agonized intelligently on both sides of the question. On the one hand, "we cannot dismiss the foster family as a mere collection of unrelated individuals," Brennan wrote. On the other hand, any recognition of a constitutional protection for the relations in such a family would create "virtually unavoidable . . . tension" with the rights of the biological family. Brennan's solution was to sidestep the conflict by finding that New York City's new hearings were constitutionally adequate, and that even the informal procedures available outside the city were good enough, when taken together with the foster parent's right to participate in the family-court review mandated by New York state statute after eighteen months.

Lowry called it a "Pyrrhic defeat." For Gans, it was in some ways a Pyrrhic victory. She deeply resented the time and energy absorbed by what was at best a defensive case, and one that proved to be of little precedential value to her side.

So much passion and principle had been poured into the one thousand pages of briefs and affidavits that made up the court record. But the core debate, of biological parents versus foster parents, dealt with the exception, not the norm, of foster care. Of all foster children transferred in any given year, 80 percent went to another foster placement, and only 20 percent back to a biological parent. Moreover, foster parents were far more likely to be requesting a child's transfer themselves than battling to keep a child. Few children in foster care had even one adult competing to love them, let alone the two or more necessary to set up the Solomonic choice that stirred such public interest and legal conflict.

SEVEN

I N THE SUMMER OF 1977 LAMONT AND THE FILS-AIMES FLEW
to Tampa, Florida, rented a car, and drove to Disney World. They had
planned and saved for this as the ideal family vacation. Later they would
look back on it as the idyll before the fall. But in photographs from that
summer, Alicia's face looks almost frozen in anxiety. In every picture, a
little frown pinches her brow, as though she were concentrating very hard
on staying still enough not to spoil the frame. When Frantz appears, he is
unsmiling, too, his eyes almost closed against the glare of the Florida sun,
his thick mustache, bald head, and stiff bearing giving him a look both
aggressive and aggrieved.

Something was happening in their marriage that they had not yet
grasped. Alicia felt herself wanting to grow and change in ways that
Frantz's love did not accommodate. She was the vessel of his physical
desire, not a companion of the spirit in the way the Scriptures envisioned.
Simply to be herself, she needed more and more time outside his presence. Later that summer, taking the children with her, she stayed for a
month in Puerto Rico at her mother's house.

Frantz would maintain afterward that he never knew what precipitated
the rift in their marriage. Perhaps he had not transformed himself sufficiently, he thought. In order to marry her, he had had to give up his religion and follow hers. But the prohibitions of the Baptist Church remained
alien to him. No liquor, not even a glass of wine with good food. No dancing. No music except certain approved songs and hymns. When a holiday
or family birthday came around, he would take Alicia and the boys to celebrate with his Catholic relatives, where the wine flowed and people

danced with abandon. And yes, he would join in, flouting the look of disapproval he thought he saw in her eyes. It was true that when she was away, he had friends of both sexes over to the apartment without her knowledge. He suspected that a neighbor woman later reported this to her, and that that was why she suddenly changed toward him.

Alicia knew about the sexual privileges that men of his class enjoyed in poor countries. They could get anything they wanted with their money. He came from a society where it was considered normal for married men to lead a double life, to have a wife to respect and come home to but also another woman as a mistress on the side. She could not tolerate the knowledge that he was looking at other women; it made her feel all the more that she had become his possession. She was angry, but most of all she felt so hurt that her very skin was raw to his touch.

Eventually they sought counseling from their pastor at the Mount Eden Church. In the presence of the pastor, Frantz made what Alicia understood as an admission that he had strayed—though in later years he would deny that he had ever been unfaithful.

"You should take time away from each other," the Reverend Cesar Ramos told them, a suggestion Alicia thought was very good. "She's been very hurt, and when you are hurt like that, you cannot feel loved—you need time for healing. So don't approach her," he said to Frantz.

In the beginning, Alicia saw that Frantz was trying. But then he got impatient. The more she sought a healing distance, the more he feared losing her altogether and pressed for an intimacy she could not bear. She suggested that he go somewhere for a while, maybe to his sister's, until she could feel better about being close to him. He refused to leave. She asked him to sleep on the living-room couch and she closed the bedroom door against him.

They didn't really fight in front of the children. He was the kind of person who would say exactly what he thought when he was angry, and two minutes later be happy again. She was more likely to say nothing, but then to brood over one of his outbursts long after he had forgotten it. Tension filled the small apartment.

Seeing Frantz on the couch in the morning in a tangle of sheets was strange for Lamont and Henri. As though to defuse the uneasiness of the sight, the boys threw themselves on their father in wrestling horseplay, and he responded in kind. Soon they were shrieking with laughter, taking flying leaps that made the couch shudder, flailing wildly with pillows as Frantz grabbed them by the knees to pull them down again.

Suddenly there was a crash. The noise brought Alicia running from the bedroom. A painting hanging behind the couch had been knocked from its hook and had tumbled to the floor. It was a Haitian pastoral scene painted on a wooden board in brilliant colors, the ocean very blue and the green hills dotted with small houses and tiny people. Alicia had brought it back from a trip to Haiti that she and Frantz made early in their marriage. Now it lay broken in two pieces. Her face, usually so impassive, grew contorted. She had loved that painting, with its languid peace and lush color. She had imbued its deceptive simplicity with her best memories of being a newlywed. How could Frantz, a grown man, have been so irresponsible as to endanger what was precious to her? She was very angry, angrier than the boys had ever seen her. They ran to their room, but through the thin walls, they could still hear her voice vibrating with barely suppressed rage.

Later, Alicia tried to reassure them. She explained that she and their father weren't getting along well, but that it had nothing to do with them. She told herself that the children's lives had not really changed. When the boys became increasingly quarrelsome with each other, she blamed it on late-blooming sibling rivalry.

Before their Florida vacation, the Fils-Aimes had told Kihara that they wanted to adopt Lamont. Wasn't he already a part of their family? Adoption would legally seal what had already grown together. But by winter the caseworker wrote in her report to the city that the crisis in the Fils-Aimes' marriage made adoption problematic. The long process of freeing Lamont for adoption had formally begun in October 1977, when Sheltering Arms requested the city's approval to seek a termination of Shirley's parental rights. In November, the city sent its approval. In January 1978, a Sheltering Arms attorney filed the petition for termination, and the wait for a court hearing began. By that time Kihara considered the foster family's situation "somewhat tenuous." She advised the Fils-Aimes of the requirement that both spouses in a marriage agree to a child's adoption, or, alternatively, that a divorce be final for only one to adopt.

Alicia was a little concerned that Lamont, then three and a half, still wet his bed at night, though he was toilet-trained during the day. "We suspect that he is under tension perhaps due to foster family's marital situation," Kihara wrote. "Also, it may be that foster family has high expectations from child and may be pressuring him beyond his abilities. We hope to learn from psychological testing about child's functioning. He seems intellectually to be a bright normal or above average child." She also noted in her report that if the Fils-Aimes were to adopt Lamont, it would likely be with an adoption subsidy, since the family's income was small. But she did not, apparently, discuss a subsidy with them directly.

In February, Lamont scored 105 in a Stanford-Binet Projectives test, confirming Kihara's impression that he was bright-normal. He was thirty-nine inches tall and weighed almost thirty-eight pounds—big for his age—so that when people heard him speak so clearly and so well, they tended to think he was older than his years. Alicia had tried to enroll him in a city-funded day-care center at the First Spanish Methodist Church in East Harlem, near a bilingual institute where she was taking noncredit refresher courses in hopes of eventually going back to college. But because Lamont was a foster child, she was told, he was not eligible without the city's approval. Kihara made a special request to the Allocation and Accountability office on his behalf, pointing out that this intelligent child would benefit from the stimulation of structured activities with other children and that there were no neighborhood nursery schools that took children his age, other than another city-funded day-care center fifteen minutes' walk away from the Fils-Aimes' home, where he would also be ineligible as a foster child. The answer that came back was a pennywise negative: only a child with "special needs"—mental retardation, for example—was allowed to receive both foster care and day care.

Alicia gave up her courses and spent more time in church, taking Lamont with her. But Mount Eden no longer felt like a refuge. The Reverend Ramos took Frantz's side now. Not only was it her Christian duty to forgive, he made clear to her, but as the woman, it was her task to make the marriage work, and her fault if it foundered. She had always been bothered by the authoritarian way the pastor ran the congregation, and by his restrictions on the roles the women could fill. Women were elders of the church Alicia had joined in Puerto Rico, but Ramos had declared that no woman could serve as an elder in his church unless the last man was unavailable. His was a finger-pointing type of preaching, she felt—judgmental sermons that left her soul still thirsting for spiritual comfort.

When a guest pastor from a Methodist church preached, she was struck by the contrast. This Methodist preacher, Juan Sosa, spoke of a God who was always present, who was always there for you. She began to visit his church, Saint Stephen's, in the afternoons. It felt like a liberation. There she was free to be herself. It was a beautiful old wood-and-stone church building with room for everybody, more tolerant, more open than Mount Eden, she thought. After the conservativism of Baptists, these Methodists shocked her sometimes. People here not only spoke of feeding the hungry, they asked *why* they were hungry; they mixed the Gospel with social action. She began to attend church meetings and to go on every retreat that was offered. Her mind and spirit were engaged in a new way. But as she grew mentally and spiritually that winter, spring, and summer of 1977–78, the stony ground of her marriage seemed to her even more unyielding. When she looked back on it, her relationship with Frantz appeared empty and false from its beginnings. There was nothing to go back to, and yet the only way forward was over a precipice.

Not only was divorce proscribed by the Baptist Church and anathema to Frantz's Catholic family, but it would leave her to earn her way as a single mother at thirty-six with no marketable skills and little education or experience. Her mother, her friends, her church were all against it. A woman without a man is not much in this world, she thought bitterly.

Scanning the bulletin board at Saint Stephen's Church the summer after Lamont's fourth birthday, she noticed that the Hispanic Methodist churches were planning to sponsor a Labor Day camping retreat near Montauk, Long Island. She determined to use that weekend to come to some decision about her relationship with Frantz.

The weather was unseasonably chilly for the beach on Labor Day weekend that year. Lamont and Henri went into the water anyway, splashing and jumping in the surf. When Lamont emerged, he was chilled and shaking. Alicia rubbed him down with a towel and dropped back on her bare heels to watch him run in gleeful circles on the sand, chasing seagulls with boundless hope. Henri was at the shoreline, digging. For a long moment Alicia felt as though she had left her body and was outside it looking in, with an honesty she had not permitted herself before. She knew then that she could not be reconciled to staying in her marriage.

On their return, she called Frantz into the bedroom so the children wouldn't hear them talking. She told him she could no longer live with him. She told him she wanted a divorce. He became distraught, angry, then defiant.

"I'll never give you the divorce," he shouted. "You'll always be with me. I'll never leave."

The last weeks were the worst. He alternately berated and taunted her and begged her to change her mind. But finally, in October 1978, he moved out. Alicia began a government-sponsored CETA job-training program in office skills the same month. A good friend agreed to watch Lamont and Henri while she was at class.

ALL THIS TIME, Lamont's status had remained uncertain. On May 15, 1978, Surrogate's Court, which handled terminations of parental rights, had approved continued foster care pending court action on the agency's four-month-old petition. Eleven months after the petition had been filed, the court was still waiting for a report from the lawyer appointed as Shirley's guardian ad litem in the matter, Jonathan Sulds. Sulds, whose role was to make sure Shirley's legal rights were respected, had determined that she was the only parent with a right to notice of the termination proceeding. Although Shirley had alleged that Prentis Smith was the father of her child, he had never acknowledged paternity or made payments on Lamont's behalf. Sheltering Arms contended that the required notice to Shirley was complete as of the May 15 court review. Sulds didn't want to sign off on termination without talking to her himself. But it was far from the most pressing matter among his cases, and he did little to try to track her down until the end of the year. Eventually he obtained the usual telephone numbers and left word with Shirley's stepmother that she should call him. In early February 1979, she did.

Shirley and the lawyer spoke twice by telephone. She insisted that she didn't want Lamont placed for adoption and maintained that she had never received a copy of the petition. She told a confused story of having had lunch with Lamont at Sheltering Arms as recently as June 1978, and of waiting in vain to hear from the agency about setting up a schedule of regular visits—a claim flatly contradicted by Kihara's affidavit. Sulds stressed to the teenager the importance of keeping him informed of her whereabouts and the need for them to meet to review the petition together so he could contest it. They agreed to speak again in about a week to set up a meeting. Ten days later, when Sulds tried to contact her at the telephone number she had provided, no one answered. He tried five times a week, at different hours of the day and evening, but it just rang and rang. Later the line was disconnected, and a registered letter sent to the address was returned unclaimed.

In March, while Sulds was still trying to reach Shirley Wilder, Alicia Fils-Aime found a clerical job at a local business. The friend who had been watching the boys said that Lamont and Henry were fighting so much now, they would be better off with separate sitters. Alicia began dropping Lamont off at the apartment of an older woman named Rose who baby-sat for several young children in a neighboring building. On weekends, Frantz came back to spend time with the boys; Alicia tried to stay away from the apartment while he was there, to avoid his renewed entreaties for a reconciliation.

At times she would be overtaken by panic at what she had done and would pray for strength. One terrible moment came shortly after she began her new job. Since her duties included making out the payroll, the company's finances were quickly revealed to her. She realized it was on the verge of bankruptcy, and that she would soon be unemployed again. Frantz was very bitter toward her these days, still fighting the divorce every step of the way, and hard pressed for cash besides. She couldn't depend on him for enough money to keep the household afloat. If she lost her job, she would be a candidate for welfare.

It was at this point, with Lamont two and a half months away from his fifth birthday, that Sheltering Arms gave Alicia an ultimatum: adopt Lamont now, or give him up. Alicia pleaded for more time.

"Listen," she told Gertrude Kihara, "at this time I'm going through a divorce. At this time I cannot make a decision like that. When you are going through a divorce, especially if you come from a very strong Christian background, you are in no condition to make big decisions like that."

But the powers-that-be at Sheltering Arms insisted that no further delay was possible. For almost five years, delay had been endemic in Lamont's case; now speed was suddenly of the essence. A caseworker from Sheltering Arms's adoption unit urged Alicia to think about Lamont's best interest. If, as a single parent in emotional turmoil, she was reluctant to make this commitment, wouldn't it be better for Lamont if she gave him up? The ideal for the boy, of course, was a two-parent family, a home with a father as well as a mother. Lamont had been close to Frantz, and there was no question that he was now missing the day-to-day attention of a father.

There were other reasons to insist on a decision, reasons the agency didn't share with Alicia. In truth, age five was the borderland of unadoptability for black boys. If Lamont was to be adopted by strangers, it had to happen soon, or chances were it wouldn't happen at all. In 1977 New York Spaulding for Children, an agency specializing in finding homes for children considered "hard to place," had offered to assist ninety-four child-care agencies in finding homes for more than two thousand foster children waiting for adoption. A spokesperson for Spaulding said that it had been deluged with referrals of black boys past the age of seven. "These boys are the least desirable," the *New York Times* reported, "because they are prejudged unmanageable." The agency had called a press conference to announce a demonstration project in adoption recruitment. One of the children put on display at the news conference was a ten-year-old black boy they called Jimmie Johnson, who had been in foster care since the age of thirteen months. Exceptionally handsome and very bright, he had lived in several foster homes, the longest for eight years. But after two years of litigation to free him for adoption, his foster parents had finally declined to keep him. He began to have behavioral problems and, after another failed placement, was now living in a Children's Aid Society group home on Staten Island. That was the kind of scenario Kihara wanted to prevent by securing a stable home for Lamont now.

THERE WERE OTHER PRESSURES felt by Sheltering Arms and agencies like it. Foster care was becoming one of the city's hottest political issues. A piece in the December 18, 1978, issue of *New York* magazine by Nicholas Pileggi raised the temperature. "Who'll Save the Children?" the headline asked. "Certainly not New York City," the story answered, "even though it gives $300 million each year to private and religiously affiliated agencies to care for the homeless, abandoned, and neglected young." In many ways Pileggi's article echoed the 1975 *Daily News* series "Big Money, Little Victims," which had revealed the agencies' multimillion-dollar stock portfolios and tiny expenditures on children's food and clothing, highlighted their dismal record on adoption, and blasted the city's failure to hold them to fiscal account. Pileggi also drew on the published findings of advocacy groups and commission reports, as well as ongoing audits by the city comptroller's office, which had issued its own highly critical assessment of foster care the year before. But if many of the story's elements were old, its overall effect was electrifyingly new. Pileggi had succeeded in painting the voluntary agencies as a kind of municipal version of the military-industrial complex, and was heralding a new season of big-league political scandal.

"New inquiries could call into question the whole private reimbursement system in New York and bring into the open the intense rivalry that goes on behind the scenes between various religious organizations for control of government-funded hospitals, medical schools, and universities," Pileggi wrote. "The revelations may also call a halt to Mayor Edward I. Koch's plan to turn the city's widely divergent and politically volatile community-based anti-poverty programs over to religiously affiliated agencies."

In other words, this was an issue with real mileage for a reform-minded Koch rival. That point wasn't lost on David Tobis, the new social-services director for City Council President Carol Bellamy. On Tobis's first day of work, January 2, 1979, Bellamy had given him three months to find her an area in the social services to focus on. The Pileggi piece came to mind immediately: "It was a perfect issue for Carol. She could save money and help kids at the same time." Her decision to go with it was clinched when she learned that another Koch rival, Manhattan Borough President Andrew Stein, might beat her to the punch if she delayed.

Tobis enlisted Judy Schaffer, formerly of the Council on Adoptable Children, to compile and summarize the findings of fifteen years' worth of studies, both in New York and nationwide. Her compendium showed that the problems with foster care had been exposed ad nauseam; now the focus had to be on the remedies. The solution had to include tough, enforceable standards and control over placement. The shift in power that Carol Parry had wanted and that Marcia Lowry was still trying to win through the courts was finally within political reach, Tobis believed.

By April 1979, Tobis and other members of Bellamy's staff had drafted a series of new rules for the city's foster-care contracts. The key provisions required the city's Special Services for Children to set minimum-performance standards for the care of children, to impose sanctions on agencies that fell short, and to place children in the better agencies, thus shrinking or closing the worst ones and eliminating their excess beds. The resolutions called for city contracts that would make the city the final arbiter on the appropriateness of a child's placement with a voluntary agency. They also outlawed the automatic contract renewals, extensions, and rate increases that had become commonplace. Instead, under the resolutions, every contract would have to be approved by the Board of Estimate, the powerful budgetary arm of New York City government, whose members included the mayor, the council president, and the comptroller, with two votes each, as well as the borough presidents of Manhattan, Queens, Brooklyn, the Bronx, and Staten Island, with one vote each.

The comptroller, Harrison Goldin, agreed to jointly sponsor the foster-care resolutions with Carol Bellamy. His motives were not entirely altruistic, in Tobis's view. Despite Goldin's scathing 1977 report on foster care, "The Children Are Waiting," he was himself vulnerable on the foster-care issue. His office was responsible for fiscal audits of the foster-care agencies, but by 1979, when he had been in office five years, many agencies had not been audited for eight years or more. The few audits that were conducted frequently showed hundreds of thousands of dollars in overpayments by the city, but Goldin's collections had been less than vigorous in the face of protest by the politically powerful religious federations. In addition, Goldin was under investigation by several city and state agencies for misuse of public office;* taking a leadership role on a good-government issue would give his public image a needed boost. This way, too, he could attack a mayoral agency's management of foster care rather than provoke individual foster-care agencies in thankless audit battles.

Before the resolutions were formally introduced, Bellamy and Goldin secured enough votes, from four of the five borough presidents, to guarantee their passage. As the reforms gained the political momentum of a train leaving the station, Mayor Koch came aboard. His new commissioner of the Human Services Administration, Stanley Brezenoff, and Carol Parry's successor at Special Services for Children, Beverly Sanders, both had sympathy for the resolutions. More important, because Bellamy and Goldin had taken the lead, they, not Koch, would draw most of the political fire from the foster-care agencies, while Koch would share credit for a popular measure that promised to save tax-levy dollars.

As foster-care reform by the Board of Estimate took on an air of inevitability, the administrative staff of Special Services for Children made the design of new foster-care regulations a priority. In the past it had used vague standards, periodic site visits, and subjective impressions to make

---

*Goldin would weather all these investigations, rejecting reports that criticized him.

judgments about agency performance. Now it proposed to measure performance strictly by the numbers, including, among other variables, the
percentage of children adopted or discharged home.

Two days before the Board of Estimate vote, behind closed doors at the
comptroller's office, opposition from the religious federations and foster-
care agency organizations was fierce. The proposed accountability system
would only add another layer to the multiple reporting requirements that
already robbed caseworkers of time better spent with children and families, representatives argued. The Board of Estimate resolutions would
have devastating financial consequences for the agencies, and children
would be harmed. Agency directors were especially unhappy about provisions that would impose financial sanctions and freeze reimbursement
rates until money found owing in past fiscal audits was paid. At a private
meeting that same day, May 2, 1979, the foster-care agencies won a
promise from the comptroller that these provisions would be applied
only to future audits. Goldin also agreed to add an audit-appeals procedure that opened a back door for the exercise of political muscle. But the
agencies' efforts to kill the resolutions entirely failed. The best they could
do was demand language making it clear that if the city could terminate a
foster-care contract, so could an agency. "In part, this addition was a
threat to the city that the private agencies would cease providing foster-
care services if they were pushed too far," Tobis later wrote in his unpublished Ph.D. dissertation about the foster-care reforms.

On May 4, the day of the hearing before the Board of Estimate, everyone jumped aboard the reform train. The foster-care agencies that had
privately battled to have the resolutions tabled now testified in favor of
their passage. Monsignor Robert Arpie, director of child care for Catholic
Charities and its twenty-two foster-care agencies, called them "workable
guidelines" and asked that the city use them in an "atmosphere not of
indictment or of allegation, but of mutual respect and confidence that
together we can do the impossible."

The final vote was unanimous, and the press coverage congratulatory.
Goldin termed it a revolution in the care of children in public custody,
predicting that "the system is going to be set on its head and changed from
top to bottom." For the most conscientious caseworkers in agencies like
Sheltering Arms, the crescendo of public support for reform that spring
can only have added to a growing sense of urgency about adoptions that
had been promised on paper but not fulfilled.

WHEN GERTRUDE KIHARA SPOKE about Lamont's need for an adoptive family, Alicia felt again how little value she had as a woman alone. Why, after all, should they let a woman on the edge of welfare adopt such a promising child? she thought. And was her love really enough to compensate for what she couldn't give him? It was true that he needed a father, and the best might be one with dark skin like his own. Since the age of three, Lamont had shown increasing awareness of the color difference between him and the Fils-Aimes. He fantasized openly about changing his skin shade so he would look like them. Alicia had tried to handle it in a calm, realistic fashion, telling him matter-of-factly that that was impossible, that she loved him as he was, that people came in all shades and were all equally pleasing in God's eye. But she saw that he was not convinced.

She tried to imagine Lamont with another family, and she envisioned a warm black couple with a loving marriage and steady employment, the father always ready to play catch with the boy after school, the mother not tormented by conflicts between her religion and her life. Surely this family would be happy to let Lamont visit her and Henri during school breaks and on occasional weekends. Perhaps they would all go to Puerto Rico together on vacation and become part of her extended family.

She sensed that in the view of the caseworker and her colleagues, life with a newly divorced woman could not be in Lamont's best interest. In truth, to provide better than a hand-to-mouth existence, she needed more education or training. That would mean working and attending school at the same time, a grueling schedule that would leave little time for the children. The best solution might be for the children to go live with her mother in Puerto Rico for a while until she got on her feet. But of course the agency would not approve such a plan for a foster child, and even if she agreed to adopt Lamont, he would legally remain a foster child for many months to come. Yes, it was selfish to want to hold on to him now, to put him through the hardship ahead. Maybe the Reverend Ramos was right; maybe she was a selfish woman who had failed in Christian sacrifice for others.

She wept when she told Kihara her decision, but the caseworker assured her it was for the best.

EIGHT

LAMONT WAS PLAYING WITH A HULA HOOP, TRYING TO MAKE it spin around his middle the way Alicia's niece Diana had shown him. In his eyes, Diana had special powers. When she was nine and he was so little that the steep church stairs still frightened him, Diana had carried him down. Even when she slipped and fell, she held on to him the whole bumpy way so he wouldn't get hurt. Now the hot-pink circle seemed to hover effortlessly around Diana's swaying hips. But when Lamont tried it, the plastic just dropped with a clatter to the asphalt. He tried again and again, but the hoop always went clumsy in his hands, and some of the other children laughed at him.

A curse word came out of his mouth, a bad word he had heard on the playground that he knew was forbidden to him. Instinctively, with a quickening of guilt, he looked up. Squinting against the sun, his eyes found the fourth-floor window where his mother often stood to keep an eye on him and the other children on the playground below. The window seemed so high up, so far away, yet he could feel Alicia's presence hovering over him.

The moment stayed in his memory long afterward: the hula hoop, the curse word, the instant belief that his mother would know and care what he had said, the unique meaning of one window among so many in a high-rise apartment building in a big city. Later the memory became something to turn over in his mind like the icon of a forgotten faith, like a rare artifact from a vanished universe.

LAMONT LIVED IN A WORLD in which words still carried almost magic power. Because he was bright and articulate, it was easy for adults to forget that as a four-year-old, he had a worldview not so far removed from a toddler's, in which a child can be sucked down a bathtub drain or lose his bodily integrity by eating a broken cookie. Four-year-olds typically dream of omnipotence but fear the power of their own destructive impulses, of the bad wishes and angry thoughts that can suddenly overmaster them. It's not only that their hard-won measure of self-control is threatened by such surges of emotion, but also that they are afraid their most terrible words and wishes have power over the real world. When a four-year-old wishes that his beloved father were gone so he could have his mother all to himself—as little boys commonly do, according to Freud and his successors—reassurance comes mainly from the discovery that wishing won't make it so.

"Parents—including those who have never heard of an Oedipal complex—play a vital role in the resolution of these conflicts," child psychiatrist Selma Fraiberg writes in *The Magic Years,* a classic account of the psychological world of early childhood. "Reality (and this includes the parents who are certainly part of the child's reality) plays the decisive role. A little boy cannot have his mother all to himself now—or ever. [He] cannot get rid of his father and have his father at the same time, and since he's really very fond of his father, he relinquishes his futile day-dream in favor of another that offers real possibilities of satisfaction. He can become *like his father.*"

Reality offered Lamont no such reassurance. His daddy truly had been banished from home, and surely that was Lamont's fault. Lamont had jumped on the couch and broken Alicia's painting. He had been bad in other ways, too, sometimes in secret. He had at times, in jealousy or anger, wished for his father's disappearance. Clearly his parents could not protect him from the forces his own fury could unleash, since they, too, were crushed by what was happening.

One evening after a weekend visit, Frantz drove Lamont around until darkness fell and it was long past bedtime. Finally he stopped the car in front of their apartment building and sat staring out the windshield. Then he hunched over and began to cry. Lamont had never seen such a thing before. Later he told someone his father was sad because he had to live in his car now.

That spring Lamont found a book of matches in his baby-sitter's apartment. He was fascinated by the power of grown-ups to call forth flame from a little stick, and though he knew it was forbidden, he wanted to try it himself. He was going to a private nursery school in the afternoons now. A yellow school bus picked him up at Miss Rose's building, and another yellow bus drove him back. Alicia came to pick him up and walked him home while he chattered about what he'd done all day and gave her the drawings he'd made in school. The teacher was happy with him; she said he was learning to share. But the matchbook was not something he could share with anyone.

Miss Rose, a grandmotherly woman, didn't notice when he slipped away into the bedroom by himself; perhaps she was busy with the other children, or in the kitchen preparing a morning snack. To make sure she didn't catch him being bad, Lamont crouched down between the bed and the wall, near a pile of old newspapers.

It was dark and quiet in his hiding place. He held the match tightly, rubbing it hard on the black strip. Suddenly flame spurted from his hand and he felt excited and scared by his own power. He waved, and the fire went out, leaving a little trail of smoke and a smell that tickled his nose. He tried again, awkwardly gripping the match close to its colored tip. Now the fire darted closer, burning his thumb and forefinger. The pain made him drop the match, and still burning, it fell on a newspaper. Immediately a black hole grew where it had fallen, bigger and bigger, until the paper burst into big flames that leapt to the edge of the bedspread and set it alight. The room filled with black smoke. Lamont cowered in the farthest corner behind the burning bed, afraid to move.

"Lamont, Lamont!" Miss Rose was screaming. "Lamont, get out of there!" Finally the old woman's voice broke through the paralysis of his guilt and terror, and he scooted under the bed and out the door into her arms.

Firemen had to break the outside windows to train their hoses on the flames. What with the fire, the smoke, and the water damage, most of the bedroom's contents were destroyed. Miss Rose tried to get Sheltering Arms to pay for the damage, but she never got a penny. It was an unfortunate accident, the caseworkers said, which would have been prevented by closer supervision.

Alicia was surprised that the agency did not provide some kind of counseling for Lamont after such a traumatic experience. But from the agency's perspective, it must have seemed a sensible decision: the last thing to add to the file of a candidate for stranger adoption was a psychological or psychiatric diagnosis occasioned by a fire. And without such a diagnosis, therapy could not be justified for Medicaid reimbursement. Psychiatric or psychological referral in itself tended to raise concerns in prospective adoptive parents that were difficult to dispel. A four-year-old who had "needed" psychological counseling was by definition a less attractive candidate than a child who hadn't, regardless of the reason for it. Like Alicia herself, caseworkers saw the incident as a matter of a normal child playing with matches. Why blow it out of proportion? What Lamont needed as soon as possible, they felt, was what they were working on already: an adoptive family.

Susan Leaf, an adoption specialist, was brought in to prepare him for the transition. She gave him an empty photo album with a red imitation-leather cover. Together they would paste in photographs of his life with the Fils-Aimes. She planned to use it as a device to help him review his history, make a separation, and move on to a new placement. Too many foster children had no way to look back and see what they were like in infancy, no pictures to anchor memories of the past. Leaf saw her job as giving permanence to whatever good memories foster children had of their biological family or subsequent foster families, then helping them form an explanation of why they had been placed and why they had to move again now. Sometimes the adoptive family sent its own book, and the two sets of photos could be merged in a third album after the child was placed, memorializing the merger of different lives into a new, permanent family.

Permanency was the byword of every child welfare conference and workshop Leaf attended in those days. Lamont's length of stay in foster care was all too typical: the mean in 1979 was 4.86 years. That spring, newspapers were full of articles and editorials decrying the damage such impermanence did to children—and its waste of public funds. Leaf could feel proud that her own work was at the cutting edge of change. Lamont was unusually easy to work with, too, because he was so friendly and so verbal. She and Kihara agreed that he conversed with them almost like an adult, deliberate and serious.

"Lamont knows that he has a natural mother and that the Fils-Aimes are his temporary parents," Kihara wrote in a report to the city in June 1979. "He has been well aware of these facts since there are color differences. He shows some confusion as to his acceptance of himself as being a Black child, but hopefully this process of adoption preparation can serve to strengthen his ego. In addition permanency with a sense of really belonging to a family should help him in terms of his feeling of security and stability."

For Lamont's fifth birthday, Alicia hosted a party at McDonald's. It was a neighborhood party, shared with two other mothers who regularly took their sons bowling with Alicia, Henri, and Lamont. Alicia kept a photograph of the occasion that bursts with high spirits. One of the boys holds a baby brother too young to join in the merriment, but the other five boys, all wearing birthday hats, are caught between grins and gleeful laughter. Lamont is in the middle, close to Henri, his eyes turned to someone outside the frame, his delighted smile very white against his dark skin. A large rectangular cake with white icing is beside him, its candles not yet blown out.

Three weeks later, on June 26, 1979, a court terminated Shirley Wilder's parental rights to her son. Jonathan Sulds, Shirley's guardian ad litem, had filed his report at the end of May, at last consenting to the agency's long-standing petition. He noted, "While my ward stated several times during our two telephone conversations that she wished to oppose Lamont Wilder's being placed for adoption, her failure to support the infant and failure to visit him on an ongoing, regular basis appear to constitute an abandonment within the meaning of sections 371 and 384 of the Social Services Law. More specifically, my ward has known since February 1979 of the pendency of this matter and since then, apparently, has neither visited Lamont nor provided his support. Such abandonment is a ground for the commitment of the custody and guardianship of the infant to the petitioner."

A judge of the Surrogate's Court signed the papers. Two caseworkers from Sheltering Arms brought Alicia other things to sign, meeting her in the parking lot next to her job. Alicia was too upset to read the documents. She wrote her name hurriedly, choking back tears, fearful of changing her mind.

About a week later, on a hot July day, the Millers were waiting in the lobby of Sheltering Arms when Alicia brought Lamont down on the subway to see them. They were white people, very fair-skinned and large, their plump faces shiny with the heat. The father wore a suit, and when he sat down, his paisley tie dipped and rose over the broad expanse of his belly. He had a reddish-blond mustache, straight reddish-blond hair, and small blue eyes. The mother had dark hair, cut short, and a pug nose in a round and shiny face. There was a son, too, red-blond like his father and taller than most of the nine-year-olds Lamont knew. They sat on the couch and watched Lamont play with the toys in the sparsely furnished waiting room.

The Millers would be his new mom and dad, caseworkers from the agency had told Lamont. The son, Ian, called the new dad Bill instead of Daddy or Papi, but Lamont called them Mom and Dad right away. He was used to language that gave him more than one set of parents. He had learned to repeat that his mother was "Shirley," though he didn't really know what she looked like anymore, except that she had eyes like his, and dark skin. He knew, too, that Alicia was his foster mother, but what did the extra word really mean? She had always been Mommy to him. He liked to talk to adults, and he had no fear of strangers. He showed the new mom and dad the way he could build a block tower and make a car race across the rug. A caseworker gave him a camera to take a photograph of them, and he did, catching them askew, almost falling off the edge of the picture frame, with startled smiles on their faces and cartoon owls from a mural peering over their heads.

The next day they picked him up at home to take him to the Bronx Zoo for half a day. Near the giraffes, Lamont got to ride on the new dad's shoulders, clasping his hands under the big man's pale, round chin and letting his legs dangle against his chest. The Millers spoke a different kind of English than everyone Lamont knew, slow and cool, with no peaks and valleys of inflection and no sprinkling of Spanish words. They had come to New York on an airplane, they told him, and he would get to ride an airplane, too, when they took him back with them to Minnesota, tomorrow.

That night Alicia packed him a small suitcase according to the agency's instructions. Four changes of clothing, a pair of pajamas, and the photo album. There would be no room for toys on the airplane.

The panic she had felt when she first saw the Millers washed over her again. Never had she imagined that the agency would choose for him a white family in a distant state. The Millers had promised to write, to let her know how Lamont was doing, but it would be news from an unfamiliar world, filtered through the eyes of strangers. Carefully folding into the suitcase the T-shirt and shorts Lamont had worn at his birthday party, she thought of the easy affection that surrounded him that day, the hugs and kisses and jokes from the other mothers. One of them had stopped by to give him a good-luck charm as a good-bye present, her eyes wet as she fastened it around his neck and embraced him one more time. Alicia remembered how Bill Miller had stayed on the couch at the agency, asking Lamont questions from a distance instead of getting close to him on the carpeted floor. Something in the man's face made her uncomfortable. He seemed very serious and very stern. But she had tried to keep her reactions hidden from Lamont. She didn't want the child to feel as though these people were kidnaping him. She had dutifully exclaimed over the photographs they showed of a house that looked like a child's drawing, with an oversized roof, a window on each side of the front door, and a stretch of grass in front. Lucky boy! He would have a yard of his own! She had echoed their upbeat talk about the airplane he would take there, bigger and better than the ones that had taken him to Florida and Puerto Rico when he was little. All along she knew he didn't understand the real difference: from this departure, there would be no return.

At bedtime she read him a Bible story and heard his prayers, as she always did. She heard him cry out in his sleep in the middle of the night; that was the signal for her to walk him to the bathroom and back to bed again, still half asleep, so his sheets would be dry in the morning. Alicia's sister had been a longtime bedwetter, too, and this had been her own mother's nightly ritual. But tonight she couldn't go back to sleep herself. She sat at the kitchen table and reread the poem she had written at work two days before.

> Lamont
> My love, my dear child
> you will always be in my heart.
> Across the miles your beautiful,
> friendly face will be vivid in my mind.
> Your loving eyes will see other faces
> And the familiar faces will be no more.
> Remember that you will never be forgotten

and we will always love you very much.
I loved you as my own from the day I saw you.
There is part of you in me and part of me in you.
I pray the Lord He will keep you under his loving care.
May you be very happy and love God because he loves you
I will always love you

—ALICIA

Under her name she wrote the date: July 10, 1979. It was five years to the day since she had brought him home from the hospital. She had copied out the poem twice. One copy she slipped into Lamont's photo album. The other she put in the drawer where his first baby sleeper still lay folded.

It was dark when the airplane took off. Lamont had been excited at the prospect of flying again in one of the silver machines that passed high above the tallest buildings in the Bronx. But after the first steep climb with engines throbbing, there was nothing to remind a tired child that he was amid the clouds. Soon the lights in the plane were turned off, and everybody fell asleep. In the darkness below, New York City was left far behind. The Appalachian Mountains rose and fell. Hills and valleys and smokestacks of cities gave way to the vast waters of the Great Lakes. Eventually the plane bore him north, over the flat fields of Wisconsin to the Mississippi River and Minnesota.

OTHER CHILDREN HAD MADE this journey a century before him, on "orphan trains" that shipped "west" some two hundred thousand children of the eastern poor in a cavalcade spanning seventy-five years. The orphan trains drew on American faith in the power of a fresh start, and an idealized image of life "out West." In much the same way, Sheltering Arms's choice for Lamont had been colored by an unexamined belief in the wholesome advantages of Minneapolis, of a white, middle-class, two-parent family, of a house and yard far from the New York City projects. But the enduring sentimental appeal of that tradition obscured its uglier underpinnings.

From the beginning, in 1853, Charles Loring Brace, the idealistic Yale theologian and city missionary who is considered the father of foster care, paired his pleas for Christian responsibility toward New York's "great multitude of unhappy, deserted, and degraded boys and girls" with warnings that if these offspring of the "dangerous classes" were not drained from the city, they would poison society. His solution was dependent on demand for farm and domestic labor in the sparsely settled prairie states and Northwest Territory. Its social acceptance was rooted in extremes of economic inequality that allowed the urban poor to be viewed by the wealthy almost as an alien species.

Most of the orphan-train children were not orphans at all, and Brace's version of "placing out" fell into a gray zone between indenture, which legally bound a child to serve a master until a certain age, and adoption, which was not codified in several midwestern states until after the Civil War. Brace's fiercest critics were the Catholic clergy, who saw his Children's Aid Society as a bigoted organization that, under the guise of nonsectarian charity, stole Catholic children from their poor parents' faith. Catholics struggled to found their own orphanages and immigrant-service programs as the Civil War increased the supply of destitute women and children in cities and boosted the demand for children's labor in farm states depleted of men. But after 1875, when New York City ended relief to families in their homes and New York State barred children from the almshouses where their parents took refuge (to save the young from the ill effects and stigma of poorhouse life), Catholics established their own orphan trains. "Children are sent neatly dressed free of expense to destination and will be taken back at any time up to the age of twelve if found unsatisfactory," the nuns of New York Foundling announced in a Minnesota newspaper in 1879.

Orphan trains played both to the myth and to the market the railway boom had created: the overly rosy view Brace and his fellow reformers had of frontier life was in part the product of advertising campaigns to lure settlers to the "virgin territories" that the railways crossed, and to boost railway bond sales. And at a time of increasing protest by New York's organized workingmen, the orphan trains also confirmed a basic tenet of scientific charity: family relations, not the low wages and unemployment of unrestrained industrial capitalism, were responsible for the growing misery of the poor. Orphan trains became a pet project of the fashionable rich; by 1884, Mrs. John Jacob Astor III had personally sent 1,113 children west. Brace never publicized the fact that he collected more than half of the Children's Aid Society's operating budget from public sources—a mix of county taxes, Board of Education money, and state funds. By emphasizing private donations rather than taxpayer contributions, he could command public gratitude without public accountability.

Modern defenders of the orphan trains correctly point out that at the time, thousands of ragged children swarmed New York City streets, subsisting as scavengers, prostitutes, beggars, peddlers, thieves. Child labor was considered not only normal but ennobling, provided it took place on a farm in the Midwest rather than in a corrupting eastern city. But even some of Brace's contemporaries viewed his enterprise with a jaundiced eye, drawing parallels to slavery. Another criticism leveled by the 1880s was that Brace was polluting the West with the refuse of the East, dumping delinquents who eventually ended up on the public charge or debasing midwestern genetic stock. The underlying issue was that the midwestern states, too, were by then confronting problems of urban poverty. Like the interstate trade in unwanted children that boomed a century later, the orphan-train movement turned several states into both importers and exporters of poor folks' kids. By 1893, even as Ohio continued to accept orphan-train riders from New York City, orphanages in Ohio's bigger cities were sending hundreds of children a year on trains to Indiana. And Indiana was dispatching its own indigent children to Nebraska, "that state of vast possibilities"—even though one thousand of Nebraska's children were living in that state's industrial school and "Home for the Friendless."

The orphan trains stopped running in 1929. Fifty years later, Lamont's journey to Minneapolis was like the whistling echo of their long ride across America.

WHEN THE PLANE LANDED, it was still dark. Between sleep and waking, Lamont looked out at the lights of a city where no one knew his name.

NINE

BILL MILLER HAD NEVER THOUGHT OF THIS PRAIRIE-STYLE bungalow in southwest Minneapolis as anything special—just a 1950s house set back in the middle of a quiet block marked by old trees and wide lawns. Now, arriving home from the airport, he compared it to the project housing he'd seen in New York.

Nann Miller led Lamont upstairs to the large, airy room under the eaves that he would share with Ian. Unpacking his suitcase, she decided every piece of clothing in it was too small. She helped the sleepy child take off his shirt and saw that he was wearing some kind of gold necklace with a symbol hanging from it: a serpentine, like a windy road or an elongated S. She thought she had seen the symbol before on Hispanic people, but she didn't know what it meant. He didn't want to take the necklace off before putting on his pajamas, and since it seemed important to him, she let it go. It was just one of the many little things she hadn't thought to expect, like his New York–Spanish accent and the fact that sometimes he used words she simply didn't understand. But all that would change soon enough. They would love him just like Ian, and treat him just like Ian, and he would learn all their family ways, she thought. She looked back at the two boys as she left the room, lying there in narrow beds opposite each other, Ian's hair glinting on his pillow, Lamont's face against the white sheets darker than the room's dusky shadows.

NANN AND WILLIAM MILLER had never made a decision to adopt a black child. No one in their families seemed to understand that. They had decided to adopt, period. They weren't fanatics, Nann would tell friends, but they were concerned about the world population explosion, and they had one biological child already. Bill hadn't forgotten that Nann used to talk of wanting four children, before she suffered morning sickness every day for five months during her pregnancy with Ian. In any case, they agreed that adoption seemed a better way to add another child to the family. Bill was an only child, and he didn't really want his son to be one.

But after years of discussing adoption, when they finally applied, they were turned down. They were living in Iowa at the time, Bill's native state, and the adoption agency told them he was on the road too much to qualify as an adoptive father. He was a fund-raising consultant for non-profit organizations: Kiwanis clubs, humane societies, a children's hospital here and there. It meant his going into a town as a stranger and working with a cadre of local people to mount a fund-raising campaign from start to finish. He came home every third weekend and every summer, but the relationship he had with his family depended heavily on long, nightly telephone calls. In the mid-1970s, with so many other families competing to adopt a shrinking pool of Iowa babies, the adoption agency said that wasn't good enough.

The agency eventually reconsidered, but by then, in 1977, the Millers were moving to Minneapolis. There they eventually applied at Crossroads, a new agency that specialized in foreign and interstate adoptions of hard-to-place children. This time they were quickly approved. The question at Crossroads was not so much what kind of child you wanted, but whether there were any children you would refuse to consider. The Millers could see no justification for ruling out a child because of race. They did rule out a child with a major health problem because their insurance was so limited. They ruled out a foreign child because the travel costs and fees involved were unaffordable. They ruled out an infant because Nann was working full-time as an interior designer at Dayton's, Minneapolis's largest department store, and they needed her income. They decided they couldn't handle major emotional problems, nor were they ready to take on a sibling group.

It was almost like buying a house, Nann Miller had thought, paging through an interstate photo book of children available for adoption. There was a picture at the top of each page and a description, and you had to learn to read between the lines. Some were listed as having minor problems that turned out on inquiry not to be so minor. Some were already gone by the time Crossroads called the out-of-state agency with the listing. But like a good real estate agent, the adoption worker at that agency might propose another child who had just become available instead.

Lamont seemed a good prospect for fitting in with their family. He was almost five years younger than Ian, which was about right. The fact that he had been in only one foster home was a plus; many available children his age had been in two or three homes already. He was a perfectly fine kid, from all accounts. Only this one little problem: he had tried to start a fire at some day-care place. But that was just curiosity, they were assured, an ordinary case of playing with matches. For one reason or another, the other candidates fell away, and it came down to this one. And this one, it just so happened, was black.

That certainly raised eyebrows on both sides of the family. Nann's people were staunch Congregationalists. Catholics were OK, Grandmother would allow, but of course you shouldn't marry one. Grandmother had probably never spoken to a black person in her life, Nann thought. Nann put Bill's parents in the same category; like her grandmother, they had grown up calling people of color "darkies." But surely they would accept Lamont. It was a process more of education in the face of ignorance than of overcoming prejudice, she believed.

Bill considered Nann's parents more conservative than his own. His mother had been a teacher in a one-room schoolhouse before she married a man with a fourth-grade education, and she had given her son a liberal upbringing—liberal, at least, for Dubuque, Bill felt. Bill once described the awakening of his social conscience this way: "You grow up in a family where you didn't call blacks niggers, you called them Negroes, but you're in Dubuque where there are only fourteen of them, and you go off to college during the civil-rights movement and go to a church staffed by a Yale Divinity graduate." Bill spent a summer constructing a home for Hungarian refugees and building a bridge across a streambed for farmers in southern Italy. Later, as a conscientious objector, he did his alternative service in Chicago at an inner-city storefront church. Bill, born the same year as Marcia Lowry, would look back on that time wistfully. "It was the Kennedy-type generation of leadership and change," he would say. "Oh, I was a radical!"

He was twenty-four, and Nann twenty, when they married. They had met at a campus church house for students, and for years it seemed that at least one of them was always in school. Bill went to work at a YMCA college, moonlighting on the grounds crew of the campus arboretum when he went back to graduate school to earn a master's degree in administration. For a few years after Ian was born they lived in a two-room apartment in a rented house shared with three other families, with a collective count of twenty children under two. The stress was terrible. It was only when Bill started his traveling job, with its combination of base pay and commissions, that they could afford a place of their own.

When they moved to Minneapolis, in 1977, the city's population was 92 percent white, mostly descendants of the Scandinavians and Germans drawn to the Northwest Territory after 1860 by railway agents' glowing prose and steep fare discounts. The Millers bought one of the smaller houses on a street of large, well-kept homes on the city's southwest side, in the kind of liberal, middle-class community that would eventually support two food co-ops, a vegetarian take-out store, and an "open" kindergarten. The few black children in the public elementary school Ian attended five blocks away were almost all from white adoptive homes— or, as the parents preferred to put it, from interracial families. These families were all very supportive when the Millers told them about the possibility of their adopting Lamont. So was a black friend from college whom Nann called. He worked for the federal government and moved a great deal—Chicago one year, New Guinea the next—but the Millers had stayed in touch with him. Sure, he said, he'd be happy to come visit them for a couple of weeks next summer to help the boy with his racial identity.

Race was really no problem, Nann thought. An agency group meeting for parents adopting transracially did nothing to change her view. The one point that stuck with her was the need to use Eucerin cream to keep a black child's skin moist so it wouldn't get that chalky look. If there was any discussion of the psychological or sociological issues involved, she didn't remember it. For the Millers, a far greater concern than race was the impact of Bill's long absences on the adopted child's adjustment to the family. But the family system they had evolved to accommodate Bill's job had worked just fine with Ian. He had learned early that he had to share the household chores with his mother, and that fatherly concern mainly came over the telephone.

Distance suited Bill's style. His own father was a stoic man who believed in correction more than conversation. Bill was not one to express emotion much, but he took his paternal role very seriously. His attitude when he listened to Nann's account of day-to-day family problems was always, "This has got to be fixed," and to suggest ways they could improve things. "Bill always feels it's his role to help us do the best we can," Nann would explain. Every spring, even when Ian was quite small, they would sit down as a family to talk about what was really important to each of them. Over a restaurant dinner, they would discuss what they had to do to achieve their goals, and make up a list for the coming year. Then Bill would post the list on the bulletin board behind the kitchen door. One year Bill talked about his awareness that his mother and father were getting old and were going to die; he wanted more communication with them. So he wrote out a reminder to call his parents and affixed it, along with their Dubuque telephone number, to the list behind the door. Mostly he was mindful of what the others wanted for themselves, and took responsibility for prodding them to meet their own interim goals, much as he pushed his Kiwanis clients in their capital fund drives. The family had always been able to work things out.

Nann, who had to go back to work, had enrolled Lamont in Southwest Minnesota Learning Tree Center, a day-care place on a main thoroughfare a few blocks away. It was part of a day-care chain but was located on the lower level of a church. She could leave Lamont in the morning and pick him up after she left work at 4:00 P.M. Lamont was the one black child among thirty-nine fair-skinned children at the preschool. In Nann's eyes the problem was not the lack of black peers but the fact that Lamont seemed to think *he* was white, too. Sheltering Arms had warned Crossroads about this in a brief biographical sketch: Lamont wanted to be white, pretended to be white, and might need additional exposure to blacks in order to accept his racial identity. So after Nann discarded the shirts and shorts in Lamont's suitcase, she made a point of taking him shopping for new clothes at the downtown mall, where he would likely see some blacks, rather than at the nearest suburban shopping center, where he wouldn't. And on Sundays, instead of going to the all-white Quaker meetinghouse they had regularly attended for love of its silent meditation, the Millers began taking Lamont to a Methodist church with a racially mixed congregation.

The Millers were only dimly aware of the national controversy surrounding adoption across racial boundaries. Minneapolis had a pioneering tradition in transracial adoption going back thirty years. Adoption itself had not come into its own as a child welfare service in America until well into the twentieth century. Historically, it was designed to meet demand from infertile white middle-class couples, rather than to serve the needs of children without parents. In a reflection of the broad influence of the eugenics movement's theories of racial improvement, only those couples deemed worthiest of reproduction had been eligible to adopt, and children whose traits didn't match those of the agencies' rigidly defined elite clientele had been automatically excluded from the adoption pool. Adoption agencies offering only the "best" babies weren't eager to identify their supply with charitable programs intended to rescue the children of the incompetent poor, even when notions of "bad blood" and "degenerate racial stock" had fallen out of fashion. Child welfare agencies kept their adoption units quite separate from their foster-care programs—that is, if they did adoptions at all. As late as 1973, for example, forty-four of the seventy-seven child-caring agencies sued in *Wilder* had no adoption departments. But from the late 1950s through the 1960s, dramatic demographic changes disrupted traditional patterns of supply and demand in both child welfare and adoption programs, and transracial adoption suddenly became their common ground.

The integrationist message of the early civil-rights movement and the War on Poverty galvanized this nascent transracial-adoption movement. By the late 1960s, such parent-run organizations as the Open Door Society and the Council on Adoptable Children had affiliates around the country promoting interracial adoption and lobbying traditional agencies to change their matching policies. In 1969, the Minnesota Public Welfare Department had so many requests for mixed-race adoptions that it imported three hundred black and biracial children from Milwaukee, Wisconsin, to meet the demand.

All the while, the number of white babies available for adoption nationwide was dropping precipitously. More white women chose to keep their babies. Only 18 percent of white infants born out of wedlock were given up for adoption in 1971, compared with an estimated 65 percent in 1966. By 1972, when the U.S. Supreme Court made abortion legal, the infant shortage was so acute that some agencies had shut down their adoption units completely. Others had expanded their foster-care programs to replace lost income from adoption. Some sought out new sources of supply to meet the increasingly desperate demand from their white, middle-class, infertile clientele, arranging adoptions of Korean, Vietnamese, or South American babies and tapping the domestic supply of minority and mixed-race babies that had been ignored before.

According to one estimate, transracial adoption tripled between 1968 and 1971. Of all black children placed for adoption nationally in 1971, 35 percent were adopted by whites. But 35 percent was only twenty-five hundred children—an indication of just how few black children were being officially adopted by families of *any* race. Both the surge in transracial placements and the low level of black-family recruitment by traditional agencies drew strong criticism from black child welfare professionals in the late 1960s. In 1972, at an adoption convention in St. Louis full of white couples cuddling black babies, the controversy exploded. The president of the National Association of Black Social Workers issued a harsh condemnation of transracial adoption as "cultural genocide" and told white parents they could never give their black children the racial pride and survival skills necessary to cope with a racist society. So tumultuous, swift, and regionally uneven was political change on racial issues during this period that southern state statutes forbidding transracial adoptions under segregationist Jim Crow codes were still being struck down as unconstitutional while black child welfare professionals in border states were demanding a halt to transracial adoptions.

Nationally, the adoption of black children by whites plunged to 831 out of 4,172 black adoptions in 1975, but then edged up again in 1976. Public agitation over the problems of foster care—its instability, high cost, damage to children—kept intensifying the pressure on agencies to find adoptive homes for "hard-to-place" children. A white adoptive home might be a second-best choice for a black child, but wasn't it better than a childhood spent in foster care? The Child Welfare League of America retreated from earlier statements encouraging transracial adoption but endorsed the idea that it was still preferable to a significant delay or denial of adoption when no black home could be found. Left unstated was the corollary, that agencies would ask adoption applicants to take a "hard-to-place" child they never would have considered had a more "desirable" one been readily available.

Local black militancy in Minneapolis was negligible, in part because the black population was so small and the state's political culture so progressive. Transracial adoption had continued to flourish in the state, promoted by organized adoptive-parent groups and strengthened when foster parents won a right to preference in the adoption of their longtime foster children, even across racial lines. Crossroads had been started in 1976 at someone's kitchen table, launched by a group of parents who had adopted Korean children. They considered traditional agencies rigid and arrogant because they excluded families that deviated from the old-fashioned ideal when the world was full of "imperfect" children waiting for parents. Their credo, a founding member recalls, was "Love is enough, and permanence is the key."

Crossroads social workers took pride in the openness of Minnesota families to children of different races and in the speed of the agency's own placements. The Millers were a little shocked at how abruptly Lamont was handed over to them, but it reinforced their sense that the adoption posed no special problems.

THE PROBLEMS WEREN'T special at first. Every morning, Lamont's sheets were soaked with urine. Every morning Nann Miller hoped the bed would be dry. Stripping the bed became a morning ordeal. Enforcing consequences, the Millers gave Lamont the responsibility of taking the sheets down himself whenever they were wet. Sometimes he wouldn't even mention it. His stricken face would just appear over the clammy heap as he struggled down the stairs with the load. Washing the sheets became the daily ritual that underlined what they already knew: Lamont hadn't yet adjusted to their family.

They knew so little about him. He didn't seem able to pedal a tricycle, let alone a bike. The medical information they had received was so sketchy. There was something about his having had seizures or spasms as a newborn—"jittery extremities"; they assumed his mother had been on drugs. Still, when they took him to a T-ball program for little kids in a park two blocks away, he did fine. In fact, he excelled. He was taller, stronger, and better at hitting the ball than the other boys his age. A tough, macho little kid, Nann thought. His command of language was fine—accented and not genteel, but not full of swear words, either. Yet he could be standing next to a puddle of milk he had just spilled and deny that he was to blame. "We don't lie within our family," Nann would tell him firmly, beginning one of the long lectures that were a hallmark of Miller family discipline. And he would just get this faraway look on his face. He was there in body, she thought, but mentally he had just removed himself.

People told Nann she had the lowest anger quotient of anyone they'd ever known. Even when Ian was little more than a toddler, she had reasoned with him in her calm, cheerful voice, enlisting his advice on how to punish persistent transgressions. "This is totally unacceptable," she would say of some misdeed. "Just what do you think we ought to do about it?" Once, when her son was only three, he had astonished her into suppressed giggles by answering in the same reasonable tone, "Well, we could just fuck it."

But Lamont's response to the same kind of question trailed bits of a dark past. He blurted out that his foster father once hit him with a belt. Another time he talked about how he and Henri were playing in the living room, and how you're not supposed to throw pillows in the living room, and they broke something, and she—his foster mother—was really angry.

Nann and Bill had spent an hour at most with Mrs. Fils-Aime. There had been a divorce, that much they knew. Some caseworker later suggested that Mrs. Fils-Aime hadn't kept Lamont because he would have handicapped her search for a boyfriend or a new husband. Nann, who considered herself highly independent, thought of Hispanic women as male-dominated. She vaguely remembered seeing crucifixes on the walls of the Fils-Aime apartment and assumed the family was Catholic, like other Spanish-speaking people. She had no memory of books in the apartment—at least nothing like the glossy-jacketed art and American history volumes that filled the modern bookshelves in their own living room, interspersed with pottery and Indian artifacts. She assumed Lamont had never had books read aloud to him at night.

As a fiber artist who did her own weaving on a loom, she sometimes traded her work for other people's crafts, like the graceful tower of handmade oval Shaker boxes that stood in another corner of the living room. Of course Lamont had to be taught that these things were not to be handled like toys. What he seemed to like best in their house, however, was the big upright piano that dominated the front hall, its warm brown wood gleaming under a Vasarelli print. Neither Nann nor Bill knew how to play, but Lamont sat at the keyboard for as long as they let him, striking chords that never quite resolved into any tune they knew.

One evening Nann found Lamont sitting woebegone at the foot of the stairs opposite the piano. Yes, he admitted, he was thinking of his New York family. "Why did I have to leave?" he asked, gripping his knees and looking back from the middle distance into her face.

"I don't know, exactly," she replied. "I'm sad that you had to leave. Are you feeling sad?"

"Oh, very sad."

"Do you miss your family?"

"Yeah."

"Do you want to talk about them a little while? Do you want to remember things about them?"

"Yes."

They looked at his photo book together. What else was there to do? Sheltering Arms had told Crossroads there should be no direct contact with Lamont's former foster home; a clean break was best. Once a month, Nann wrote a letter about him that Crossroads sent on to a caseworker at Sheltering Arms. Supposedly it was to be passed along to the Fils-Aimes, but she doubted that ever happened. Certainly the Millers had received no response from his old foster home.

"This is your family now," she told Lamont firmly, "and you won't ever have to leave again."

Such conversations were repeated many times over the next weeks. Lamont would furrow his brow until Nann asked if he was worried about something. Yes, he was worried about his family in New York, about his brother and especially his foster father. "He had to sleep in the car," he confided. "She said he had to go, and he didn't want to go."

A day or two later, they'd have the same talk. "Why did I have to leave?" he would ask. "I don't understand." Nann didn't really understand herself, so she focused on present reassurance. This was his family now. He was here for good. They would always be his mom and dad, and Ian would always be his brother.

In the morning, his bed would be wet again.

"We don't do that in our family": that was the other refrain all summer, as the five-year-old broke basic household rules, borrowing Ian's things without asking permission, leaving the block without saying where he would be, not doing his chores, lying when he was called to task. "You try to talk for a while, but there comes a point when it has to be corrected," Bill told Nann. He was leaving for another season on the road, and he wanted to get Lamont on track before his departure. With Ian, a third offense meant some type of punishment—being sent to his room or a spanking, whatever seemed appropriate at the time. Bill saw no reason to treat Lamont any differently.

The closeness he'd imagined having with an adopted son just wasn't there. He remembered the glow he had felt from the easy trust small ghetto children accorded him when he was doing parish work in Chicago. Maybe he was being too idealistic. He was close to Ian, but of course he had worked at it when Ian was little, taking breaks between campus jobs when he was a graduate student to come home to his baby son. Once, still covered with sweat and dirt from the arboretum grounds crew and with no time to shower, he took the toddler to get a photo ID. He still recalled the pleasure he felt, perching his clean, rosy son on the knee of his mud-stained work pants.

When he took Lamont driving across town, the boy wasn't interested in conversation. First he was fascinated by the compass on the dashboard, watching how the trembling needle always found its way home. Then, looking out the window, he would let parks and lakes go by without remark. But at some business corner with a stoplight and a few lighted signs, or a few painted letters above a two-story shop in a semiresidential area, he would suddenly grow alert. "This looks like New York," he'd say.

Later, Nann wondered if she'd underestimated his loss. Moving more than thirty times as a child herself—her father was a farm-implement dealer, and the family followed his work—she'd grown used to having people and places disappear. She had become adept at making friends in a new school in the middle of the term, gotten used to never having the same textbook or the same gym for a whole school year. Of course her family had stayed the same, while the dimensions of Lamont's old family had ebbed and flowed in ways he couldn't possibly understand. A few times he talked about visits to Puerto Rico and spoke the names of people who might be relatives. These seemed to be happy memories.

The cousins taught him how to jump the waves and play tag among the palm trees. Alicia's grandmother made him her special rice and praised his appetite. She scared him once by taking out her teeth, and everybody laughed and hugged him. Sometimes, in endearment, the family called him Lamontcello. They were stretching his name with warm Italian syllables absorbed into the air of El Barrio like the fragrance of the paticcerías that outstayed an older generation of immigrants.

"Lemon Jell-O," Nann heard Lamont say. "They used to call me Lemon Jell-O." He was smiling, really smiling. But it was strange, because when Nann made lemon Jell-O for him as a treat, he didn't like it at all. Later she and Bill decided the words might be Spanish. *La mancello,* perhaps— whatever that meant. They didn't know Spanish, they told Lamont. Would he teach them some? Would he say something in Spanish?

"No, no no!" he cried.

One day Nann noticed that Lamont's necklace was gone, the gold necklace he never took off. Where was it?

"Well, I lost it," he told her.

She wondered later if he had pulled it off in anger and hurled it far away.

THE LEARNING CENTER suggested that Lamont not go to public kindergarten in September. There had been a few problems. He was a little aggressive with other children—nothing terribly serious, but with his June birthday, it was reasonable to hold him out another year, until he was more settled and socially mature. But Nann felt that wouldn't be wise. He was already large and strong for his age. And there was the cost to consider, too. She went ahead and enrolled him in the public elementary school, Robert Fulton–Lake Harriet, where Ian was starting fifth grade. At the end of the regular school day, Lamont could go to a "latchkey" program there until she returned from her job.

There was a brief period that fall, after Bill went on the road and they hit their seasonal telephone rhythm again, when she thought they'd all turned the corner. Lamont told someone at school this was the best mommy he'd ever had, and Nann felt great when the story came back to her. For several nights one week, he didn't wet the bed. Then, on the first weekend in October, she took Lamont and Ian up north to the lakeside cabin that used to be her grandparents'. It was a four-hour drive, and she was very tired when they arrived. It was dark, and the weather had turned icy. Striking match after match, she couldn't get the heater lit. The boys looked so little and cold in their sleeping bags, she decided it would be better if they all slept together in the double bed.

She was lying in the middle, wearing a T-shirt and long underwear, when Lamont started groping her breasts. To her mind, it was not unpracticed groping. She had to tell him twice to stop before he did.

"Lamont, we don't do that," she said, trying to keep her cool. "I don't think this is appropriate."

From that moment, she believed he had been sexually abused.

People didn't talk much about sexual abuse in Minnesota in 1979, but Nann had her own point of reference. She vividly remembered being sexually molested by a family member at family reunions. As she told it, by the time she was five she consciously decided that this was not something she wanted to be a part of, and from then on, she managed to avoid the perpetrator. Ever afterward she had been especially sensitive to signs of sexual abuse in others.

Back home, she tried to ask Lamont leading questions, but she got nowhere. She called the Crossroads caseworker, Myrna Otte. "I think Lamont was sexually abused, and I need help," she told her. Myrna heard her out, then dismissed Lamont's behavior as a five-year-old's curiosity.

That was what Sheltering Arms had said about the fire: curiosity. An accident. Now Nann was not convinced. Fire setting was a classic symptom of sexual abuse. She started watching the way Lamont related to women. His after-school caretaker, for example: he was always climbing up in her lap and cuddling. Five-year-olds do that, of course, but there was a different manner to this, she thought—something too sexual. But everybody told her she was wrong. Meanwhile, after one whole week of being dry, Lamont was back to bedwetting without abatement. After listening to her suspicions over the telephone as he lay in a motel room near a freeway, Bill talked about new strategies for improving Lamont's behavior.

Nann was never sure what normal five-year-old experiences were foreign to Lamont. Halloween, for example. She always made Ian an original costume; often he was a bat. In case Lamont hadn't celebrated Halloween in the projects, she tried to explain the concept of dressing up. "What would you like to be?" she asked him. "You could be a dirty sock, a candy bar, a pumpkin. . . ."

A candy bar, he decided.

"What kind?"

"A Hershey bar." He could remember eating a Hershey bar in New York City.

How awkward, she realized suddenly, for her as a white person to dress this brown child as a Hershey bar! "Are you sure?" she asked him. Yes, he was sure. Fine, fine, she thought. That's what he wants; let him be what he wants to be.

It was a very successful costume, and he seemed perfectly happy wearing it.

IN NOVEMBER, simmering kindergarten problems boiled over. Lamont attended a school-within-a-school. The main program was in an old-fashioned three-story brick building; Lamont's 1960s-inspired "open" program was in the annex, a squat, one-story addition set in the large asphalt playground. It was supposed to provide a holistic, multiage approach with a lot of freedom and was conducted mainly in one very large room, with a single teacher for twenty-five children. The teacher was still learning how to handle an unstructured classroom. Lamont was her nemesis.

She would call the circle meeting, and all the other children would sit down on the floor and take turns talking. But Lamont would be off doing his own thing on the other side of the room. He would run out the door and hide in the hallways, and she would have to hunt for him, after begging another teacher to watch the class. He was such an unhappy child, she thought, and he had so much else going on in his life, that she couldn't reach him and teach the others, too. She felt like a failure.

One morning he took apart a section of the geodesic dome in the classroom and threw the plastic pieces at the window, breaking the glass. As Nann described the incident to Myrna Otte, it had been a game of playing sword, and he had been copying an older child. Still, it could not be described as an accident. In a conference with the teacher and the principal, Nann learned that Lamont did not look at books in class and did not finish his work. They would all have to push him harder. The school social worker reported that on the playground he did too much problem-solving through punching. Later Nann learned from Ian that Lamont was provoking older black kids with derogatory racial remarks, just as if he weren't black himself. Mindful of her own suspicions about sexual abuse, she made a forceful request for Lamont to be evaluated by a school psychologist. In December, the school said his behavior had grown worse, but the request for a psychological evaluation was still pending.

Crossroads had little help to offer. It had no counseling arm. Its social workers were not required to document anything. They kept progress notes on scraps of household paper—"pathetic notes," Myrna Otte would call them later, sifting through her meager written account of Lamont's placement with the Millers. Halting and fragmentary, her narrative mainly reflected faith that everything would work out in the end. "Perhaps a low level of hyperactivity," one scrap read. "One of his statements: 'When I be a man,' things will be better—referring to the bedwetting. Settled down after Christmas. Not so many problems in latchkey [program]. Poor small muscle coordination. Things are getting better."

Another scrap: "January 15. Finalization papers came Saturday. Final time for decision. Lamont said he was going back to New York. Then later said he'd decided to stay here."

The Millers postponed the formal adoption for another six months, to the one year maximum allowed. By then, surely, everything would have worked out.

GAY HALBERG, the school psychologist, began to observe Lamont in his classroom in early spring. His teacher was completely baffled. She couldn't imagine any future for this five-year-old. "Anything he puts his mind to do, he does," she told the psychologist. "He's such a strong-willed child. Is he ever going to get an awareness of right and wrong? Is there any chance for him in the world?"

The psychologist later told the Millers that she thought the teacher was prejudiced against black children. Halberg herself maintained Lamont's problems could be overcome with time and patience. He had a short attention span and poor self-esteem; when he felt bad, he became destructive. By now a nurse's 1974 notation about Lamont's "jittery extremities"—quite normal for a premature newborn—had been interpreted to mean that he had suffered seizures, possible evidence of brain injury or drug exposure. This was cause for concern, Halberg said, and it was possi-

ble that Lamont was mildly hyperactive, but she believed most of his difficulties were related to the unresolved adoption.

Later she would tell Myrna Otte that Lamont was socially as sophisticated as a ten-year-old but emotionally no older than three. He still felt
abandoned by the first family, and his anger about that colored everything
else. He rejected Bill Miller as a father. It didn't help that the Millers were
uncomfortable with feelings, their own as well as the child's. Feelings
were not OK in this family, Otte would write in her notes. Feelings were
not safe. Feelings were to be hidden and insulated by layers of reasoning
and detachment.

IT WAS DARK in the latchkey room at school. The other children were
watching a movie, but Lamont tiptoed to the back, where the gerbil lived
in a metal cage. It twitched its whiskers at him, brown eyes appealing for
release. Carefully, Lamont slid the cage door open and took the gerbil
out. It lay warm and soft between his hands, the pulse of its heart like
undemanding love. It was content to have its fur stroked, and Lamont felt
each caress as though he, not the gerbil, were being gentled. He cuddled
the creature, seeking the comfort that had eluded him all these months in
Minnesota. And the gerbil bit him, hard.

The unexpected pain was like the opening of a sluicegate on the boy's
rage. In an instant, he dropped the gerbil to the floor and stamped it.
If the animal cried out, no one heard it. Its small, broken body lay still
on the linoleum beside Lamont's foot, its life extinguished by his overpowering anger. He ran from the room and hid in the boys' bathroom.
Like the gerbil in its cage, he crouched in a corner and defecated on the
floor.

THE SCHOOL CALLED NANN AT WORK. Lamont had killed a gerbil,
they told her. No, no one had seen him do it, but everyone was certain he
was to blame. Nann was very upset, but when she got him home, she
questioned him in her usual tranquil voice. Lamont told her the gerbil had
run away and he had thrown a rock at it. He didn't know if he'd hit it or
not, he said. She pretended to accept his account. She was never sure
what had really happened.

She certainly didn't trust the school. Lamont's behavior at home was reasonable. Yes, he still wet the bed. He still sometimes took things without asking, and lied about it. But that was all within the realm of normal for a child adjusting to adoption. There was nothing at home that involved violence. At school, she believed, he had been neglected by uncaring teachers and had come under the dangerous influence of older kids. The principal didn't seem to have any control over the situation. The school didn't keep Nann informed, and when people there did call her, it wasn't clear what they expected her to do.

One day, for example, Nann got a phone call telling her that Lamont was on the roof of the school. It was the flat roof of the annex, actually— the one-story addition attached to the main building by a low, enclosed passageway. Finding toeholds between the bricks and the metal drain spout, the kindergartner had shinnied up there from the playground.

"What do you want me to do?" Nann asked the caller. "Do you want me to come?"

"No, we just thought you ought to know," she was told. "The kids are out there playing. Kids have done this from time to time."

Why are you singling him out, then? Nann wondered. *Do you call the other parents, too?* She was amazed that Lamont had not been better supervised on the playground. But she didn't ask her questions out loud.

About four days after the roof incident, she got another call from the school: "We can't find Lamont. He's missing." He soon turned up, but only after Nann learned for the first time that he hadn't spent an entire morning in his classroom since the start of the school year. The teacher had never bothered to tell her. While the other kindergartners were learning how to read, Lamont had been allowed to wander through the hallways.

Nann didn't know what to do. Night after night, talking on the phone with Bill, she'd ask, "What do I do with him, what do I do with him?" Bill wanted her to be tougher. They argued over it. There were other arguments, too. Ian was getting into fights at school to protect Lamont. When Bill was home and tried to discipline Lamont himself, Ian objected, challenging his father in a way he had never done before. That spring, Nann found herself crying at work for no reason. A woman she didn't know very well, but whose husband also worked at Dayton's, called up one night and asked with hushed concern, "Are you guys OK?"

They were not OK. Their life was being torn apart by a small child they had promised to keep forever.

"ARE THERE ANY PROBLEMS?" their family doctor asked after Lamont's checkup. When he heard that the boy wet his bed every night, he examined him more closely. The problem could be solved with minor surgery, he said. Lamont had a condition known as pinhole meatus—the opening on his penis was too small to pass urine normally, so he hadn't developed the capacity to hold and void in the quantity necessary to stay dry at night. The Millers scheduled the procedure for the end of May.

It never took place. The last straw came earlier that month. Once again, the school called Nann at work about Lamont. The story this time was that Lamont had used a knife to slash the tires on cars and bicycles parked near school. It was almost beyond belief that a five-year-old, even a five-year-old from the Bronx, would *think* of slashing tires, let alone have the strength to actually *do* it. As usual, Nann felt she couldn't get the full story. At first the principal claimed that Lamont had brought the knife from home, but the Millers had never owned such a knife. Another version had him finding the knife on the sidewalk on his way to school. Lamont himself said an older child had given him the knife and ordered him to slash the tires. His teacher accused him of taking knives from the art room and dropping them into the gas tanks of teachers' cars.

Lamont was to be sent home, Nann was told. She had to leave work to get him. He had been so badgered by the school by then, she felt, that she couldn't get the truth out of him anymore. Maybe Bill would do better. Bill was in Minneapolis that week, not by choice, but because it had been a bad year for fund-raising assignments. Money was tight, in fact, and it didn't help the family tension that their insurance wouldn't cover the cost of the psychological counseling they had begun with Gay Halberg.

"Lamont!" Bill shouted as soon as he walked in the house. "Lamont, come here! I want to talk to you."

Lamont was hiding in the bathroom. Bill charged up the stairs and went in after him. Lamont would always remember what ensued between them as a fight, but how does a child just shy of six years old fight a grown man?

In the small, tiled space, Bill Miller towered over Lamont. His face red, his breathing hard, he demanded surrender. But Lamont resisted. The heavyset man grabbed the child and dragged him from his hiding place. As Lamont recalled the struggle, Bill Miller kicked him in the eye and cut his finger.

Nann saw no blood. She did see her husband pick Lamont up by both arms and carry him down the stairs. As a stranger to anger herself, she classified the tone in his voice as very firm and loud. "Bill was not happy," she would allow later.

Bill was, in fact, beside himself. He told her, "This child has to leave here. It's either him or me."

He didn't mean next month. He meant right away.

MYRNA OTTE COULDN'T BELIEVE what was happening when Nann called her at Crossroads that afternoon. At Sheltering Arms, workers estimated that 20 percent of their "hard-to-place" adoptions unraveled, but for Otte, still a relative novice, this was the first such disruption ever on her caseload, and it seemed to come out of the blue. Lamont was a charismatic child; he was bright, he was cute, he was articulate. Sure, there had been a few problems, but nothing to justify or even explain a decision to toss him away. When she got over her astonishment, Otte became angry and adamant.

"You guys are crazy," she told Nann. "Do you know what you're doing to this child? You're going to destroy him." She talked about her own adopted sons, two street boys from Southeast Asia who had never completely adjusted to family life. She hadn't given them up, and Nann shouldn't give up Lamont. If she could make it, so could the Millers.

Nann didn't want to give up, but she was tired, and Bill was unshakable. Lamont had been with them for almost a year, and things were getting worse, not better. The deadline for finalizing the adoption was upon them, and the whole family was falling apart. The marriage itself was at stake. She tried to consider her alternatives calmly. Bill thinks Lamont has to go, she thought. If I say no, Bill says he can't survive in that situation. Divorce would leave me with a house and two children and no way to support them. Bill doesn't make a lot of money, but he's a white male, and I'm not. My job at Dayton's is above minimum wage, but barely. Jobs in the arts for which I qualify pay no better.

For Bill, it was as though the child's very presence threatened his sense of identity. Had he glimpsed himself in the bathroom mirror as he confronted the defiant boy? Perhaps the face he had seen reflected there belonged not to the stoic, rational father who could orchestrate family life long-distance, but rather to a man possessed by rage against a five-year-old. Bill insisted that someone from Crossroads take Lamont away that very day.

Out of the question, Myrna Otte told him. "We can't do this to a child. We can't move him in an afternoon. You have to work through this. We need to prepare him for the move. You have to say good-bye." The least the Millers owed the child was time for the agency to find him another family and an explanation for the adoption's failure that would absolve him of blame. How could they be so inflexible, so rigid? How could Otte have misjudged them so badly?

She won a few days' grace. She instructed them to tell Lamont it was not his fault things hadn't worked out. Not trusting them, she arranged for them to inform him in her presence. They all sat in the living room, Lamont perched on the couch next to the social worker, Bill and Nann in armchairs on the far side of the coffee table.

To Nann, it seemed obvious that words and emotions were in conflict: Everything's fine, but you have to leave. She saw Lamont watching them with those big eyes, saying nothing. They had all assured him this was his family forever, that he would never have to leave. They had lied. She and Bill felt it was morally wrong to terminate the adoption, but they were doing it anyway. It was, Nann would say later, "like choosing to have one of your children die."

Lamont had already lost one life. Once he had been the favorite parishioner of the Mount Eden Baptist Church, the baby cousin who fell down the stairs unscathed, the boy standing inside a magic circle of pink plastic under his mother's omniscient gaze. Once he had been Lamontcello.

Two days after his sixth birthday, carrying a small suitcase and his photo album, Lamont moved to his third home in twelve months.

TEN

THERE WAS NO COMPASS IN MYRNA OTTE'S CAR. LAMONT looked out the window as the house fell away and the park where he had played T-ball vanished. The car entered a freeway and passed one green sign after another, a long stretch of river fringed in green, an elevated railroad track, a traffic light. Eventually the car turned right, onto a side street shaggy with trees. Halfway up a hill, it stopped in front of a reddish house that seemed to lean into the slope. This was the Wassermans', and he was theirs now.

Otte took him inside and made the introductions. Sherri Wasserman seemed enormous. Instead of having a sleek cap of dark hair like Nann, she had a big blond hairdo that looked like a wig. Albin Wasserman had a dark pompadour and glasses that made his farsighted hazel eyes huge and blurry. Their son, Kevin, was a pale, blond eight-year-old whose shy smile was missing a tooth. They lived in a house so crowded with everyday debris that at first Lamont couldn't tell which room was which. On a dining table near the front door, the odds and ends were spread several inches deep—newspaper circulars and school-trip advisories, bills, baseball cards, an artificial rose, photos, cough drops. The smell of dog and cat rose from the worn carpet, and a whistling chatter came from big bird cages in the next room.

Where the Millers ran a tight ship, Myrna Otte had concluded, the Wassermans were laissez-faire. These were good-hearted, undemanding people. They lived in unfashionable Fridley, a white blue-collar suburb north of Minneapolis. Al Wasserman sold canvas boat covers and venetian blinds from his pickup truck throughout the upper Midwest. The Wassermans had adopted Kevin as an infant from another agency because Sherri couldn't have children. She had always wanted more kids, but mainstream adoption agencies looked askance at an overweight woman who was a careless housekeeper and a Lutheran married to a Jewish traveling salesman. The Wassermans owned their home, but they had little money in the bank and no college degrees. They were, the social worker thought, just the kind of family Crossroads had been founded to serve—not the elite, blue-ribbon family of adoption tradition, but people with enough love and tolerance to parent some of the nontraditional children waiting for families. Scrambling for a home for Lamont on short notice, she had been very grateful to find their names on a waiting list to adopt an older child of any race. The sooner Lamont could settle into their household, the better. So Otte said her good-byes and drove away.

Al Wasserman could see Lamont was scared. It had to be hard for a six-year-old to be kicked out of one family after another. But even with that frightened expression on his face, he was a really good-looking kid. The color made no difference, Al thought. There was no problem with their being prejudiced or anything. The neighbors were pretty good. Besides, he and Sherri didn't worry about other people's opinions. They were already alienated from most of their relatives.

Al's own family life had been rotten. All his parents did was fight. All he ever heard growing up was "You're never gonna amount to nothing, you're a no-good." It wasn't the nurturing Jewish family of stereotype. His mother had come to the United States from Russia with her family when she was eight or nine, and his father's parents were from Germany. They were both disappointed in him from the start, and with his brother, born ten years later, too. Al had been bar mitzvahed, like all the boys in their Jewish neighborhood in North Minneapolis, but he hadn't attended a synagogue in years. His parents had refused to come to his wedding, and for years they didn't speak to Sherri.

Al had been twenty-two and Sherri eighteen when they married. Her father had run away to California with a younger woman when she was sixteen, and it had broken her heart. She insisted on driving out west to find him after the wedding, and they had tried life in California for a couple of years to be near him. Both California and Sherri's dad had fallen short of their hopes, though, so they moved back to Minnesota. Sherri's mother came to live with them. Al went to work in his father's canvas manufacturing business, returning from long days on the road to the old man's endless stream of bitterness and recrimination. Al had sworn never to treat his own kids the way his father treated him.

Kevin showed Lamont the bunk beds they would share in the small back bedroom. The narrow stairs up to his grandma's room started there, too. It was kind of a dark room, but the window looked out on the creek that ran through their backyard and drew kids from all over the neighborhood. Having Lamont join the family would be like having a friend sleep over every night, Kevin thought. Only days before, his parents had asked if it would be OK if they adopted a brother for him. "Yeah, I think that would be cool," he told them. Did it matter if he was black? They showed him a picture. The boy in the photograph looked like a decent kid, so he gave his approval. Now he took Lamont outside to meet his friend Davey, and they shot some baskets together in Davey's driveway.

That night Sherri told Lamont that since he was being adopted into a new family, he could choose a new first name to go with his new last name if he wanted.

"He wants to be called Bobbi," she told Myrna Otte in a happy phone call the next day. That was how she wrote it, *Bobbi:* Sherri loved unconventional spellings. It was part of the romance of reinventing oneself, of wiping out an unsatisfactory past and starting over. It did not occur to her that Lamont might have taken her suggestion as a strong hint that neither his old name nor his old self was good enough for this family. Officially, he would become Robert Ryan Wasserman.

He called them Mom and Dad and followed Al around everywhere that first weekend. New aunts and uncles kept showing up to get a look at him. He didn't wet his bed the first night, Sherri reported proudly to the social worker. Perhaps it was because he never went to sleep.

A child in Lamont's position tries very hard to be perfect at the beginning, Myrna Otte had warned them. Uncertain of the household rules, fearful of a new rejection, he places unbearable pressure on himself to be on his best behavior. Finally he can't keep all the hurt and anger bottled up a minute longer, and the feelings erupt in episodes of bad behavior. Or, as he begins to feel real attachment to members of the new family, he panics because it recapitulates the vulnerability that ended in rejection before. So he strikes out, pushing them away before they can get close enough to hurt him. Each eruption also serves as a test: Are they really committed to him?

Of course Lamont soon began to wet his bed again. His bedwetting continued to be seen by Crossroads staff as a sign of emotional maladjustment; somehow the diagnosis by the Millers' family doctor never followed him to the Wassermans'. Perhaps the Millers never mentioned his need for surgery. Perhaps it was lost among the scratch-paper notations that accumulated in Myrna Otte's kitchen between the telephone and the toaster. But Kevin was a bedwetter, too, and unlike the Millers, the Wassermans didn't take enuresis personally.

The second week Sherri sat down with Lamont and wrote an upbeat letter to Sheltering Arms and the Fils-Aimes. Afterward, as they were about to drive somewhere together, Lamont stood on the car's tailpipe and broke it off. The honeymoon was over. Later he asked to call Nann and Bill. The phone just rang and rang. So he called a boy he had known in the latchkey program. When he got off the phone, he cried and coughed and said he felt bad. The cough persisted, so the Wassermans took him to their doctor, who said he had asthmatic bronchitis, and prescribed medication.

One minute this child was affectionate, the next minute defiant, Sherri reported to the social worker the third week. After hugs all around one evening, he had picked up something to throw at the TV screen. When they threatened to give him a spanking if he didn't put it down, he retorted that he had been hit in the face and the back at the Millers'. Then he told a story about his being blamed for stealing Bill's beer. He told of yelling and fighting between Nann and Bill. As he talked, he grabbed Sherri's robe and seemed sincerely fearful. So what should they do to punish bad behavior? Sherri asked him. He told her spanking was not fair, but it was nice. He loved Nann, he added suddenly, and he missed her. What a mixed-up kid he was, Al thought. Later he and Sherri quarreled about how to handle his misbehavior.

Lamont/Bobbi seemed most at ease with Kevin. There were nights that summer when the two boys stayed up late talking and playing with toy cars in their bunks. They made a big chair in the living room into a fort using pillows; they watched late-night TV and ran back to the chair to feign sleep when Al and Sherri came in to check on them. They spent long afternoons by the creek. One of their companions was a deaf boy who lived up the road; Lamont never forgot how the boy's mother would blow a whistle loud enough so the air's vibrations called her son home. Sometimes, on a weekend, Al told the boys to put on their bathing suits and took them fishing down at Moore Lake off Highway 65. They would catch bullheads and call to Al to get the fish off their hooks. Another time they threw popcorn into Lake Harriet to feed the big openmouthed carp at the foot of the dock.

They were playing baseball in the yard one day when Lamont suddenly hit Kevin across the stomach with the bat. It was completely unprovoked. The older boy dropped to the ground, crying out in pain. He struggled to his feet and ran into the house, sobbing and calling for his mother. Sherri gave Lamont a swat on the rear and sent him to his room. Later she made him apologize. "I'm sorry," Lamont told Kevin. "I'll never do it again."

One night when Lamont was fooling around at the supper table, Sherri warned him that if he didn't eat his dinner, she'd sell him to Farmer Jones down the road. She'd said the same thing to Kevin many times; it was an old family chestnut, a joke. But Lamont heard it as unforgettable confirmation that his place in the Wasserman family was tenuous.

Sherri was no disciplinarian. She was the kind of soft-hearted mother who would let her son skip school to go see *E.T.* in a theater the day it opened. She forbade Kevin to wade barefoot in the creek for fear of the nails thrown in the water when the house was built, but when he disobeyed her to go frogging with the other kids and she caught him lying about it, she couldn't bear to ground him for more than three hours. Al would have been stricter, but Al was on the road. Sherri's relaxed approach had worked fine with Kevin, a stolid, good-natured child who adored his mother. But Lamont didn't respond the same way. Caught in a lie, he was likely to tell another one. Sent to his room in disgrace, he daydreamed or pulled at his hair, ripping out the "peas"—those little matted, nappy bits that grew out of the uncombed ends. Or he found escape under the covers, in masturbation.

Just before Lamont made the move to the Wassermans, Myrna Otte had arranged for them to meet the Millers over lunch. Nann had shared her suspicions about Lamont having been sexually abused. She advised the Wassermans to seek counseling for him as soon as possible. Over the summer, Sherri and the social worker decided that Lamont probably had had some inappropriate sexual experience in New York, but they felt he was handling it well, and no counseling was necessary. One August day the Wassermans drove Lamont to his old neighborhood for a visit with his latchkey friend, who was also black, and had been adopted as an infant.

His parents told Sherri and Al that Lamont was a great kid, and that the Millers were oddballs.

But when school started in September, Lamont's most troublesome behaviors increased. He was enrolled at Adams Public School, where his teacher, Mrs. Young, was a calm, motherly woman with five children of her own, who knew that even for a child without special problems, first grade was a difficult adjustment. Especially for little boys, just sitting still for long periods and following directions posed a challenge. Lamont's disruptiveness, however, was of different order. He was certainly capable of learning, but it was very hard for him to settle down and pay attention for more than a few minutes at a time. He craved attention and always wanted hugs—his teacher had never seen a child who sought hugs so insatiably. Yet on the playground he was always beating up one child or another.

One morning at the start of class he hid under Mrs. Young's desk and wouldn't come out. "You know that we want you here, and you know that we love you," the patient teacher told him. "And when you're ready to come out, you'll come out and talk." Then she just turned her back on him and went on teaching. Eventually he crawled out and took his place.

Mrs. Young, who came from Massachusetts, could hardly overlook the fact that Lamont was the only black child in her classroom, even the only black child in the school. But like other adults in Lamont's life, she treated that fact as though it were unmentionable, or of too little importance to merit discussion. The child's-eye view was quite different. Kevin's old friends had basically accepted "Bobbi," but in the Wassermans' immediate neighborhood there were other kids who targeted him for abuse because he was black. One in particular, a big, heavy boy three times Lamont's size, went too far one day. He called Lamont "Nigger" while they were all waiting at the bus stop. Kevin watched in amazed admiration as Lamont turned around and punched his tormentor until the bigger boy toppled to the ground. But on the Adams School playground there was an endless stream of children ready to taunt Bobbi as "Blackie," "Brownie," or "Nigger." Sometimes he had three fights during a single recess. Once he stuffed toilet paper in the mouth of a kid from a special-ed class until the child could hardly breathe.

Still, at Crossroads the overall impression in September 1980 was that the Wassermans were coping beautifully with Lamont, proving their own parental competence and indirectly demonstrating the Millers' shortcomings. So when another of the agency's adoptive placements suddenly fell apart, leaving a thirteen-year-old Chippewa Indian girl without a home, Crossroads turned to the Wassermans again. Would they be willing to add this girl to their family? Sherri, who had spent years longing for many children and dreaming of a daughter, couldn't say no. Al was ready to go along with whatever Sherri wanted. They would clear out the attic storage room and fix it up as a bedroom. Three months after Bobbi's arrival, he and Kevin would acquire a sister.

The boys were enlisted to help move stuff out of the attic—an old chandelier, discarded toys, broken furniture. Perhaps Lamont/Bobbi was suddenly overwhelmed by memories of his own arrivals and departures. Perhaps he was gripped by fear that the newcomer would displace him. As though he simply couldn't fight his emotions any longer, the six-year-old broke down and cried for an hour and a half. Then he grew very quiet.

"Have you noticed how I've shaped up?" he asked Sherri that night.

The three days surrounding his new sister's arrival were Lamont's most chaotic. Nothing the Wassermans tried in the way of discipline worked with him, and all the old stories came up again: being hit with a belt by the Fils-Aime father, being hit in the face by Bill Miller, sexual nightmares— or were they memories?

"I feel like he wants to be hurt," Sherri told the social worker. "He hates being black." That Friday at school he did anything for attention, including chasing another kid with a protractor. When he came home, he asked if he could ever go back to the Millers.

Al and Sherri picked up the new sister on Saturday. She was tall and round-faced, with slanting eyes and long, straight black hair. Her name was Vera Ellen James, but Sherri offered her the chance to change it, and Vera Ellen James became Melissa Onewa Wasserman. Onewa meant "Morning Star" in the language of the Ojibwa, or Chippewa, as the European settlers pronounced one name for the tribe. Sherri soon turned Melissa into "Missi." In truth, the thirteen-year-old liked the name Vera Ellen and had wanted to keep it, but she sensed that the name change was important to Sherri, and at that point pleasing Sherri was her overriding goal. Melissa was the name on a necklace she spotted in a department store where Sherri took her shopping for clothes that first weekend.

The whole family was thrilled with Missi, Sherri reported later to Myrna Otte. Missi liked to laugh. She played the trumpet. She was very personable.

She was also more deeply troubled than the Wassermans knew. As they learned about her background in bits and pieces, it seemed far worse to them than anything in Lamont's past. But Lamont and Missi recognized each other, like survivors of separate shipwrecks washed up on the same shore.

VERA ELLEN WAS BORN on the Roseau River Indian Reservation, west of Lake Superior, near Minnesota's border with Canada. Like so many reservations, it was a place of degraded poverty, alcoholism, and broken families. Once the seminomadic Chippewa had held sway over a great swath of Great Lakes country and parts of the Great Plains. They were the Indians of wigwams and birchbark canoes whose nobility was celebrated in Longfellow's "Hiawatha." But the black-robed Jesuit missionaries had come to them from France, and then the fur traders who made John Jacob Astor's fortune. As part of the fur trade's cutthroat competition, white men plied Chippewa trappers with whiskey, weapons, and European goods until the game was all but gone from their forests and young braves no longer knew the traditional ways of living. Then came the federal agents of white civilization, and the ax-wielding copper miners, lumbermen, farmers, and town-builders. In 1854, the same year Charles Loring Brace sent the first orphan train to Dowagiac, Michigan, the commissioner of Indian affairs forced the lake Chippewa bands along the shores of Michigan, Wisconsin, and Minnesota to relinquish most of their ancestral hunting grounds to white developers. Scattered on small reservations too rocky and harsh for profitable farming, their forests felled and their lakes polluted, their old economy forcibly changed from food gathering to money gathering, the ruined Chippewa survived into the twentieth century at the mean edges of what had become the world's greatest industrial hub.

Vera Ellen was the oldest of three girls; their parents divorced when she was five. At first she and her two little sisters, who were twins, lived with their mother. But their mother moved in and out of relationships with different men, and one day she decided the children were too much to handle. The girls were abruptly shifted to their father's house, where he lived with a woman they would call "our wicked stepmother." Vera was beaten with a two-by-four. She was sexually abused by her father and her grandfather. She contracted venereal disease before she was nine. She and her sisters were left alone for weeks on end, fed by the woman's mother sometimes, and sometimes forced to scavenge for what they ate. Eventually neighbors complained to the authorities, and a social worker came to take them away.

"We're just going into town to talk," the social worker told them. Instead she put them in a foster home. Not long after, social workers removed Vera from the foster home, too. They said they would bring her back to see her sisters, but they never did. The three had been so wild, so used to being on their own, that perhaps the authorities decided to separate them. Or perhaps when Vera's VD was discovered, the foster parents didn't want her anymore. For years afterward Vera wrote letters to the twins. They never answered.

Vera was placed with a Catholic French-Canadian family in Ontario. "You're the perfect child in the first foster home," she would say later. "I just wanted a mother figure. In my mind, I figured this was going to be my home forever. My grades were the only problem."

Or almost the only problem: she was also sexually molested by her foster father. But she told no one about that; "I figured if I told someone I'd be taken away from my mom." She was removed anyway. The foster parents had begun to have marital conflicts. After two and a half years in their home, then nearly twelve years old, Vera was reassigned to a family ready to adopt her in Cannon Falls, Minnesota, a white suburb near a reformatory.

"When I was told I was going to leave my mother [in Ontario], my world was just crashing. When I moved to the adoptive home, that's when everything went wrong. I was trying to keep something I wasn't going to have anymore. The [Ontario family] accepted me the way I was, but the [Cannon Falls family] didn't. The kids at school never accepted me. I couldn't get along with people my age, only with adults. I completely forgot my Indian heritage. People would say, 'You're colored, we don't want you here.' I'd go home and try to scrub myself white. After I learned their ways and accepted their ways, they rejected me anyway."

Every three months or so, the adoptive parents, who were Baptists, threatened that Vera would have to leave if her behavior didn't improve. But she kept taking out her anger and frustration in destructive ways. Once, coming back from school, she was so angry that she took off her jeans and tore them up at the crotch. After she calmed down, she tried to sew the pants up again. The adoptive mother was furious when she found the damaged jeans in the wash. As Vera would tell it later, the woman threw her to the floor and jumped up and down on her back. The father wanted to give her another chance, but the mother called Crossroads and demanded that the girl be removed within twenty-four hours. She had lived with them for a year and a half.

"I woke up, and they just said, 'Pack your clothes. You're going.' I didn't even get a chance to say good-bye to my friends or to get their addresses to write. It was really awful. I figured I'd try to correct my mistakes and do whatever people would tell me, and maybe they wouldn't reject me."

The Cannon Falls couple had been very neat, highly organized people who kept pets confined to the basement and did not allow children to run in the house. The Ontario foster parents had been more laid-back, with a basement room the kids could wreck, a family room that had to be picked up and vacuumed from time to time, and a parlor for guests only. Adjusting to the Wassermans' life-style was extremely hard for Vera/Missi. At first she just lived from day to day.

When Sherri came into her room to say good night, Missi would leap to the other side of the bed and cower in the corner. She slept with her glasses on—the better to see anyone who came after her in the night. Recognizing signs of past trauma, Sherri tried hard to win her confidence, but she made a mistake early on. "Once I told her a secret," Missi would recall later. "Next thing I knew my aunt knew. She broke my trust."

One afternoon Lamont overheard Missi and Sherri talking. Sherri was pressing Missi about her past—prying, in Missi's view. Finally the girl blew up, burst into tears, and ran outside.

Lamont went after her. He put his small arms around the weeping girl and hugged her. "It's going to be all right," he said.

"You will never be able to understand what I went through," she cried.

"You're wrong," he said. "I can understand, 'cause it happened to me, too."

Standing by the creek, he told her then what he wouldn't tell anyone else for another decade: his foster father Fils-Aime had sexually fondled and abused him.

Here's this little six-year-old telling me this, Missi thought. *This is bizarre.*

Kevin, too, tried to reassure Missi in his own way. He saw that she was scared when Sherri trotted out the old threat about Farmer Jones down the road. "Don't worry," he told her. "She said that to me, too, and she never did it. It's a joke." Missi wasn't convinced. "I thought, Oh, they're going to get rid of me. I thought, I'm going to push these people away before they push me away.

"I was trying to push them to a break, to see how much it'd take for them to get rid of me. Whatever my mom hated, I did just because she hated it. But she put up with it."

Years later, after the Wassermans had stuck by her through defiance and drug abuse, ignored professional advice not to adopt her, toughed out her runaways and her sexual promiscuity, and adopted the out-of-wedlock baby she had with a black man, one question would still haunt Missi: Why had they put up with her?

Looking back, she would see herself as Lamont/Bobbi's silent partner, getting away with the same acts that were his downfall. Once, for example, she picked up the Wassermans' guinea pig, and it bit her. "I smacked it down in the cage and broke its leg, and it died. The folks didn't even know. They knew it died, but not why." Another time Sherri found all the heat registers stuffed with tissue and toilet paper. She summoned the children and warned them that this could cause the furnace to overheat and start a fire in the house. Then she punished Bobbi by sending him to his room— she was certain he was to blame. Missi said nothing, but she had been stuffing registers with paper, too. She didn't know why; just to see what would happen, maybe. It was like starting a doodle on one of Al's tax documents. She could be thinking, "This is an important paper. I'm writing on it. Oh, shit, Dad's going to get mad." And all the time her hand would go on tracing concentric circles, bigger and bigger on the page.

She remembered Sherri getting really mad at Bobbi for sleeping with a knife in his bed. But Missi had taken knives to bed with her, too, because she felt she couldn't handle anybody abusing her again. In one recurrent dream—or was it a hallucination?—she would see a big man standing in her doorway, and she would scream and scream. "I wouldn't trust anybody. If I did love somebody, I would do mean things to them."

She had a terrible time at Coons Rapids High School and was forced take a series of psychological tests. "Write 'yes,' even if it only happened once," she was instructed. She didn't find out until three years later that the tests resulted in a psychiatrist's recommendation that the Wassermans not keep her. "He kept saying I was crazy and they should send me back, that I don't belong in a family, I don't deserve to be in a family."

But they didn't send her back. They would send Bobbi away instead.

BEFORE CHRISTMAS, Myrna Otte paid a rare home visit to the boy she still thought of as Lamont. He was understandably very anxious about the visit, and she talked with the Wassermans about the need to finalize his adoption to relieve some of his insecurity. The six-month minimum waiting period was coming to an end. He was doing better in school. The new school psychologist had talked to Gay Halberg, his predecessor, and was going to test Lamont to see if he was dyslexic. Meanwhile, he attended a class for learning-disabled kids twice a week and was on an incentive program: he got a nickel for every worksheet he finished in school.

But this time the biggest problem was his behavior at home, not at school. Most disturbing was his sexuality. He had developed a sore on his penis from the combination of masturbation and bedwetting, and Sherri had to dress it with antibiotic cream. He told her he liked her to care for the sore and wanted her to continue to rub his penis after it was no longer necessary. Any mother would find it unsettling to discover she was inadvertently giving a six-year-old sexual pleasure by medicating a sore, but it is hardly surprising that the boy would enjoy the sensation of having cream rubbed on his penis. Past sexual fondling by an adult could only make it more likely that he would experience such attention as sexual. And even for a child who had never been molested, and who had not repeatedly lost his father, the other side of such pleasure would likely be fear or guilt.

One night—perhaps in an effort to stop him from masturbating?— Sherri threatened to cut off his penis, and he started crying. He reported a dream in which he had sex with his foster mother, and other dreams in which people cut off his penis and he awakened screaming. A few times he was caught trying to peek under the door when a female in the house went to the bathroom; a Freudian interpretation might understand this as an effort to observe what was left on the bodies of those who had "lost" their penis.

Later he really did injure his penis on the metal springs under his mattress, hurting himself so badly that he needed a bandage that had to be changed twice a day, and the school nurse had to be enlisted to help. According to Missi's memory, that injury was a matter of innocent high jinks gone awry. Bobbi and Kevin liked to remove the mattresses from their beds to jump up and down as though the metal springs were a trampoline. Bobbi, already undressed for bed, was leaping around when his legs went through the springs and he found himself stuck in the most painful way. Missi remembered him shrieking for Mom, and Mom applying antiseptic in the bathroom. Kevin would have no memory of such an accident. In any case, school personnel eventually came to think of it as a bizarre form of self-mutilation. Stories about Lamont's past had begun to circulate. It was said that he had choked a gerbil at his Minneapolis kindergarten and thrown its body off the school roof. He was rumored to be the child of Jamaican drug addicts, brain-damaged in the womb. He had been sexually abused and beaten in a New York City foster home, the teachers whispered, and he had burned the house down.

In January, the school psychologist advised the Wassermans to have a complete psychological workup on Bobbi before they went ahead with an adoption. He had confided to the school psychologist that he loved to play with matches. He loved to watch flames and firemen, and he had dreams at night of people burning on poles and being stabbed. At home, they had caught him being mean to the family dog, holding her head down so she couldn't breathe, and giggling. Yet at other times he was so sweet, so affectionate, and so eager to please.

"It's like he has two personalities," Sherri told Myrna Otte on January 19, 1981. "There's Bobbi and then there's Lamont." She said she had found him dancing around the kitchen that day, stabbing a knife at the cupboards. He told some fantastic stories about himself; she didn't know when he was lying and when he was telling the truth.

The following day he had a perfect day at school. There was a party in his classroom, and the teacher said he behaved beautifully.

That night Sherri woke up to overpowering heat. The temperature in the house felt like a hundred degrees. She groped for the clock. It was four in the morning. She jumped out of bed and ran to the living room, where she found Lamont sitting on the couch, rocking back and forth. "I'm waiting for the fire to come," he told her, and he laughed. He had turned the thermostat as high as it would go. He had stuffed all the registers with paper again. He had torn up newspapers and left them in different corners of the house. For the first time, she felt real fear.

At 6:00 A.M. Sherri telephoned Myrna Otte at home. The social worker started calling psychiatric hospitals. Only one had a bed available immediately, and a psychiatrist ready to admit the child on an emergency basis: Golden Valley Health Center.

ELEVEN

GOLDEN VALLEY HEALTH CENTER WAS SET ON A HILL BE-side a lake, at the end of a dead-end road that cut through a huge wooded property. It had been founded in 1937 as a private psychiatric hospital for adults. In the 1950s it had added a pediatric wing and expanded into medicine and surgery. By 1981 it relied on inpatient psychiatric care of children for much of its income. Within a few years of Lamont's stay, it would close down the last of its nonpsychiatric functions, turn into a for-profit operation with ties to a California-based insurance company, and ride the boom in the psychiatric hospitalization of juveniles through the 1980s.

Thomas Wilson III, a lawyer who represented numerous children confined in its psychiatric units during the 1980s, called Golden Valley a "money machine." As long as your child was covered by insurance, he used to say, Golden Valley would admit the youngster, but sending kids there was like putting them in Marine Corps boot camp. Bob Johnson, a former psychiatric social worker who visited Golden Valley's wards as a patient advocate for the Minnesota Mental Health Association, considered it worse than boot camp. The Marine Corps, after all, modified behavior in order to turn out soldiers. Golden Valley kept children until their insurance ran out, and prepared them for nothing so much as life inside some other total institution.

Its emphasis was on "aversive treatment"—what most people think of as punishment. "They would have a child sit in a chair for hours," Wilson said. "They would roll a child up in a mat and leave him rolled up for hours. They would lock up children." Ultimately, any juvenile who resisted by getting angry or "acting out" could be physically overpowered by staff and shot up with enough major tranquilizers to serve as a pharmaceutical straitjacket.

The escalating scale of aversion could be triggered by any small rebellion. A sign in the adolescent unit's dining room read Do Not Make Fun of the Food. "My God, even the army is smarter than that," Bob Johnson said when he saw it. "On that day, as it happened, there were bananas for lunch. A boy, one of the leaders among the kids, said, 'I bet I have the biggest banana on this unit.' The staff sent him to time-out."

A girl said, "Eric, I know your banana is bigger than anybody else's." She, too, was sent to time-out.

"Why did you do that?" Johnson asked the staff person.

"That was inappropriate," came the reply. Such was the attitude that pervaded the institution's milieu therapy.

Johnson never went inside the "Valley Youth Center," at the back of the property, which Golden Valley's program director officially described as a "free standing cottage designed to evaluate children ages 2–14 for behavior and emotional problems." From the outside, Johnson thought it looked like a bunker on the Maginot Line.

There are few independent sources of information about a locked psychiatric ward for children aged two to fourteen. Children under fourteen had no right to a patient advocate like Bob Johnson. Even children confined for years in a state mental hospital were legally considered voluntary patients, with no civil-liberties interests separate from those of the adults who had placed them there.

For a brief time in the midseventies it had looked as though a Georgia class action might change that. But in 1979 the U.S. Supreme Court ruled otherwise in *Parham* v. *J.R.* (442 U.S. 584). "The statist notion that governmental power should supersede parental authority in *all* cases because *some* parents abuse and neglect children is repugnant to American tradition," Chief Justice Burger wrote in the majority opinion, which emphasized "the family as a unit with broad parental authority over minor children."

In a dissent to the *Parham* decision, Justice Brennan, joined by Justices Marshall and Stevens, contended that "the presumption that parents act in their children's best interests, while applicable to most child-rearing decisions, is not applicable in the commitment context. Numerous studies reveal that parental decisions to institutionalize their children often are the results of dislocation in the family unrelated to the children's mental condition." In calling for adversarial review, he concluded, "Fairness demands that children abandoned by their supposed protectors to the rigors of institutional confinement be given the help of some separate voice."

But even if that dissenting view had prevailed, the case would not automatically have applied to children in private psychiatric hospitals like Golden Valley.

LAMONT WOULD always remember it as the scariest place he'd ever been.

The first night, he was under twenty-four-hour observation. It was like jail, he would say much later. But when Myrna Otte called to ask about visiting hours, she was told by the staff that he had slept well and without nightmares. He was said to have praised the good food and to have exclaimed, "I love it here." Otte passed on the reported comments to Sherri. "What a trouper!" Sherri said.

Within a couple of days, the reports were not so good. Lamont was soiling his pants, Myrna Otte wrote in her notes. He liked to antagonize people. He was throwing cars—toy cars, presumably.

Everything about the treatment of children at Golden Valley Youth Center was considered confidential. But by chance, a complaint investigation by the Minnesota Office of Health Facility Complaints documented an incident that took place at Valley Youth Center the same week Lamont arrived there.

"An activity leader refused a twelve-year-old patient permission to go to the bathroom," the investigator noted. "This action resulted in his having a bowel movement in front of his peers January 19, 1981."

Someone complained to the state that nursing notes related to the incident had been removed from the patient's record by administrative staff. A state investigator found that four days' worth of notes had indeed disappeared from the twelve-year-old patient's chart. But after admitting that the bowel movement incident had occurred and dismissing the activity leader responsible, Golden Valley's administration claimed not to know what had happened to the missing notes. The complaint was closed as "undeterminable."

A few months later, another complaint alleged that Valley Youth Center staff routinely restrained patients by throwing them on the floor and sitting on their chests, and that one fourteen-year-old girl restrained in such a manner had been told she had to "eat on the floor." Like nearly every other complaint filed against Golden Valley during this period, it was closed as "unsubstantiated—insufficient evidence." Golden Valley was not subject to any regular inspection or certification by any state agency. Under Minnesota law, as long as it was accredited by the Joint Commission on Hospital Accreditation, it was deemed to be in compliance with all licensing requirements.

This was the place where Lamont was to spend three months for a diagnostic evaluation that cost the Wassermans' health insurance company thirty thousand dollars.

There is a looking-glass quality to Golden Valley's official evaluation of Lamont. What *is* a normal reaction to being left or rejected by a succession of eight parents, with or without a little sexual abuse, a fire, and racial confusion thrown in for good measure? It didn't matter, since no reaction would be perceived as normal in this setting. Not fear and not anger, not a craving for affection, not fantasies of empowerment and revenge. Not even a sad expression.

"Bobby sought mothering from female staff," a nurse therapist dictated in a report signed by the admitting psychiatrist. "He tries to please, seeks hugs from all staff. There are times when he attempts to manipulate staff by looking sad or cute when he has been confronted. . . . Initially on admission, Bobby seemed to settle in very quickly. He, however, tested the unit limits, used rude language, made threatening gestures toward his peers, and was involved in name-calling."

It was a teenaged black boy in the unit who drew most of his name-calling. A pigment problem had left the youth's brown skin mottled with large, sickly-looking pale patches. It was as though Lamont's racial self-hatred and confusion had been made flesh. How could he not want, like Missi, to scrub away what set him apart? But here was that wish made manifest, and it turned out to be an ugly, piebald adolescent.

"You look like someone threw bleach on you," Lamont/Bobbi told the youth, and he pestered and taunted him until the teenager hit him.

"Generally, he has responded to limits well," the report conceded. "When supervised, Bobby's peer interactions have been appropriate. He has been noted when unsupervised to be in frequent peer conflicts. Bobby often tells stories about himself that are exaggerations or lies. At one time, he focused on whipping people with a belt. This seems to be the content of a fair amount of fantasy and probably reflects past experiences of abuse. . . .

"We have noted an obsession with fire. He has talked about setting the staff on fire in a joking manner. He has said that he likes fire, the way the flames come up and pop out of the windows. On more than one occasion, he has talked about setting staff on fire to warm them up.

"Bobby has been caught in the bathroom with two other male peers and did admit to sexual play twice. We have also noted that he has protested when a boy made sexual gestures toward him. He has started to talk regarding the sexual and physical abuse in the past with the aid of a coloring book which deals with just these issues. He has been interested and motivated for one-to-one talks and shows much understanding."

The boy who wanted to please adults did not tell the staff what he had told Missi about his foster father, or at least those who evaluated him did not write it up that way. Instead, the "possible sexual experiences" first suspected by Nann Miller were now tentatively blamed on Alicia Fils-Aime. It was as though Nann's ideas about Alicia had received an Oedipal spin. With the foster father out of the household, the narrative went, the foster mother might have turned to the child for sexual gratification. Wouldn't that fit with the report of Lamont's "practiced" groping of Nann Miller's breasts? The "groping" incident had been dismissed by Myrna Otte at the time as normal curiosity. But in light of Lamont's problems in the Wasserman home, neither Myrna Otte nor the consulting diagnosticians at Golden Valley took such a benign view any longer.*

Lamont's diagnostic evaluation occurred in an era when the prevalence of child sexual abuse had been newly rediscovered. The point is not that

---

*In fact, a few years later a study by Alvin Rosenfeld, director of child psychiatry at the Jewish Child Care Association in New York City, would find that almost all boys and girls between the ages of two and four in the sample group had tried to touch their mothers' breasts and genitals, and most had tried to touch their fathers' genitals. Behavior sometimes used as evidence of sexual abuse thus appeared instead to be part of normal childhood curiosity.

allegations of sexual abuse are not to be believed, but that the automatic credence and power accorded expert evaluations in the child welfare system are completely out of proportion to the stuff those evaluations are made of. The problem isn't only with the suggestibility of children. Studies have shown that when diagnosing identical patients in identical settings, no two psychiatrists agree more than half of the time. Training in psychiatry, for example, predisposes practitioners to diagnose a mental illness for which drugs can be prescribed, and the particular school of psychiatry to which an examiner belongs almost predetermines what illness he will find. A patient already in a hospital is more likely to be diagnosed as mentally ill than the same patient examined in another setting; a patient believed to be poor is more likely to be diagnosed as mentally ill than the same patient credited with a higher income.

Ten days after he was locked up at Golden Valley, "Robert Wasserman" was given a battery of psychometric and projective tests by a consulting psychologist who measured the boy's responses to Rorschach blots, Bender pictures, and achievement tests, against what was expected from a child who had experienced a normal childhood. Any deviation would automatically become evidence supporting the foregone conclusion that something was very wrong with Lamont.

The psychologist's report reads as an exercise in reconciling this "rather typical-appearing black child who was somewhat hyperactive, but otherwise rational, cooperative, and well-motivated throughout the testing procedures" with the delusional, fire-obsessed child in the admission record. Parts of the report show empathetic insight into why a six-year-old subjected to Lamont's experiences might seek refuge in fantasies of power and revenge. But because the boy was good at words and bad at blocks, and better at talking than at writing, the psychologist included the suggestion that the source of some of his problems might be inside his brain rather than in his life. The psychologist hedged his bets by covering all the bases and sprinkling his speculation with conditionals, sometimes three at a time: "I am *inclined* to *suspect* the *possibility*." Take your pick, he was saying: early-childhood deprivation (a black foster child from New York City—what could be more likely?) or "minimal organic overlay" (i.e., a small, unspecified brain glitch that might have some unspecified connection to the reported behavior at the Wassermans'). The supporting evidence? Reads better than he writes. Intellectual growth greater than "emotional integration." For good measure, the psychologist included a kind of blanket approval for medicating the boy for hyperactivity "if Robert is viewed by others as being a hyperkinetic child"—though the implication was that he himself didn't find Lamont hyperkinetic.

DIAGNOSIS: Adjustment reaction to childhood. A delusional, angry, perhaps organically dysfunctional child.

RECOMMENDATIONS: 1. Continued hospitalization at Valley Youth Center for therapy, evaluation, milieu support, and behavior shaping.

2. Outpatient family therapy, casework supervision, and follow-up.

3. Robert should be helped by everyone to verbalize his frustration and anger directly, and also to respond more acceptably to these feelings.

As the weeks went by, reports from the hospital classroom said that Lamont—now "Bobby" instead of Bobbi—had begun to do more work and was less distractible and impulsive. He showed good classroom skills but "demonstrated poor fine motor skills in cutting with scissors. . . . His self-esteem is low and he has difficulty in peer relationships. He requires much positive attention and affection."

Golden Valley sent to New York City for Lamont's child welfare records. The documents that came back included Dr. Anna Vanderschraaf's diagnosis of eleven-year-old Shirley Wilder, who had admitted talking with her dead grandmother at times of distress.

CHILDHOOD SCHIZOPHRENIA

As Golden Valley's psychiatrist prepared his case summary, those two words written down three years before Lamont's birth took on new significance. They loomed larger, it seemed, than the psychologist's report, the nursing staff's notes, or the boy's hospital-classroom progress. They cast an ominous light over ever-more-sinister summaries of hearsay about Lamont's past.

The one-paragraph family history included in Golden Valley's official evaluation declared that the boy had been severely beaten and scared in his New York foster home, had been whipped in the morning when his bed was found to be wet, and had set a house on fire. "Bobby came to Minneapolis from New York and was placed in another adoptive home here. . . . He was reported to have very similar problems there and, at one time, he killed a gerbil. He had been found on the roof of the school and needed continual care. He did not show remorse or guilt. Mrs. Wasserman reported that the adoptive father had hit Bobby and two of his teeth had been knocked out; he had also been hit with sticks and belts and at this point, he entered the Wasserman home."

At first the Wassermans had said they wanted Bobbi to come home to them when he was discharged from Golden Valley. They took Kevin to visit him there once. The boys played floor hockey together in the hospital basement. Then visiting hours were over, and it was time to say good-bye. Kevin thought Bobbi looked very small and unhappy sitting alone on his bed. Later Bobbi told the psychiatrist that he wished the Wassermans would visit more often than they did, and that he was homesick.

But as stories began to seep back to Sherri from the hospital through Crossroads, she became more and more frightened. It was said that the boy's parents had been Jamaican fire-worshipers and this was "reflecting on his mind," as Al would put it. Or perhaps the fire-worshipers had been in the first foster family, and the locale some other Caribbean island, but anyway, it seemed the family had killed animals, maybe as part of a cult. Satanism? Was that what lay behind the gerbil's death and Bobbi's treatment of the family dog?

"He was a nice boy, but this scared my wife to death," Al would tell people later.

"This has been a very difficult time for the Wassermans," the psychiatrist wrote in his discharge report. "They have felt guilty and reluctant to decide what they will do (to continue with the adoption or to terminate it). We have encouraged them to meet with Dr. John Vancini at the Golden Valley Psychiatric Clinic to assist working through these feelings. They have canceled two appointments with him because Mrs. Wasserman was too anxious and on one occasion her blood pressure was elevated. They said they would meet with him after hearing our recommendations."

Those recommendations were unambiguous.

DISCHARGE DIAGNOSIS:

1. Schizophrenia, latent type.
2. Fire-setting.

PROGNOSIS: Guarded.

RECOMMENDATIONS:

1. We recommend that Bobby be placed in a residential treatment center for behaviorally and emotionally disturbed children.
2. We recommend that Bobby not be placed in an adoptive home following treatment. We, instead, recommend a foster placement owing to the severity of this boy's problems.

For a while, the Wassermans talked about placing Lamont in the group setting that Golden Valley recommended and trying to remain his "advocates" or foster parents while he was in treatment. But the residential center was going to cost at least a thousand dollars a month, and they didn't have that kind of money. By now Myrna Otte was convinced that the New York City agency had withheld information about Lamont's background, covering up the pathology of his foster home and the problems he must have had before he came to Minnesota. She told the Wassermans he should never have been up for adoption in the first place. He would not be listed in the interstate book again, she said; he would stay "in care" for the balance of his childhood.

ONE DAY IN EARLY APRIL 1981, there were official telephone inquiries from the New York State Department of Social Services about Lamont. A lawyer, Marcia Lowry, had been asking questions on his birth mother's behalf. Where was Lamont? Was he adopted and well cared for? Perhaps these questions triggered the decision to discharge him; perhaps it was a coincidence. The Wassermans' insurance for an inpatient psychiatric stay was running out. On April 10, 1981, Lamont had to leave Golden Valley.

Myrna Otte and a colleague went to pick him up and transport him back to Sheltering Arms in New York City. He was very subdued.

"Where am I going to stay now?" he asked them. Like the staff at Golden Valley, the two social workers couldn't say.

"We don't know," one of the women told him. "But we're taking you to these people who are going to find a place for you to live."

He was very compliant on the airplane. He was a trouper. As instructed, the social workers hailed a taxi at La Guardia Airport and took the boy to Sheltering Arms. They all waited in the lobby for a few minutes. There were toys on the floor, and people coming in and going out. Somebody emerged from an office and took Lamont by the hand. The two women said good-bye and left.

1981–1983

ONE

INSIDE THE MANILA FOLDERS FILLED WITH PRINTED FORMS and typed reports that made up New York City's child welfare record of a boy named Lamont Wilder was a sheet of lined yellow paper, scribbled over in black ballpoint pen. It was a list of twenty-three foster-care agencies hurriedly telephoned in a search for somewhere—anywhere—to send a black, Protestant, schizophrenic fire-setter, aged six years and ten months, being returned from Minnesota.

Agencies contacted included Madonna Heights, the same Catholic residence for girls that had twice rejected Lamont's mother; Abbott House, the agency with a group home for disturbed teenagers that Marcia Lowry had helped develop with Bellevue Hospital; and Cardinal Hayes, a residence for the mentally retarded.

The page spoke of an approach to placement so haphazard that some children, with a guarantee of payment attached, were simply up for grabs.

Children's Village—rejected . . . JBG [Jewish Board of Guardians]—no firesetters—rejected. Graham Windham—interested—wants interview . . . Astor Home—no response . . . Childville—interested—wants interview . . . Green Chimneys—written material forwarded . . . Pleasantville—too young . . . Brooklyn Catholic Society—rejected . . . Harlem Dowling—rejected . . . St. Dominic Home—no response . . . Society for Seaman Children—rejected . . . MIV [Mission of the Immaculate Virgin]—rejected . . . St. Agatha's Home—rejected . . . Cardinal Hayes—only take developmentally delayed . . . Children's Aid—couldn't reach 800 number . . . Abbott House—too young . . . Pius XII—not a candi-

date . . . St. Christopher—no openings . . . Little Flower—no answer . . .
St. Cabrini—no N.Y. children . . . McMahon Services—rejected . . .
Madonna Heights—girls' school . . . Spence-Chapin—take a written
summary.

The scribbled list buried in the city's confidential files was eerily reminiscent of the one Justine Wise Polier summarized when she sent Shirley
to the training school at Hudson almost a decade earlier. The percentage
of black children in some of these agencies was higher now since the pool
of poor white children in the city had continued to shrink. But the system
Marcia Lowry had set out to transform in 1973 was fundamentally unchanged. And in the spring of 1981, the *Wilder* lawsuit had only recently
emerged from years in a legal no-man's-land.

TO MARCIA ROBINSON LOWRY, the worst period was the ten months
in 1978 when *Wilder* actually disappeared. At Judge Robert Ward's suggestion, Lowry had agreed to withdraw the suit and refile it with a new
set of juvenile plaintiffs to escape the legal swamp left by Ward's predecessors. It became *Parker* v. *Bernstein.* Blanche Bernstein was then head of
the Human Resources Administration under the new mayor, Edward I.
Koch. Barry Parker was an eleven-year-old black boy who had become
suicidal after his abusive stepfather beat his mother so badly she had to be
hospitalized; rejected by Jewish and Catholic residential treatment centers, he had been shuttled between a violent temporary shelter and men-
tal-hospital wards. The only silver lining in *Parker* v. *Bernstein,* as far as
Lowry was concerned, was that Legal Aid took the opportunity to quietly
drop out of the litigation. Determined not to let *Wilder*'s enemies be rid
of it so easily, Lowry hunted down Shirley Wilder, added her as an adult
plaintiff claiming damages for irreparable harm, and persuaded Judge
Ward to retitle the case *Wilder* v. *Bernstein.* People sometimes called it
Wilder Two, like the sequel to a hit horror movie. The horror, to Lowry,
was that Judge Ward still wouldn't rule on anything.

One sunny Saturday morning in the spring of 1980, when the defense
motion to dismiss and Lowry's motion for class certification had both
been fully briefed and pending before Ward for nearly two years, Lowry
ran into journalist Steven Brill at the Jefferson Market, a fashionable and

quirky Greenwich Village grocery store. Lowry had just joined the national ACLU office at the invitation of Ira Glasser, taking the Children's Rights Project with her. She had seen child-care principles she espoused unsuccessfully in court make their way into legislation, notably in the state's 1979 Child Welfare Reform Act and its national counterpart, the Adoption Assistance and Child Welfare Reform Act of 1980, which required diligent efforts to keep families together or to find new permanent families for children. At thirty-nine, she was about to marry Fritz Mosher, a midwestern-born WASP who was a program officer at the Carnegie Foundation, nine years her senior, and, quite improbably, the son of a (liberal) Republican congressman. But that day in 1980, as she and Brill stood together near the checkout counter, what Lowry talked about was only *Wilder*.

Not long afterward, Brill—the man who would go on to create Court TV—recounted *Wilder*'s embarrassing judicial saga in an article for the *American Lawyer*.

To Brill, Judge Tyler voiced more sympathy for the substance of the case than he had ever shown from the bench, and claimed he had expected a settlement. "This is an odds-on case of legislative default," he complained. "The legislature has to face the fact that the old traditional agencies, for good reasons, have favored their own, and that black Protestant kids are dumped into inferior homes. The courts shouldn't have to step in. . . . But I really thought I'd worked something out. If not, there's no question I'd have had to do something for these black kids."

Then again, perhaps not. "This is a fascinating case," Tyler told Brill, "but not one you love as a judge. You have all these nice people—do-gooders—on the boards of all these religious organizations who were very upset. I'd get all kinds of anguished mail from them. I was really depressed about this case."

Not as depressed as Lowry. By then she had decided the problem with her case was that it was too good: "I was so right on the law, and the consequences of my being right were so radical, they didn't know what to do with me."

Brill's piece finally seemed to shame Judge Ward into action. He denied the defense motion to dismiss the case, granted Lowry class certification, and told the parties to get on with a fresh round of discovery. This case, he declared, was really moving to trial.

Belief in *Wilder*'s urgency recurred in Lowry like a toothache. Eli Gilbert still feverishly updated the numbers. By 1981, in a system that was as a whole only 14 percent white, children in the Jewish agencies were 65 percent white and 24 percent black, with the non-Jews twice as likely to be white as black. The Catholic sector looked better on the numbers overall—about 48 percent of the children in Catholic agencies were black now—but some Catholic agencies were nearly all white, others disproportionately black.

So here she was again, on March 4, 1981, about to confront her enemies once more in the offices of Davis, Polk & Wardwell. But this time a grown-up Shirley Wilder was at her side.

Shirley was twenty-one now, and she looked great—a woman free to occupy her curves without apology, serene in the confidence that the lawyers who would interrogate her on this day had no power over her. In fact, she seemed enormously pleased with herself, Lowry thought, proud to be part of something so important.

The substance of her deposition was not of much legal significance to the case, Lowry knew. But the event had great symbolic importance. The system's powerful allies had done their best to kill *Wilder*. Well, *Wilder* was alive and kicking. And here, walking into their loftiest precincts, was Shirley Wilder herself to tell them so.

THEY EMERGED FROM THE ELEVATOR into the hush of thickly carpeted law offices. On one side was a library with Persian rugs and wide rows of leather-bound books. Straight ahead was a sweeping harbor view. Shirley Wilder gasped when she saw the Statue of Liberty in the distance. They stood there for a few minutes, breathing in the smell of old money, before being ushered into a small, windowless conference room for the deposition.

There were women among the *Wilder* defendants' lawyers now. Floran Fink and Myra Karban had replaced Leonard Sand, who had been appointed to a federal judgeship; Lorna Goodman and Michele Ovesey represented the city. The table seated more than a dozen lawyers, and still more crowded in to watch from the row of chairs that lined the walls. This was obviously a hot item, Lowry thought, eyeing the Davis, Polk associates coming in to see the show. In addition to Lowry, three lawyers present were on Shirley's side: Lowry's ACLU colleagues Michael Mushlin and Mary Sandoval, and Chris Hansen of the NYCLU office.

Kevin Simmons, a fair-haired, very junior lawyer with Davis, Polk, was the lead questioner. Before the day was over, as Lowry fiercely and repeatedly objected, Simmons and other opposing counsel would question Shirley about her first sexual experience, ask the names of her sexual partners, the number of times she had had sexual intercourse at Pius XII–Holy Cross Campus, whether she had ever used condoms or foam, whether it was true that she had been raped at age nine. This last was one of the questions Lowry instructed her not to answer, vigorously challenging its relevance.

What were they trying to do here? Certainly they had to depose her, to see that Shirley Wilder was not a phantom or a no-show. But this kind of grilling was only for harassment purposes, Lowry thought. So what if Shirley had screwed around? It had no legal significance. But they had decided to make this as unpleasant as possible; she could almost hear them chortling about the juicy parts behind closed doors.

Shirley never faltered, never lost her poise. At times she even showed flashes of defiant wit. There was a kind of indomitable dignity in her conviction that she had been wronged by the system these men and women were defending.

The eighty-first paragraph of the latest *Wilder* complaint charged, "Solely because she is black and neither Catholic nor Jewish, plaintiff Shirley Wilder has been permanently and irreparably damaged." Flo Fink read the passage aloud.

"Shirley, can you explain to me how you have been permanently damaged?" she asked.

Neither the question nor Shirley's answer was completely relevant, Lowry interjected, because some damages were based on violations of constitutional rights. But she let Shirley answer anyway. And in her own way, Shirley struggled to convey the hurt of lived injustice.

"I was refused in different Catholic institutions, ones that I thought I agreed to go to," she said. "I wanted to change my life, and I was refused." Madonna Heights was the only name she remembered among many, perhaps because the words exemplified the lofty promise of all the places that had turned her down. In disgust, she said, she had stopped listening in court as she was remanded back to detention again and again because she had been denied entry into all the places Carol Sherman praised for their fine schools and understanding counselors.

"How would this have changed your life?" Flo Fink asked her.

"Because, because the institution that you did send me to, the only thing is——"

"*I* didn't send you."

"Well, whoever sent me there, it didn't do nothing for me, and my schooling——I have no education at all."

Had she ever attempted to go back to school?

Yes, in 1977 she had tried to enroll at Empire Technical School for job training, but she was rejected because she didn't have a GED or high school diploma.

Why hadn't she taken extension or high school equivalency courses since? one of the lawyers demanded.

"I had to keep on making a living for myself. At the time, I didn't have a permanent place to stay." She had worked as a barmaid and was now employed by a Mr. McCann in a corner saloon called the Rainbow, she said.

They kept pressing her for evidence of other damage. The more they pushed, the more bleak details she gave them, all weighted with her stubborn sense of fairness and the experience of impotence in the face of wrong. She told, for example, of the time at Spofford when an assistant supervisor smacked her in the face and split her lip.

How did that come about? they wanted to know.

She and the other girls had tried to go to the office to speak to a supervisor about a counselor who kept cutting their recreation short, but the assistant supervisor stopped them in the hallway.

"One of the girls had snuck by him to go in the office and he picked her up and threw her on her back. She had just had an operation——she didn't *just* have an operation, but she had a pin in her back——and I went to pick her up because she was in pain, and he slapped me in my face."

"Did he say anything?"

"He said, 'Didn't I tell you to get over there?' I said, 'She is hurting. Furthermore, you are not supposed to put your hand on us.' "

That was Shirley, all right, Lowry thought——the mix of impulsiveness and self-possession, the defiance that sprang from some innate, un-crushed sense of human entitlement and that so often got her into trouble. What a waste of potential, the lawyer thought, as she had so many times before, listening to kids who had grown up lost in the system.

To Shirley, the opposing lawyers seemed strangely ignorant about life inside an institution. How could other students attack her at school? one asked after she described an incident in which she'd been jumped by a gang of girls at Holy Cross. Where were the teachers? "Teachers were getting beat up just like the average kids," she told them. She had to explain solitary, too.

"There was no window, just sort of an open room with screens?" Lorna Goodman asked. She sounded slightly incredulous.

"Yes."

"Any heat in the room?

"No."

"What time of year was it?"

"Winter. Winter—all year round, same thing."

GOODMAN PRESSED HARDEST on the question of irreparable harm. How had Shirley been injured by the failure of the staff at Holy Cross to give her birth-control devices? she asked at one point. "Did you get pregnant because of that?"

"No."

Then how had she been injured?

"Because I had asked them that because I wanted to protect myself. When I asked them why I couldn't get birth control, they told me, because it was Catholic, and I told them that even [so] I am not Catholic, if I go off campus, on my own time—"

"I understand that," Goodman broke in impatiently, "but how—"

Lowry stopped her. "Would you not interrupt the witness when she is trying to answer your question!" Shirley smothered a grin. She loved having this fierce advocate at her side. "Marcia's a bitch in court," she would inform someone gleefully later.

"She is not being responsive to my question," Goodman complained. She asked again. Once more, slowly, Shirley tried to explain.

"I wasn't injured in no way physically, but I felt that in another way, I did [get injured]."

"What other way?

"I felt that they—because of the place being Catholic, by me being Baptist, I felt they was wrong to deny me because I really did want it at that time."

Why, asked Kevin Simmons, whose Catholic clients included Pius XII–Holy Cross Campus, had she needed birth control there in the first place?

"I didn't want no more kids," she replied evenly.

Even after establishing that she had had sex on campus, he demanded to know how often sexual relations had occurred. When Lowry objected, he insisted that the question was relevant because "the extent of the relations would somewhat establish the need for the birth-control devices."

"Once is enough, according to what I learned," Lowry countered with pointed sarcasm. "I don't know. Maybe it's different at Pius, but that is what I learned."

"You might be right," Simmons allowed.

AND MAYBE NOT SO RIGHT AFTER ALL, Marcia Lowry thought later. She had always been quite clear that she herself wouldn't have a child. "Marcia doesn't like children except as a class," her aunt, a flinty matrimonial lawyer, would explain to those who wondered why. But before her wedding to Fritz Mosher, who had three grown sons from his first marriage, she had warned him that she might want to have a child after all. He was worried but willing. Now, at nearly forty, she had decided to have a baby. The fear that she had come around to the idea too late was a strange counterpoint to some of the questions and answers heard in the conference room that day.

The interrogation had started slowly. Shirley Wilder's name, age, and address; her occupation.

"How many children do you have?"

"One."

"What is the child's name?

"His name is Lamont."

"How old is Lamont?"

"He is six years old."

"Where is Lamont living?"

"I don't know. . . . He is in foster care."

Had it troubled Shirley to say that? Perhaps so. After the deposition, she asked Marcia Lowry to try to find out what had become of her son. She had never wanted to give him up, never consented to his adoption. In her vague account of what had gone wrong, it seemed almost as though somewhere along the way, he had just been misplaced.

TWO

L IKE A BABY DROPPED ON A DOORSTEP, LAMONT WAS SCOOPED up by the Sisters of Charity until something else could be arranged. The order's New York Foundling Hospital was the only institution Sheltering Arms found willing to take a black, Protestant, six-year-old fire-setter with no family.

It was understood that this would be a strictly temporary placement while Sheltering Arms pursued referrals to long-term residential treatment centers. But for now Lamont had a bed. He would join fourteen other children in what Foundling called Blaine Hall, an apartmentlike residential diagnostic unit for emotionally disturbed children aged five to ten. It had only recently been opened on the ninth floor of Foundling's main building, a big brick edifice on Third Avenue and Sixty-eighth Street in Manhattan.

Sister Theresa Kelly, the tenderhearted and strong-willed nun who ran Blaine Hall, was determined to teach these children, nearly all of them poor, that you didn't have to be rich to be neat and clean or to keep a nice home. Sometimes the city's child welfare auditors complained that the quarters were kept a little *too* neat and clean to reflect good child-care practices, but Sister Theresa felt that part of the staff's task was teaching these children how to live in a proper home, where beds were made every morning and people did not put their shoes on the couch or punch holes in the wall. For a play yard they had Central Park, four long blocks to the west, to which they were walked nearly every day.

Blaine Hall had a supervising psychiatrist as well as the services of psychiatric fellows from St. Vincent's Hospital, which had no children's psychiatric ward of its own and welcomed the teaching opportunity. But at age forty-seven, Sister Theresa didn't need a psychiatrist to tell her what ailed most of the children who came through the doors.

They were heartbroken, she told people. They missed their mothers. They all loved their mothers, no matter what. Right away she had realized that the ones who were dragged in kicking and wailing did better than those who stayed dry-eyed, carefully examining the bedspreads and the sunny dining room and declaring Blaine Hall a nice place to live. Invariably, the ones who didn't cry were children who had already been through the foster-care mill. She rarely knew the details of their histories, but some had such a buried store of anger, guilt, and anxiety from past losses that they were afraid to give in to their feelings at all or, worse, had disconnected them. She was always ready when they broke, taking even the biggest boy on her lap and holding him close to her bosom while he cried, rocking him through his great keening sobs like a toddler.

She had been a "baby nurse" for five years in the booming Foundling nurseries of the 1950s before joining the Sisters of Charity herself at twenty-three and becoming a teacher. Much later, reading the classic studies of maternal deprivation in young children by the British psychoanalyst John Bowlby, she recalled the staff shortages of those days uneasily. More than three hundred healthy babies were in the nurseries then, and many stayed for more than a year, fed by a changing cast of teenaged child-care students, nuns, and volunteers.

The care of babies born out of wedlock had been a proud part of Foundling's identity ever since Sister Mary Irene Fitzgibbon took in the first abandoned infant from the doorstep of her Twelfth Street convent mission on October 11, 1869. The nuns of the Foundling, dedicated to preserving the reputations of young unwed mothers as well as to preventing infanticide, placed a crib in the vestibule of its first asylum building so infants could be left "without inquiry or observation."

Police statistics and other data from that time show that more than 990 infants per year were being abandoned in the city's streets by their parents. The upper class blamed the immigrants who are now enshrined as the hardworking great-grandparents of American self-sufficiency. "It is they who leave babies at other people's doors; who expose them in the street; who abandon them to neglect, or even murder them to avoid the expense or trouble of taking care of them," Junius Henri Browne wrote in his popular book *The Great Metropolis,* in 1869.

The immigrant poor of Browne's day were overwhelmingly Irish Catholics. Between 1854 and 1860, an average of 69 percent of relief recipients and almshouse residents were Irish, as were half the residents in the city's lunatic asylum and most of those in jail. In a period when African Americans did not figure at all in concerns about poverty, it seemed obviously to native-born reformers that Irish destitution and dependency were caused by deeply ingrained cultural shortcomings, if not by outright "racial" inferiority. They were quick to view Catholicism as part of the problem. After the 1863 draft riots, both church and city money flowed to Catholic endeavors that promised to rescue and discipline the next generation.

The evidence that foundling homes were unhealthy for children mounted during New York Foundling's first decade, when more than half of its babies died each year despite the Sisters' policy of encouraging mothers to stay and nurse their own and one other. In response, Sister Mary Irene devised what has been called the city's first foster boarding-home program, an elaborate system of wet-nurse homes for up to fifteen hundred Foundling babies under the age of three. A daily allotment of thirty-eight cents per child, financed through city taxes, allowed poor nursing mothers of all religions and races to perform wage work without leaving home by breast-feeding Foundling babies along with their own. Although some foster mothers begged to adopt the children they had nursed, they were not allowed to do so. At age three the children had to be returned to the institution, which sent many on to distant homes by orphan train.

There were never enough wet nurses to meet the demand. As the Foundling grew to house over two thousand young children, more of them continued to die each year than were discharged. By the 1880s, physicians in New York realized that the problem went beyond the lack of safe artificial formula and the inadequacy of nineteenth-century medicine in the face of contagious disease. Even when mothers were unable to nurse and had to bottle-feed their infants, for example, nearly 80 percent of those babies survived, compared to less than 25 percent of children bottle-fed without their mothers, physicians at the public Infant's Hospital observed in 1883. The more the physical care of babies in all institutions improved, the more obvious it became that lack of maternal nurturing also imperiled their healthy development. Yet institutional pride, religious and ethnic loyalty, shortages of foster homes or fear of their inadequate supervision, and the demand caused by the absence of public relief in the homes of the New York City poor between 1875 and 1931 all kept institutions open. As late as the 1920s, for instance, the administration of the Home for Hebrew Infants was embarrassed but defensive when critics described the average three-year-old raised in that institution as "lacking even the elementary knowledge of the normal eighteen-month-old baby in the poorest home; completely apathetic, or else so desperate in his need for affection and attention that the average adult could not handle his problems." Psychiatric studies undertaken in the 1930s and 1940s told the same sad story, and in 1952, Bowlby published the first of his seminal articles about the long-term negative effects of maternal deprivation.

But in those days, Foundling could do no wrong. It was the favorite charity of Cardinal Francis J. Spellman, which assured that it was also the favorite charity of many of the city's rich and powerful. In 1958 Cardinal Spellman gave Foundling a new $11 million building, debt free, with baby nurseries on every one of its eleven floors. Not until 1980 did city officials become insistent: healthy babies did not belong in an institutional nursery, no matter how well it was staffed. The nuns reluctantly closed the last baby nursery and opened Blaine Hall in its place.

In 1980, concern about the psychological perils of institutions for young children was refreshed by the publication of the last volume of Bowlby's three-part opus on childhood mourning, *Attachment and Loss*. One of the book's classic anecdotes was about Reggie, a two-and-a-half-year-old who had already lost a number of mother figures while growing up in a wartime residential nursery in Hampstead, England. When a nurse to whom Reggie had become attached left to get married, he was reported to be "lost and desperate." When the same nurse returned a fortnight later, he refused to look at her, though he gazed longingly at the door when she left again. Later he was heard to remark, "My very own Mary-Ann! But I don't like her."

After repeated, unresolved losses, such a child would react with intense anxiety and intense anger to the prospect of a new attachment. This was what Bowlby called the anger of despair, which eventually supplanted "the anger of hope" in a child who had experienced terror that he would have no one left to care for him. Bereaved older children were also vulnerable to such despair and anger, especially when they felt pressure from new caretakers to "forget" their grief. Overactivity and aggressiveness in response to loss almost always reflected the child's hidden sense of guilt for being in some part responsible, Bowlby suggested—a guilt often based on a thoughtless comment by a distraught parent, rather than on some deeply harbored hostility, as traditional Freudians assumed.

The children of Blaine Hall were the walking wounded of such traumas. Less often acknowledged was that placement there inflicted additional injury. Officially, the purpose of the program was diagnosis and planning, but most children stayed for at least a year. Sister Theresa, who made it her mission to bond with every child, felt torn when her charges left. Just mentioning a favorite child's recent departure to an acquaintance, the nun would sometimes feel her hazel eyes fill with tears. "My Craig," she would say softly. "My Ruby Lee." She kept snapshots of some of them for years, not knowing whether they were dead or alive.

But Lamont's picture was not among these. If he ever cried in Sister Theresa's arms, his tears were forgotten among so many others'. His stay lasted two months, and during that time Sheltering Arms took him for preplacement interviews at Children's Village in Dobbs Ferry, at St. Agatha's in Nanuet, and at several other far-flung residential programs. One day near his seventh birthday, in 1981, he learned that he would be leaving Blaine Hall. Lucky boy, Sister Theresa told him, he was going to the Astor Home for Children! It was a beautiful place in the countryside, one hundred miles away.

What Lamont would remember most vividly about Foundling was a view from a high window, and an image of himself alone, looking down on a green place that he thought was Central Park. In fact, what he would have seen from the Foundling was only the manicured median of Park Avenue, where the tulips had already bloomed and been discarded to make room for another row of plants.

THREE

BURT AND HELEN NEUBORNE QUICKLY REALIZED THEY WERE the only guests for dinner at Fritz Schwarz's Riverside Drive apartment. Marian—"Min"—Schwarz served something uncomplicated buffet-style, and the two couples ate casually, balancing plates on their knees.

It was the last evening of June 1983, and the Hudson River view was still luminous when Fritz Schwarz finally brought up the *Wilder* case. Helen and Min, who worked in overlapping provinces of the Koch administration, had carried their conversation into the kitchen with the dishes. The two men were finishing their beer.

Technically they were adversaries. The year before, Frederick A. O. Schwarz, Jr., had become the city's corporation counsel—Ed Koch's lawyer, as he sometimes put it. Burt Neuborne had become legal director of the ACLU at about the same time, inheriting a roster of well-entrenched lawsuits against the city. None was older or more acrimonious than *Wilder*. After months of nonstop discovery and grueling interrogatories, the ten-year-old case was now only weeks away from trial. Neuborne knew that Marcia Lowry and her team were deep in the final throes of trial preparation. But it didn't take much of an invitation from Fritz Schwarz for him to step back and take the long view. Yes, he agreed, this might be a case better settled than tried.

"We both had a sense that this was a case that had outlasted the capacity of courts to resolve it in an equitable way," Neuborne would say later. "If the thing went on, all it would mean was more bitterness, more anger. But would the kids be better off? Would the city be better off? Would the ACLU be better off? My intuition told me that if a serious set of negotiations could ensue in which the city would not be nitpicking and we would not leave a hole where the system used to be, a settlement meant a better chance for improvement than a trial."

Schwarz had thought hard about the values at stake in the case, and in his disarmingly direct way, he outlined his conclusions. On the one hand, he could not see the city giving up the use of the religious organizations, he said. He believed they provided good care, on average, and better care than the government itself was providing (though in scrupulous fairness, he noted that this might be because the government took the most difficult kids). It wasn't that he was unwilling to oppose the religious interests; indeed, he would soon be fighting the hierarchy of the Catholic Church on the politically combustible issue of job discrimination against gays in city contracts. But he was convinced that it would be utterly disruptive and harmful to children to purge the hundred-year-old foster-care system of its religious agencies.

On the other hand, Schwarz was persuaded that, intentional or not, there was something wrong with a system that didn't give black children equal access to care. No issue resonated more with him than what he saw as the system's real racial unfairness. That the courts had elected to do nothing with the case for so long was to him an institutional failure: people had simply lacked the courage to deal with it. He and Neuborne had a chance to do better.

That was what made Fritz Schwarz unique among government lawyers, Neuborne thought. He was so open and honest in his approaches and so anxious to do justice that you could do business with him in a way that you couldn't with anybody else. You could trust that it wasn't a ploy, that he really wanted a just resolution of the issues. You could trust that he meant what he said—and that he had the authority and the stature to carry it out.

"If you guys will back off that part of the complaint that says the religious agencies have to go, we will address the questions of care and access," Schwarz told Neuborne.

Within the few minutes it took for nightfall to darken the Hudson, the two men had sketched a framework of principles for a possible settlement.

"I can't do this unless Marcia agrees," Neuborne cautioned at one point. That was understood, Schwarz replied. Just as Neuborne had to talk to Lowry, he had to talk to the mayor and make sure he was aboard.

The scaffolding erected by the two men that night encompassed all the key elements necessary for a final stipulation. That, surely, was part of Fritz Schwarz's extraordinary appeal: his invitation to act, however low-key in manner, was like a summons to make history. Their battalions of opposing lawyers might be caught up in the heat of battle, eager for hand-to-hand combat after a decade mired in trench warfare, but, Schwarz seemed to say, he and Neuborne were statesmen. They alone had the perspective needed to shape a just peace.

F. A. O. SCHWARZ JUNIOR's family name was synonymous with the glorious excess of a Victorian toy emporium. But with his spare, Lincoln-esque frame, his mismatched, rumpled clothing and haphazard haircuts, the man had the same aura of austere authenticity as the Shaker furniture he collected. Schwarz was apt to protest mildly that the mayor always thought he was much richer than he really was. But he took pride in a family heritage that exemplified the potent American cross between entrepreneurial capitalism and religious freedom. His ancestry included the spiritual leaders of the *Mayflower* and of the Huguenots who fled French persecution, as well as a Dutch merchant family of early New York City and the Westphalian toy-store founder Frederick August Otto Schwarz, who came to America in 1848.

The law, too, was part of family tradition. His father had been not just any lawyer, but a revered senior partner in Davis, Polk & Wardwell. Fritz, the oldest of five children, consciously modeled himself on his father, and his *father* modeled himself on John W. Davis, the superb gentleman advocate who headed his law firm. Every Christmas afternoon of the five years before his death in 1955, Davis paid a call to the Schwarz family's house at 8 East Ninety-third Street. He was a very handsome man, six feet tall, with a full head of silver hair and an ability to quote as fluently from the Koran or the Talmud as from the Bible or Charles Dickens. When Fritz Schwarz knew him, Davis was in his late seventies and still at the very peak of his professional powers. His most celebrated defeat came later, in the last of his 180 appearances before the Supreme Court, in *Brown* v. *Board of Education*.

Four states were defending their segregation laws against the NAACP's onslaught in *Brown*: Kansas, Virginia, Delaware, and South Carolina. Davis was the voice of South Carolina—the same South Carolina where Shirley Wilder's forebears had picked cotton outside the schoolhouse door. "Let me say this for the State of South Carolina," Davis said in his fervent oral argument. "It did not come here . . . in sackcloth and ashes. . . . It is convinced that the happiness, the progress, and the welfare of these children is best promoted in segregated schools." The 1954 *Brown* decision devastated Davis, and he died soon afterward at his South Carolina vacation retreat, having graciously declined a twenty-five-thousand-dollar fee from the state and accepted instead a sterling-silver tea service.

In 1957, Fritz Schwarz wrote his senior honors thesis at Harvard College on John W. Davis. His essay, which focused on Davis's earlier career, was far more an appreciation than a critique. By the time Schwarz reached his last year at Harvard Law School, he was passionately interested in civil rights. In February and March of 1960, he and his classmate Bernard Nussbaum organized a picket line outside the Woolworth's in Cambridge, in support of the Woolworth lunch-counter sit-ins by black students in Greensboro, North Carolina. After clerking for a judge of the Second Circuit in New York City, he seized the opportunity to spend a year working in Nigeria on the implementation of that newly independent state's constitution. On his return, he was invited to join his father's firm. He declined. Instead, he joined the only law firm in the city arguably more prestigious, more corporate, and more conservative than Davis, Polk: Cravath, Swaine & Moore. In retrospect, it was all part of the complicated balance he had attained: maintaining respect for and from his father's world while working to change it in his own way.

When Ed Koch first invited him to take the post of corporation counsel, Schwarz made sure Koch knew where he stood; he spent much of their breakfast meeting arguing cogently against the death penalty, which the mayor supported, and discussing the dangers of racial divisiveness. The Koch Fritz Schwarz knew was so attuned to public opinion that he could reposition himself several times a day, adapting to breaking news cycles with no more embarrassment than a surfer riding the next wave. He was often self-indulgent and self-absorbed. But Schwarz accepted these characteristics as inseparable from some of Koch's best qualities: his buoyant optimism, his fervor for New York City, his common touch.

The New York City Law Department's 502 lawyers made the law firm the second-largest in the world under one roof (the first was the federal

Department of Justice); its cases involved the most volatile issues in urban America. The city was the defendant in many class-action suits brought by the public-interest bar. But Schwarz, who had helped the U.S. Senate investigate illegal CIA and FBI practices in the 1970s and worked for corporate clients in the early 1980s, never doubted that he could honorably serve both Koch and the public good.

"I believe in the redemption of people," Fritz Schwarz would later tell an oral historian who interviewed members of the Koch administration. "I believe in the power of logic. And I believe in keeping trying."

Those lines could have been the peroration of one of the upbeat speeches Burt Neuborne had begun giving at CLU offices around the country. "It is as important to be a civil-liberties lawyer in a period when the wind is blowing against you as it is when you're winning," he advised discouraged staff attorneys. "Because when good times come again, the point of departure for progress is defined by how much ground you held."

Many of the men and women in the CLU offices had chosen their life's work in the 1960s, when the courts seemed a shortcut to social justice. This was the generation that had seen sixty years of Jim Crow laws overruled in a day.

Neuborne had been a thirteen-year-old New York boy visiting Charleston, South Carolina, on May 17, 1954, the day the U.S. Supreme Court's decision in *Brown* v. *Board of Education* was announced. His father, a stubborn, self-taught radical who worked in the garment industry, had taken Burt south with him on a cloth-buying trip. Seeing the news printed inside a black border of mourning in the Charleston paper, Neuborne felt the power of the Court's pronouncement as something biblical, like a great prophetic voice of moral truth that had changed the world forever. Neuborne's father wanted him to be a labor lawyer, however, and when he went to Harvard Law School in 1961, that was his intention. Instead, bitterly disappointed in the unions' regression on race, and eager to impress his upwardly mobile in-laws, he went straight from graduation to a Wall Street firm to plan estates for the very rich. It was his wife, Helen, who told him he hadn't been put on Earth to make rich people richer. He arranged his departure for the New York Civil Liberties Union in 1967 as a one-year leave of absence, but kept renewing it year after year.

By the early 1980s, civil-liberties lawyers were losing more cases than they won, and even their victories came in rearguard actions, not in trail-blazing. They had discovered that the real name of the game was compliance. Implementation was where the grass retook the road. The more a court decision seemed to change the status quo, the more powerful the inertial drag of institutional resistance.

But unlike many of his peers, Neuborne had not suffered a crisis of confidence when the zeitgeist changed. During a sabbatical year in France in 1980–81, after five years as a professor at New York University Law School, he realized that as a civil-liberties lawyer, he was an existentialist. French philosophy since World War II had struggled with the difficulty of living a rational life in an irrational world. The American equivalent, he decided, was the dilemma of the lawyer who knew that it was impossible to do substantial justice in a society beset by economic inequality. He could cynically choose to make as much money as he could and just forget that the system was unjust, or he could act as though justice were possible. As civil-liberties lawyers, he believed, he and his colleagues were called upon "to make a life knowing rationally that perfect justice is impossible but refusing to acknowledge in our hearts that it can't be achieved."

MARCIA LOWRY'S LAWSUIT had already created the conditions for change, Neuborne thought. He knew next to nothing about foster care, but to him the proof lay in Fritz Schwarz's interest in settling *Wilder*. As for concessions on the use of religious agencies, he had never seen the church-state issues as central to the case; to his mind, they were simply constitutional handles for grappling with the real issue of racial discrimination. "Congress shall make no law respecting an establishment of religion, or prohibiting the free exercise thereof," the First Amendment said. But the twin clauses did not hold equal appeal for Neuborne; unlike so many of his ACLU colleagues, he could never get excited about the establishment clause. Every year, when the crèche cases came around, he argued about this with Norman Dorsen, Lowry's old mentor at NYU Law School and chairman of the ACLU board. Dorsen claimed Neuborne was soft on religion. "I didn't take this job to stamp out the Virgin Mary," Neuborne would retort.

And then, too, there were practical advantages to settlement. Looking hard at the ACLU's docket, Neuborne had noted that the impending trial of the ten-year-old case promised to be a drain on the organization's resources for years to come—and in more than the obvious ways. Traditionally, many of the CLU's donors were Jewish. The rise of the Right in the early eighties had brought in more members than were lost by the Skokie, Illinois, episode of 1978, in which the ACLU defended the free-speech rights of American Nazis to march through a community of Holocaust survivors. But *Wilder* had always been intensely unpopular with the organized Jewish groups; a full-fledged trial could only reignite smoldering unhappiness about a case that threatened to pit blacks and Jews against one another. Neuborne was far too principled to ever argue that the ACLU should abandon the case on such grounds. But these realities were part of the context that made Schwarz's overture attractive—so attractive, indeed, that Neuborne began to believe the rapprochement had been a mutual idea, maybe even his own idea, arising by chance from a social encounter. That was how he would present it to Marcia Lowry.

IN FACT, SCHWARZ HAD INVITED the Neubornes to dinner with the deliberate plan of launching a settlement of *Wilder*. The most basic problem was that the city might lose the whole foster-care system at trial on establishment-clause grounds—Judge Ward had hinted as much. Schwarz himself had concluded that black children had become majority entrants into a system dominated by agencies that didn't fully accept them. Socially and legally, he felt, it was important to find a race-neutral way to equalize admissions.

He invited Gail Kong, the latest head of the city's child welfare administration, out to his country house in Westchester to sound her out informally about the state of foster care. They swam in the family pool and sat out in the sun talking. Soon he had her pouring out her frustrations with the system she had taken over the year before. Schwarz quickly realized that in much the same way he responded to the race question, she was troubled—no, furious—that the agencies had been able to thumb their noses at her as she tried to impose some standards on their operations. The ones being hurt, she said, were the children in care.

The conversation only confirmed his determination to settle *Wilder*.

FOUR

Settling *Wilder* was the furthest thing from Marcia Lowry's mind that summer. She was working as hard as she ever had in her life, with a baby at home and two trials on the way.

In the end, it had taken only five months for her to conceive, though it seemed like forever at the time. Then, in her fifth month of pregnancy, she had almost miscarried.

Had she been working too hard? She was guilt-stricken but unable to cut back, and pregnancy won her no concessions. Litigating a class action in New Mexico that spring, feeling huge and exhausted at the end of a long day, she had responded to the judge's question about scheduling from her seat. The judge barked, "Ms. Lowry, unless your condition precludes it, you will rise to address this court!" She was up like a shot.

She did stop flying in her eighth month, after a particularly harrowing landing in a commuter plane. She became so fanatical about eating right that she passed up green tea ice cream at a Chinese restaurant for fear that it might contain caffeine. But she kept working until her due date. After two weeks of impatient waiting at home, she let the doctor schedule a C-section, and went into labor the next morning.

Avram Lev Robinson-Mosher was born on May 15, 1982, weighing an ounce shy of nine pounds. Lowry wasn't just maternal; she was mesmerized. The surprise, to her, was how interested one could be by things that were inherently uninteresting. The baby moved his arm! The baby yawned! It wasn't as though she were reading his Ph.D. thesis, she joked, and yet she couldn't have been more impressed if she were. She and Fritz Mosher both took parental leaves. They bought a country house in Warwick, a small, isolated town in unfashionable Rockland County, and spent most of the summer there in thrall to the baby.

Intellectually, Lowry believed, she had always understood the parent-child bond. How could anyone who had been a child fail to understand how special that relationship was? Once, during a case in the midseventies, the judge had interrupted her passionate argument to ask if she had children herself. When she said no, he remarked that she was extraordinarily engaged for someone who wasn't a parent. He apparently meant it as a compliment, but she resented it almost as much as the cheap rebuttal some people used in debate: "Well, how would YOU know? You don't have children." The judge had gone on to rule against her and her plaintiff, a poor, incompetent, but loving mother who had lost thirteen children to city shelters without officialdom lifting a finger to help her raise them right.

No, if having Avi made a difference to her advocacy, it was not to change her judgments but to sharpen the feelings that surrounded them. Above all, it made the relentless delays of the legal process more excruciating. The autumn after Avi's birth, one of the new cases she took on was a U.S. Supreme Court appeal of a Texas case that centered on a baby girl born eighteen months before her son. As her own baby smiled, babbled to his toes, and called out to her in the middle of the night, she had a new, visceral understanding of how much time was passing in the life of that other baby.

The ACLU's client was the baby's unwed father, who had been denied parental rights to his daughter under one of those indefensible statutes that made the Texas Family Code so notorious. On the facts and the law, it was a wonderful case, Lowry had thought when she first read the trial record. The father, Don Kirkpatrick, a twenty-five-year-old Nebraska man who lived with his parents and two sisters on the family farm, had tried everything to do right by his baby girl. He asked the teenage mother to marry him as soon as he found out she might be pregnant, but her parents refused permission and instead sent her to the Christian Homes for unwed mothers in Abilene. He tried to pay her expenses there, sent her money, wrote her letters, and when he learned that she planned to relinquish the baby for adoption, told her he wanted to raise the child himself. When Christian Homes and the mother filed a petition to free the baby for adoption, he cross-filed to "legitimate" his daughter under Texas law and win custody.

"All I can say is I love my daughter and I want her, and she's blood, and I just can't see letting her go when I want to raise her myself," the father had said at the trial, after driving all night to get there. His parents came, too, to testify that they would help raise their granddaughter. The baby's sixteen-year-old unwed mother acknowledged that Kirkpatrick was "a wonderful man . . . a good man, a hard worker," but she thought he wouldn't be as good for the baby as two adoptive Christian parents. He was often unclean after working in the fields, she told the county court; he smoked, sometimes used bad language, and lacked her religious conviction. She had been adopted herself, and she said she knew the stigma suffered by an illegitimate child. As though to drive home the point, her father testified that the return of her baby to the same small town where they all lived would be an embarrassment to the family.

Without any evidence that Kirkpatrick was an unfit parent, the court had found it in the baby's best interest to terminate all parental rights, and appointed Christian Homes to place her for adoption. The Texas appellate court had upheld the finding, citing an earlier decision that equated unwed fathers with "sperm donor[s], rapist[s], hit and run lover[s], adulterer[s], or the like, or, at best, [men] disinterested in their children." The Texas Supreme Court had affirmed the appellate decision without comment.

"This case poses with special poignancy an unsettled constitutional question of extraordinary importance which this Court has frequently noted, but never squarely confronted," Lowry wrote in her petition for a writ of certiorari. "What is the minimum substantive standard pursuant to which a State may terminate a parent-child relationship?"

A spate of recent Supreme Court decisions weighed heavily against the constitutionality of the Texas statute on both equal-protection and due-process grounds. The majority opinion by Justice Powell in *Caban* v. *Mohammed* (1979) could have been written for Don Kirkpatrick. It dismissed the argument that the legal distinctions could be justified by a fundamental difference between maternal and paternal relations, and it found no "substantial relation" between the state's interest in encouraging adoptions and a legal framework that made it easy to dismiss fathers.

Typing her brief late into the night as Avi and his father slept, Lowry even had the bittersweet pleasure of citing her own defeat in *Smith* v. *OFFER* in the list of cases showing the Court's long-standing view of the parent-child bond as "a fundamental human relationship with which the state may interfere only when it asserts a powerful justification and then only in the least intrusive manner." How gratifying it would be to balance the *OFFER* defeat—still her only Supreme Court case—with a resounding victory. And it looked as though she couldn't lose this one.

As expected, the Supreme Court granted cert. But as if they were saying to Texas, "You don't really mean this, do you?" the justices then sent the case back to the lower court. The Texas Supreme Court, defiantly committed to its statute, offered no saving interpretation of the law but ruled against Don Kirkpatrick again anyway.

It all took a lot of time. The baby, now two, was in an adoptive home, and Lowry's fight for visitation by the father had failed. Sure, they could knock out the Texas statute on a renewed appeal, and she would have her Supreme Court victory. But what about the child?

Lowry brooded about the disregard for children endemic in a system where adults had rights and children had only "needs" and "interests." She agonized over the Texas case with her colleague Michael Mushlin, who would later become dean of Pace Law School. "The kid is just too old," he heard her say. "It wouldn't be right."

Her concern for this one child in Texas made an indelible impression on Mushlin. When he started at the Children's Rights Project, in 1980, some of Lowry's bitterest adversaries had warned him that her cause wasn't children at all; it was Marcia Lowry. As the *Wilder* case heated up, he saw opposing counsel treat her as a kind of monster of self-aggrandizement. How wrong they were, he thought. Winning a case in the U.S. Supreme Court was the greatest high a lawyer could have, but she was ready to let it go rather than harm this child who had no official claim on her advocacy. Yes, she was driven, but to say that she was driven by ego was just silly. "She has real devotion," he told people. "She's a reformer. She believes passionately in what she's doing."

Despite what she said privately to Mushlin about her own misgivings in the *Kirkpatrick* case, Lowry always saw the decision not to pursue the appeal as Don Kirkpatrick's.

"What should I do?" he asked her. He was married now, and his wife was expecting. He wanted to keep fighting for his daughter, but he was deeply troubled about whether it was the right thing to do for the child. The counseling he'd sought from his minister had been inconclusive. He wanted advice from his lawyer.

He'd probably win in the end, she told him, but his daughter might be six or seven before he saw her for the first time. Like him, she said, she was troubled by the effect on the child. He did have other options. They could try to reach a settlement.

It was painful for Kirkpatrick, but he decided that was his best choice. In the settlement, he agreed to let his daughter stay with her adoptive parents. He wrote his child a letter, and the adoptive parents agreed to give it to her no earlier than her sixteenth birthday and no later than the day she turned eighteen. In careful words, he explained the circumstances of her placement, told her where he lived, and that he would love to have a relationship with her if she wanted it. It would be up to her.

FIVE

CHARTS SCRAWLED IN MAGIC MARKER COVERED THE WALLS of Lowry's office, the *Wilder* war room where they were plotting the lineup of lawyers and witnesses for the first ten days of trial testimony. Documents spilled from the sagging couch onto the floor. The detritus of too many long nights had come to rest on the sooty windowsills: cardboard coffee cups, a sticky plastic spoon, candy wrappers.

It was Wednesday, July 27, 1983. The trial was still set to start on Monday, August 1. A few days earlier Gerald Bodell, one of the lawyers for the defense, had asked for a postponement. "Absolutely not," Judge Ward told him. "I'm not postponing this for anything."

Once, right after Avi's birth, Lowry had dreamed that her office had vanished and there was no room left for her at the ACLU. But in her waking life she found no need to choose between her old identity and motherhood—and no possibility of making such a choice, either. Working toward the *Wilder* trial meant total immersion. The case was more than her crusade, Michael Mushlin sometimes said: the case was Marcia herself. Yet when she was with Avi, she was still entranced by every sound and movement he made. At fifteen months, her son still didn't sleep through the night. It was a source of amusement to her friends that the hard-nosed litigator had never been able to let her baby cry, not even for the five minutes necessary to win an uninterrupted night of rest. His fascination with the world was such a delight to her that she was almost glad to stumble out of bed for a wee-hours tête-à-tête, knowing her work would keep her at the office late the next day. It wasn't guilt; she had hired Mattie, an older black woman with years of experience as a baby nurse, while she was still pregnant. Since his birth, Mattie had always been there for Avi when his parents weren't. She was a thin, energetic woman of uncertain age and great wisdom who lived in the Amsterdam Houses, one of the better housing projects on the Upper West Side; sometimes Lowry and Mosher would pick her up there on the way back from a family weekend in Warwick and drive her downtown to their apartment on West Twelfth Street. Warm, patient, and voluble, she had held elaborate conversations with Avi before he could say a word. Now he babbled happily back.

In a kind of trance induced by lost sleep and adrenaline, Lowry had lurched from one interim deadline to the next: discovery, pretrial motions, the last date to submit expert reports. Now she and her team were laboring feverishly on the edifice of words and exhibits that they expected to present in court in less than five days' time. They had generated most of a 473-page document, "Proposed Findings of Fact," culled from thousands of pages of depositions, from cartons of coded case readings, from foster-care studies and commission reports and midnight arguments over the meaning of the numbers they'd wrested from the other side. It had been a chaotic production, accomplished on the cusp of the transition from typewriters to computers; the ACLU had no computer of its own, so to move a paragraph of text among the 1,578 findings, Lowry's secretary had to carry a disk off-site to a computer company that had made a machine available as part of a sales pitch. The finished document had to be submitted to the court no later than Friday.

ONLY TWO MONTHS BEFORE, the case had been in crisis. Their numbers wizard, Eli Gilbert, considered the statistical evidence for discrimination very strong, but Lowry believed that to win at trial they needed testimony from a nationally recognized statistician—from Stephan Michelson himself. Michelson was practically the inventor of forensic statistics in discrimination cases, and he had a long winning track record. Back in 1973, he had given Lowry's team some free help in drafting the list of documentary information to demand in *Wilder*'s first discovery phase. But he had declined to sign on as lead analyst back then because he deemed the budget for the job unrealistically meager. Now he was willing to testify as an expert witness, but he insisted on reanalyzing the ACLU's data from scratch. His draft report, when it arrived in late May, was cause for consternation. Powerfully supportive of *Wilder* in many respects, the report contained one finding that seriously undermined the plaintiffs' position: based on the most recent numbers available, Michelson said, there was no longer any statistical evidence of racial discrimination in the foster-care system's Catholic sector.

"This can't be right," Lowry had protested. "I don't believe it." They had spent all Memorial Day weekend brainstorming over the numbers in her colleague Chris Hansen's bachelor apartment, where the refrigerator held nothing but Pepsi Lite and the floor served as the only conference table. Eli Gilbert was there, too. It was one of the few times Gilbert went head to head against Lowry. "Marcia," he insisted, "this is what the data show."

Eventually Michelson himself flew in from Washington, D.C. He was an attractive, bearded man of forty-five who exuded self-confidence and still liked to list his two youthful blues guitar records on a résumé thick with academic publications and institutional affiliations: Stanford, the Brookings Institute, the Carnegie Corporation, Harvard.

Chris Hansen would tell the story later as an object lesson in why lawyers should not be awed by other professionals' expertise. "In the face of this very high-powered expert who was very certain of his results," he remembered, Lowry "was equally convinced that he was wrong, and if he was wrong, that it was our job to figure out *why* he was wrong. Marcia kept saying, 'I know this system. It's there, the case is there, we may not have found it, but it's there.'

"The meeting was all about, are we going to take Marcia's faith and keep pushing, or accept this expert's verdict? Marcia persuaded us to accept her vision, and she turned out to be right."

When one looked at the Catholic sector as a whole, as Michelson had, the proportions of black and Hispanic children now reflected the total foster-care population. But if one examined each agency separately, a very different picture would emerge. Reworking the data this way at Lowry's suggestion, Michelson found that children were clustered by race and religion in individual Catholic agencies and institutions, as though certain programs had been set aside for the diminishing number of white Catholics, others for Hispanics, and the rest for blacks. At the extremes, at a time when black Protestants made up 52.6 percent of the overall foster-care population, they accounted for less than 1 percent at

Madonna Heights, the place of Shirley Wilder's dreams, but 74 percent at Pius XII–Holy Cross Campus. In the middle of the spectrum were six New York Foundling programs, four with between 31 and 39 percent black Protestants, and the other two more than 64 percent black. Statistically, Michelson was now prepared to testify, such clustering was more than twice as prevalent as would be expected to happen by chance.

It was an exhilarating experience for them all, a turning point. Gilbert, who had argued so strongly against Lowry at Hansen's apartment, relished her vindication. Her self-confidence and tenacity had carried them through the crisis to a heady certainty: *Aha, we've got 'em.*

IT WAS LATE AFTERNOON, and the team had been working all day at organizing the trial. But everyone was too excited to be exhausted anymore. They were all high on the sense that they had a strong case, a good judge, and devastating evidence—that they were right and finally they were going to win this thing.

"We had invested so much in it," Mushlin would say later. "We were working together very well, we were having a ball, and we hated these people."

SMOLDERING ANIMOSITY had reached a new pitch during the discovery phase of *Wilder II.* The last unofficial settlement feelers from some of the defendants had only fanned the flames. In 1980, soon after Judge Ward made it clear that the lawsuit wasn't going to go away, Helen Buttenwieser had brokered a disastrous meeting between Sanford Solender, the executive vice president of the Federation of Jewish Philanthropies, and the ACLU team. It was practically an article of faith with Solender that the Jewish federation's affiliated agencies had the right to give preference to Jewish children and to offer them a Jewish experience. In a sense, he had grown up in Jewish institutions himself: Solender's mother and father had been cottage parents at the Hebrew Orphan Asylum's Pleasantville campus when he was born on the grounds in 1914, only two years after the place opened.

His father was a reformer who did not believe orphan asylums were good for children, and he had eventually closed several Hebrew orphanages in favor of foster-home placement programs, before moving on to direct YMHA centers in the community. Solender followed his father's lead into Jewish philanthropy (as his own son would later follow him), and for many years he had been director of the National Jewish Welfare Board, overseeing Jewish community centers, YMHAs, and the chaplaincy service in the armed forces, as well as sitting on key committees of the Jewish federation.

Solender championed a renewed federation emphasis on serving Jewish children in Jewish programs, and he had clashed repeatedly with Justine Wise Polier over the nondenominational direction of Louise Wise Services. After Polier refused to turn back from serving an increasingly non-Jewish, minority population, the federation slashed its modest contribution to the agency.

The Jewish federation did not exist to provide a general philanthropic service, Solender told the ACLU team. Its purpose was to support agencies that contributed to the continuity of the Jewish people. Nevertheless, without any ulterior interest in making religious conversions, high-quality Jewish child-care agencies were also helping many non-Jews, he noted. Surely this was voluntarism at its best, and should be preserved.

The underlying suggestion that Glasser detected was, Do what you want to the Catholics, but hold us harmless. This was absolutely no foundation for a settlement. Lowry, who made it a principle never to initiate settlement discussions in a class-action lawsuit, had been skeptical of Helen Buttenwieser's effort from the start. She and Glasser lost no time in disabusing Solender of his hope for a separate peace.

Solender became irritated, then accusatory. They were against voluntarism, he said. They were undermining democracy. They were engaged in an activity that threatened the survival of the Jewish people.

Glasser and Lowry were unsparing in their response to Solender. How could it be that the same folks who opposed parochial-school vouchers for Catholics wanted Jewish child-care agencies to keep taxpayer money and Jewish prerogatives, too? If they wanted to discriminate in favor of Jewish children, they should ask the Buttenwieser family to foot the bill, not the American public.

Brusquely, Solender dismissed them. There was no point in continuing this discussion, he said, his voice icy with contempt.

Antipathy seemed to color the entire case. Mushlin, an even-tempered, soft-spoken product of small-town southern life, felt that he had never before encountered from opposing counsel a hostility so unbounded by professional courtesy. After college at Vanderbilt and law school at the University of Chicago, Mushlin had worked for VISTA in the Harlem office of Legal Services and later served as head of Legal Aid's Prison Rights Project—hardly genteel environments. This was worse. On one occasion, at the start of one of the many all-day depositions, Mushlin warned the other side that he had to catch a 5:30 P.M. flight to Texas to be in court there the next morning. In any other case it would have been no problem, but this was *Wilder*. With Davis, Polk lawyers in the lead, the opposing counsel refused to adjourn the deposition and told him they were going to move to compel his presence, and would have him cited for contempt if he left.

Usually the anger came out in just such petty ways, but one deposition that winter brought the clash back into a larger perspective, as though a camera had suddenly pulled back to reveal that the two sides faced each other across a great divide of American history.

It was the deposition of Kenneth B. Clark, the black social psychologist who more than thirty years before, at Thurgood Marshall's urging, had carried his box of black and white dolls to a back-country school in Clarendon County, South Carolina, to demonstrate the psychic damage racial segregation did to black children. His doll studies might not meet current standards of research methodology, but they had won a pivotal footnote in the Supreme Court's decision in *Brown*, helping to overturn sixty years of "separate-but-equal" doctrine. Now Clark was a taxpayer plaintiff in *Wilder*, one of the official recipients of Davis, Polk's interrogatories and a signer of the voluminous answering papers mainly produced by Mushlin. The deposition took place in the offices of Robinson, Silverman, at 230 Park Avenue, a cupola-topped tower at East Forty-fifth Street, built in 1929 to symbolize the Vanderbilts' prosperous North Central Railroad.

Clark's connections to *Wilder*'s roots went back to long before *Brown*. His mother, an early shop steward in the International Ladies Garment Workers' Union, had been what he liked to call a one-woman social agency, taking in half a dozen unofficial foster children from their Harlem neighborhood at a time when virtually no private agency offered foster homes for "colored" children. In the early 1940s, Clark's wife, Mamie, then finishing her doctorate in psychology at Columbia, had worked as a volunteer in the psychiatric clinic that Justine Wise Polier helped establish in the Children's Court. The Clarks had become close friends of the Poliers', and their allies in the battle against racial and religious discrimination in services provided to poor children. At the end of World War II, when Judge Polier was decrying the lack of delinquency-prevention programs in Harlem, the Clarks tried to persuade old-line social-welfare agencies to expand into social work, psychological evaluation, and psychotherapy for Harlem kids. Universally rebuffed, the Clarks resolved to open their own clinic, Northside; it was to be the first integrated, nonsectarian child guidance center in the area.

By the time *Wilder* was filed, Clark was the head of the Metropolitan Applied Research Center (MARC), which he had founded in 1967 with money from the Field Foundation, whose board Polier was on. A 1974 research paper on discrimination in New York City foster care, produced under MARC auspices by sociologist Setsuko Matsunaga Nishi, found "drastic inequality by reason of race and religion" and concluded that "prompt and authoritative action is imperative for the restructuring of the system." That report had long been part of the *Wilder* arsenal.

The case was deeply congruent with the core conviction of Clark's professional life, that homogeneity—whether racial, religious, or cultural—was detrimental to human development and education. "I believe that variability is one of the facts of life, and if you don't teach people to cope with that, you're handicapping them," he had said in a 1976 interview with NYCLU staff to explore his possible testimony in *Wilder*. "The purpose of education is to help free the human mind from constricting parochialisms, tribalisms, and superstitions that give significance to [nonrelevant] variations among human beings. . . . I think the same disadvantages which were established and affirmed by the Supreme Court in *Brown* on the detriment inherent in racially homogeneous schools are to be found . . . in child-care agencies that are racially homogeneous."

"You don't fool the children," he added. "They know that this discriminatory pattern is operating."

Clark had concentrated his passionate activism on public education in New York City; the way he took its failures to heart was almost painful for his friends to see. By 1983, in a time of growing black separatism, the integrity of his life gave him an aura of tragic nobility.

"I remain an incorrigible integrationist," he was quoted as saying in an August 1982 *New Yorker* profile. "Or if you prefer, I remain a rigid, hardline integrationist."

Tom Aquilino, the Davis, Polk lawyer who led the deposition questioning, read this quotation aloud to Clark. "How do you, sir, describe the word *integrationist?*" he asked. "What does it mean to you?"

Clark was approaching seventy, a slender, almost elegant man of controlled intensity who chain-smoked throughout the deposition.

"*Integrationist* means to me that I do not believe in arbitrary, irrelevant distinctions," he started. "Basically what I mean by *integration* is what is promised by democratic society, what the Bill of Rights promised, what the Fourteenth Amendment promised: that there should be no discrimination among human beings based upon irrelevant qualities and characteristics. And I believe that color is irrelevant in terms of the potential of human beings in a society . . . to make constructive contributions to that society."

Aquilino was a man with a scholastic mind as sharp as his narrow shoulder blades. "Let me ask you this, if I may," he said. "The word *integration* appears in the field of mathematics, does it not?"

"Yes."

"In speaking of integration, do you ever think of it in terms of numbers?"

Before long, Aquilino had pulled Clark into abstract questions of percentages and disproportion, of "complete integration," and into the acknowledgment that no society he knew reflected it.

Lowry intervened. This extensive examination was inappropriate, she complained: Clark was here not as an expert but simply as a taxpayer plaintiff.

Aquilino was undeterred. He demanded to see a report Clark's private consulting firm had done for the Bermuda government on integrating government contracts; cross-questioned Clark about MARC's funding in the 1970s; and pressed him about his relationship with Judge Polier.

"She is a personal friend of mine," Clark said, "and her husband, Shad, was a member of my board at MARC before his death. These are people who share most, if not all—certainly not all, but most—of my values."

"Is Judge Polier engaged in any kind of project, to your knowledge, at this moment?"

Clark knew only vaguely—it was something to do with children that she and Marian Wright Edelman were doing together, involving "research and policy implications of children's rights and children's concerns."

"Which children's rights?"

"Children—they—I must tell you, one of the things I admire about people like Justine and Marian is they don't make distinctions about children. They are concerned with the welfare of children."

Again Lowry stepped in. She would not block the examination and was prepared to allow a lot of latitude, but Dr. Clark was a very busy man, she said, and "inquiry about what a personal friend of his is doing these days . . . is really bordering on impermissible infringement on his time. So I do mean we won't spend much time for such irrelevancies."

Peering over his spectacles, Aquilino gave her a tight-lipped smile and steeped his words in sarcasm: "I just want to say that was the first amusing statement I heard today. There may be more, I suspect, as we move along."

To Aquilino, it was *all* an irrelevancy, all an infringement on the time and money of the religious agencies that dealt day to day with the inevitable misery of the city and of the world. *Wilder* had become irrelevant back in 1974, when the three-judge court ruled that the New York state statute on religious placement was constitutional on its face. Lowry was a terrific advocate, he thought—smart, tough, unflappable. As for Kenneth Clark, he had no particular respect for the man, let alone any of the awe that he could see in the faces of the watching ACLU lawyers. "Kenneth Clark has made a living out of one case," he would say later. "He's not a heavyweight, but he's tried to act like one all his life—and why? Because of a footnote."

As Aquilino continued his examination, the surface of his perfectly courteous words bore the unmistakable slick of disdain.

"When you referred to children's rights, were you referring to legal rights, economic rights, cultural rights?"

"Human rights."

"Human rights?"

"Yes, the right to be respected and cared for."

"Respected and cared for?" Again the mocking echo, as though in disbelief.

"Yes."

And so it went, on and on. Questions about the early meetings on

Wilder and the funding of the Children's Rights Project, about Clark's income-tax returns and whether he had ever been subjected to an IRS audit.

Lowry was controlling anger now. "We object on the ground of relevance, and I direct him not to answer. . . . I think it is personal, and it is for the purpose of harassment and embarrassment."

Clark smiled at her. "I am not embarrassed at all," he said.

But the effort to humiliate him was far from over. Had he ever visited Angel Guardian Home? Astor Home? Any of the defendant agencies named in the suit in which he was a plaintiff? No. He had no personal knowledge of Sister Mary Chrysostom, Monsignor Edmund Fogarty, or Brother Robert Francene, did he? Yet they were just three among the many other unfamiliar people he was suing.

"Have you ever met Carol Parry?"

"That name—the name seems to be someone I might have met, but I can't tell you."

"But as you sit here today you are not able to describe for the record who Carol Parry is?"

No, he wasn't. Still Clark did not become defensive or lose his dignity. "Mr. Counsel," he said evenly at one point, "I joined in this because I have been concerned with the general problems which I break down into two major areas, namely, the use of public funds for sectarian child-care institutions, and the extent to which such institutions, with the use of public funds, are able to determine their intake and selection of children on terms other than the needs of those children. You know, there isn't anything else that I can say, and I certainly am not here—if you asked me a thousand more questions about specific schools or specific individuals I would not be able to answer them outside of this."

There was no legal requirement that Clark know the details of the case; as a taxpayer plaintiff, he only had to believe that the taxes he paid were being used for unconstitutional purposes—and he made it clear repeatedly that he did. But it was obvious to Aquilino that Clark's real role was to lend Lowry's lawsuit stature, and he wasn't going to miss the chance to cut him down to size. Naming the other plaintiffs slowly one by one, he had the satisfaction of making Clark say again and again that he could not recall if he had ever met or talked with them. Barry Parker . . . Shedrick Roberts . . . Sharon Rodwell . . . Shirley Wilder . . .

"I don't know Shirley Wilder except by name. It's been so many years. I don't think I—I don't remember. . . . This case has been going on for many, many years. . . . We thought the whole case was dead."

There was even a test of Clark's knowledge of New York's state constitution—"after all, he is a high-ranking official of the state of New York," Aquilino said when Lowry objected, referring to Clark's position on the state board of regents. What, he wasn't familiar with Article 7, Section 8? That was the section providing for placement of children in agencies operated by persons of the same religious faith as their parents, and wasn't that part of what the lawsuit was challenging? Had it never crossed Clark's mind that there might be a conflict of interest in a member of the New York State Board of Regents' joining a suit against, among others, officers of the state of New York?

For his pièce de résistance, Aquilino brought out the thick sheaf of responses to the defendants' interrogatories and triumphantly revealed that some of the very names Clark had not recognized were listed in the documents he'd signed. When Lowry protested again—"I think it is clear from the record that Dr. Clark did not himself prepare these interrogatory responses, nor are we trying to represent that he [did]"— Aquilino wrapped himself in righteous indignation. The interrogatories were "a sham and a denigration" of the rules, he said. "I find it quite unfortunate that a person of Dr. Clark's stature has been, I'm not sure of the appropriate word, but drawn into lending his name to documents which he himself has indicated he skimmed at best, and which my examination . . . indicates he has very little familiarity with. . . . These things bear the weight of one's oath and reputation."

If he thought this might goad Lowry into losing her temper, he was mistaken. "That is all very well and good, Tom," she said coolly, "and if this is your position and you think you want to take appropriate action, you are free to do so." They both knew he would get nowhere with the magistrate who periodically ruled on their pretrial disputes.

Nevertheless, all the other defendants' lawyers followed Aquilino's lead: Michele Ovesey, throwing out to Clark, one at a time, the unfamiliar names of city child-welfare officials; Floran Fink, of Robinson, Silverman, demonstrating with gusto that Clark had forgotten his brief involvement as guardian ad litem in a 1977 family-court case; Judith Kramer, attorney for the state, pressing him for specific evidence that the system classified children by race.

Once, the tenor of the exchange suddenly changed. A demand for specifics dredged up a painful memory that Clark had never thought to recount that day.

"In nineteen forty-seven, the year after my wife and I founded the Northside Center for Child Development," he began, "we had a case of a young woman who was sixteen years old at the time, and who was pregnant. And my wife and her casework associates sought to find a placement for this young woman, because she and her family did not want [her] to undergo an illegal abortion. And we got word on an excellent facility under the auspices of the Jewish Board of Guardians, and we knew Herschel Alt, who was the director. And we called him and told him about this young woman and her family and their needs. And he said to us that they could not accept her because they only accepted Jewish girls.

"As it turned out, this young lady was Jewish. Her family for generations had been Jews. They were black Jews. They had come from the West Indies, where there was a long tradition. We said, 'Herschel, she is Jewish.' That made no difference. That young lady was not accepted because she was black, and I have never forgotten that . . . and I think that may have been the beginning of an estrangement."

For Floran Fink, one of the younger lawyers on the defendants' side of the table, the dramatic story only added to the sense that Clark was an envoy from another world. His very presence invoked the historic struggle against segregation, but by the time Fink had come into political consciousness, that struggle already seemed obsolete.

Flo Fink had grown up on Long Island. She was in fourth grade when her family moved from Avenue Z in Brooklyn to Glen Cove, where she was the only Jewish girl in her class and one of the few whites in an elementary school district gerrymandered to meet pressure for desegregation. Her own memories of isolation and taunting made her identify with the position of her clients, that maintaining a critical mass of Jewish children in their agencies was necessary if Jewish children were freely to exercise their religion and maintain an ethnic identity. Surely, she thought, that meant concentrating the Jewish children, who had dropped to only 2 percent of the city's overall foster-care population.

The 1970s had witnessed a renaissance in public homage to ethnicity, from "Kiss Me, I'm Italian" buttons to such books as Nathan Glazer and Patrick Moynihan's *Beyond the Melting Pot* and Michael Novak's *The Rise of the Unmeltable Ethnics.* The new ethnicity might be read in part as white reaction to black nationalism. Supporters billed it as a celebration of ethnic pluralism's triumph over assimilation, but some critics argued that it was more like ethnicity's last gasp. Regardless of its contradictions, ethnic consciousness had flourished in popular culture and political discourse for more than a decade by 1983, and to Flo Fink it seemed almost incomprehensible that Clark could dismiss ethnic identity from the realm of a child's relevant needs. That was the point of substance that she and the others pressed him on again and again. But it was almost as though they were speaking a different language.

"When an individual wants ethnic identity to have the priority, that individual should bear the responsibility," Clark insisted. "When public officials are involved in meeting the needs of children, I feel strongly and categorically, and I am on record in writing, in lecturing, in testimony, that this is not a responsibility of the public sector. And when it is, when the public officials and decision makers enter it, they enter on the side of reinforcing racial and religious distinctions which I devoted all of my adult life to fighting with one damn glorious defeat after another. . . . Is that point clear? You know, I think that if there's any one point that I have repeated ad nauseam today, it is that. I do not think that the public sector, public funds, public officials should be involved in reinforcing ethnic distinctions in meeting public needs."

Asked for his own solution, he was unequivocal: "My personal opinion is that the city of New York should assume the responsibility for providing the necessary [foster] care." It was no different from the government responsibility for public education or corrections, he said, adding that he would hope, however, that the quality could be better than what was presently provided in public schools and prisons.

Prisons: to Fink's ears, the analogy exposed the damning contradiction at the heart of Lowry's lawsuit. City-run shelters and diagnostic centers were already prisons of sorts, she thought—terrible places where children were beaten and sodomized. Yet Lowry wanted to turn the whole system over to the very people responsible for those pits. The lawsuit ostensibly sought greater access for black Protestants to the superior programs of the Jewish and Catholic agencies. But in reality, Fink believed, Lowry was more than ready to sacrifice quality on the altar of "equality." She would be glad to trample the best interests of some children in order to make them all "equal," and Clark had lent the weight of his reputation to help her do it.

"I have no further questions of this witness at this time," Flo Fink said with distaste when the day was almost over.

But there was still one lawyer to go: Marc Bunim, who represented the small Orthodox Jewish agency named Ohel. Returning to Aquilino's tack, he proposed to take Clark page by page through the interrogatory responses, asking for clarification. For the witness, it was the last straw.

"This has reached and gone beyond the point of personal harassment," Clark exploded. "This whole thing has given the impression that I am the perpetrator of some crime. In all of the litigation I have ever been involved with, starting with *Brown,* I have never really been subjected to this type of thing.

"I want that on the record. For you to say you are now going to go through page by page on this at this time, I really—there is a point beyond which I can't even pretend to be—"

"Dr. Clark," Bunim put in, "there is a history with regard to these aside from this particular deposition."

"You have our answer on this, Marc," Lowry said.

"I have been involved in a number of cases," Clark repeated, his voice hoarse, "and I . . . really have never been subjected to this kind of thing, as if you people say I am some sort of criminal."

The deposition finally ended at 5:12 P.M., with Clark's outburst still hanging over them all like his cigarette smoke. In a sense, the smoke had never cleared.

THE AUGUST 1 TRIAL DATE was a week away. On the day Judge Ward denied Jerry Bodell's eleventh-hour plea for more time, Diane Morgenroth and Michele Ovesey went out to dinner together at Zeno's, a good Italian restaurant on Thirteenth Street. They drank plenty of wine. It was the last meal of the condemned, Morgenroth joked: "We basically decided this was going to be the end of our lives, because we were going to be starting that trial that would never be over." A day or two later, Ovesey went to work on her opening statement.

Morgenroth and Ovesey had no authority to settle a case even if they wanted to, and like so many of those who came close to *Wilder,* they had been pulled into its orbit of hostility. Their first inkling that settlement was a possibility came at a meeting at the city law department offices on Tuesday, July 26. There were five lawyers on the city's side, including Fritz Schwarz and Judy Levitt, who was head of general litigation. On the other side of the table, alone, sat Burt Neuborne of the ACLU. The younger lawyers assumed that the overtures had come from Neuborne, not Schwarz, and neither man disabused them of the idea. It was just an exploratory discussion, of course, but Schwarz and Neuborne seemed to have a personal rapport that transcended the matter at hand. They apparently had common ground for trust, at a time when *Wilder* veterans had only the mined and rutted battlefield on which they had clashed for so long.

Neuborne was quite disarming. At one point Morgenroth heard him articulate concerns within the ACLU about the cost of funding the *Wilder* case. She couldn't help wondering if he would ever have said such a thing in front of Marcia Lowry.

Years later, Neuborne would express disbelief that he could have gone to such a meeting at all without Marcia Lowry: "If I did it, it was disloyal to Marcia; I would never have been disloyal to Marcia." The meeting, however, was recorded in Fritz Schwarz's office calendar with a list of the participants.

Lawyers who have worked with Neuborne invariably use the words "very creative" when they talk about him. *Creativity* is not a word ordinarily associated with the practice of law, but Neuborne's approach to legal problems has a kind of uninhibited originality that any artist might envy. Colleagues knew that if they sought his advice on a stymied lawsuit, he would effortlessly throw out a dozen new ideas and theories to fit the known facts; some of the ideas would be bad or unworkable, but at least a few would be absolutely brilliant.

In much the same spirit, Neuborne would in retrospect offer a rapid-fire series of possible scenarios to bridge the gap between his sense of principle and his documented presence at the July 26 meeting. When his preferred reconstruction floundered, Neuborne would settle on an interpretation of his role that cast Marcia Lowry as a proud damsel in distress and him as a rescuer responding to a silent cry for help.

"I think Marcia was ready for settlement; everyone was exhausted. They approached me desperately and said, 'Is there some way to settle this thing?' " No? "Well, there's no way I would have gone down that road without receiving powerful signals from the lawyers that that was what they wanted me to do. . . . It's conceivable that I went to a meeting without telling them, but if I did, I was wrong. Ask anybody, it's not the way I ran my office. . . . I was receiving signals which Marcia may or may not be willing to acknowledge she was giving, asking me to bail her out. I may have received those signals, knowing she would never ask me outright."

KNOWING NOTHING ABOUT Neuborne's meeting with their adversaries the day before, Lowry and her colleagues worked all through the afternoon on trial strategy. Toward evening, the team shifted from Lowry's office to the small law library on the same floor. There were no Persian rugs here, and little elbow room, but the plain rectangular library table was the best place available for them to review documents together. They were still bent over the work when Susan Kaiser, a paralegal who had been Lowry's secretary years earlier, came running in. She had an urgent telephone message about Avi's baby-sitter from Lowry's husband:

"Mattie has died. Get home."

All the breath seemed to leave Lowry's body. A look of horror and then panic swept her face. Never had her colleagues seen her so stricken. In less than sixty seconds, she was out the door and in a cab speeding home.

SIX

FRITZ MOSHER HAD RETURNED FROM WORK AT 5:30 P.M. that day, as he usually did. Time as a hands-on father meant more to him at age fifty than an extra hour at the Carnegie Corporation, where he'd worked since leaving Harvard with a Ph.D. in social psychology in 1962. In a sense, he was living his life over in his second marriage, and this time he wanted it to be different.

As soon as he opened the door, he could hear Avi screaming. He was in his crib, in the little roomlet they'd turned into a nursery. Scooping up the tear-soaked child, Mosher walked into the kitchen to look for Mattie.

Her body was lying on the linoleum floor. They hadn't known she wore a wig; it had fallen off her head, and he saw that she was much older than they'd realized. The image of death was grotesque and shocking, and he instinctively tried to protect his child from it. He rushed Avi back to his crib before returning to bend over the body in a futile search for signs of life. Then he ran to summon a doctor from a medical practice in the lobby, called 911 for an ambulance and the police, and telephoned Lowry's office.

Later they surmised that she had been dead for about five hours. The doorman had seen her bring Avi in at lunchtime. It was one of the hottest days of the summer. Mattie smoked and had high blood pressure; perhaps she had felt unwell and gone into the kitchen to get a drink of water. Perhaps she had put the baby down for a nap and started to prepare his lunch. Suddenly she had dropped dead, felled by a massive heart attack or stroke. For hours afterward, Avi must have called and cried and screamed.

Horrible as it was, it could have been worse, Lowry told herself as she carried Avi to the home of close friends while Mosher waited with the body for the police to arrive. The kid could have been wandering around the apartment. He could have been in Mattie's arms when she had her seizure. Still, she couldn't stop imagining those hours when Mattie had lain dead while Avi, hungry, wet, and all alone, kept crying fruitlessly for her to come.

The police didn't arrive until eleven that night. Mattie had been separated from her husband, and it was hard to get in touch with her next of kin. Eventually her relatives and the police agreed that no autopsy was necessary, and after Mosher offered to help pay for the funeral, an undertaker finally took the body away. Only then did Lowry bring Avi home again.

He cried and fought when they tried to put him back into his crib, and their own loft bed was perilous for a toddler. So Lowry put something soft on the floor of the living room and spent the rest of the night lying there beside him.

How much did he understand? she wondered. The woman who had taken care of him for fifteen months of his life had dropped off the face of the Earth. His parents could do nothing to change that.

"Talk to him about this," a therapist she knew advised her.

"He's not going to understand anything," Lowry objected.

"He'll hear your tone of voice and her name."

But she couldn't bring herself to do it, couldn't say "Mattie is dead" when her every instinct was to try to shield him from that fact.

The next morning she knew she was not going to work; she was going to spend time with her son. It was Thursday; on Monday the trial was to start, and she would not be ready.

She remembered how Ward had refused Bodell's plea for more time. Every judge has his own particular rules about procedures and scheduling; Judge Ward's clerk had handed out a "Notice to Counsel Appearing in Civil Matters before Judge Ward": "Counsel are expected to adhere to all dates set by the Court. Adjournments will be granted where appropriate, but no attorney is to communicate with chambers to request adjournment until he or she has at least attempted to speak to each adversary involved in the matter."

Well, there was no way she was going to reach out to Davis, Polk or

Floran Fink in her hour of need. She took a deep breath and telephoned Ward's courtroom. His secretary answered. "I've had a crisis," Lowry began, "and this is what it is."

"Oh my God," the secretary exclaimed when she heard the story. "Judge Ward is on the bench; I'll put you through to him."

LOWRY COULD SEE Robert Ward in her mind's eye: the large, fleshy face, rather pale above the black robes; the high, domed forehead that met a receding hairline; the shaggy gray sideburns and bushy eyebrows hooding mild blue eyes. It was not an unkindly face. At fifty-seven, Ward had a look of benevolent solemnity that was the very image of judicial temperament. In his eleven years on the bench he had gained a solid reputation for fairness, intelligence, and human decency. Yet he was also known to have a temper that could erupt without warning and pour unadulterated wrath on some unwitting attorney. Most striking was his devotion to his wife, Florence, whose long battle with multiple sclerosis had left her confined to a wheelchair. She had taken some falls at home while under the care of a hired helper, and Ward was worried enough to begin bringing her to court with him instead. Every morning for years, he had wheeled her into his chambers; when court was in session, he wheeled her to one side of the jury box to watch. She was a very thin, stooped, frail-looking woman now, but her face still showed the prettiness of the Simmons College student he had met while he was at Harvard Law School on the GI Bill. Every so often he would look over at her with an expression of great sweetness and concern. He might come down from the bench and ask, "Are you all right, my dear?" They would confer, and if she needed it, he would call a break and wheel her out to tend to her needs himself. They ate lunch together every day at the conference table in his chambers with his law clerks. Usually he made his own peanut-butter sandwich on a bagel brought from home, and he washed out his coffee cups himself. The Wards had two grown daughters, one a lawyer. At a time when many judges still barely seemed to tolerate the presence of female attorneys, Ward was known to like and respect them.

But Lowry had not forgotten her terrifying first appearance before him, how he had bellowed that a three-day trial was going to start Monday, period. A lawyer's greatest fear, Ward once told his deputy, was coming to trial unprepared. Ward prided himself on his court's efficiency, and he considered it part of his job to shake lawyers up when a case dragged on for too long. In a lawsuit challenging a ban on night flights out of Westchester County Airport in the 1970s, he really had finished in three days a trial that the lawyers had estimated would take several weeks. Another time, frustrated that two lawyers were still stuck in settlement negotiations, he instructed that the matter was to go to trial the next morning, with jury selection to start at 10:00 A.M. It was the end of the day, and the clerk's office couldn't supply a jury on such short notice, but Ward went ahead with an elaborate bluff, having his staff set up a jury wheel and chairs in his courtroom and solemnly ordering his deputy to bring in the nonexistent jurors. The ruse worked.

"YOUR HONOR," LOWRY SAID when she heard Ward's deep, pleasant voice at the other end of the telephone. "I'm in a crisis." And she told the story about Mattie again.

He was full of sympathy. "The first thing, is the baby OK?" he asked.

"Yes, but upset."

"Of course." He would give her two weeks, he said, and she should check with everybody else to make sure that such an adjournment was OK. "I'm sure it'll be OK," he added, "and if it isn't OK, I'll give it to you anyway."

The trio of city lawyers was furious. It was a measure of the bad blood in the case that Diane Morgenroth considered it completely unfair of Ward, after denying the defendants an adjournment, to grant one to Lowry "just because her baby-sitter dropped dead."

The story of Mattie's death on the eve of Lowry's big trial became the talk of a wide circle of working mothers in New York City. Lowry received dozens of supportive telephone calls from people she hardly knew. Even among women who had never met her, the episode became legendary; it seemed to capsulize the worst fears of their bifurcated lives.

Lowry took less than a week to hire a new baby-sitter, and a few more days to help Avi make the transition. On Tuesday, August 9, she was in court again; by the end of the week she was back in the office, resuming trial preparation for the new date, August 15.

But the trial would not take place. This time the telephone call that postponed it came from Burt Neuborne. He was calling from France, where he was on a vacation. He had sent Lowry the possible framework for a settlement, drafted on the plane to Paris. Before leaving New York, he had told her that Fritz Schwarz was interested in settling *Wilder*. Now he stressed that Schwarz was acting in good faith, and they needed to take him seriously. They needed to delay the trial and negotiate. If they didn't, they would hurt themselves.

It wasn't an order; the ACLU did not have a hierarchical culture, and Lowry, as lead counsel, had the right to call the shots on her own case. Still, she could not ignore this. She immediately informed Hansen and Mushlin of the new developments. How odd, she thought, that it had taken Mattie's death and her own request for an adjournment to start real settlement talks, though the trial date had been looming over them all for six months.

After the others left, she sat quietly alone for a few moments, amid the clutter of charts and documents, feeling her adrenaline ebb away and a sense of exhausted wariness take its place.

SEVEN

WHEN LAMONT FIRST ARRIVED AT ASTOR HOME FROM New York Foundling in June 1981, shortly after his seventh birthday, he was said to show "evidence of problems forming attachments." Changing that was one of the goals of his treatment, an Astor Home caseworker wrote in the report that had to be submitted to the city every six months to justify the cost of his care, which ranged from $64 to $119 a day over time. It was Goal 1C: "Lamont will learn to relate to women with less anger and anxiety and will exhibit more real spontaneous affection." In an adjacent box was typed a "method/service task" to be used to meet the goal: "Female child care staff will spend individual time with Lamont."

There were other goals, too, of course. Goal 1A was "Lamont will decrease his teasing, verbal baiting, tattling and instigating of peers. Lamont will be given a two to five minute period of 'time-out' each time he teases or instigates." Goal 1B was to reduce the boy's "lying and excessive denial" through staff intervention. All of these were subparts of Goal 1, "Lamont will demonstrate appropriate positive peer and adult relationships."

Goal 2 was "Lamont will understand his past history and gain a better sense of identity." Goal 3 was "Lamont will stop nighttime enuresis." All were to lead to the "permanency goal," listed as adoption. The "anticipated completion date" for adoption was given as August 1984, when he would be ten. It was all part of his Uniform Case Record Reassessment and Service Plan Review, known as the UCR, the first of many such reports that would be filled out on Lamont by Astor Home, reviewed by city caseworkers, and kept on file in the downtown offices of New York City's child welfare agency.

Eventually the city's official record on Lamont would grow to be four volumes thick. Really just dog-eared manila folders, the volumes were held together by metal fasteners that carelessly speared each document. Beside the stiff yellow pages of his UCRs lay the thin onionskin paper of reimbursement-eligibility studies, with sheets of carbon paper still attached. From time to time hand-scrawled scraps of memo would be added to the mass of printed forms, artifacts of the improvisation that underlay the bureaucratic formulae.

The forms were meant to bring businesslike supervision and account-ability to a fragmented system in which, it was generally agreed by 1981, children had been left to drift for years at great public expense and emo-tional cost. Both state and federal law required that diligent efforts be made to find new permanent families for children who couldn't go home, and that periodic checks be done to see that children whose own behavior was an obstacle to "permanency" were getting the treatment they needed to make progress toward that goal. The state Department of Social Services tried to monitor the city's compliance by auditing UCRs. The forms reflected the tenet that Astor Home was being paid not to keep and care for Lamont during his childhood, but to heal him psycho-logically as quickly as possible so he could return to a normal family life. Yet the forms also revealed abiding confusion over who was ultimately responsible for managing his future.

Within two months of Lamont's arrival at Astor Home, a Sheltering Arms adoption worker named Barbara Davis called Sister Margaret Ann McSweeney, an Astor Home social worker, demanding to know why the nun had not written to the Wasserman family in Minnesota about con-tacts with Lamont. Sister Margaret Ann explained that it was her under-standing that this was a shared case, and that Ms. Davis was to serve as the contact person for the Wassermans. Ms. Davis disagreed. "In effect, seems like case is ours for now," Sister Margaret Ann wrote in her casework notes for August 20, 1981.

"Lamont will understand his past history," Astor Home had pledged as its Goal 2. But what *was* Lamont's past history? The records sent from Sheltering Arms were sketchy, and New York Foundling Hospital in Man-hattan had never had the full story. Through the rest of that first summer and fall, Sister Margaret Ann made a series of telephone calls to Minnesota seeking clarification about this ostensibly friendly, cooperative, and verbal child who called himself a "fighter" and reported dreams in which he was killed and chopped to pieces. She obtained casework summaries from Myrna Otte, the Minnesota social worker, and had a long talk with Mrs. Wasserman, who was obviously still in emotional pain over the family's failure with Lamont. Indeed, the first letter Mrs. Wasserman sent to Astor Home for the child would not do; Sister Margaret Ann had to send it back with corrections that would deliver a clearer message of closure. The treatment team had agreed that Lamont needed to lay to rest any false hopes of adoption by this family if he was ever to move on to another.

On October 19, 1981, four months after Lamont's arrival, the grave-faced nun took the seven-year-old from his classroom in the middle of the day and walked him down the long, narrow corridor to her office.

He would never be going back to Minnesota, she told him. The people in the last home he had known there wanted to be his friends, but because of his behavior, they couldn't be his family. She kept peering at his face as she talked; he had to swallow hard several times to keep from crying in her presence.

"They'll still write you letters," she told him.

"Could you ask them not to write in cursive?" he said at last. "Because I can't read that."

She said she would. Then she talked about the behavior problems he had to work on: teasing, fighting, telling lies, fidgeting in class, wetting his bed at night. "We are all here to help support you in this difficult time," she told him.

The good-bye letter that arrived later from the Wassermans was clearly printed. There was no room for it inside his album, he told Sister Margaret Ann, and she promised to get him a new one. She never did, though. Like many other adults he came to know at Astor Home, she would move on long before he did, leaving him behind in a place that would never lose its power to frighten him.

ASTOR HOME WAS NOT what modern eyes saw as a place particularly suited to young children. Stamped with the grandeur of old-fashioned benefaction, its sweeping staircase, high-ceilinged reception halls, massive furniture, and blood-red carpets silently demanded humility, if not gratitude, of its charges. From the outside, even on a bright day, there was something gloomy about the redbrick mansion with Tudor chimneys, standing on a slant to the road at the edge of town, just north of the Rhinebeck cemetery. A fast-moving creek known as Landsman Kill ran right under the road and through the property, cutting a rocky gully beside the building. The land fell away steeply, so that the blacktop playground was on a kind of plateau below the building; beyond it stretched dark woods.

Passersby often assumed it had been a millionaire's country seat before being donated for charitable use. In fact, it had been built expressly for needy children by the heir to one of the great American fortunes at a time when he himself had just reached adulthood.

Vincent Astor was a twenty-year-old Harvard freshman when his father, John Jacob Astor IV, went down with the *Titanic* on April 15, 1912. Vincent's inheritance was so vast and so rich in Manhattan real estate that it was hard to measure. But the Astor heir had grown up as a poor little rich boy, with a cold, absent mother who was divorced on the ground of adultery, and a demanding, uncommunicative father in whose approval he had never felt secure. The happiest days of his sad childhood had been spent on school holidays with his father at Ferncliff, the family's Dutchess County estate. When Vincent was about ten, his father commissioned the era's most celebrated architect, Stanford White, to add a Ping-Pong court to the grounds. What resulted in 1904 was an unprecedented sports casino in Palladian style, including a neoclassical marble swimming pool behind a plate-glass wall, squash courts, a billiard room, a library, and a two-hundred-foot tennis court with a glass ceiling equipped with canvas panels that could be rolled back and forth by servants to provide shade for the players. Vincent called it the "playhouse."

When the grief-stricken heir searched for a fitting memorial to his father, he learned that Holiday Farm, a charity started "for the little waifs of New York City" by his parents' social set, was in need of a new home. Opened in 1902 on the other side of Rhinecliff, it had as its stated purpose "caring for children between three and twelve years of age, at the critical time when, weakened by illness, they are discharged from hospitals and would otherwise return to the unwholesome surroundings of the tenements." Holiday Farm then accommodated about twenty tenement children in a large frame house, but it was in the way of the Rhinecliff railroad station's planned expansion.

Combating the noxious effects of tenement housing had been a recurrent theme in charity work since the 1840s. By the turn of the century, when 1,585,000 people lived in 42,700 such dwellings in Manhattan, the tenements had come to represent all that ailed the poor. They were also a major source of the Astor wealth. The founder of the family fortune was Vincent's great-great-grandfather, the first John Jacob Astor, who had bought fur pelts from the Chippewa for trinkets, guns, and rum. With his profits he obtained Manhattan farm acreage cheap and subleased it to developers of tenements. When he died, in 1848, as the wealthiest man in America, his real estate holdings included nearly all of the congested Lower East Side and much of the West Side, too.

The heir to all this wealth bought Holiday Farm for one dollar, purchased a piece of property east of the river from his future in-laws, and commissioned a leading architect to build what was officially called the Colonel John J. Astor Memorial Home for Children and Holiday Farm. The large brick and stone building that resulted in 1914 may have seemed quite cozy to Vincent, who was used to the vaulted halls of Ferncliff. But its essential unsuitability reflected more than just good intentions gone awry; it was emblematic of the distortion that philanthropy brought to child welfare.

This was an exculpatory philanthropy indifferent to the harmful consequences of its chosen form of largesse, unconsciously or willfully blind to the connection between wealth built on poverty and the gaping inequities that put so many poor children at risk of harm in the first place. Like the orphan-train endowments of Mrs. Astor, Vincent's chosen charity required that children be physically separated from their impoverished homes. And so, out of the thousands living in the profitable slums, a few dozen waifs would arrive upstate each year, sickly and scared, and in the name of Vincent Astor's father, they would pine, in splendor, for their mothers.

Eventually, in the post–World War II era of antibiotics and Aid to Dependent Children, the Holiday Farm concept would come to seem obsolescent. Vincent Astor gave the institution to the archdiocese of New York in 1946, and it became the site of a state-financed pilot project to develop techniques for the residential treatment of emotionally disturbed children. Vincent Astor was chairman of the board when this new version of Astor Home opened on January 5, 1953, with seventeen emotionally disturbed boys in the care of the Daughters of Charity of St. Vincent de Paul. After Vincent died childless, in 1959, his widow added the St. Vincent Chapel in his memory.

Astor Home enjoyed the special favor of the church hierarchy: the New York archbishop, Terence Cardinal Cooke, was chairman of its board, and the director of Catholic Charities, Monsignor Robert Arpie, served as its treasurer. It was ensconced in a wealthy, desirable community that gave it charitable support. And in the early 1980s, it remained predominantly white and Catholic. If the *Wilder* lawsuit, in its narrowest sense, was about giving black Protestant children an equal shot at the best the system had to offer, then it was about giving them a fair chance to enter Astor Home. That would become part of the double-edged meaning of Lamont's years there: within the system, he could have hoped for nothing better.

LAMONT LIVED IN A PLAIN BRICK ANNEX to Astor Home's main building, hidden from view by the chapel of St. Vincent de Paul. The chapel, completed in 1962, was a modern circular building with walls of stained glass, ringed by a dozen white stone statues of saints. They formed a benign guard during daylight hours, but as soon as darkness fell, Lamont saw the silent figures grow sinister in his imagination: the stone nun ready to join those moving invisibly in the attic; the Saint Francis, whose animal companions were like shades of fiercer beasts lurking in the forest; the archangel Michael.

Night after night, it was the archangel who chased Lamont in his dreams, those great stone wings beating the dark air, the sword upraised to chop him into pieces. Lamont began to fight to stay awake, lying rigid in his bed, scanning the shadows with wide-open eyes. But sleep would always overtake him. At least twice a night, in an effort to keep him from wetting his bed, a changing roster of third-shift child-care workers would come to shake him awake. Usually he was wet already, and he would stumble to the bathroom clammy and shivering, his nightmares pursuing him down the narrow corridor.

EIGHT

THERE WAS EVERGREEN ROPING ON THE BANISTER AT ASTOR Home that first Christmas, and a large wreath on the front door. A decorated Christmas tree appeared in a corner of the big parlor known as the red room, and the carpet was heaped with gifts wrapped and donated by church groups and charities. But what Lamont would remember later was that the Santa Claus who handed out the presents was a teenager with a phony beard, and that the toys inside the shiny boxes broke quickly.

He was one of very few children who spent the whole holiday at the institution. Many went home with their local volunteer families for Christmas, or visited relatives. Lamont had neither. On January 8, 1982, half a year after his arrival, when a caseworker from Sheltering Arms called to ask if Astor saw Lamont as being ready for a home, Sister Margaret Ann said no. "He is showing some signs of pathology which came out in his last placement," she wrote into her notes in explanation.

Later the same month, Lamont achieved one of his three treatment goals through the simple operation a Minnesota pediatrician had recommended almost two years earlier. In the interim, he had awakened to the sad, sour smell of wet sheets on more than six hundred mornings, and been roused from bed in the darkness of nearly as many nights. "No longer enuretic due to surgery," the next UCR form informed the city.

Lamont was fearful before the operation, but it was performed under a general anesthetic, and he told Sister Margaret Ann at their counseling session afterward that he had felt only the sting of the needle in his arm. That session was one of their best. Noticing the photographs the nun kept on the desk in her office, Lamont decided to get his album and went slowly through each picture of the Fils-Aime family. Then he came to the Millers.

"Mr. Miller got mad at me a lot," he explained to the nun, before quickly flipping to the back of the book to look for Wasserman pictures. Some seemed to be missing, he told her. Later he turned to one of the games she kept in her office for play therapy. When the hand-eye coordination it required proved too difficult, he settled on a book instead, reading half of it aloud to her. He began to droop, and she offered to read the rest to him herself, taking him into the curve of her arm. He obviously liked that.

Two days later, Sister Margaret Ann filled in most of the form requesting a local volunteer family for Lamont. Surely this seven-year-old would benefit from the individual attention a volunteer could provide. The only question was what to include about fire setting. She consulted Lamont's therapist. The record from Minnesota was full of fires threatened or fantasized, but in discussing his case the women realized they were both in the dark about the only real fire in his past. Had Lamont merely been in that fire, they wondered, or had he actually set it? At Sister Margaret Ann's request, Sheltering Arms checked its records. What came back was not good news.

"Lamont did set a house on fire when he was three and a half or four years old," Sister Margaret Ann wrote in her notes before relaying the information to his therapist. "Not clear whether this was foster home."

Fire-setter: the label was fixed now, and even finding a volunteer to take the child home occasionally might not be so easy.

The next week, on February 4, 1982, Sister Margaret Ann got an unexpected telephone call from a woman who identified herself as Mrs. Fils-Aime, Lamont's former foster mother. In a soft, low voice with a Spanish accent, she asked for information about him and said she wanted to visit.

The rules of confidentiality made it impossible for her to share anything about Lamont, Sister Margaret Ann said firmly. But if the former foster mother wished to pursue the matter further, she could contact a social worker named Mrs. Beaman at Sheltering Arms and have her call Astor Home. Together, the social workers of the two agencies would see what could be worked out. Mrs. Fils-Aime's voice became strained, and after choking out a thank-you, she hung up.

Mrs. Beaman called from Sheltering Arms a little later the same day. She reported that it was documented in the record, in a letter written by a former Sheltering Arms supervisor, that Mrs. Fils-Aime wished to remain involved with Lamont.

But Astor Home had no such letter in the rather skimpy material the agency had sent along with Lamont. In fact, Astor had received no information at all about his placement with the Fils-Aime family. That was the very reason she had needed to call to ask about the fire, the nun pointed out with irritation. She requested a meeting as soon as possible to share and discuss the missing files.

Mrs. Beaman seemed uneasy. She would have to check with her supervisor, she said.

LOSING LAMONT HAD BROUGHT deeper and more long-lasting sorrow to Alicia than she had ever imagined at the time of his abrupt departure in the summer of 1979. The Millers had promised to write, but she had received nothing from them, and she had no way of contacting Lamont in Minnesota; when she initially inquired, the Sheltering Arms caseworker said his address was confidential information. In her first year as a woman alone, her feelings about Lamont were among the many layers of guilt and grief that she numbed with the dogged effort to earn a living and an education. Finding work as a church secretary in the same United Methodist congregation where she had found spiritual comfort, she was able to bring her son, Henri, back from his grandmother's in Puerto Rico by the end of the summer of 1980. But Henri's return only brought Lamont's absence into sharper focus. She felt it like a physical ache, a painful yearning.

The neighbors never stopped asking after him. They had not forgotten the adorable child with the winning smile, and Alicia found herself brooding again and again over the agency's decision to ignore his ethnic and community ties. Still, she kept telling herself, Lamont was adopted and happy, and her own pain was not too great a sacrifice.

Then, two and a half years after Lamont had left, she received an invitation from Sheltering Arms to attend a meeting of foster parents at the agency. It was described as a forum on feelings about the foster-care system. When she arrived at the gathering, she wondered if her invitation had been a computer error. All the others in attendance still had at least one foster child from the agency; Lamont had been her first and last.

Alicia was often shy in group discussions, preferring to say too little rather than too much. But when the discussion turned to adoption, she seized the chance to speak out. She described Lamont's five years in her home and his sudden placement with a white family in Minnesota. "My issue is, I know this child, but nobody ever approached me about whether Lamont would be able to handle this," she said. "We are the ones who know those children and their needs. What we know should be taken into consideration when those children are free for adoption, but it seems foster parents have no rights."

As the meeting broke up, the Sheltering Arms staff took Alicia aside. She was escorted to a small office by two women who asked to talk with her. One, who seemed to be a supervisor or therapist with authority in the agency, wasted little time on preliminaries.

"Did you see any signs of disturbed behavior in Lamont when he was in your care?" she asked.

No, Alicia told them.

Her denial was like a signal for attack. Suddenly both women were accusing her, saying things so terrible that Alicia's protests were soon strangled by her sobs.

Lamont had not been adopted. Lamont was not happy. And as far as they were concerned, it was her fault. She had abused the child, they implied. He had suffered traumas in her care. All those months, she had imagined he was doing well. Instead, they were saying in so many words, "He's having a lot of problems, and you are to blame."

She was still crying when they left the room. After the supervisor went away, the other woman seemed to feel sorry for her and came back with some tissues. Alicia clutched the soggy remnants on the long subway trip back to the Bronx, trying to hold her grief in check until she made it home. For more than two years she had sought comfort in an image of Lamont smiling up at the Millers. Now, as she wept, she envisioned him alone, crying and uncomforted.

The next day, she tried to reach Miss Kihara, the Sheltering Arms caseworker who had supervised Lamont's care in her home for almost three years. Surely Miss Kihara would remember how loved and happy he had been in the family; surely she would tell Alicia where to find him. But Miss Kihara was gone, and a stranger answered her old number at the agency. Perhaps because this caseworker was new, she readily checked the record and told Alicia that Lamont was living in a group residence upstate called the Astor Home for Children.

Alicia placed the call to Astor Home from the church office where she worked. When she was directed back to Sheltering Arms, she held on to her composure; but as soon as she put down the telephone receiver, she began to sob again. The people at Sheltering Arms would never agree to let her visit Lamont, she knew. To them, she had turned into some kind of monster. And Lamont, would he not see her as a monster, too, by now? After all, she had failed him. Her pain had been not a sacrifice to buy his happiness, but only a prelude to more pain for them both.

One of the pastors saw her distress and asked what was wrong. Without intending to, she recounted the whole story. He offered to help and wanted to press the issue. But in the end, she told him no. She didn't think it would help anyone, she said.

ON A COLD DAY in late February 1982, Lamont stubbornly maintained that he and all the other Astor Home children who had passed through Foundling's Blaine Hall were going back there. He had the information from Craig, a small, blond, blue-eyed boy who had recently arrived from Blaine, and Craig had it from Sister Theresa herself, Lamont insisted. His child-care workers asked Sister Margaret Ann to set him straight.

She was gentle but firm. She was his social worker, she told Lamont, and she knew there was no such plan. And even if there were, Sister Theresa would go through workers, not through other kids.

At first Lamont refused to relinquish his conviction. Sister Theresa had brought Craig to Astor Home herself, sitting in the backseat of the car while Craig rode in front on the long drive up the Taconic Parkway. Craig knew, Craig must be right, because Sister Theresa had said it.

Maybe Craig had misunderstood Sister Theresa, the social worker said at last. Maybe Sister had told Craig, Wouldn't it be nice if the kids could come back? And maybe Craig thought that meant they were all going back.

Finally, Lamont gave in to her logic. For him, it seemed, there was never a way back to the people who had let him go.

A few days later, Sister Margaret Ann was pleased to inform Lamont that a possible local volunteer had been identified for him. Her name was Mrs. McKinnon, and she would come to meet him on Wednesday, March 3. If all went well between them, she would become his special friend, inviting him to her house sometimes on weekends.

But at the last minute that Wednesday, Mrs. McKinnon called to cancel the meeting. By Friday, Lamont's disappointment had erupted into misbehavior. Sister Margaret Ann saw him by chance in the stairwell of the school wing, and he said he had just finished being physically restrained in his classroom.

"I lost it today," the boy told her.

Many of the children at Astor Home experienced such eruptions. The constant effort to keep emotions under control and the rule-bound friction of group living made outbursts of anger a kind of routinized discharge of excess frustration. Staffers called it "going off," and they had a systematic response: physical restraint by two staff members, followed by the child's isolation in a "time-out" room. Teachers and the child-care staff, which included several large men, took courses in the gym on how to wrestle children to the floor safely, two on one. The child's arms would be wrapped around his body by one adult, crossed as in a straitjacket, and his hands held firmly behind his back. Another adult would help lay the child stomach-down on the ground, hold his legs, and sit on him if he was still struggling.

It was like being in a fight without getting hit, Lamont would tell someone later. It hurt to be restrained, but some staff members hurt you less than others.

Sister Margaret Ann knew that for a child who had suffered the repeated loss of parental figures, even a small snub could trigger overwhelming feelings of rage and despair, as the child emotionally relived earlier abandonments.

"I know you're disappointed about Mrs. McKinnon," she told Lamont. "But she'll come on Monday."

Unfortunately there was a staff mixup on Monday, and Mrs. McKinnon did not come to see him. It took another nine days to arrange their first meeting. "Lamont did well with her," the nun wrote in her notes. "She seemed to be quite willing to take him out once in a while."

The first time Mrs. McKinnon took Lamont home, on Saturday, March 29, 1982, he seemed to fall apart. He came back claiming that he had been hit by a car outside her house. It was an obvious lie: he was unscathed, and Mrs. McKinnon had reported no such incident. Yet Lamont kept insisting that it was true, that a passing car had bumped his knees while he was playing in the road outside the McKinnon house. Later, after being reprimanded for lying, he set some paper on fire in his bedroom. There was no real damage, but the signs of a psychological emergency were unmistakable. The car story now seemed more like a hallucination than a lie; the fire confirmed all the worst aspects of Lamont's record. At an emergency meeting with staff, Lamont was told that the visits to Mrs. McKinnon would be suspended.

"After only a few hours of visiting with a volunteer family, Lamont let loose a high degree of aggressiveness which he had been keeping in check," Sister Margaret Ann reported in the next UCR sent to the city. As to his relationship goals, "Lamont has made no progress," she added. "He has instead become much more openly aggressive with both peers and adults."

After nearly a full year at Astor Home, Lamont was suddenly worse instead of better. When his group crossed the road to the playing fields near the cemetery, he courted danger, lagging behind as though trying to be run over, and threatened to run away. "Staff is now alerted to Lamont's need of constant vigilance to contain his apparent self-destructive tendencies and physical aggression toward others, particularly younger peers," the nun wrote in the UCR. "He will be referred to the RTF unit where he can be more closely supervised."

Lamont had been living on the third floor of one of the annex buildings, in the coed unit for the youngest children, known as the Immaculites. Now he would be moved to the second floor of the main house, into the Josephites, a unit recently designated as a "residential treatment facility," or RTF, where the most emotionally disturbed younger boys were to receive the institution's highest levels of staffing and restriction, at the highest rate of city reimbursement.

Most children at Astor Home lived in the annex buildings, in small bedrooms off low-ceilinged, dimly lit cinderblock corridors. Their food was delivered from the central kitchen in wheeled blue plastic bins and eaten at utilitarian tables and benches bolted to the floor in a corner of each unit. Each unit, named for the followers of a saint, also had its own small television lounge. The dozen boys in the Josephites were the only children left in the original Astor Home building, where the sunny playrooms, sleeping porches, and dining room commissioned for children by Vincent Astor had long since been taken over by administrative offices, reception areas, and a research library for psychology students.

When Lamont informed Sister Margaret Ann of his impending transfer, he assured her that it was OK. He had asked for the move himself, he told her, to get a later bedtime. It was typical of his ego defenses, the social worker thought.

WHEN HE FIRST ARRIVED AT ASTOR HOME, Lamont had been diagnosed as having conduct disorder, socialized aggressive type, and attention deficit disorder with hyperactivity. Now, a month before his eighth birthday, the treatment team sought another psychiatric evaluation, citing "increased incidents of aggression toward staff and peers, threats of running away, hallucinatory experiences, increased somatic complaints, violent fantasies, mood swings and an incident of fire setting." According to the evaluation, dated May 10, 1982, "he was found to have a very active fantasy life around themes of violence, getting hurt and being a savior. Fantasy and reality were poorly differentiated and he exhibited grandiose and magical thinking, perceptual distortions, impulsivity, poor judgment and hallucinations. Ego defenses included denial, rejection, flight into fantasy and counter-phobic defenses. He showed mood swings as well."

This was the kind of language usually employed to describe psychosis. But viewed through the lens of John Bowlby's research, Lamont's behavior could have been understood as a normal reaction to frustrated mourning. For that matter, much of the behavior that had puzzled or frightened his teachers and caregivers in Minnesota was understandable as a response to successive losses that he had never been allowed to grieve.

Although Bowlby's work had successfully challenged the view that a traumatic loss was best resolved in adulthood, little attention had been paid to how parents and social workers could help children mourn and resolve such losses. Bowlby saw anger as a normal, even biologically determined, reaction to separation, with two likely evolutionary functions: assisting in overcoming obstacles to reunion, and discouraging the loved person from going away again. The mother who searches frantically for a missing child and then scolds him furiously when she finds him is perhaps the most familiar example of the phenomenon. Anger may serve no practical purpose when separation is final, but in children, too, it erupts in response to loss. Yet the child moved from a foster home to an adoptive home often receives the message that in order to please he must act as if nothing bad has happened. During a honeymoon period, the child does everything possible to ingratiate himself with the new caretakers. Denial may eventually give way to yearning for the lost parent figure, which is often also manifested in a kind of restless, aimless moving around, a constant searching and scanning of the environment. Many such children, followers of Bowlby note, are medicated for hyperactivity when their behavior is in fact merely a normal reaction to loss. Other common symptoms in bereaved children include nightmares and night terrors. The sadness and anger can be so strong as to make the child fear that if he gives in to his feelings he will lose control and destroy himself or someone else. The child's anxiety is compounded when caretakers imply that sadness and anger are unwelcome.

"Looking after a grieving child is exacting and unrewarding work," Bowlby wrote, "and it is small wonder that caregivers become impatient and irritable. After a small child has lost a parent, therefore, it is by no means unusual for him to be subjected to strong pressure to 'forget' his grief and, instead, to become interested in whatever his current caregiver thinks may distract him." Yet even as he becomes attached to a new parent figure and tries to please her, the yearning for the old one persists and returns, accompanied by intense bursts of anger. In such circumstances, children often become accident-prone or exaggerate physical hurts, which serve as substitutes for the unbearable sense of emotional vulnerability that comes with the revival of suppressed feelings and the danger of a new rejection.

Lamont's account of being grazed by a car could have been seen as a metaphor for the threat posed to his precarious emotional detachment by the visit—his first to any family in more than a year. From a Bowlby perspective, he needed to be reassured through the support of a loving caregiver or insightful counselor that it was now safe for him to feel, safe to mourn the Fils-Aime family and his other losses, and safe to release his store of sadness, anger, and self-blame without opening himself to fresh rejection. But the child-care staff at Astor had been instructed to intervene with logic and reason whenever Lamont lied. Instead of showing that his emotional needs would be met this time, they in effect denied his vulnerability with logic and reprimanded its expression as a falsehood.

His brief refuge was a fantasy of omnipotence and self-destruction, in the flames that he could summon from the end of a match.

A MONTH AFTER LAMONT was moved into the Josephites, Sister Margaret Ann and his first therapist both left Astor Home. Lamont started therapy anew with Greg Barker, a tall, full-bearded young psychologist who looked to him like the Marlboro man. "Cognitive behavioral and relaxation techniques were introduced as ways of controlling his anger in the classroom," a summary of Lamont's therapy recounted later. "He also wrote an autobiography and discussed his experience of being rejected by several foster families. He expressed considerable ambivalence about another foster placement, fearing that it would lead to yet another disrupted attachment. Lamont also explored the conflict and anxiety generated by attachment to staff members. He had developed a strategy of maintaining distance or, when threatened by the possibility of attachment, of rejecting the other party before that person could reject him."

For months, no social worker replaced Sister Margaret Ann, who had left due to budget cutbacks. At one point late in 1982, however, Sister Marie Thurlough, Astor Home's social-services director, reviewed Lamont's file and made this notation: "I see Lamont in his group. He is a nice looking boy. Whenever I've seen him he appears to be in good shape and pleasant. However, he is in the RTF unit and is described as seriously disturbed, a fire setter. Though photolisted, we have received no requests." She meant that Lamont now appeared in the illustrated interstate adoption brochures that the Millers had likened to real estate listings, but that no one had even asked to know more about him.

On November 12, 1982, Lamont, then eight and a half, asked to see Sister Marie Thurlough privately. "He talked of wanting a family," she wrote into his file afterward.

AT A HEARING IN Manhattan's family court on March 21, 1983, the city's custody of Lamont and his placement at Astor Home's residential treatment facility were extended for another eighteen months. No one present at the hearing actually knew the boy. Gertrude Burns, the new social worker representing Astor Home in court, had never met him.

The decrepit old Family Court Building where Shirley Wilder had appeared time and again had been replaced in 1976 by an eleven-story structure of polished black granite in Lower Manhattan. The waiting rooms were full of light, their contoured plastic seats bright orange. But just like the dreary waiting rooms in the old building, they overflowed with the barely contained chaos of families in disarray.

In theory, the requirement for extension hearings on children in foster care ensured that such children would not drift in care indefinitely. It forced the agencies involved, including the city's child welfare agency, Special Services for Children (SSC), to account to a judge for the nature of a child's treatment and to offer a plan for the future. But in reality, most such hearings were routine and hurried affairs, squeezed four at a time into the breaks between delinquency hearings. When a parent was still in the picture, a few judges might make it a point to challenge a foster-care agency for failing to work with the family on the child's return home; others might demand to know why there had been no termination of parental rights so the child could be adopted. But in a case like Lamont's, those issues were past. Despite widespread concern that agencies kept children in care too long and did too little to find them adoptive homes, it was rare indeed for a judge to deny a request to extend custody when there were no ready-made alternatives.

IN THE EYES OF ITS SUPPORTERS, Astor Home's setting alone made it a good spot for damaged children. If nothing else, they thought, years spent at Astor provided a respite from the emotional turmoil of changing foster homes, disintegrating families, and bad neighborhoods. Above all, they believed, it served as a place of stability and a safe haven.

But to Lamont, who would be moved half a dozen times within the institution and have a score of different caregivers before he left, Astor Home came to seem like a place where children were defenseless and in danger.

In the section where he lived one year, on the partially-below-ground floor under the school wing, there was a boy named Philip who could feel his seizures coming on at night. Philip would run up and down the corridor in the dark, screaming, "Help me, help me, no! no!" before passing out in the shakes. His cries would echo through the dreams and waking terrors of the other children. In their cell-sized rooms off cinderblock hallways, they would lie listening for the sound of a heavier footfall on the worn linoleum, for the tread of any paid employee who could give Philip his injection.

Many of the children at Astor Home experienced grief and anger almost the way Philip experienced seizures. "Fuck you," a small boy named Sean would scream at the staff when he went off, tears streaming down his face. Sean, a very light-skinned African American boy, was always being restrained. Released, he would be at it again, throwing things and flailing at staff members, who had already been dealing with his outbursts for two or three years and were obviously fed up.

Restraints, Lamont discovered, could easily escalate into time-outs that lasted not for five minutes or twenty, as the rules specified, but for hours. The worst time-out was in the main house, in a small, confined space on the second floor with a window to the outside that had been covered over with hard metal mesh. They would take a child's shoelaces before thrusting him inside and sliding the steel bolts shut.

For a moment, light would still shine through the small square window cut into the door. Then some staff members would switch the light off and leave. Lamont tried to detach from his feelings of fear in the dark. Once he found a metal screw on the floor and played with it to pass the time, dropping it, picking it up, throwing it against the wall as the hours went by. Later he would remember seeing moonlight filtered through the window grid, and the strange shadows that tree branches cast on the floor.

That was the year an Astor Home child died. One Saturday in June 1983—it happened to be Lamont's ninth birthday—counselors took a group of children to the Rhinebeck community swimming pool. At about noon, Marcus Little, a twelve-year-old black boy from Lamont's group, was found submerged near the bottom. He never regained consciousness.

The next week, Gertrude Burns invited Lamont into her office for one of the "face-to-face" bimonthly meetings that state social-service rules required. Usually they played checkers or Spin the Top and talked about impersonal things. Once, after a sketch of Athens and Sparta caught Lamont's eye, they had discussed the Athenian-Spartan conflict. "He is very bright verbally," Burns had noted after that particular session.

This time Lamont told her he was looking forward to summer. He spoke wistfully about a summer he had spent at the beach with his family in Puerto Rico. Almost half his life had passed since he jumped the waves with Alicia's nieces and nephews, but he had not forgotten.

Burns filled out another UCR semiannual review for the city the same day. Lamont had made minimal progress, she wrote, and he continued to need RTF placement. Word for word, she copied nearly everything that Sister Margaret Ann and Sister Marie had typed in previous reports: the "time-out" of two minutes to be imposed each time Lamont teased or instigated his peers, the staff intervention when he lied or showed aggression, the permanency goal of adoption. Goal 2 now stated, "Lamont will gain a better understanding of himself," and Goal 2A, "Lamont will develop an awareness and expression of feelings."

Lamont's happiest feelings at Astor Home were evoked by Reuben Contero. Reuben was a child-care worker, one of the few whom Lamont would remember hugging him and the other boys. Reuben delighted in inventing games the children could play in their cramped quarters, like the one that involved throwing Frisbees from doorways through the hall, or the version of tackle football tailored to their small lounge. When they got funky from running before bedtime, he sometimes broke the rules and gave them a bath—"I'm going to treat you like I would my own kids," he would say. Once Reuben, who played in a Latin jazz band on the side, even helped them make guitars out of glitter and cardboard and put on a talent show. And when he caught Lamont at the keyboard of the piano in the red room, he told him, "Sure, go ahead, fool around."

Another person Lamont liked was Walter Joseph, a bear of a man who was promoted to assistant executive director of Astor Home in 1983. In the summer, Walt Joseph led a nine-year-old Lamont and a few other boys on a series of camping trips into the woods. He taught them how to pitch a tent, how to cook their food, how to follow a trail. Upward Bound, he called the program, which culminated in a twenty-one-mile, five-day hike into the Adirondacks.

"Same philosophy as the Marines," said Joseph, who had grown up in Brooklyn and been a Marine himself in the 1970s. "Stretch them, push them, they grow, they get a sense of mastery."

One of the preparatory hikes was at Bash Bish Falls, where the trail ran high above the gorge, with handrails to steady the way along the falls. One minute Lamont was staring down at the cascades, surrounded by the group; the next minute the others were gone and he was alone. Walt

Joseph had instructed the boys to sit down wherever they happened to be if they ever got separated from the group. The hike leaders would eventually notice you were missing and retrace their steps to find you, he said. But Lamont was afraid to sit alone on the trail, perched between the chasm and the deep woods. Once, on an earlier hike, he had taken a crap on the trail in front of the others rather than go off into the trees by himself.

The sky darkened and the rumble of thunder grew louder than the falling water. It began to rain. By the time the group missed Lamont and doubled back, he was gone.

Walter Joseph was about as scared as the nine-year-old had been. He was sharing supervision of the boys with a recreation leader on the Astor Home staff. They both began searching in earnest under a strong summer rain, the other boys in tow. Finally, with his heart in his throat, Joseph scrambled down into the gorge to look among the rocky places for spots where a falling boy might have lodged. He found nothing and knew he had no choice but to telephone Astor Home to say, "We lost Lamont."

But when they got down to the parking lot, there he was, near a group of departing boy scouts. Lamont had quietly joined the other hike when it crossed his path, following the scouts downhill to their bus rather than waiting alone for people who had left him behind.

On the summer's last camping trip, the five-day expedition to the top of Mount Marcy, Lamont suddenly realized that he wasn't feeling scared anymore. They were sitting beside the campfire in the immense blackness of the mountain. Walt Joseph told them that he could perform open-heart surgery with a pocket knife. Lamont had never felt so tough and self-sufficient before, and he wanted never to feel vulnerable and powerless again.

Come fall, Lamont was moved away from Reuben Contero and the RTF to the less restrictive program in the Cottage, the old frame house below Landsman Kill that had been built in 1919 as an isolation building for contagious children. His photo album disappeared in the move, but he told himself he didn't care.

The woods near the Cottage were small compared to Mount Marcy's forested gorges. The fast-moving creek was just a shadow of Bash Bish Falls. Yet in the evening, when Lamont rolled plastic bins of food for supper down the hill to the Cottage from the kitchen in the main house, he still felt fear prickling the back of his neck.

Often, at dusk, when he saw the old cemetery outlined against a lowering sky beyond the playing fields, Lamont felt more vulnerable and more alone than ever. Then he was sure that Astor Home was haunted. It was haunted, he thought, by the suffering of other children, long dead or long forgotten.

PART FOUR

1984–1989

ONE

From the tall windows in her second-story living room, Justine Wise Polier could see through bare tree branches to the dark earth of the garden's flower beds. It was a gloomy day in late January 1984. When spring came, she would be eighty-one years old. Today she had no feeling of celebration. She was full of anger and disappointment over the latest turn in the *Wilder* lawsuit. She had recently learned that the ACLU was preparing to settle with the city, and in her eyes, the terms were tantamount to surrender.

In essence, the ACLU had abandoned the claim that the city's sectarian system operated in violation of the First Amendment. In exchange, she believed, the city had offered up a lot of formalistic nonsense that purported to guarantee children equal access to the best foster-care services available, regardless of race or religion. Even from these questionable provisions, the settlement exempted a category of "specially designated" agencies for children "whose religious beliefs pervade and determine the entire mode of their lives, regulating it with detail through strictly enforced rules of the religion." That loathsome paragraph was designed for Ohel, the Orthodox Jewish agency, which would thus remain all-white, pervasively religious, and publicly funded.

Polier was waiting to confront Ira Glasser and Marcia Lowry. She had asked them to come and explain themselves in person. A draft of the stipulation of settlement lay on one of the two long refectory tables in the room. She had marked it up fiercely, circling or underlining all the "weasel words" that would make it ineffective and unenforceable. She had drafted an eighteen-page affidavit denouncing it, which was lying out of sight in the study that was also her bedroom. She had offered the document to her son Steven Tulin, urging him to go to court and formally oppose the settlement in his role as counsel to Louise Wise Services. Like a number of other nonsectarian agencies, Louise Wise had reserved the right to intervene when Marcia Lowry agreed to dismiss it as a defendant in the lawsuit in 1975. But Steve didn't want his mother's affidavit. To tell her tactfully that it wouldn't work, he'd sent Donald J. Cohn to see her one recent evening. Cohn, a partner in the law firm Webster and Sheffield, which represented the Children's Aid Society, was such a good friend that he called Polier by her family nickname, Bobsey, based on Steve's baby version of "Mommy."

"It's terrific, Bobsey," Cohn had told her. "You should publish it in the *Harvard Law Review*. But it isn't an affidavit. It's a brief."

Cohn and Steve Tulin would indeed intervene in *Wilder*, objecting to the proposed settlement on behalf of nineteen nondefendant child-care agencies, but they would do it in their own way, with affidavits from the agencies' directors challenging the settlement more from a therapeutic perspective than on constitutional grounds. Principally, they were against the new power the settlement would give the city over private agencies.

Polier could take little satisfaction in their resistance to the city's push for greater control. Not that she had any illusions about Special Services for Children; but she wanted it fixed, not written off. All her life she had fought to get the public sector to assume greater responsibility for children in need. Sitting in judgment over delinquent children and neglectful parents in family court, she had always felt that she might herself have committed any of the offenses they were charged with. That she had not, she'd told Shad once, was "largely a matter of luck, privilege, and always feeling loved." Recently she had tried to convey this to a young woman with a tape recorder, an oral historian from Radcliffe's Schlesinger Library.

"We demand of poor people in this country more than we demand of ourselves," she had said. "We're not a poor country. Yet there is no country among the developed Western nations that doesn't provide a family allowance as a matter of right when a child is born, except the United States. We talk about the importance of the family, the moral values of the family, but we're not willing to provide the underpinnings to which every child is entitled. We're much more willing to give money to the aged, the blind, the disabled. Children get the lowest amounts of money support in this country. . . . The self-image of a child who feels his parents are not anything, and that nothing good is going to happen to him, is probably the most destructive ethos to which any child can be exposed."

These were the abiding problems left untouched by all the fads and fashions that had swept through child welfare and juvenile justice in her lifetime. Years before, she had welcomed the shift from orphanages toward foster-home care, and later, too, the attack on foster care for leaving children in limbo, and the movement to broaden adoption services to include nonwhite and older children. The crusaders of the sixties and seventies had not been wrong to champion due process, or to try to restrain an overreaching state, she thought, but she faulted them for focusing too narrowly on the juvenile court system and grim juvenile institutions, when they should rather have concentrated on deteriorating social and economic conditions, inadequate public education, and poor health services.

She had even tackled Judge Harold "Ace" Tyler personally about the *Wilder* case one afternoon in the midseventies when she was visiting a friend whose property in northern Westchester County abutted his. Years after he had left the bench, Tyler would still remember Polier's intensity on that occasion, and her unwillingness to let him rest on generalities about the good works of religious agencies since Dutch colonial days. "She was very unhappy about what had happened to this Wilder child," he recalled.

She had been fierce and unsparing, too, in her two days of deposition as an expert witness in the case, on April 29 and June 21, 1976. In truth, the deposition had unfolded more like a lecture than an interrogation; at times the attorneys couldn't get a question in edgewise. But she had so much to say, so much disinformation to correct.

At the time of the deposition, in the spring of 1976, she was seventy-three. For three years after her retirement from family court, at seventy, she directed the Juvenile Justice Division of the Children's Defense Fund for Marian Wright Edelman, a friend since the early 1960s. Polier had agreed to work three days a week and had produced three national studies: one on the harmful use of jails for juveniles, another on the children of women prisoners, and a third on the fate of children shipped to institutions outside their home states. In South Carolina, she had started a federal class-action lawsuit against the practice of jailing white children with white adults, and black children with black adults, after documenting the rapes and abuse that resulted. In Louisiana, she had met with corrections officials ordered by a federal court to end cruel and unusual practices in the prison they called Angola; before long she was fighting the mass IQ tests used there to exclude more than thirty-seven hundred of the prison's four thousand inmates from its one tiny, all-white educational program. She had also thrown herself into a Connecticut case, *Roe* v. *Norton,* drafting an amicus brief to help challenge a law that would have jailed for up to a year any mother on public assistance who refused to identify and prosecute the absent father of her child—a law that would thus have deprived children of their only caring parent.

She had planned to work only part-time after retirement and to take more time for her hobbies. She had planned to spend more time at Lake Placid, at the family's rustic retreat upstate. But as Shad had often remarked during those three years, her retirement meant that she worked only eight days a week.

Dear Shad—irascible, impatient, a fighter to the end. He was seventy, and still putting in nine-hour days at the law office he shared with Steve, when he died quite unexpectedly of a heart attack, alone in the house. It happened on June 30, 1976, only nine days after her second *Wilder* deposition.

Everything in her life had seemed to shrink after that, beginning with the house itself. Unable to afford the real estate taxes and loath to leave the brownstone in which she had lived since 1941, she vacated the top three floors and turned them into a rental apartment. It took her weeks just to clear out the books. Every night she brought them down by the armful and sorted them into piles to give away. Much of the child welfare history went to her foster daughter, Trudy, who was by then Trudy Festinger, a professor at the NYU School of Social Work in the midst of an in-depth study of former foster children. It was only fitting that Trudy should have become a defender of foster care, and particularly of the possibility of a strong psychological bond between foster parent and child. Growing up in the Poliers' household, she had dutifully visited her refugee father once a week, conscious that she was all he had left. But she had never lived with him again, and she considered the Poliers her family. She was an adult, a mother herself, divorced and remarried, when her father died and they could finally establish in law what had been true for so long in fact. Trudy joked that she was the oldest adoptee in history.

Some of Shad's books went to Steve, who seemed more like his stepfather every day, and others to their son Jonathan, a lawyer, too. Polier did not keep the lost treasures that turned up among her father's books, not even a tiny volume in Hebrew with thick leather covers studded with tiny stones. But in old age, she felt more than ever that she was her father's daughter.

She had always prided herself on eschewing the diplomatic silence, the politically astute compromise, no matter the cost. She had never stopped being a woman of her convictions. She didn't think of herself as a crusader; she was "just a hard-working old dray horse," as she put it—undeterred by defeats and disappointments, incapable of retreat. The key was not to give up on one's principles. That was the message she had for her ACLU visitors.

TWO

T HEY HADN'T BEEN INVITED; THEY HAD BEEN SUMMONED,
Lowry thought as she and Ira Glasser followed Justine Wise Polier
up the small spiral staircase to her library. Polier showed her to a straight-
backed leather armchair and sat down opposite her, on the sofa beside the
windows. Glasser, who usually sprawled, perched on the other end of the
couch like a penitent schoolboy.

In her deep, expressive voice, Polier attacked the settlement they had
painfully carved out during half a year of negotiations. She cared deeply
about racial discrimination, she said, but that was not the only wrong
cloaked and perpetuated by the system's sectarianism. In the days when
the city's poor children were mostly white, she had seen New York's
sectarianism champion large, regimented institutions long after more
enlightened states had shifted to foster homes. She had seen religious
organizations block the development of public adoption services while
hundreds of babies and small children languished in hospital wards and
shelters. She had seen religion and power politics become so intertwined
that the state abdicated all meaningful supervision over the spending of
public funds and turned a blind eye to the suffering of children of all
races.

Why, she demanded to know, had Lowry abandoned the lawsuit's legal
core and greatest strength, the establishment clause of the First Amendment? How could the ACLU—the ACLU!—countenance a settlement
that jettisoned the principle of separation of church and state? And in
exchange for what? For the plaintiffs' lawyers had given the defendants
language that would allow them room to dodge any real accountability
for their treatment of individual children.

Imperious was the word Lowry had always associated with Polier, and she was imperious today. But the tone of her scolding wasn't "Listen to me because I'm a big shot," Lowry thought; it was "Listen to me because I care deeply and I've dedicated my life to these issues." What made it so painful for Lowry to hear was that in many respects she agreed with Polier.

From the beginning, Lowry had seized on the legal claims in *Wilder* as a means to an end, a way to attack the entrenched problems of the city's foster-care system. Still, the constitutional principles she had invoked in the lawsuit were not just a device. Seeing how sectarianism played out in child welfare had made her, like Polier, a strict separationist of strong conviction. Lowry had never thought of *Wilder* as primarily a lawsuit about racial discrimination; she had never defined her goal as simply getting more minority kids into the better foster-care programs. She saw the whole system as dysfunctional, and like Polier, she was convinced that its resistance to change was rooted in a sectarian structure that violated the establishment clause.

Lowry's original position had been that there was no way, except in violation of the Constitution, that the city could fulfill a government obligation (child placement) by financing agencies whose mission was religious. She still believed that. But the history of the *Wilder* case demonstrated that no judge was going to come to the same conclusion, since that would mean dismantling the foster-care system. Her legal position was correct, but if she had learned any lesson in eleven years of litigating the case, it was that in the real world, being correct on this point would get her nowhere, slowly. Wasn't it better, then, to settle for what she could get?

There was no way to convey to Polier how passionate and arduous the settlement process had been. The result was not an abdication but the outcome of hand-to-hand combat on three fronts.

First were the surreal negotiating sessions with the city. One, scheduled to run from 5:30 to 8:30 P.M., had lasted all night long instead, from Thursday evening to Friday morning of the 1983 Labor Day weekend. When the lawyers stumbled into daylight from the windowless sixth-floor conference room where they had spent thirteen hours, they still had no agreement. Of course neither Fritz Schwarz nor Burt Neuborne had been with them that night, down in the trenches. Later it seemed fitting that only the soothing patter of Ike Saunders, an articulate black newcomer to the case from the child welfare administration, had kept the negotiations going when tempers exploded and the city lawyers almost walked out. Saunders, whose résumé included Columbia Law School and a stint as a second deputy mayor in Detroit, was so impressive overall that Neuborne had added his name to a short list of potential faculty appointments at NYU Law School. He was so likable that Diane Morgenroth loaned him money to go visit his family on Cape Cod the first week she met him. But months later it turned out that the city had failed to check his references. Saunders had no law degree, no family on Cape Cod, and no record of government service in Detroit; what he did have was warrants outstanding for his arrest on fraud charges in two states. *Wilder*'s star negotiator was a con artist.

Perhaps only a flim-flam man could have been so conciliatory, given the fundamental contradictions under discussion. It was all very well to talk abstractly of the natural tension between the establishment clause and the free-exercise clause, but as the settlement talks ground on, the practical details became increasingly inflammatory. Should a crucifix hang in the room of a Jewish child placed by the city at public expense in a Catholic-run agency? Should a black Protestant child in a Jewish-run agency be denied a ham sandwich? What about a picture of Moses crossing the Red Sea—was that the same kind of religious symbol as a cross over a child's bed?

The other religious issue that emerged as a crucial stumbling block was birth control. Here, the city lawyers were much more sympathetic to the ACLU's position. Adolescents placed by the city in foster care should have equal access to family-planning services, they agreed, no matter what agency they were placed in. For the government to rule otherwise was to favor the tenets of one religion over others, in violation of the establishment clause—not to mention to invite unwanted pregnancies.

Still, the city lawyers could see that legally the Catholic agencies were also right: requiring them to provide birth control and abortion counseling in violation of their own religious beliefs would contravene the free-exercise clause of the First Amendment. Lowry argued that no one was forcing the Catholic agencies to contract with the city. If they accepted public money, they would have to accept the government's rules, too. If they chose to forgo $50 million or so, the money and the children should go to agencies willing to do the job the way the city wanted it done.

But Fritz Schwarz wanted to keep the religious agencies in the foster-care system—that was his main reason for pursuing the settlement. It was he who finally crafted compromise language on religious symbols and family planning that was acceptable to Monsignor Arpie, the director of child care for Catholic Charities, and to lawyers from Davis, Polk. Children in care had to have meaningful access to the full range of family planning, according to his terms, but the agencies did not have to provide it themselves, just make the children available for instruction by others. An agency could convey its moral precepts on such matters, but only as part of religious instruction. Religious symbols, meanwhile, would not be barred, but only those requested by the child should be in the child's room, and in common areas they should not be "excessive," a provision that Lowry would trumpet as a victory in the ACLU press release but that she knew very well was unenforceable. Despite the hours spent wrangling over such questions, Lowry accepted these accommodations without distress.

For her, the part of the stipulation that was hardest to swallow was the Orthodox Jewish exemption, covering those agencies serving children "whose religious beliefs pervade and determine the entire mode of their lives, regulating it with detail through strictly enforced rules of the religion." The number of children involved was small—about two hundred in the agency in Brooklyn known as Ohel—but the principle at stake was important to Lowry. If permitting discrimination by some publicly funded religious agencies and not others didn't constitute the government's favoring one religion over another, what did? But the city negotiators considered Ohel a deal breaker. The Orthodox Jewish community was politically very powerful, and legally, it had a strong U.S. Supreme Court decision on its side: in a 1972 case, the high court had made a similarly big exception for a discrete religious community on free-exercise grounds. That decision, *Wisconsin* v. *Yoder,* had allowed Amish parents an exemption from compulsory-education laws so they could keep their children home from school after the eighth grade. Chief Justice Burger's majority opinion even explicitly likened the pervasively religious practices of the Amish to Talmudic dietary laws. The legal argument in *Yoder* wasn't palatable to Lowry. If anything, her views were more in tune with the partial dissent by Justice William O. Douglas, who said the children involved had a right to be heard by the Court before their parents were granted a religious exemption that would inevitably "impose the parents' notions of religious duty upon their children." But she ultimately accepted her colleagues' view that *Yoder* made her hard-line position untenable, especially since the practical problem of integrating Orthodox Jewish children into other agencies was a real vulnerability in her case.

The result was the settlement provision for "specially designated" agencies that Polier loathed, and with good reason. A lawsuit that was supposed to promote public accountability and inclusion had created a huge loophole for the most sectarian, least racially integrated, and least ecumenical programs taxpayers' money could buy.

Polier said she didn't believe in sacrificing principle for what was politically possible. There was no other way, Lowry countered hopelessly. She was willing to go down in flames if there was a shot at victory, and Ira Glasser was, too. But by now it seemed obvious to both of them that the risk was much bigger than it was worth. The courts were retreating. The country had shifted to the right.

"We cannot win now on the strict First Amendment position, if we ever could," Glasser told Polier. Whatever they might win with Judge Ward, they had a high chance of losing on appeal. "The appeals will take years, and we can make bad law," Lowry put in. "I am not sanguine about getting the Supreme Court to dismantle the New York City foster-care system. The bottom line here is services to kids."

Yes, under considerable pressure from her own colleagues at the ACLU, she had compromised. In Lowry's own opinion, the compromise was unconstitutional, but she believed it was the best they could do.

Backlit by the window, Polier seemed to gather herself to her full height.

"There is no compromising with the First Amendment," she said.

It was a memorable phrase, and a terrible reproach, Lowry thought. And it was true.

To Glasser, there was something marvelous and moving about Polier's anger. For twenty years the ACLU had been suing the hell out of everything her generation represented, dismantling the very concept of the state as parent and attacking the discretionary power that had accrued in the name of benevolence to juvenile courts, mental-health professionals, and ladies bountiful. Yet he and Marcia were Polier's protégés, and she was saying to them, "You dropped the ball."

They left feeling very sad. You had the sense, Lowry thought, that she was passing the baton, and already they had stumbled.

THREE

O N MARCH 13, 1984, A FRONT-PAGE ARTICLE IN THE *NEW York Times* presented the *Wilder* settlement as a fait accompli. "We're happy to have signed this," Fritz Schwarz told the *Times*. "The principles are exactly what we set out to agree to." A two-column photograph with the story's jump caught him in midgesture at the press conference in his office, in shirt sleeves and a sweater vest, his hair falling in lank clumps over his forehead. He came across as the winning architect of an outcome that had no losers. Lawyers for Catholic and Jewish foster-care agencies were still reviewing the proposed agreement, the article noted, and they had been given two weeks to suggest amendments, but "they said they would be likely to accept the settlement if it provided that foster children's religious preferences would be respected, whenever possible."

There was no suggestion in the article that John Joseph O'Connor, a bishop in Scranton, Pennsylvania, who was about to become New York's eighth archbishop, might take a harder line. But a *Times* editorial appearing the same day denounced the "highly offensive implications" of remarks the bishop had made on a Sunday television news program, comparing "the killing of four thousand babies a day in the United States, unborn babies," to the Holocaust. Telling of his visit to Dachau, O'Connor had said, "Now, Hitler tried to solve a problem, the Jewish question. So kill them, shove them into ovens, burn them. Well, we claim that unborn babies are a problem, so kill them. To me it is really precisely the same." He seemed to be suggesting that Jews were a genuine problem and only Hitler's remedy was evil, the *Times* said, and that women who made the painful choice of abortion were "practicing Nazi genocide."

O'Connor appeared willing to provoke civic uproar in the passionate service of doctrinal principle. It seemed that in *Wilder,* however, no principles at all were at stake anymore. Under the settlement agreement, children would be placed in foster-care agencies on a first-come, first-served basis, regardless of their race or religion. But the agreement allowed children whose parents expressed a religious preference to be placed in homes observing that religion. "If no such placement is available and the situation is not deemed an emergency, the child will probably be put on a waiting list," the *Times* explained. The settlement provided, too, for an outside consultant to evaluate and classify city foster-care agencies, ranking them by the quality of the services they offered. According to the article, "The findings are to be used to insure that foster children have equal access to the highest quality care available." Final approval rested with Judge Robert J. Ward, of course, but the *Times* piece made this sound like a formality. Who could be against equal access to quality care?

Shirley Wilder herself publicly expressed satisfaction with the agreement, though on a more poignant note. "Miss Wilder, who is now twenty-four years old, still lives in New York City and attends a computer school. She said in an interview that she was pleased that a settlement had been reached. 'I'm happy because it will make a change in the agencies,' she said. 'But it really hasn't done anything for me. Back then, I was looking [to] people for help.' "

In retrospect, the *Times* article represented the high-water mark of agreement. The settlement of a lawsuit that had subsided from an assault to an annoyance was a complicated legal and political minuet. And on March 19, 1984, when John Joseph O'Connor took his seat in Saint Patrick's Cathedral as archbishop of New York, the carefully crafted *Wilder* stipulation became anathema.

MONSIGNOR ROBERT ARPIE AND MARCIA LOWRY made an odd couple as they walked through Rockefeller Center in the spring of 1984, the Catholic prelate in his cassock, the woman lawyer in a dark tailored suit. They had just emerged from the taping of a television talk show, a local public-affairs program called "Positively Black" that was doing a feature on the *Wilder* lawsuit.

Arpie, the director of child care for Catholic Charities, was feeling particularly frustrated by the experience. For more than half of the thirty-minute show he had been left to cool his heels in a secluded room off the WNBC set while Lowry and the two black hosts talked about *Wilder* outside his hearing. By the time he joined them, it was hopeless for him to try to redress the imbalance. He felt set up.

A wiry man with a fair Irish complexion and the energy of a boy, he was sixty-three, twenty years older than Lowry. He had known her since her days as one of Barbara Blum's lieutenants in the city's child welfare office. They had actually worked closely together to devise new residential programs for the "hard-to-place" teenagers who deluged the childcare system in the late sixties and early seventies. But by now, he thought, he saw her for what she really was: a marvelous advocate for the disposition of theoretical stances that held absolutely no benefit for children.

After eleven years of *Wilder* litigation, whenever Arpie met with lawyers in the case, he thought about what their millions of dollars in legal fees might have bought for needy children.

"Marcia," he said to Lowry as they passed the golden statue of Prometheus in Rockefeller Plaza, "we in the Catholic group have been open to the black Protestant children, even over the Catholic children we serve, and the statistics show that."

She made some noncommittal response, and he went on with his careful probing. "It seems to me," he said, "that you have much more concern about the whole issue of placement of children according to religion. Disbanding the New York pattern, that was your goal."

"Oh, yes," she readily agreed.

"Marcia," he continued. "You really have a much more far-reaching goal in mind—the end of public funding to all religiously sponsored services, specifically, in this instance, hospital services under Catholic auspices, or any religious auspices."

As he would remember and recount her reply afterward (Lowry herself would not later recall the conversation and would deny its substance), she did not miss a beat: " 'I have no problem with answering that question. The answer is yes.' "

Before them now were the soaring spires of Saint Patrick's Cathedral, built by the pennies of the Catholic poor and the fierce determination of New York archbishops over the course of half a century. Here in stone and stained glass was a testament to the power of religion and its ineradicable place in the city's history. But he didn't think Lowry saw the humor in the situation.

She had zealously collected examples of public child-care money spent for religious purposes, including Astor Home's $6,000 in chapel repairs, Madonna Heights's $200,000 claim for construction of a new chapel, and the $4,980 spent on stained glass for the church at the Mission of the Immaculate Virgin (MIV), the agency that Arpie himself was now directing. To support her contention that New York City's child welfare system unconstitutionally promoted religion, she had quoted MIV's mission statement, among others: "Each one of our adolescents in this Unit is a very special person, closely identified with our Lord and Savior and sharing intimately in his cross. . . . The Mission speaks of a life that is greater than one's own and a power that can transform present suffering and pain into the joy of Easter. People, Christ is risen, Alleluia."

Catholics of Arpie's generation, brought up to be on guard against Protestant onslaughts, had never stopped seeing themselves as a beleaguered minority. He had felt a sense of historical déjà vu in 1975 when Marcia Lowry began asking him in *Wilder* depositions why elderly Daughters of Charity were being housed rent-free at the Astor Home for Children, and how the Catholic agencies could claim "reimbursement" from the city for the salaries of Sisters who were not, in fact, being paid. Was public money going straight to the mother house of the nuns' religious order, to archdiocesan coffers, or perhaps to Rome?

It was all evocative of an inflammatory episode a lifetime earlier, the infamous "charities investigations" of 1914–16. The Mission of the Immaculate Virgin had been the largest of twenty-six private children's institutions held up to disgrace during that period by a would-be reform mayor. The controversial list also included fourteen Protestant agencies, among them Sheltering Arms. To Justine Wise Polier and her progressive forebears, the investigation had represented a noble, evenhanded effort to hold powerful private interests accountable for the care of the city's wards. But many Catholics saw it as an attack on their religion and on their political success in winning public tax support to care for poor children. They felt particularly insulted by the implication that under the public-subsidy system, the nuns were holding children hostage in inferior institutions at public expense in order to enrich their own religious orders. The voters blamed the reform mayor, John Purroy Mitchel, though he was a Catholic himself, and promptly put him out of office, in a lesson later-twentieth-century mayors had not forgotten.

Even after F.A.O. Schwarz, Jr., stepped in to orchestrate a settlement, even after the ACLU agreed to drop its establishment-clause claims, Lowry had continued to insist that any settlement must bar religious symbols from the common areas of child-care agencies; they were oppressive to children of other faiths, she said.

The religious-symbols issue had been on the agenda when Arpie led the Catholic contingent to the corporation counsel's office to discuss the settlement negotiations with Schwarz in September 1983. He was accompanied by Dick Nolan, the senior lawyer on the case, and Tom Aquilino, the junior lawyer from Davis, Polk who had been so tough on Kenneth Clark. It was immediately apparent that Schwarz knew nothing about child care. He did not even realize that the initials MIV stood for Mission of the Immaculate Virgin. When they told him, he blurted out, "My God, we're paying for that?"

Arpie did not like or trust Fritz Schwarz, with his patrician nonchalance and his arrogant remove from the concerns of those who actually cared for children. In Arpie's eyes, Schwarz embodied the Protestant establishment that his own forebears had struggled to overcome. Arpie's parents had been servants to very wealthy Protestant families summering in Oyster Bay, Long Island, when they met, his Irish mother a lady's maid, his father, the son of Italian immigrants, an undergardener ("which means he worked variously on manure piles," Arpie put it dryly).

For Aquilino, the sense of antipathy toward Schwarz was even more personal. Aquilino had studied engineering at Cornell and political science at Drexel and the Free University of Berlin; he had clerked with a federal judge after graduating with honors from Columbia Law School. But he still referred to himself as a "Guinea lawyer," and at Davis, Polk, where Schwarz's father had been revered, he felt like an interloper. Appearing before Judge Tyler in the earliest stages of the *Wilder* suit, Aquilino had been acutely aware that his youngest uncle, Joey, was the gardener at the judge's Westchester County home, and that Mrs. Tyler bought vegetables from his paternal grandmother at a roadside stand.

Aquilino's mother, a committed atheist who traced her Presbyterian roots back to Aaron Burr, had been disowned by her father for marrying the devout Catholic son of an Italian immigrant groundskeeper.

Aquilino's father had risen through mechanical genius and military service to head airplane maintenance at La Guardia for American Airlines, but he was never good enough for the "English" side of the family. Aquilino had grown up hearing about his maternal grandfather as the prototypical WASP, a man who had advised J. P. Morgan, made a fortune on Wall Street, and kept his sense of superior caste long after losing his money in the Depression. Schwarz was like the living emblem of this rejecting heritage.

"Fritz Schwarz was the Judas," Aquilino would say of the corporation counsel's decision to settle *Wilder* with the ACLU. "Fritz came along when we were in the trenches and in his infinite conceit said we ought to try to settle this case, as though we hadn't tried to do it for the past ten years."

Of the three visitors in his office on that day, only Dick Nolan felt at ease with Schwarz. A few years earlier they had worked closely together on the merger of two steel companies, and their joint coup had been finding an expert witness on the steel industry who also happened to be a Jesuit priest. Nolan not only respected the younger man's legal skill and personal integrity, he valued his friendship. For Nolan, Fritzy Schwarz would always be his father's son, and F.A.O. Schwarz, Sr., had been one of his idols. Distinguished and charming, the older Schwarz was the partner who had given Nolan the last in the requisite battery of interviews before Davis, Polk hired him in 1957. Nolan was the son of an Irish-American printer active in the Brooklyn typographers' union. For him, winning a partnership had been an uphill fight. Along the way, in dress and in manner, he had himself become the epitome of the Wall Street lawyer.

But with an unlawyerly passion, Nolan loathed Marcia Lowry and her case. One of their clashes became emblematic of the raw hostility she could evoke from her adversaries. Neither witnesses nor participants could remember the specific topic under discussion at the time, but Nolan became so angry that Lowry herself thought he was either going to reach across the conference table to strangle her or have a stroke. Red in the face, veins bulging in his neck, the craggy corporate lawyer slammed his hand down on the burnished wood table and screamed at her, "Who do you think you are? The czarina of foster care? You can't run our system!"

Arpie himself became angry at the idea that this woman wanted to ban the crucifix from precincts that had been dedicated to Christ's work for more than a century. Even Fritz Schwarz had agreed at the September

1983 meeting that such a thing would be insulting, and he had suggested a phrase to surmount the problem: a stipulation that there should not be "excessive" religious symbols in common areas. "I would agree with that aesthetically," Arpie had responded with a broad smile, and the phrase had become part of the boilerplate of successive stipulation drafts.

But when the newly invested O'Connor read the stipulation for the first time in March 1984, he saw the "excessive religious symbols" clause as an outrage perpetrated by the ACLU and its Protestant ally, Fritz Schwarz. The birth-control solution included in the stipulation was no better in his eyes.

Arpie was on record maintaining that the standards of behavior set by Catholic values were part and parcel of the Catholic agencies' benefit to children of all colors and creeds. It was never in the best interest of a child to have a contraceptive device available, he had told Lowry in 1975, in the first of his three depositions.

"We are concerned not to support such promiscuity," he had said. "You could say this is basically religious in its derivation. . . . I say to you it's out of concern for the human condition." He had told the *Times* in 1975, "Shirley Wilder doesn't need contraceptive devices. She doesn't need abortive devices. She needs supervision."

But Arpie was a practical man, and a moderate. In fact, the church's reach had shortened considerably since the death in 1968 of Cardinal Spellman, who had openly scoffed at the "shibboleth of separation of Church and State" and traded real estate with Robert Moses as though they were playing Monopoly. In the larger American Catholic community, 90 percent of sexually active Catholic women had used methods of contraception that were not approved by the church, according to a National Center for Health Statistics survey in 1982; a quarter of the 1.5 million women who had abortions each year were Catholic. Catholic Charities did not monitor the implementation of its policy on contraception. Many youngsters in care went home on weekends; there they might resort to birth control or abortion without their agency's knowledge or approval. In any case, neither Arpie nor his two lawyers had objected to Schwarz's solution when it appeared in successive drafts of the stipulation they circulated back and forth: it allowed Catholic agencies to satisfy the requirement of family-planning access by making children available to the city for instruction, rather than having to provide such services themselves.

O'Connor's reaction to the same clause was to threaten to close down all Catholic child care rather than compromise his religious principles. What the ACLU had been unable to do through the Constitution, it seemed, the new archbishop was prepared to do in the name of God.

Other new players had already complicated the settlement. The non-sectarian agencies, represented by Justine Wise Polier's son Stephen Wise Tulin and Don Cohn, had won the right to be heard by Judge Ward. The two lawyers were orchestrating an outcry against the compromise by such clinicians as Morton S. Rogers, executive director of Louise Wise Services, who argued that the placement scheme central to the agreement treated children "like so many ears of corn." And as the Catholic agencies' lawyers scrambled to toe the harder line taken by the new archbishop, Jewish philanthropic organizations were waging an intense lobbying campaign of their own against the settlement in private meetings with the mayor.

And then, quite suddenly, less than two months after the settlement announcement, Mayor Koch told Fritz Schwarz privately that he had changed his mind.

IN HIS HIGH-CEILINGED OFFICE at New York City Hall, the mayor defended a nineteenth-century accommodation by religion, politics, and social need. He really believed in the religious agencies' right to decide on the basis of religion who they were going to take in, he said, and he wanted Schwarz to withdraw the city's signature from the *Wilder* stipulation of settlement.

"I can't do that," the city's lawyer replied.

He knew Koch had never been enamored of the settlement. In an account of the *Wilder* controversy included in the 1989 book *His Eminence and Hizzoner,* produced in tandem with by-then Cardinal O'Connor, Koch would write that his "intuitive belief in the value of the religious dimension in the provision of foster-care services" made him sympathetic to the Catholic Church's resistance to the notion of first-come, first-served assignments. It also seemed reasonable to him, he would write, that Jewish organizations considered it their first raison d'être to take care of Jewish kids. Sure, the social services they provided were paid for in great part by taxes, but also involved were large sums that the organizations had raised themselves. "Why, they argued, should they provide any services at all, since they no longer would be able to have a minimum, let alone a maximum, number of Jewish kids in their system? It didn't make sense," Koch would assert.

Nevertheless, just that winter, in a series of meetings with Schwarz and his legal team, the mayor had fully approved the *Wilder* settlement as both sensible and politically desirable for everyone concerned. On February 29, Koch had personally OK'd plans for handling the press coverage of the settlement announcement. It had gone off perfectly, garnering articles in all the papers and a favorable editorial in the *Times*. It was only after the agreement had been signed, sealed, and delivered to the court with the agencies' foreknowledge and acquiescence that the same agencies began demanding a trial and threatening to pull out of the foster-care system entirely if the mayor did not scuttle the settlement.

Schwarz knew immediately that unless he could bring Koch back on board, he would have no choice but to resign. He would not repudiate an agreement that he had already signed and still believed was right; he could not put the case back on the trial calendar for political reasons and keep his integrity. But at this moment he was not going to tell Koch so. Under the circumstances, he thought, if he said, "Look, I'm going to have to leave," Koch might very well react emotionally and tell him to go ahead.

"The problem is a legal one," he reminded the mayor. "If we go into the case saying public money should be used to allow religious organizations to do this, there's a very substantial likelihood the case will be lost."

He knew the other man respected his judgment. Despite the bluster and ego that prevailed in the mayor's public image, Koch was an excellent listener in private. Many of the people around him assumed they had to second his opinion to win his favor, but Schwarz saw in Koch a man prepared to be convinced by substantial disagreement, and to respect dissent as long as it came from someone he judged to be loyal.

But this time Koch was not interested in being persuaded. In moments, the meeting was over.

On purely political terms, the *Wilder* defendants were Koch's natural allies, the very core of the winning coalition he had used to build and consolidate his power. White ethnic fear of being outnumbered and disempowered by lower-class blacks and Hispanics, a key theme in the *Wilder* outcry, was also a key component of Koch's electoral success. Not that Koch was unwilling to cross his political allies or to anger large campaign contributors; in fact, he was already embroiled in a politically volatile legal battle with Archbishop O'Connor over gay rights. This conflict centered on the mayor's Executive Order 50, of which a crucial provision forbade those contracting with the city to engage in employment discrimination on the basis of "sexual orientation and affectional preference"—a measure that in effect added homosexuality to the protected categories already recognized in federal and state law, including race, creed, disability, and gender.

To O'Connor, E.O. 50 and *Wilder* raised fundamentally the same issue. Schwarz also saw the similarities and was struck by the difference in the mayor's resolve: "On gay rights, Koch's position was, 'Well, the city's providing the money.' On that front, the mayor never wavered at all. He would say to [Archbishop] O'Connor, 'We'll just have to disagree.' On *Wilder*, he was much more torn personally."

WHEN SCHWARZ RETURNED to his own office that afternoon, he summoned his *Wilder* legal team. There were some rumblings at city hall, he told them, and he was very upset—so upset that it looked like he might resign. He asked them all to come to a meeting at his apartment early the next day to discuss the memo he planned to write to the mayor over the weekend, laying out all the reasons that the city should not change course now.

In the end it was an extremely effective twenty-page brief, its austere authority enhanced by Schwarz's private decision to resign if he could not persuade the mayor to change his mind. Schwarz did want to let Koch know indirectly that his resignation hung in the balance, however, so he told Stan Brezenoff, the deputy mayor in charge of social services, confident that Brezenoff would inform him in a psychologically more effective way than he could himself. It was the mayor's prerogative to ignore his advice, of course, "but I couldn't stay on as corporation counsel if I couldn't do what I thought was legally right, and right as a matter of principle," he said. He gave Brezenoff a copy of the memorandum. In a cover memo to Koch, dated May 17, he summarized his stance:

(1) What we have done is correct on the merits;
(2) In any event, the agencies' rights will be fully protected at the forthcoming hearing before the Court;

(3) Finally, we made a considered judgment to sign and, under those circumstances, we cannot defend or justify attempting to withdraw our signature.

Among the most damning sections of the document itself were those detailing Schwarz's view that the present foster-care system was constitutionally indefensible. He dissected the agencies' practice of "self-referrals," by which a parent of the preferred religion could win a place for a child by approaching an agency directly, thus jumping the waiting list of children already approved by the city's Special Services for Children as needing placement. "Certain programs are of higher quality than others and black children are being denied equal access to high quality programs and are being relegated to lesser quality ones simply because they are not of a certain religion," Schwarz wrote.

One of the plaintiffs' major claims was that Special Services for Children, through its lack of control over the private agencies, facilitated and condoned discrimination. "Plaintiffs will be able to prove that the manner in which the City operates the foster care system has a discriminatory impact on black children," Schwarz said flatly. Indeed, he contended, "pulling back from our agreement would be proof positive that the foster care system is in fact run by the agencies and not by the City. Plaintiffs could prove that SSC does not control the system and allows the agencies to determine what children they will serve. This . . . may even rise to knowing and reckless discrimination. More importantly, Judge Ward would view the City's withdrawal of its consent to settlement as a sign of extreme bad faith, weakness and proof of plaintiffs' underlying claims." In attempting to retract the agreement, he added, city hall would be perceived as succumbing to the political pressure of the agencies. "There are no magic words which could effectively paper this over," he wrote. "The City's bargaining position in future cases and the professional reputation of its Law Department would also be seriously damaged."

Schwarz left unstated that his resignation would turn it into a political scandal, which would be even more damaging to the mayor. Instead, he pointed to the public good at stake:

"The *Wilder* settlement represents a culmination of SSC's efforts to gain the upper hand in its relationship with the agencies. Retraction of the *Wilder* settlement would result in a tremendous setback . . . and would make it extremely difficult for SSC to push through changes in the system which the agencies do not like, but which are in the public interest."

BREZENOFF WARNED KOCH about the strength of Schwarz's feelings. "Fritz is really troubled about this," he told the mayor. "We really ought to sit down with him and go over the issues." A meeting was set for May 23, 1984, a Wednesday.

Brezenoff himself shared Schwarz's view of the settlement and had a New Deal belief in government's potential for the public good. He saw the distinct possibility, even the probability, that some agencies would opt to leave the system. Given the abysmal record of city-run shelters and diagnostic centers, he, Schwarz, and the mayor all harbored grave doubts about the city's providing more of these services. The question was how to keep what were probably the best agencies in the city: the premier Catholic and Jewish agencies. But Brezenoff and Schwarz told Koch forcefully that the risk of losing in court outweighed any downsides of settlement, even if some agencies did bow out—and Schwarz insisted they were bluffing, anyway.

"Suppose the whole system was thrown out as a result of a full court review?" Brezenoff said. "We then would be faced with a worst-case scenario—a direct-care municipal system in a much shorter time frame."

As Schwarz had pointed out in his memo, the settlement would minimize change, increasing control of placement by the city but leaving the sectarian agencies great discretion once children were in their care. If the city proceeded to trial and lost, it would also lose control over the scope of the relief imposed by the court. "The ACLU and the Court could become de facto administrators of SSC and, given Judge Ward's reluctance to handle these matters himself, he probably would vest plaintiffs with substantial oversight authority," the memo noted. That meant that Marcia Lowry—or whichever special master she chose—could truly become the czarina of the foster-care system.

"All right," the mayor finally told Schwarz, "you can go ahead with *Wilder*. I don't like it, but I accept it."

Brezenoff had no illusions about what had carried the day: "Believe me, it wasn't any of the arguments that Fritz and I made about the substance of *Wilder*. It was, 'We're going to lose, and you'll lose the whole thing.'"

FOUR

MARY ZUVIC WAS A TWENTY-ONE-YEAR-OLD COLLEGE SE-
nior with long, flowing hair when she was assigned to Lamont
Wilder as part of a social-work course at Marist College in the fall of
1983. She had grown up fourth in a Catholic family of five children in the
Hudson River town of Cold Spring, New York, free to explore the coal
yards and the riverbank in the long summer afternoons. Astor Home
struck her as a place of skinny corridors, narrow-minded nuns, and children whose lives were impossibly regimented. But she was enchanted by
nine-year-old Lamont. Of all the children she had been assigned to work
with, he was her favorite—"such a good kid, full of life and energy, and he
had nobody."

Their weekly sessions felt more like friendship than social work. She
had won his trust from the beginning, when she made it her special mission to find his lost photo album. He began to tell her about the people in
the pictures, about feeling angry and sad, about wishing he could be
adopted again. He showed her a kite he had made, and she took him to the
park to fly it. They watched the movie *Robin Hood* together when it was
shown in the gym; they walked in the woods, shot baskets, and built a
rocket ship for his room.

She couldn't understand why Lamont had no family: "*I* wanted him. I
wanted to adopt him. There was no way."

As her senior year drew to an end in the spring of 1984, Mary was
supposed to begin what her social-work supervisor called termination—
preparing Lamont for her departure from his life. She did tell him in early
April that she would soon be leaving. As a farewell gift, he gave her a col-

lage he'd made of tiny tiles. But when the time came to terminate, she just couldn't. She took him out to visit FDR's home in Hyde Park and bought him lunch at McDonald's. And she told him that though she was no longer his student worker, from now on she would be his volunteer. That meant that she would be allowed to visit and telephone him regularly, even to take him out on weekends and holidays, when the children with families were allowed to go home. Lamont was very happy, because he believed her.

Soon afterward her mother was diagnosed with cancer. Doctors at Albert Einstein Hospital in the Bronx said she had only a 30 percent chance of pulling through. Mary stayed with her mother at the hospital when she had her operation, and drove her back and forth for treatment. She skipped her own college graduation because she didn't want her mother to have to sit at the ceremony for three hours. All summer, her mother was her first concern. She never did find time to call or visit Lamont.

That was the summer Lamont's therapist, Greg Barker, left Astor Home. In May his social worker, Gertrude Burns, had also left. The new one eventually telephoned Mary Zuvic because Lamont kept asking after her. Three weeks after his tenth birthday, she sent him a card. By the end of the summer, when her mother was better, Mary was told that Lamont didn't need a volunteer anymore because he was going to be placed in a foster family. She was very happy for him.

MRS. MARTIN WAS WAITING for Lamont in the Astor Home library at their first meeting, on a hot day in mid-August 1984. She was a stout black woman, as dark as Lamont himself, in her fifties, with bright black eyes behind her glasses and a high, gentle voice.

"I think I'd like to have you come live at my house," she told him as the two social workers smiled and nodded.

I can finally get out of here, Lamont thought. He hated it at Astor Home. He hated the child-care supervisors fresh from college who enforced every single rule, and the more laid-back, hippie types who pretended they cared and then vanished. He hated the middle-aged volunteers, who wanted to brag to their friends that they helped poor little children, and the rich donors who traipsed through on self-congratulatory tours. He even hated the holly tree that grew just outside the chapel door. The first summer its glossy green leaves had looked so pretty he caressed them; but in winter, when he tried to grab a handful, the leaves had pierced his hand. He saw then that the vein of each leaf ended in a thorn.

He did not want to be one of the crazy Astor Home kids, did not want to belong with children who mutilated themselves in secret, who sat twitching in corners, who erupted in violent temper tantrums. But whenever he was taken into the real world for two or three hours, on a group trip to the Kingston Mall or into the streets of Rhinebeck, he felt like such an outsider. It wasn't only that his color made him stick out like a raisin in a slice of white bread; it was that he didn't really know how to conduct himself in the world anymore. He didn't know how to live in a family. For years he had longed for one. Now he was scared.

Lamont's most recent psychological evaluation had found him "coherent, cooperative and in good contact." His diagnosis had been revised to "atypical pervasive developmental disorder, in remission, conduct disorder, socialized aggressive, in remission, and mixed personality disorder." He had not been on medication for a year and a half, and Mary Zuvic, who had filled out his UCR in December, had written of his "tremendous progress" and expressed the expectation that he would soon move to a treatment foster home and could be adopted by the end of 1984.

Time was running out. On October 5, 1984, after only two overnight visits, Lamont was discharged to the "family treatment home" of Mrs. Margaret Martin and assigned to attend a Kingston public school.

MARGARET MARTIN HAD ALWAYS KEPT a houseful of kids at 216 Catherine Street in Kingston, usually four foster children and two of her own. She had started as a foster parent out of necessity, soon after her husband left her with two little girls in diapers. When she applied for aid, the welfare investigator who came poking around her house told her to sell her car, the washing machine, and the children's bedroom set, and not to come back for help until the money was gone. "How can I sell that stuff from under my children?" she asked. For a while she had tried to scrape by doing other people's housework, leaving the girls to be watched here and there. Then she noticed a flier from the Astor Home for Children on a lady's kitchen bulletin board, with the telephone number.

Astor Home paid about $400 a month per foster child, and $250 twice a year for each one's clothes. It wasn't much, really. You had to feed them, and they went through underclothes like Grant went through Richmond, she pointed out to friends. Licensed for six, and a mother of two, she could have as many as eight children in her home at once, though that was rare. "They only release so many children from Astor Home," she told people. "They hang on to them to have the money."

For years now, Mrs. Martin had also worked making computer chips for IBM on the four-to-midnight shift. It was rough, but it worked out, even after her firstborn daughter left home. Martin would cook dinner for the kids before she left and tell the two oldest girls to serve it up— Yvonne, her teenaged younger daughter, who was still at home, and Loretta, a foster girl who had come from Astor Home when she was twelve. The children could play outside after supper, but they had to be back in the house by eight o'clock, and she would telephone from work then to check. Her second husband would not be around. They were living separately by now, with a divorce planned; when he wasn't at work or stepping out with other women, he lived around back. He was a hard-working Jamaican with a farm job in an apple orchard, but he was younger than she was and had proved to have a roving eye. She should have known better, she told herself. Hadn't her own father been too young and flirtatious to be reliable when he was left a widower with three little girls?

"We kind of raised ourselves," Martin would tell anyone who asked about her childhood. "We were hungry and raggedy. We'd run from house to house at suppertime to see who we could get a meal from. After a while, the neighbors would stop feeding us, because they said, 'As long as we keep feeding these kids, that father's not going to do nothing for them.'

"I had a rough life, a ROUGH life," she would say, falling into the cadences of her church. "Me and my sisters climbed up the ROUGH side of that mountain. The school we went to, they'd send you home for lunch. We would go home, but there was no lunch for us. We would go back to school the same way we came: hungry. We kept it private. We would say, 'Don't tell anybody. Keep it to ourselves.' "

One white teacher, whose family ran the grocery store in Glasco, used to bring her own lunch to school every day and usually kept an apple or orange sitting on the windowsill. If she left it there, Margaret would make it her business to sneak back in and steal it. She was seven or eight at the time. One day the teacher caught her taking an orange and admonished her, "Don't ever steal. Ask for what you want. If ever you're hungry again, come to the store and ask my mother."

"I never did," Mrs. Martin said. "I had too much pride."

Her oldest sister left home at fifteen to live with her grandmother in New York City. The middle sister married at sixteen, to have better. After eighth grade, Margaret herself went to New York to live with a god-mother and finish high school.

She'd never liked the city. In recent years she had traveled down there only to pick up her emergency foster-care cases, children placed with her at a moment's notice by the Mother Cabrini Home, another Catholic agency. Her favorite had been the youngest, a baby girl under two whose grandmother had been feeding her alcohol to shut her up. When Mrs. Martin walked into the agency office one day in the late 1970s, the little thing came to her with arms open wide to be picked up; they said she'd never done that before. The poor baby was an alcoholic, shaking so from withdrawal in the first days that you could hardly put her down.

The agency staff had told her, "If you take a young child and the parent doesn't show up in a two-year period, you can file for adoption." That's what she did, but all it brought was heartache. The case lingered on and lingered on, and still she didn't get to adopt the little girl she had let her-self love. After four years went by, the caseworkers found the mother and started taking the child to visit her in the city. The girl would come back crying that she didn't want to go back there. She had to sleep with her mommy and the man, she said.

"Don't you have your own bed when you go there?" Mrs. Martin asked her. "No, Ma," the child answered. All the children called her Ma.

Mrs. Martin reported it. The child didn't have no business sleeping with her mother's boyfriend, she told the caseworker. The mother was maybe eighteen by then, if that. She wasn't capable of caring for that child. But the caseworkers said the mother was going to get her own apartment, and the child would have to go live with her.

When the day came, the little girl was standing there and screaming that she didn't want to go, she didn't want to go. They were both in tears. Mrs. Martin told her, "Honey, I don't have any choice." She wrote a letter to the mother and put it in the child's suitcase, asking would she please let her come visit on holidays or for a couple of weeks in the summer. But she never heard a word back.

She had not been able to adopt Calvin, either—the baby her foster daughter Jackie had put in her arms when he was two days old. Jackie had married, and her husband wouldn't accept Calvin, so he stayed with Mrs. Martin until he was about four. Then Mrs. Martin injured her back on the job at IBM and needed an operation, so she sent him to live with his mother and stepfather and baby half-sister in Poughkeepsie. Within six months Calvin called her up and cried to her that his stepfather, Norman, kept beating on him, and Mrs. Martin drove right over and took him back. Norman ordered Jackie not to associate with Mrs. Martin anymore, and Jackie stopped visiting her son. She didn't even send him presents at Christmas or on his birthday. Because Calvin had never been part of the foster-care system and Mrs. Martin didn't get a penny for him, they could have handled an adoption privately. But after Mrs. Martin had a notary draw up all the papers, Jackie didn't sign them. Still, Mrs. Martin considered Calvin her own. The children from Astor Home were not.

"When you get those foster children, they don't give you the history," she would tell people. "They just put them in your house and expect you to do wonders with them. You just got to pray to God and do the best you can."

She had argued about it with the nuns sometimes. How were you supposed to work with these children when you didn't know their background or what triggered them? she asked. But the Astor Home people would answer that they didn't know too much themselves, and what they did know, they couldn't tell her. In the beginning, she had put a lot of energy into getting those children calmed down. "After a while, you develop a technique," she would say.

She preferred the girls; they were easier to manage. The boys, well, most of them she had to send back. But it seemed like she wasn't getting girls anymore since she had told off Sister Marie in 1982 or 1983, during an argument about one of her foster girls who got pregnant. The girl was about fifteen. She had been raped on a home visit to New York City. "They wanted me to go with her to get an abortion. I said, 'Why don't you take her?'

" 'No, that's against our religion.'

"I said, 'It's against my religion, too. I'm having nothing to do with it.' "

All she had to do was accompany the girl to the clinic, the nun pointed out.

"If it was to take her across the street to get a drink of water to help her do it, I wouldn't," Mrs. Martin countered. Not that she doubted the girl's word about the rape, but it was still a human being.

"I'm just as religious as them Catholics—more religious," she said later. "I know enough to know it's taking a life. I have enough to pray about now."

In the end, one of the city caseworkers took the girl for the abortion, and the girl went to live somewhere else. From then on, it seemed like Sister Marie sent nothing but boys, the worst kids the agency had. Mrs. Martin already had Richard and Junior, young teenagers from Astor Home who were becoming a handful. But Lamont was a beautiful boy, and she could see that he was very, very bright. Maybe next time Sister Marie would relent and send her a nice little girl.

LAMONT'S TWO VISITS to the Martin house in Kingston that August were like a taste of the childhood summers he had seen in the movies. The house was only blocks from Rondout Creek, the Hudson River tributary that served as Kingston's port, and a crisscross of railroad tracks ran nearby. It was a *Stand By Me* kind of place, he would say later, where boys in jeans and T-shirts could roam around all day, get into mischief, and come home safe again. It was his first sense of freedom.

I really want to grow up here, he thought when he saw the cozy two-story frame house, on a sloping street shaded by trees. When he was older, he would recall all the best times in Kingston through a summer haze. "I was just a regular kid in a town where there was so much to see, so much to do. The Hudson—you can never get bored. You get tired of the quarries, you go to the creek; you get tired of the creek, you throw rocks at the tankers or you go in the woods."

But by the time Lamont was moved to Mrs. Martin's, on October 5, the weather was already turning cold. He arrived with nothing, she complained—no winter coat, no suit pants, no jacket, shoes, or shirt for church, no school clothes. A different social worker, Kathy Lago, had taken over his case when he was transferred to Astor's foster-home division, and she put in a request at the institution for the items. Three weeks went by before she got a few things as well as sixty dollars for Mrs. Martin to outfit Lamont. He finally started going to school on October 24. By then Mrs. Martin was demanding medication for him, something to keep him calmer. An Astor Home doctor prescribed twenty-five milligrams of Thorazine to be taken at noon every day.

"When he first came to me, Lamont was a very confused little boy," Mrs. Martin would recall. "He tried so hard to do the right things because he liked it at my house. You could see him trying and scuffling to do the right thing. 'OK, Mommy,' he would say, 'I'm not going to do that anymore.' But he just couldn't control himself."

Mrs. Martin believed in corporal punishment. "I'd take a switch off the bush out there," she said. "I did my kids the same way. I would just sting their bare legs with it when they didn't want to mind. They had to obey me, because I was a single parent. I had to work. There was nothing easy about my being a foster parent raising my two kids. I have no regrets and no guilty conscience."

As Lamont remembered the beatings, they were with a belt. He was beaten for all sorts of things, he said: not cleaning his room, messing up in school, staying out past supper. One day he broke Calvin's Speak & Spell toy and they both got a beating because they didn't want to tell on each other. "I figured that was just the way foster care was," he would later say.

The school staff felt Lamont had real potential and belonged in a more challenging class. But in late November, Lamont's teacher called Kathy Lago to tell her he was having a bad day. The social worker picked him up at school and took him out for a snack. "He said he wanted to return to Astor," she wrote in her social-work notes. "He said he wasn't happy at Mrs. Martin's. He said she was mean to him, and that she hit him."

Lago took him to Mrs. Martin and repeated everything he had told her. "Apparently some of the things she had said were misunderstood by Lamont," the social worker wrote. "We were both firm about his having to obey regarding going off across town without permission, etc. It became evident that he was concerned about his position in the family, if there would be room for him on Thanksgiving, etc. He was reassured."

Lamont had asked in October if Lago could arrange for him to join the Kingston YMCA. In early December, she recorded that a Y official had said Lamont was too young for a general membership but could be in a latchkey program two afternoons a week for $10.70 weekly. There might be a scholarship available in January if Astor Home wouldn't cover the cost. She promised Lamont that a latchkey program at the Y would be set up for him after Christmas. But whether because of the cost or because Kathy Lago left the agency a short while later, it never happened.

Mrs. Martin herself had other things to worry about. For years she had been asking her bosses at IBM for a day shift, and that winter she was finally assigned to work from seven in the morning until three in the afternoon. Her sister Helen Washington, who had several foster children herself and watched her grandchildren besides, agreed to baby-sit for Lamont, Calvin, Junior, and Richard. But apparently the new arrangement wasn't discussed with Astor Home beforehand. Kathy Lago first noted Mrs. Martin's new work schedule on January 7, 1985, when the Kingston principal complained that Lamont was acting out in school. "Lamont has been angry lately and when he gets angry he deliberately upsets the class," the social worker wrote. She contacted Mrs. Washington, his baby-sitter, who was surprised to hear about Lamont's school misbehavior, because he had been doing very well at her house, she said.

The school had distributed the class gerbils before Christmas vacation, and Lamont had brought one home. He was keeping the animal in the plastic top hat from his old magic set, one of the few playthings he had brought with him from Astor Home. He asked Mrs. Martin if he could buy the gerbil a proper cage when Astor Home sent his allowance. He saw the check before Mrs. Martin cashed it: it was for thirty dollars, which seemed like a lot of money to a ten-year-old. He was sure the cage couldn't have cost that much, but Mrs. Martin never gave him any change. He brought up the matter when Sister Marie came for one of her rare home visits. When the nun left, he got a beating—for complaining, he believed.

He began recording each beating on a little notepad, with the idea of writing to Sister Marie. But he didn't really know how to send a letter through the mail, and anyway, he soon heard from the other children that Sister Marie might not be sympathetic. She was known to say, " 'Yeah, sometimes these kids, they need it.' "

Because of his misbehavior, Lamont was not transferred into a more academically challenging class. He was a little frustrated in school, Kathy Lago wrote before she left, at the end of January 1985, but otherwise he seemed to her quite happy. "I discussed with Lamont the fact that I would be leaving the agency. He said he was sorry to have me leave, but people are always coming and going."

January was also the month Astor Home displayed Lamont's photograph at a Catholic Charities adoption meeting. Its own reports to the city suggested that Lamont had improved enough to be in an adoptive home by now, and the Astor staff demanded an update from Sheltering Arms on its efforts to recruit one. A Sheltering Arms caseworker replied that one possible family had withdrawn because of the boy's history of fire setting, but there were other possibilities to be discussed. Meanwhile, Astor obtained an extension of Lamont's care from the court through April 1, 1985.

Kathy Lago's replacement didn't even meet Lamont and Mrs. Martin until April 1. Again, Lamont asked about the Y after-school program, and the new social worker promised to call about it. Mrs. Martin announced that she was going away on vacation for two weeks. She said Lamont and the others would be under the supervision of her daughter.

It was mid-May before the social worker spoke with Mrs. Martin again. By then the foster mother was full of complaints about Lamont. He had been put off the school bus for bad behavior and missed a week of school. Since she was working the seven-to-three shift, she certainly couldn't afford that kind of thing. He had left home without permission and come back at seven at night with a case of poison ivy. She was frustrated by her lack of communication with the boy. She had warned him that if he didn't behave himself, he would have to go. Worst of all, Mrs. Martin felt Lamont was a bad influence on her foster grandson, Calvin, now six.

Poor Calvin: recently rejected by his mother, he kept asking who his father was. Mrs. Martin knew the man, a fellow named Jerry who drove a taxi in Kingston. He had never given Calvin a nickel, but she asked him now if he would mind being introduced to the boy as his father. No, he wouldn't mind. He went up to Calvin and said, "Hi, man, how you doing?" and gave him a dollar. About two weeks later, when Calvin and Lamont and some neighborhood children were out playing, Calvin saw Jerry's taxi and said, "Oh, here comes my father." The other children crowded around Jerry, who was dropping off a fare on the block.

"Are you Calvin's father? Are you Calvin's father?"

"No, I'm not Calvin's father," Jerry said.

Calvin ran into the house crying. Mrs. Martin did her best to comfort the boy, but he pushed her away. "My mother said I'm not your grandson," he told her.

How could she respond? "We're the ones who take care of you," she said.

Lamont listened and said nothing. Where were the ones who were supposed to be taking care of *him?* He could tell from Mrs. Martin's threats that his days at her house were numbered. Where were they all, he asked himself—his mother, his father, his grandparents? Where were all the aunts, the uncles, the cousins, and the step-relatives that other children seemed to have?

He was almost eleven, and big for his age—too big, Mrs. Martin told him, to be always playing with a six-year-old like Calvin and leading him into trouble. As the weather warmed up now, he hung out instead with Junior and Richard and their teenaged buddies, the town bad kids and greasers. They'd bring beer to the old quarry; they'd smoke cigarettes. Sometimes they all pushed motor bikes down the hill that ran from the church to the Martin house, or threw rocks at the big tanks by the river to scratch and dent them.

June came. On the Sunday after Lamont's eleventh birthday, Mrs. Martin drove off to visit friends, leaving Yvonne, sixteen, in charge of serving dinner. Lamont had eaten at church that day, and he wasn't hungry. He told Yvonne to put his dinner back in the pot. She demanded that he eat it, and he refused. The confrontation quickly escalated. She dared him to slap her, and he did. It turned into a fistfight, and Junior had to break it up. When Mrs. Martin telephoned to check on things, Yvonne was crying.

"Lamont's going crazy in this house," she told her mother. "He didn't want to do what I said."

"Yvonne tried to boss me around," Lamont yelled. "She's not my mother."

Mrs. Martin drove home as fast as she could. She was furious. This was the last straw. Lamont needed to be someplace where there was a man, she decided. He had been at her house eight months, and he just kept getting worse and worse. Hadn't she smelled smoke the day before? She had found matches in the pocket of his jeans when she did the wash. No, she would not let him stay another night.

Lamont ran outside and hid when he saw her coming, fearful of a beating. Junior soon coaxed him inside again, but Mrs. Martin had already called Astor Home to announce that she was bringing him back to the institution.

"Get in the car," she told him.

He didn't argue. They drove over the Kingston–Rhinecliff bridge in silence, as twilight darkened the Hudson and deepened the blue of the hills in the rearview mirror. She left him at the reception desk, and she didn't look back.

ON MONDAY MORNING, Astor Home staff made telephone calls to other residential treatment centers that might take Lamont Wilder. The short list was copied into the social-work notes: *Greg Staten——no room; Leake & Watts; Graham Windham; Abbott House; St. Christopher's.* Sheltering Arms was notified; if adoptive prospects were still in the pipeline, they would be diverted to other children.

New psychological and psychiatric evaluations were ordered. They found no evidence of thought disorder or psychosis in Lamont, and the treatment team decided to keep him for a while, back in the most restrictive and expensive RTF unit of the Astor Home.

"Lamont was able to verbalize some sadness, but not anger, about the foster placement's failure," the social worker wrote after a treatment-team meeting on June 28, 1985. "Some of his interaction had a manipulative and defensive flavor. Lamont was guarded about making attachments to people as his past experience of being moved or taken out of foster homes or residential environments has been re-awakened resulting in his anxiousness and disruptive behavior."

There was one striking new development since his return to Astor Home, the social worker noted.

Lamont kept asking about his mother.

FIVE

A S THE SUMMER OF 1984 HAD PASSED INTO FALL, AND FALL given way to a bitterly cold winter, Judge Robert Ward had kept his patience. Never had he invested more time in the settlement of a case or participated more personally in the excruciating process of revision and re-revision necessary to move from conflict to agreement. But he felt that the historic grandeur of *Wilder,* its potential for good, and its complex and delicate interplay of constitutional, statutory, and administrative problems demanded nothing less of them all.

There were all-day hearings interspersed with negotiating sessions that lasted half the night. There were long, aggrieved speeches couched in terms of large principles, and pointed colloquies that stripped some objections bare of the smallest constitutional fig leaf. There were moments of simple eloquence and murky, grueling debates over footnotes and colons. In office negotiations, the lawyers for the foster-care agencies fought Fritz Schwarz and Marcia Lowry or each other over nearly every phrase. In court, Ward painstakingly hammered out their differences. It would take more than two years to construct a final *Wilder* settlement from the stipulation Lowry and Schwarz had signed, and a third year to turn that settlement into a court decree.

Along the way, despite Lowry's own regrets about the settlement's compromises, the agencies' opposition confirmed her belief in its strengths. "After decades of largely unregulated and uncontrolled public funding, the voluntary child care agencies which contract with the city are now faced with a comprehensive effort to subject many of their activities to rigorous scrutiny," Lowry had written in her memorandum of support. "And unlike other, fledgling attempts to impose order on the many divergent parties in the child welfare system, this settlement, if approved by the court, will be enforceable through the jurisdiction of the court without being subject to the kinds of political pressure that have marked other efforts at foster care reform."

Inside the modest fifth-floor courtroom, under the steady gaze of a federal judge with a lifetime appointment, Lowry could believe that was true.

The shift and reconfiguration of power taking place had been palpable to spectators at the first hearing, on August 6, 1984. They could almost feel the floor tilt toward the plaintiffs every time Fritz Schwarz rose to endorse what Lowry had said or to add his own limpid reasoning to the force of her arguments.

"The system as it now exists remains legally vulnerable," he said, "not because of any conflicting analysis of facts but because of the simple principle: why shouldn't the black Protestant child have the same chances to get access to the agency which is best for that child as does a white Jewish or a Hispanic Catholic child?"

Watching from the defendants' table at the first day's hearing, Tom Aquilino saw the two of them maneuver seamlessly together to outflank his boss, Dick Nolan, and the combative counsel for the Jewish Board of Guardians, Floran Fink.

There was no way around what Schwarz had cited as his ultimate reason for seeking a settlement: "We simply did not think it was right, just, or lawful to have a governmentally funded foster-care system that does not recognize that all children should have an equal chance to get the best." The settlement had been carefully crafted to ensure the protection of both equal access and freedom of religion, Schwarz maintained.

Again and again, both Nolan and Fink cited the religious-matching provision enshrined in state law, which gave Catholic and Jewish children in their clients' care a right to in-religion placement "when practicable," and which had been upheld by a three-judge panel in 1974. But the same decision left the lawyers boxed in. To find the provision constitutional, the panel had read it as *permitting* religious matching but not *mandating* it. The phrase "when practicable," Judge Ward himself pointed out, could hardly be construed to allow discrimination against black Protestants— "that is, a greater likelihood of placement in lower-quality facilities."

Somewhere in the convergence of law and real life, race had trumped religion. Even as the Catholic agencies argued that religion should not and could not, under New York law, be reduced to just one of many factors to be considered in placing a child, they acknowledged that they themselves placed children in foster families less according to religion than according to race. MIV, for example, had 52.9 percent of its black Catholic children in out-of-religion foster-family placements, but no white Catholic children similarly placed. The city itself seemed far more likely to honor religious matching in its own foster boarding homes, where only 54 children out of 1,810 (or 3 percent) were with families of a different religion than their natural parents. The social and political construction of religion as a marker for class had been teetering under its own weight. Not even the free-exercise clause of the Constitution could shore it up now, when race ruled the discourse of identity.

Nolan, Fink, and Aquilino did their best to cast the *Wilder* settlement as a race-conscious remedy that could not be approved in the absence of a prima facie showing of discrimination. Since Lowry and Schwarz kept citing *Brown,* they invoked *Bakke.* The *Wilder* settlement was really about a Jewish child losing his rightful place in a Jewish treatment center so a black child could take his bed, Fink seemed to be saying. On a gut level, their argument did echo emotions in the case of Allan Bakke, the white middle-class engineer denied admittance to a California medical school that had reserved places for minorities until 1978, when the Supreme Court ruled its quota unconstitutional and ordered the school to accept him.

There was just one problem: it was the Jewish and Catholic children who benefited from affirmative action in the system at hand. The plaintiffs were not seeking a racial advantage to compensate for past disadvantage, Lowry pointed out. They were not seeking equal results. All they asked for was equal treatment.

To Ward, it became obvious which side really wanted a quota when Nolan offered a dual waiting list scheme, in which agencies would be allowed to admit every other child from a list of those with a religious preference. The lawyer cited the approval of similar lists in an employment discrimination case.

"That was to remedy past discrimination," the judge reminded him. "What bothers me about your dual-waiting-list proposal is that it struck me as an attempt to give preferential treatment on the basis of religion, not to give equal treatment."

"With all due respect, I don't think it gives preferential treatment," Nolan said.

"Of course it does," the judge retorted. He had known Nolan for years and felt warmth and respect for the man, who was only four years his junior, but he spoke to him now as though to a backward pupil. "There are two lines. There is a long line and a short line. If you get on the long line, you are at the end, but if you express your preference and get on the short line, and it is one, and one and one"—here he pointed from one imaginary line to another and back again—"you are going to go up a few notches, and you've got to be accepted at an earlier point in time. I visualized it."

Theoretically, Nolan put in hopefully, the in-religion line could be the longer one. "It could work either way."

"As a practical matter, it wouldn't," Ward said flatly.

As a practical matter, only one in four hundred children in foster care was Jewish, and such children now had a 95 percent chance of placement in a publicly funded Jewish agency. This near certainty would surely shrink if the settlement equalized opportunity.

IT WAS NO SECRET that Ward was Jewish, though his name was not. He had always practiced his religion openly, and he believed its philosophy pervaded his thinking as a judge. Like Ed Koch, Ward had first witnessed southern-style racial segregation when he did his military service. It had been a shock, getting off the train south of the Mason-Dixon Line in 1945 and seeing the signs on water fountains and restrooms in the station. It was also in the service, on a light cruiser in the Pacific in the navy, that he heard remarks like "I'm going to Jew him down" from people who had never seen a Jew and didn't know he was one. On the GI Bill, he went to Harvard Law School, where he heard casual slurs about "Jewish shyster lawyers." But unlike Dick Nolan, he had never had to make his way past such attitudes in a white-shoe law firm, because he deliberately chose public service—first the Manhattan D.A.'s office, then the U.S. Attorney's office for the Southern District of New York.

Looking now at Nolan's frowning face, the judge tried to put him out of his misery. "I don't think, with all due respect, that the dual-waiting-list solution is the answer."

"I would like to hear another one," the lawyer shot back.

"The answer is rather simple," Ward replied in his measured, avuncular way, shaking his head, "and we just don't have it available to us. The answer is obviously more funding, more facilities, so that there would be a lot more give in the system, but in this day and age I must suggest it is most unlikely we will reach that point. It is another thing I don't think we will see in our lifetime. I think what we have to do—and this I know is troublesome and I recognize the thought and the effort that have been put into this problem by everyone over the past more than ten years—it seems to me that if you stick to a concept of first come, first served, and if you stick to a concept of best available or alternatively best available consistent with the wish for in-religion preference, on a first-come, first-served basis, pure and simple, it is basically the least complicated way to go, and in the final analysis, the fairest way to go."

It was also the way the settlement had gone. When Nolan sat down, he was flushed with frustration. "It was like watching a wave come in," he would say later. "There was nothing you could do."

OUTSIDE WARD'S COURTROOM, the waters were still too choppy to tell which way the current was running.

Affidavits and letters filed in support of the *Wilder* settlement had come from past and current leaders in the government's foster-care-reform wars: from Lowry's old ally James Dumpson and her onetime boss Barbara Blum; from Stanley Brezenoff, Carol Bellamy, and the Board of Estimate; and of course from Gail Kong, director of the city's Special Services for Children. To them all, the settlement was part of a decade-long pattern of increased public supervision of foster care, a pattern that was finally beginning to pay off.

Equal access and religious freedom were the rights at the heart of the lawsuit, Lowry had told Ward, but "to make these rights meaningful the settlement establishes centralized control of the placement process in the hands of the public agency. It attempts to make real the City's obligation to determine what agencies each child shall go to and what child is most appropriate for what particular bed. . . . Equal access to the best available services [is] meaningless unless there is a fair and neutral way of determining what the best available services are."

But two months earlier, in June 1984, the private foster-care agencies, representing 93 percent of all foster-care beds, had refused to sign new contracts with the city, citing the unresolved issues of the *Wilder* settlement. The city had little choice but to grant short-term contract extensions on the old terms. And as representatives of nineteen nondefendant agencies, Don Cohn and Stephen Wise Tulin had made what Ward would later call a "comprehensive, concrete critique" of the settlement from a clinical and practical perspective. They marshaled scathing affidavits from agency administrators and a wide range of clinicians opposed to the compromise.

These foster-care veterans, too, saw the *Wilder* settlement in the context of a decade of reform, but for them it was the apotheosis of all of that reform's failures: bureaucratic rigidity; an ever-increasing burden of meaningless paperwork that drove professionals from the field; and a further usurpation of power by a distant public agency that had consistently proved its callous incompetence. Above all, they saw it as a codification of the hated PAS preferred-placement system imposed by Gail Kong.

The Program Assessment System, known as PAS, was an attempt to compare and grade agencies on the basis of objective performance benchmarks and systemwide data. Agencies would be scored on such measures as the average number of home visits made by foster children in their care and the average length of time taken to complete an adoption. "Preferred placement" meant that the city would place more children in the agencies with better scores, and fewer children, or none at all, in those that scored badly. Thousands of children who had entered temporary care at a young age were lingering through troubled adolescence with the goal of "discharge to own responsibility." Giving preference to agencies with better PAS scores was an effort to change the large-scale patterns that would consign yet another generation of foster children to the same fate.

Someone on Kong's staff had come up with the idea of delivering a copy of each agency's preliminary PAS report to the home of its board chairman. These were mostly rich and important men used to hearing from their executive directors how wonderful their agencies were. They went to agency Christmas parties and basked in the glow of gratitude, but they didn't have a clue as to what was going on from day to day. Suddenly PAS obliged them to see how their good works stacked up. It made them all very uncomfortable. Such discomfort, Kong's troops believed, was what finally boosted the system's anemic record on adoption, for example: in 1984, 1,511 foster children were adopted, three quarters by their foster parents, up by almost a half from the 1,019 adopted in 1982.

But the agencies themselves never accepted the notion of aggregate measures. They saw the PAS teams as accountants checking boxes, indifferent to the nuances of individual cases and to the professional judgment of the social workers who knew the children. The closing of agencies that had repeatedly flunked PAS had occasioned some debilitating political battles. For three years, Gail Kong had expended her political capital on foster-care reform, only to run short in 1984 when a crisis erupted in child protective services.

An inspector general's report released in April of 1984 criticized the city's child protective services' field offices for mishandling fifty-one abuse and neglect complaints, including eight cases in which children had died. Scathing press coverage intensified in August when workers in a city day-care center were charged with sexual abuse. The mayor saw that Kong, whose ouster had been sought by the foster-care agencies for months, was poised to take the fall. On August 6, the first day of the *Wilder* hearing—and the very day that proponents of the settlement advised Judge Ward that it would empower Kong's agency to fix foster care—Mayor Koch told the press he had no confidence in her. She formally resigned in disgrace the next day. Few in the child welfare world doubted that the underlying reason was her vigorous pursuit of PAS and her support for the settlement of *Wilder*. And they expected her successor to be mindful of her fate.

INSIDE WARD'S COURTROOM, however, objections to the settlement kept falling away. The city and the ACLU had been willing to add phrases and provisions that would answer some of the intervenors' therapeutic concerns, and Steve Tulin and Don Cohn were eager to keep negotiating. Their purpose, they said, was to craft a document that could serve as a guideline for improving all child-care services in New York.

Ward threw himself into the effort. Judge and lawyers talked through nine hundred pages of transcripts between August and the end of October (the months, as it happened, when Lamont Wilder was shifting from Astor Home to Mrs. Martin's house). Whenever the whole process seemed in danger of coming unglued, Fritz Schwarz would step up to the plate. "Your Honor, I think we must keep our eye on the ball and not slip off," he might say before redefining the incremental problem at hand in some simple and well-rounded way that made it seem quite close to resolution.

By December, though the general outlines contained in the original thirty-two-page stipulation remained exactly the same, the new forty-page version was so successful in assuaging the intervenors' clinical concerns that they not only withdrew their opposition but voluntarily consented to sign the document and to be bound by its terms—if just one or two more conditions were met.

To approve the settlement, the judge had to find it a fair, reasonable, and adequate resolution of the underlying legal dispute. The main purpose of judicial review in a class-action settlement is to make sure the rights of absent class members are not prejudiced by an agreement that primarily benefits the named plaintiffs or their lawyers. In *Wilder,* that was the easy part. Certainly, Ward thought, no one who had witnessed Lowry's spirited resistance and effective advocacy during the negotiations could doubt the competence, vigor, and independence of class counsel. But in a settlement with such far-reaching institutional consequences, the judge also had to consider the fairness of the settlement's likely impact on the objecting agencies, on the city's child-care system, and on the public at large. That the nondefendant agencies had done an about-face and now supported the settlement went a long way, in Ward's mind, toward establishing its fairness and adequacy.

The state Department of Social Services also withdrew its legal objections to the settlement. That meant the Catholic and Jewish defendant agencies were left isolated in opposition, clinging to objections that had been demolished more than once by the judge himself in his polite but pointed Socratic style. Once, after Nolan again cited the majority of non-Catholics of color in the care of Catholic agencies, the judge had put in, "You have a majority because the supply is such. I mean, I have to be observant. Who are the people numerically who require this care?"

And Nolan had to reply, like a dutiful student, "The people numerically who require it in the city of New York in this day and age are predominantly blacks and Hispanics."

TWO WEEKS BEFORE CHRISTMAS 1984, Koch invited Archbishop O'Connor to share the podium with him at what was supposed to be a feel-good news conference about housing. The archbishop, who had been privately complaining to Koch about the family-planning provisions of the *Wilder* settlement and its language on "excessive religious symbols," took the opportunity to declare his threat to abandon the city's foster-care system, in connection with his gay-rights dispute with Koch.

"We will not sell our souls for city contracts," he said when a reporter at the press conference asked about Executive Order 50. If the courts decided against the archdiocese, O'Connor added, he would somehow find a way for the church to continue caring for children without government money.

"That's impossible," the mayor blurted out, taken by surprise.

That month, the number of children in foster care reached a historic low of 16,230, about a quarter of them in Catholic care.

Then the numbers began to climb again. It was barely noticed at first. Typically, the number of children in care rose in February, after the holidays, peaked in April, and declined through the summer and autumn. But by the spring of 1985, as the number went back up to 17,000, the city was already struggling with a bed shortage. An average of seven children a week were being placed in "overnight" beds because no longer-term placement could be found for them. The increase in children coming in the front door was still quite small, but discharges had dropped sharply. Agencies, it seemed to their critics, were hanging on to the children they already had.

The word *crack* appeared for the first time in the *New York Times* on November 17, 1985, on page 12 of the B section. The same word had been percolating through the city's child-abuse and -neglect complaints, and babies born cocaine-positive were accumulating in city hospital wards. The city had to plead with the private agencies to expand, even as the state's new reform-inspired reimbursement formula penalized expansion.

Inexorably, the balance of power shifted with the numbers. "The city's effort to get greater leverage was a feasible effort for as long as there was excess capacity," according to Steve Cohen, who had overseen the city's contract relations with the agencies under Kong and left in 1985 to work for a Jewish agency. "The moment the numbers exploded, the message to the city was, 'You can be assessing people until you're blue in the face, who cares when you're using every bed they have?' You can't regulate anything when the suppliers control the market."

As the city's small measure of control over placement and quality vanished in the face of the bed shortage, Kong's successor, Eric Brett-schneider, became desperate to implement the *Wilder* settlement. He needed what he dubbed a "vacancy-control system," a computerized way for city placement workers to identify foster-care vacancies system-wide, which would allow them to place children rationally and plan new direct-care programs—and would make it impossible for an agency to claim it had no beds while actually reserving some for preferred customers.

The proposed *Wilder* settlement called for the development of such a computer information system. There could be money for it, driven by the *Wilder* court. In the same way, Brettschneider believed, the first-come, first-served requirements of the settlement could help him clarify and apply major policies, such as placing children close to home or keeping brothers and sisters together. He wanted to use *Wilder* as broadly as it had been intended, as a tool to fix foster care.

But the *Wilder* settlement was still in Judge Ward's chambers, awaiting his decision.

AS WARD HIMSELF READ the First Amendment, the New York religion-matching statute was unconstitutional on its face. But he was not writing on a clean slate; the decision of the three-judge panel upholding the statute was the law of the case. Still, if he believed the settlement authorized conduct illegal under the establishment clause, he could not approve it. His decision had to be guided by the variable views of the United States Supreme Court on the whole subject.

"I think we are trying to build on somewhat shifting sands," Ward told Nolan in one of their early colloquies, "and we have to try to make the structure as fair as possible on the theory that if it is fair, it will be balanced, and if it is balanced, it will stand."

On July 11, 1985, the shifting sands had thrown up *Grand Rapids* v. *Ball* and *Aguilar* v. *Felton*. In these decisions, the U.S. Supreme Court ruled unconstitutional two different attempts to provide publicly funded educational programs to children attending private religious schools. In *Grand Rapids,* the Court found that the government scheme supplied impermissible aid to religion. In *Aguilar,* in contrast, it found that the very effort on the part of government to *avoid* aiding religion created an impermissible entanglement of church and state. In a 5–4 decision, the Court ruled unconstitutional a seventeen-year-old New York program that allowed publicly paid teachers to teach remedial courses on parochial-school premises, in "desectarianized classrooms," under extensive government monitoring aimed at ensuring the absence of religious content. Ward asked for legal briefs on the meaning of the two cases for the *Wilder* settlement.

The defendants argued that the combination of *Wilder I* and *Aguilar* rendered the settlement unconstitutional. It should be disapproved, and the lawsuit dismissed.

"They are half right," Lowry replied in her brief, filed in November 1985. If under *Aguilar* the settlement involved an impermissible entanglement with religion, it should, of course, be disapproved. "But in that case, *Grand Rapids* renders the present system of massive government aid to largely unregulated sectarian institutions equally unconstitutional." The only way that public funding of the foster-care agencies could be justified, she maintained, was under the painstakingly crafted settlement proposal.

Reading her brief, Ward could feel Lowry itching to toss aside the settlement and go for broke again. But in the end she renewed her request for its approval.

ED KOCH TRIUMPHED in that November's election, winning an extraordinary 78 percent of the vote. The city's economy was surging. Greed was good on Wall Street. It was as though New York City itself had become a money-making machine. Tax abatements, zoning changes, and capital improvements were feeding an orgy of real estate development. Since 1982, sixty new office towers had risen in Manhattan south of Ninety-sixth Street, and high-rise luxury housing loomed at the edges of the slums. But 40 percent of the city's children were in poverty, and as the ranks of the homeless grew to sixty thousand, squalor vied with the glitz of a new Gilded Age on the sidewalks of New York.

Two days before Christmas 1985, the mayor made an appeal to New Yorkers to become foster parents. The city was running out of private homes for the growing number of children in foster care, he said on the steps of City Hall. Children who needed foster-family care had to go to group homes instead, and groups of three or more siblings often had to be split up. An effort to place children near their own neighborhoods had been abandoned.

In the new year, as the Koch administration fell hostage to a major municipal scandal, the seasonal rise in foster care became a torrent. On April 23, 1986, sixty caseworkers stormed into Brettschneider's office to demand more foster-care beds. These workers and their colleagues now had to deal with newborns bounced through six different foster homes in a week, and angry teenagers who spent their days pacing the office corridors and their nights being shuttled from one temporary bed to the next. The average caseload was thirty children, and to place one child for as little as one night, workers often had to make up to thirty telephone calls, using a frantic mix of begging and salesmanship, digging into their own pockets to feed kids stranded between placements.

That evening, city administrators dragged office furniture from a windowless sixteenth-floor conference room at Special Services for Children and turned it into a makeshift nursery.

In the month of April 1986, the city would acknowledge later, there were at least 421 overnight placements of children of all ages; Legal Aid put the figure at 739. During that month, group homes and residential centers were virtually full, but registered foster homes under the auspices of the voluntary agencies were at only 79.9 percent of capacity. Agency spokesmen insisted that this figure did not reflect real vacancies, but rather took into account foster parents who were no longer interested in taking children, including some who had adopted their former charges. Lawyers at Legal Aid charged that the agencies were deliberately withholding beds as part of a power struggle with the city over placement, and over *Wilder*.

On May 20, 1986, Legal Aid filed *Doe* v. *NYCDSS* in federal court in Manhattan, charging that in violation of state law, the city social services department failed to provide a bed for every child in foster care. At least one child in the *Doe* class had gone through more than sixty-five "placements." More than a thousand children had experienced between five and nine "placements" within one fourteen-month period.

ON OCTOBER 8, 1986, after more than three years of debate, negotiation, revision, and pondering, Judge Ward issued a 118-page opinion approving the *Wilder* settlement. His approval, however, was conditioned on the city defendants' documenting additional hiring goals.

For a few weeks the city's response seemed uncertain. Cardinal O'Connor renewed his threat to pull Catholic agencies out of the foster-care system, and in reaction Mayor Koch publicly repudiated the settlement that his own corporation counsel had labored so long to craft. "I don't agree with those people who want to take the religious element out of these agencies that are providing services," the mayor told the press, and he called the settlement "bad."

Then, on December 20, a white mob chased a black man to his death on a busy highway for venturing into "its" Queens neighborhood—known, as the incident itself would be, as "Howard Beach." Suddenly racism, which had begun to seem an old-fashioned issue, was hot again. On the last day of 1986, in the midst of a wave of citywide concern over racial conflict, the city supplied the necessary affidavit to settle *Wilder*.

Ward also required the plaintiffs' counsel to submit an affidavit from three current class members to show that a live dispute still existed. Two of the three children Marcia Lowry chose had not yet been born when *Wilder* was first filed. The family-court judge who wrote a supporting affidavit for one, a twelve-year-old girl, had taken the bench a decade after Justine Wise Polier's retirement.

Judge Ward at last issued the finalized *Wilder* settlement decree on April 28, 1987, two weeks after Polier's eighty-fourth birthday. She would die three months later, on July 31.

SIX

W HEN LAMONT WAS TWELVE AND ALREADY TOO BIG FOR his age to belong at Astor Home, some members of the staff called him the "gentle giant." In the winter of 1986–87 they often brought him along as a helper when they took the youngest children, the Immaculites, sledding at Crystal Lake. Standing guard by the first big tree near the bottom of the hill, Lamont would catch the little kids to keep them from hitting the tree trunks as they careened squealing down the slope.

But as he approached his thirteenth birthday, he knew that no one was waiting to break *his* fall. "He impresses as a fairly well put together young man with a pseudo-mature air about himself," a psychologist reported. "Underneath that facade is a scared youngster with a lot of uncertainty about his future plans."

It had been a year of uncertainty for Astor Home, too. In March 1986 David Hoffman, Astor's longtime chief of psychological services, had been arrested for sexually molesting small boys in his care. Hoffman, forty, soon admitted to investigators that he had experienced the need to touch the genitals of children since he was in high school, and had regularly fondled his Astor Home patients for his own sexual gratification. In his mind, the child protective investigator reported him as saying, "he did not feel that he had seriously hurt anyone."

Hoffman was fired. Police interviewed many Astor Home boys, and at least four, all white or light-skinned, including Lamont's roommate that year, related incidents in which the psychologist had used his professional authority to "check" and manipulate their genitals. Hoffman eventually pleaded guilty to sexually abusing two of the boys, one nine, the other thirteen. A presentence report recommended prison, based in part on the psychologist's failure to perceive the impact of his conduct on his victims. Under state law, the maximum prison sentence possible was two and a half to seven years. But three of Hoffman's former colleagues wrote to the judge on his behalf, including a close friend who had succeeded him as Astor Home's senior psychologist. They praised his dedication to his job and described him as an excellent candidate for psychotherapy, suggesting that he had already suffered enough. Accepting the terms of Hoffman's plea bargain, the judge sentenced him to fourteen weekends in the Dutchess County jail and five years' probation. For Lamont, the scandal only confirmed a distrust of psychologists that had already become second nature to him. He saw a kind of bitter joke in it: his dark skin had spared him molestation because Astor Home's chief psychologist, though a pedophile, was also a racist.

During personality testing that same spring of 1986, another psychologist had characterized Lamont as guarded and oppositional: "Projective testing revealed a child who is emotionally constricted and detached from his emotions. He appeared unlikely to form close attachments and unaware of his emotional needs. Spontaneous affective expression was limited and unmodulated. . . . There was considerable evidence of low self esteem and of depression; the latter was denied."

But Frank, Lamont's roommate that year, a white boy from Long Island who had been punished after he called Hoffman a faggot and refused to go back to therapy with him, remembered Lamont as a gentle, sincere kid whose empathy and sense of fun helped him through a tough period. When Frank broke down and cried after a bad phone call with his father, Lamont tried to cheer him up. Mostly they were buddies, joking around, wrestling, breaking the rules together to listen on Frank's radio to the "Dr. Demento Show," which was broadcast Sunday nights at ten, after bedtime. It featured their favorite Weird Al Jankovic numbers and songs like "Monster Mash" that turned scary creatures into something they could laugh about under the covers.

Most fear was not funny to Lamont that year. One Friday afternoon just as the Hoffman scandal was dying down, the Immaculites were trooping out the school door behind the mansion's annex when one of them, a five-year-old girl named Erica, slipped and fell. A bread truck backing up to make a delivery ran over her head, killing her instantly.

Every time Lamont passed the place, he would envision Erica's small body lying broken on the ground.

The world seemed like an increasingly dangerous place. Crack had hit the news media, and every night on television there were stories about drive-by shootings, demonic drug dealers, and children of color caught in the crossfire. Some members of the Astor Home staff worried openly about Lamont's safety should he be returned to the city. But in February 1987, as Judge Ward was putting the last touches on the finalized *Wilder* settlement decree, Astor Home decided that Lamont should be transferred to Serena House, a group home for young teenagers run by the Astor agency in a relatively quiet part of the Bronx.

By then he was too tall for the clothing purchased in bulk and distributed to Astor Home residents in quarterly "shopping" sessions in a basement laundry room. A woman staff member took him instead to the Hudson Valley Mall and bought him a new aviator-style jacket just before his departure. It was the height of fashion, and he was proud to be wearing it on the van trip down to the city. The rest of his possessions were in a plastic bag.

On Lamont's first day at the group home, an older teenager grabbed his new jacket in front of a staff member and walked off with it.

"Go out and get your jacket," the counselor told him. "If you don't go out and fight that kid, I'm going to kick your ass myself." It was his introduction to a new way of life.

TO LAMONT, IT SEEMED LIKE EVERYBODY in the group home and at school was trying to hurt him. A staff report from this period reflected unhappiness, even irritation, that the boy was such a misfit in the black urban street culture of his new peer group. "Lamont is no longer the 'shining star' that he was in his previous setting," the staff reported in a UCR dated July 10, 1987. "This group of young men [is] able to confront and challenge him." Lamont was said to "take an elitist attitude," to "hide behind the air of grandiosity he projects," and—when he became a target of a violent gang in his junior high school—"to aggravate the more hostile students in class to the point where he needed to be escorted to the bus by an adult on a daily basis." The same report called his relationship with staff members superficial, adding, "They have concentrated on teaching him that life in the city is different from that in the communities where he was residing before."

Eventually Lamont realized that he came across as a country boy groomed by white people. In Rhinebeck he had been too black to belong; in the Bronx he was too "Rhinebeck" to be accepted as a black boy. For at least 150 years, philanthropy had favored removing neglected poor children to country or suburban settings like Astor Home's. But Lamont felt he was living a catch-22. "As soon as you're too old for one of these manor-type places in the country, they move you to the city," he said. "It's like taking me when I'm a baby animal, taking my claws out, and putting me right back in the jungle."

The prospect of a foster or adoptive family did still hover briefly on the horizon. The last chance, when he was fourteen, was with an unmarried black man who had seen Lamont in a photolisting of available children and considered adopting him and another boy simultaneously to create an instant family. But after Lamont ate dinner at his house in Brooklyn, the man lost interest.

One day when he was fifteen, Lamont saw his own face on television on a public-service show about children available for adoption. Such television programs were an extension of the photolisting requirement in cases where children had in effect been legally orphaned by the court's termination of parental rights but remained unadopted and in agency custody.

"I'm not going to let you exploit me and market me like a piece of meat," Lamont yelled in anger at agency staff. By then he was officially old enough to sign a waiver to halt adoption efforts permanently, and he did so. Soon afterward, he was transferred to another Astor group residence in the Bronx; this one, at 954 East 211th Street, was called Seton Group Home, and it was designated for older teenagers with the goal of "independent living."

Lamont spent most of the summer of 1989 in the streets, getting into trouble—drinking, smoking marijuana, taking a joyride that ended in a car crash. At Seton, he watched a stream of teenagers come and go as "overnighters," churned through as many as thirty temporary foster placements in a single month. One nomad kid, he noticed, carried a cup and pillowcase as his most precious possessions. Seton counselors frequently locked all the residents out during the day, and it was common knowledge among the boys that certain staff members were sneaking women into the house, using drugs, and skimming money from the residents' clothing accounts. Eventually, several staff members left under a cloud of scandal. One child-care worker absconded with the children's personal savings; Lamont himself lost $225. It took a year and a formal complaint to the children's rights unit of the Child Welfare Administration for him to get the money reimbursed.

In July 1989, Astor sold all its Bronx group homes to Leake & Watts, a Protestant agency. The kids went with the property, of course. The sale had been envisioned for several years as part of the archdiocese's strategic response to the *Wilder* decision. Rather than implement the family-planning provisions of *Wilder,* Astor Home preferred to shift its adolescent group homes to a non-Catholic agency such as Leake & Watts, according to the confidential contingency plan produced for the city by consultants in 1987, when an exodus of Catholic and Jewish agencies from the foster-care system seemed likely because of the *Wilder* settlement.

Dire projections of this exodus, and of the millions of dollars that the city would have to pay to duplicate Catholic facilities, were often cited in press accounts of the *Wilder* controversy to explain Mayor Koch's efforts to placate Cardinal O'Connor. But to the surprise of the consultants, the practical problem looked much smaller on examination. Many non-Catholic agencies were prepared to expand to take up the slack if Catholic programs closed, and they would be able to take over their buildings and staffs rather easily because, without city contracts to occupy them, these would be an economic drain on the archdiocese. Few Catholic agencies showed signs of actually bowing out, anyway. One option open to many agencies, including the main program of Astor Home, was to arrange for the relabeling of children in residence, shifting wards of the city's Special Services for Children to the state's Office of Mental Health or its semicorrectional Division for Youth.

Lamont noticed that while the name of his agency changed to Leake & Watts, the Astor group-home administrators and social-work supervisor stayed on. By then he had learned to second-guess every statement made by the counselors and psychologists who passed through his life, knowing that his responses would evoke judgments that would be preserved in a confidential file. One day he stumbled onto his own record on a social worker's desk. Flipping through it, he saw Golden Valley's diagnosis of schizophrenia and Astor Home's references to hallucinations. "I never had hallucinations," he protested. "I remember I used to have tons and tons of nightmares. I was labeled as crazy. That's what happens when you're in care."

The staff was upset that he had seen his file. One social worker, Baxter Brown, did his best to defuse its impact. A lot of psychological tests were bogus, he told Lamont, and subject to dramatically different interpretation by different doctors. Besides, he added, it was likely that Lamont himself had sometimes been playing around with the doctors when they examined him. Yet it was obvious to Lamont that the judgments in the file continued to follow him, and that decisions about his future were being made on the basis of his answers to new tests.

Lamont had become a chameleon. First he had dropped his Megadeath T-shirt for the vest-and-baggy-pants look of a popular rapper called Kwame. He used bursts of gangsta street slang to replace or break up the upstate speech patterns that had marked him for ridicule as a "black white boy." For a few months he had even "run money" for drug dealers, until he grew bored with it and decided that he didn't have the heart to be a criminal. When a social worker mentioned that his father's name, Prentis Smith, sounded Jamaican, he began hanging out among Rastafarians and added a Jamaican lilt to his speech. Later, when Spike Lee's movie *School Daze* brought the "club style" craze to the high school he attended, he dyed half his head blond and wore polka-dot shirts.

Fitting in was more important at Truman High School than academic achievement. The school had seven floors, which made it easy to cut class without being caught. Lamont, who had loved to read as a child and at nine had happily discussed Athens and Sparta with his social worker, soon fell behind in accumulating the credits he would need to graduate. For a time he was on the school's wrestling team, but then he was cut in favor of better wrestlers. He lingered on the fringes of a black fraternity but was not invited to join. At last he found affinity with a brotherhood of aspiring musicians and actors, one of whom introduced him to the Mind-Builders Creative Arts Center in 1989.

Mind-Builders had been founded in a former Yeshiva by Madaha Kinsey-Lamb, a black woman, to give artistic opportunities to children in the Bronx neighborhood known as Williamsbridge. Lamont taught himself to play the piano in one of the center's practice studios, a big, airy place with burnished hardwood floors. He hung out with its theater company, the Positive Youth Troupe, which performed all over the city. He found a mentor in the troupe's musical director, Sefus Henderson, a tall, lean, light-skinned black man who wore African garb and belonged to an Africanist religious society based on Islam. Lamont, who had declined to be a Catholic altar boy and could not remember why or when he had been baptized Lutheran, now shunned pork and tried to fast at Ramadan.

Henderson saw Lamont as a natural musician and potentially charismatic performer whose talents were losing out to a paralyzing fear of failure. He recognized the little lies Lamont told to boost his self-esteem and worried about the aimless anger that seemed increasingly to consume him. For two years Henderson tried to persuade Lamont to perform with the theater company. Instead, he joined its technical crew, serving as an assistant sound person paid twenty-five dollars a show.

After Lamont turned eighteen, in 1992, counselors at the group home and at Truman began encouraging him to drop out of high school. He was so far behind in credits, they said, that he should think about taking an exam for a general-equivalency diploma instead. His discharge goals from foster care included getting a high school diploma or the equivalent, a full-time job, a place to live, and a bank account containing a thousand dollars in savings. Until fairly recently, foster children had aged out of the system automatically at eighteen. But in the 1980s so many former foster children had been found among the young adults living in homeless shelters and in the street that Doug Lasdon, director of the Legal Action Center for the Homeless, had filed suit against the city on their behalf. The named plaintiff in the lawsuit was William Palmer, who at eighteen had gone straight from foster care to sleeping in shelters and public places. *Palmer* v. *Cuomo* had resulted in a judgment requiring the city to provide supervision for thousands of young people between eighteen and twenty-one who had left foster care. New state regulations had followed in August 1987, obligating the city to train foster children for independent living, to supply counseling and vocational services until they reached twenty-one, and to offer them transitional housing for up to a year after their discharge.

A new category of independent-living programs was supposed to bridge the gap between life as a ward and life in the real world. But the city had been slow to fund such programs. Once again, Lamont was running out of time.

PART FIVE

1990–2000

ONE

O N THE SATURDAY EVENING OF MARCH 20, 1993, ABOUT twenty of Marcia Lowry's closest friends and colleagues gathered in the low-ceilinged living room of Ira and Trudy Glasser's apartment for a party to celebrate her twentieth anniversary with the Children's Rights Project. Some had not seen one another since the 1970s, and they shared old jokes and memories with the rueful, tender self-deprecation that middle-aged people often adopt toward their younger selves. The ceremonial part of the evening was brief. Glasser's speech was a little bit like a roast, yet inspirational and respectful, too. The room brimmed with laughter, affectionate admiration, a sense of shared pride.

And then Lowry spoke. As she looked around her after twenty years, she blurted out, she felt like a failure. What had she accomplished? What had it all been for? She had set out to fix the child welfare system, and the system was not fixed. They had wanted to make a difference for children, but they had failed.

Many in the small audience were stunned. It was a kind of brutal honesty that was not appropriate for moments like this, Glasser thought, even if what she said might be true. He felt people shift and look away in embarrassment from Lowry's mournful face. In his eyes, such open unhappiness was almost a form of self-indulgence. It went without saying that one's youthful ambitions didn't come to pass, but personal disappointment could not be allowed to shadow the common enterprise. And the worst one could say, even for *Wilder,* was that it was too soon to tell.

For the first ten years, from 1973 to 1983, the city, like most of the agencies named as defendants, had contested the lawsuit. For the next five years, after the remarkable turnabout led by Fritz Schwarz, the city had negotiated the settlement that became a federal court decree. The decree had finally been upheld in its entirety in 1988 after an appeal by the religious agencies. Yet for the past five years, at every step of what was supposed to be implementation, the city had asked for more time. Now city officials were arguing that the decree was obsolete. The city's demographics of poverty, drugs, and AIDS had nearly tripled the total number of children in the system, even as they had reduced the percentage of white ones to the vanishing point. Agencies that wanted to stay in business had little choice but to fill their foster homes and beds with black Protestant children. And the system itself was now headed by Robert L. Little, a black man, himself a former foster child, and youngest brother to Malcolm X. How, *Wilder* detractors asked, could a case originally pegged to discrimination still be important?

"Time has passed this case by," Joel Berger, the latest assistant city corporation counsel to handle *Wilder,* would assert. "Listen to the dialogue in this courtroom—it's not relevant to the issues confronting the city. We're dealing with a very different world, with homelessness, crack, children sleeping in offices. Back in 1984, nobody ever heard of boarder babies, just as one example."

The *Wilder* case itself, once so controversial, so cutting-edge, now seemed becalmed in a lulling pattern of bimonthly hearings, flow charts, and schoolmarmish memos from the *Wilder* panel, which had been set up to oversee the settlement's fulfillment, but had somehow been sucked into the very bureaucracy it was supposed to prod. Mary Ann Jones, a professor of social work who was a panel member, called it "the most frustrating thing I've ever been involved with. It's a quagmire. I can't even explain it to myself at the end of the day."

No wonder lawyers joked that it was like the case out of *Bleak House*: "*Jarndyce and Jarndyce* drones on. This scarecrow of a suit has, in the course of time, become so complicated, that no man alive knows what it means. . . . Fair wards of the court have faded into mothers and grandmothers; a long procession of chancellors has come in and gone out; . . . but *Jarndyce and Jarndyce* still drags its dreary length before the court, perenially hopeless. *Jarndyce and Jarndyce* has passed into a joke. That is the only good that has ever come of it."

And yet, to Lowry, *Wilder* still went to the heart of a chaotic system.

"You focus on overnight kids, you focus on boarder babies, you just put them on another train to the same place," she would argue. The boarder babies, in fact, were the perfect example. Relentless bad publicity had forced the city to focus on removing them from the hospital wards to which they were being relegated for lack of homes, tethered to their cribs and pining for attention during the cresting crack epidemic of the mid-1980s. But in 1989, well after the news media had moved on to other stories, a follow-up study by the city comptroller's office had found that most of these babies, by then three and four years old, were still haphazardly bouncing around the foster-care system, without permanent homes.

"Discrimination is no longer the issue," Lowry would say. "This is a system that serves almost exclusively minority kids, and serves them badly. The decree sought to restructure the child welfare system and change the way the city did business."

But the decree had not changed the way Mayor Koch did business. In an effort to appease Catholic and Jewish Orthodox agencies, he even sought to overturn the state regulations that required the provision of birth-control information and services to foster children over twelve. As for the supposedly declining significance of race, skin shade was now being used routinely as a placement criterion, and by black as well as white caseworkers, at both the Child Welfare Administration's own Office of Direct Care Services and the private agencies. That was one of the most discouraging findings in a hundred-page report by Theodore Stein, a professor of social welfare hired by the *Wilder* plaintiffs to interview city caseworkers and examine fifty case files chosen at random in 1989.

According to Stein's report, hit-or-miss telephone brokerage, not first come, first served, remained the dominant method of placing children. In its defense, the Child Welfare Administration argued that the rise in emergency placements limited its ability to implement *Wilder*. But the Stein report showed that many of these emergencies were in fact created by the city's own failure to evaluate children's needs.

Lowry filed the first notices of contempt against the city in 1989, Koch's last year in office, but her motions were not ready until after David Dinkins's inauguration in January 1990. In deference to the new administration, Judge Ward postponed any judicial reckoning, holding in abeyance Lowry's first motion, on the city's failure to enforce the family-planning provisions of the settlement, and absolving the city of the obligation to respond in March 1990 to the second motion, which argued that the Child Welfare Administration had made no progress toward fulfilling *Wilder*'s key provisions.

Robert Little became head of the Child Welfare Administration at the end of 1990. It immediately became clear to him that as long as the city relied on the old-line agencies to provide the vast majority of care, he could exert no lasting authority over what programs they offered. This was a conclusion so similar to the one Lowry had reached before she filed *Wilder* in 1973 that the two of them seemed like natural allies. In fact, they were on a collision course.

Little saw the traditional foster-care agencies much as Catholics of the nineteenth century had perceived the Protestant child savers, across a divide of political and class conflict. Like the Catholics who had parlayed their growing political power into public support for their own child welfare institutions, Little, backed by the city's first black mayor, endorsed the already staggering growth of "kinship care"—that is, placement in homes where relatives were paid as foster parents. He soon translated the expansion of kinship care into a quintupling of his own direct-services staff and the creation of new black-run social-service agencies. As old-line foster-care agencies were left with empty beds to fill, they had to accept the more difficult children the city sent them. Little tried to shift the balance of power still further, redirecting money from institutional care in foster-care agencies toward a program of "family preservation," a form of short-term, intensive help for the families of children at imminent risk of foster-care placement. And for children already divided among different foster homes, he championed sibling reunification at all costs.

It was an agenda driven by his own family story.

"I truly believe that if ever a state social agency destroyed a family, it destroyed ours," the man born Malcolm Little had told Alex Haley for *The Autobiography of Malcolm X*. "We wanted and tried to stay together. Our home didn't have to be destroyed."

When Louise Little suffered a breakdown in 1938 and was committed to a state mental hospital, Robert, the youngest of her eight children, was no more than an infant. Malcolm X blamed his widowed mother's disintegration on the pain of seeing her children dizzy with hunger, on the humiliation of state charity and the oppressive interference of Michigan welfare workers. The six younger children, including Malcolm, were scattered to four separate foster homes. "A Judge McClellan in Lansing had authority over me and all my brothers and sisters," Malcolm X told Haley. "We were 'state children,' court wards; he had the full say-so over us. A white man in charge of a black man's children! Nothing but legal, modern slavery—however kindly intentioned."

As Little saw it, however, the foster home in which he and his sister Yvonne had grown up was the equivalent of modern-day kinship care. They were the only ones placed by their mother's arrangement with friends of hers from the West Indies, in a foster home that would continue to be a gathering place for the Little siblings even after Robert aged out of foster care at nineteen. His foster father was a janitor who never earned more than fifty dollars a week in his life; Robert was glad that his foster-care check was contributing to the family economy. But he grew up feeling that the social workers who trooped through the house twice a year were an extension of oppressive white authority, like the courts, the police, and the prisons.

State foster children had very limited health benefits at the time. Michigan's dental plan for them paid only to have teeth pulled, not filled or cleaned. By the time he was a teenager, Little had lost eight or nine teeth that way. "People thought I was hostile," he recalled. "Hell, I wasn't hostile! I didn't smile a lot because I was ashamed of my teeth. Only after I was grown and working and got insurance could I afford to get them fixed. It cost me thousands of dollars and literally hours of agony to repair the damage done to me in a system that didn't give a shit about the children."

That was one of the stories he told regularly in speeches now. It was part of the preface to the happy ending: how he had returned to run the same social-service system that had controlled his childhood, and added preventive dental care to the health benefits of all foster children. As the chief administrator for state social services, he had also ordered up his own foster-care record. Reading through the file, he found the names and notes of thirty-five different social workers. One had classified him as mentally retarded—and now that man was working for him.

"When you were my worker you didn't treat me too well," Little told the man. The social worker replied, "If I'd known you were going to be my boss, I would have treated you better." In telling the story, Little would add, "My life is like, what comes around, goes around."

The phrase had an edge to it. Keenly aware that five of the ten New York City child welfare commissioners preceding him had lasted less than two years in the job, he was quick to see enemies, quick to distill racial politics out of any disagreement, and ready to fight back on those terms. What often struck Little when he walked into Judge Ward's courtroom, for example, was that he was practically the only black person present. *Wilder* had become its own little industry, he thought, generating legal fees and paid consultancies, and nearly all of its beneficiaries were white, like most of the board members of the foster-care agencies that he considered his adversaries.

By March of 1993, 43 percent of all children placed by the city went to kinship homes. Little heard critics complain that foster care was now being used as a form of economic development for the black community, a back-door method of income redistribution. But he saw nothing wrong with that. For years black children had been the raw material for a white-run foster-care industry that treated them to second-class service. Why shouldn't money for their care stay within the black community instead, and help their own kind? AFDC (Aid to Families with Dependent Children) benefits had declined by 20 percent in real terms since 1979, and the kinship-care debate made manifest the dramatic difference between the meager amount government was willing to pay to support poor children living with their own mothers and the more generous stipends it would pay for them to be anywhere else. In an implicit government acknowledgment that the welfare allowance was inadequate for raising children, the basic foster-care rate was more than triple the AFDC grant, and many children in kinship care qualified for a special foster-care rate of up to seven times more.

In many ways the issues echoed the child welfare conflicts of Josephine Shaw Lowell's era. Then, the same native reformers who had barred children from poorhouses and cut public aid to families complained that irresponsible Catholic immigrants were too willing to have their children raised at taxpayer expense in orphanages run by their own kind. Now another ethnic succession seemed to be under way, with battle lines drawn along racial instead of religious lines. As new minority-run agencies sprang up, Little began to transfer kinship-care cases by the score to those that he found deserving of support. Wasn't this just another version of what Gail Kong had called preferred placement? Since children in kinship care brought along an eighteen-dollar-a-day administrative fee, the transfers were a way of ensuring the survival of fledgling black-run agencies, some of which flunked even the diluted version of PAS, the city's evaluation system. Soon, citing budget cuts, Little eliminated PAS altogether. Its standards, he said later, were based on a "Eurocentric model of family life" that ignored the special strengths of African American communities.

Privately, Little acknowledged that the kinship program was in disarray: many homes had not been visited by a city caseworker in years. Children often had severe medical and educational needs that were ignored until the crisis point. But Little believed that the old-line foster-care agencies had ulterior motives for attacking the program: now they wanted a piece of the action. And Lowry, who insisted that the *Wilder* decree applied equally to all foster children, including those being slotted in kinship care, had placed herself squarely in the enemy camp.

FOUR MONTHS AFTER HER ANNIVERSARY PARTY, in July 1993, Lowry filed a new motion in *Wilder,* asking Judge Ward to appoint a receiver to take over the city's Child Welfare Administration. Little struck back hard. He told a reporter from *New York Newsday* that Lowry's contempt motion was a calculated effort to discredit Dinkins on the eve of the mayoral election, a racial power play to put a white judge in authority over three black officials (Little, Barbara Sabol, the commissioner of the Human Resources Administration, and Dinkins himself) and over the overwhelmingly black and Hispanic children in their charge. "It's about power and control, not about minority children," he declared. "I sit in that court, and other than myself and a panel member, I don't see any person of color in this process. I just see a lot of money and a lot of fees being paid to a lot of people for a long time."

Lowry, with her tin ear for politics, was astonished—but not intimidated. She fired back a scathing letter to *Newsday*'s editor and, behind the scenes, sought out the perfect special master: black, female, and hardnosed about systems that hurt children, no matter what the race of those nominally in charge.

But the sense of failure that had gripped her at her anniversary party had lingered. She saw the kind of change she had set out to make in 1973 not as an artifact of youth but as the goal that still drove her life. It was easy to understand the appeal of bricks-and-mortar philanthropy, she thought, because if you ever wondered what you had accomplished you could go and look at the building. The *Wilder* decree was no orphanage on the Hudson. How, the city's lawyer asked, could anyone but Marcia Lowry argue the priority of setting up an elaborate agency classification and vacancy-control scheme in the middle of a foster-care crisis? She could only argue back, "You've got to see beyond where you are to where you should be."

Twenty years. Boarder babies, siblings wrenched apart or wrenched together, nomad kids dragging their possessions from place to place in garbage bags, toddlers battered to death in hotels for the homeless under the city's blind eye—virtually all these children had been born into the *Wilder* plaintiff class. What good had it ever done them? What good had it done Shirley Wilder's own son, that lost child evoked by a newspaper reporter's inquiry that spring and by a rare telephone call from Shirley herself?

Shirley had never stopped caring about the case brought in her name, though long ago, as part of the settlement that was supposed to benefit all children, she had agreed to give up any claim to monetary damages. About the time of Lowry's anniversary party, Shirley had expressed her feelings of gratitude to the reporter. "I feel if it wasn't for Marcia, I wouldn't be here today. Marcia was there through thick and thin for me."

When the words were repeated to Lowry, she felt stricken, just as she had when Glasser praised her. What she had done for Shirley and a few others was so little. Some of these kids, a lawyer who would take their phone calls was the best they ever got.

Lowry's contact with her named plaintiff had been only intermittent over the years. For long stretches Shirley Wilder had disappeared, her last phone number invalid, her new address unknown. Every so often, every three years on average, she would call again. Usually she asked about her son.

"I don't want him to feel I gave up on him," she said this time, in the spring of 1993. "Marcia, can you find Lamont? Marcia, can you find my son?"

TWO

T HEY FIRST RECOGNIZED EACH OTHER ACROSS FOUR LANES
of traffic. Shirley Wilder saw the baby she'd lost to foster care stride
toward her as a tall young man of nearly nineteen. Lamont saw that the
slim woman in jeans, with tears running down her face, was the mother
he'd never known. Speeding cars were nothing compared to the years of
yearning, guilt, and anger bridged by that first embrace in the middle of
Gun Hill Road.

There had been times when Lamont hated her. The angriest memory
was from the summer he turned twelve. Astor Home had let him play Little League baseball in Rhinebeck, and he'd made the all-star team. "I was
the only black kid," he recalled. "Everybody else's parents were there, and
I was all alone."

For Shirley, every year had days she dreaded. She hated Mother's Day.
She hated his birthday: "I felt bad as a mother. I knew he was out there
somewhere."

But when they ran to each other on May 6, 1993, their roles seemed to
reverse. Like a child, she sobbed uncontrollably against his chest. Like a
parent, he held her close and tried to comfort her. The reunion three
days before Mother's Day had been arranged by a newspaper reporter
and photographer, go-betweens of a media age. But the presence of
those observers seemed incidental to the awkward intensity of their first
meeting.

They were the closest of strangers. He looked so much like her, this
tall, handsome young black man with wide-set eyes and an open face. Yet
he was completely foreign to her imagination. He had the suggestion of a

mustache and goatee, a high forehead defined by meticulously cut hair, a sturdy frame dressed in jeans, Jamaican rugby shirt, and khaki photographer's vest. A name in gold hung from a chain around his neck: *Lamonte,* it said. After receiving the misspelled necklace as a gift from a former girlfriend, he had simply adopted the extra letter at the end of his name. At the time it seemed no more arbitrary than the spelling conferred on him at birth by a woman who had vanished from his life. "Growing up without a family leaves you kind of without an identity," he said. "In the system, you just feel like a number. And when you leave, somebody else gets your number."

Sometimes in Lamont's fantasies his mother was an heiress who brought him birthday gifts, one for every year they had been apart. No one watching them embrace in front of the graffiti-scrawled metal shutters of a Bronx street front near his group home could have mistaken Shirley Wilder for a rich woman. But she looked like *him,* and Lamont had spent his childhood thirsting to look like somebody.

She seemed almost like a teenager herself, this thirty-three-year-old woman in tight, faded jeans, black sweatshirt, and high-heeled strap shoes, her hair pulled back tight from high cheekbones, a smile now illuminating her whole face. Impulsive, needy, and resilient still, she lived like an interloper in the East Harlem apartment of a fifty-nine-year-old man known as Mister Al. He was a thin, grizzled black man with a military pension and heart disease, who had taken Shirley in two years before when she needed a place to stay and he needed help with his three youngest children; their own mother, a crack addict, had vanished. Shirley called him Daddy.

Her real daddy, James Adam All, had died on November 11, 1978, just before her nineteenth birthday. He had been beaten senseless by security guards while he was a patient being treated for cirrhosis of the liver at North General Hospital. The details of the incident were murky, but after he died of a cerebral hemorrhage from his injuries, the family sued, and the hospital settled out of court. Shirley got fifteen hundred dollars. She would have been hard pressed to give a coherent account of her life since then, and she didn't try now.

"I thought you'd be short and fat," she told Lamont with a burst of laughter, eyeing his muscular build and describing the bowlegged, portly baby she remembered.

"I'm still bowlegged. They say I walk like a cowboy. At Astor they used to laugh when I tried to run. But I ran anyway."

Their arms around each other, they sat in the backseat of the photographer's car as it drove past common landmarks of their parallel lives, and talked so fast they tripped over each other's words. Lamont pointed out his junior high school, J.H.S. 142; she had attended the same one. "I was bad in that school," Lamont told her. "I was a humdinger," she shot back.

She shared her few memories of him: his birth, his first haircut, the day she fed him all her French fries. She told him about Mister Al's children, now fourteen, thirteen, and six, but added fervently, "You're different. You're from me. I can't love 'em the same way."

"I went through the same thing," he exclaimed. "They tried to put me in different families, but I couldn't love them like they were mine. I'm probably just as defiant as you are."

As the car sped toward the East Harlem housing project where she lived, they spoke of time-out rooms, behavior-modification units, and foster-care agencies with a cynicism they had both learned young. "It's just a paycheck to them," Lamont said. "I learned with organizations like that, if you keep the kids in placement, there's more money being generated."

Stammering, he tried to convey to her the emotional essence of his adolescent years. "I was just angry, angry about everything. Then I learned how to be angry, but to say it in words. I learned from being verbal to manipulate people. I could sell you the moon—that's what music's about."

He did not mention that he had dropped out of high school six months shy of earning the credits he needed to graduate, or that in taking the exam for a general-equivalency diploma earlier that spring, he had fallen short of a passing score in math. All along, his greatest fear was that she would find him wanting. When she asked him what he planned to do next, he said, "I'll probably go to college or something. I wanted to study music or law. At one time I wanted to be a cop."

"No baby, not that," she protested, hugging his arm. "I just got you back."

In the living room of Mister Al's modest East Harlem apartment, Shirley grew languid and loose-limbed. She draped herself against Lamont as they sat on the plastic-covered couch, near the framed graduation photos of Mr. Al's ten grown children and the freezer big enough for a side of pork from his family's farm in Langley, South Carolina. Wariness and anxiety filled Lamont's face, and he sat up very straight. Still she beamed, her eyelids drooping.

"I didn't get no sleep at all last night," she said, and unselfconsciously swung her legs over his lap.

She meant no harm. It was a kind of ignorance, a failure to recognize the borders between closeness and sexuality, that reflected some long twilight of childhood need and exploitation. But Lamont hardly knew where to look. He began talking rapidly about his girlfriend.

"She's acting crazy," he said. "She makes me so mad."

"You don't hit womens, do you?" Shirley asked, alarm in her voice, pulling away. She had been beaten up too many times by too many boyfriends not to flinch at the thought of blows from this broad-shouldered stranger.

"No," he said vehemently.

"I would die for you," she whispered.

It was growing dark when they walked into Mind-Builders together. The sound of drums and woodwinds wafted down the stairwell. Shirley took her place beside Lamont at an upstairs piano. With love and pride shining in her face, she listened as he played her a piece called "Tender," and then a jazzy, half-finished tune of his own invention. Her hair had begun to work free from its pins. Her eyes seemed glazed with fatigue, but she could not stop smiling. "That's my son," she marveled. "He's everything."

Sefus Henderson, regal in his African robes, stopped by to be introduced. Only the week before, Lamont had told Henderson that his long-lost mother was a wealthy woman living in an East Side skyscraper. Meeting her, Henderson immediately suspected the truth:

Lamont's mother was a crack addict.

IN THE EARLY 1980s, when cocaine still cost a hundred dollars a gram and was known as the drug of the rich and famous, a barroom dancer called Sparkle had taken Shirley down to a party in a Village brownstone. After a guard checked them for weapons and let them through a metal security door, they entered a big parlor full of well-dressed men and sexy women having a good time. Most were white; several were freebasing—a method of ingesting cocaine that had been used in some affluent circles since the 1970s. Then a man walked through the crowd offering cocaine "rocks" from a tray, like canapés. Shirley had never seen that kind before.

"No, mama, you can't sniff that," the man told her. "I'll show you how to do it."

That was Shirley Wilder's first crack high. Three months later, on a day when she felt despondent, she remembered the intense, brief rush of euphoria she had experienced at that swanky bordello party in the Village. Asking around, she discovered that the same precooked stuff was sold right at her Harlem corner for ten dollars a chunk. Later the price dropped to five dollars, and finally to three or even two. A few blocks from the bar where she worked, under the elevated train tracks at 125th and Park, the price of a hooker dropped accordingly.

When the epidemic of crack coverage seized the news media in 1986, smokeable cocaine was often depicted as a new and instantly addictive drug, a danger to society comparable to the "plague in medieval times." But as sociologists would eventually point out, and as Shirley's own experience underlined, crack was essentially a marketing innovation: the repackaging of an old upscale commodity (powder cocaine) into small, cheap units sold on the street to a new class of consumers. Its customer base was the urban poor, a segment of society that had always been in the market for an inexpensive high, but whose vulnerability to drug abuse had grown enormously over two decades of widening inequality and family disintegration.

By 1993, when Lamont Wilder went looking for family roots and a future after foster care, crack ruled Shirley's life. For her, trying to remember the years since crack was like gathering shards of broken glass: a few scenes glimmered, but their sequence was almost random, and every memory had jagged edges. An outdoor party in Puerto Rico, all flowers, palm trees, and layer cake, she liked to call her wedding. But it only marked the best stage of her relationship with Pedro, a man who soon forbade her to wear shorts or short dresses, beat her, and put her to work in his business transporting drugs between New York and Puerto Rico. She remembered smoking crack for hours with Pedro's sister in a hotel room in New York. She remembered a church in Jersey City that she joined when she was trying to quit, and a job cleaning rooms at a

Quality Inn. But which came first and how long it lasted, she could not tell. Every recollection ended with fist against flesh, blood in her mouth, tears and remorse. Finally, when the beatings got too bad, she ran back to her old neighborhood and found Mister Al.

At first she could go two weeks at a time without getting high. That shrank to a week, then to four days. Again and again Mister Al threatened to throw her out for good, only to relent once more when she showed up street-soiled and repentant after a two-week binge, sobbing that she had really hit bottom this time.

"Stop it or otherwise get the hell out of my house," he yelled. "You go on a mission, don't come back here because I'll pack up your clothes and leave them out in the hall. I'd rather give up on you than hurt my children."

Recovering her own lost child had seemed like a promise of deliverance from the drug. In the better times, when a stint of detox and outpatient treatment brought temporary relief from the cycle of crackhouse binging and strung-out desperation, she imagined Lamont as the missing piece that would make her life whole. But what did she have to offer him after eighteen years?

She would welcome him from the shadows into the bright dream of rural domesticity that Mister Al had cast over the tenement apartment, where pickled pigs' feet gleamed in a glass jar on the dinette table and collard greens grew in a plot across the street. On good days, treading on the heels of her light shoes as though they were bedroom slippers, Shirley would walk over to survey Al's crops in the Operation Greenthumb garden reclaimed from urban rubble, loudly greeting neighbors in English and Spanish, her eyes seeking the taut lines of string that marked off his well-tended plot from five others. Rosettes of cabbage grew in a raised row, and there were sprouting cucumbers, tomatoes, sunflowers, hollyhocks, even chickens hatching their chicks in a hutch behind the rain barrel.

But just around the corner, where young men lounged meaningfully in front of a bodega called Tu y Yo, her other world was waiting to claim her. The crackhouse on the fourth floor had lost none of its pull. A reinvented motherhood proved a flimsy anchor against that tide.

On Mother's Day Lamont did not show up at four o'clock for the special dinner she had cooked him, and didn't call with his lame excuses until ten. She cried and raged. "He really hurt me. If he's going to try to get back at me, he don't know—I will turn into an iceberg."

Instead, over the next week, she called and called the beeper number he had given her. Once, he did not return her message for seven hours. Was he trying to punish her for losing track of him in the system? "I can't give you back eighteen years," she told him. But she dreamed of doing just that.

"I'm going to get a job with Marcia and buy you a car over the summer," she promised. Her only income was a $176 public-assistance check every other week, usually doled out bit by bit by Mister Al. The job was per diem office work paying $7.58 an hour. Lamont was not impressed.

"I did the best I could," she told him. "I couldn't raise you. Don't be angry about what happened in the past. I can't do anything about that, I can only do something about now."

Lamont's return had laced her struggle to control her crack craving with old guilt and fresh anger. Sometimes when she was mad at herself, she would impulsively run up to the tarred roof of Mister Al's building to survey the horizon. Barefoot, naked under her bathrobe, she would stand with her head flung back in the breeze off the East River, taking in the jumbled urban landscape and the pale sky. Her eyes would seek out the building where she had traded herself for crack in a fever of need, and beyond it the cross and church spire that marked the Sisters of Charity convent on 116th Street. She knew that nuns lived there; she didn't know that one of them was her own Sister Dorothy Gallant of the Holy Cross Campus and the Hudson River train rides, who now spent her days ministering to homeless women in city shelters, many of them drug addicts who had lost their children to foster care.

By the third day without a high, Shirley's craving would become so intense that the best she could do was stay indoors, knowing that if she left the apartment her feet would take her to where she had sworn not to go. By the fourth day she couldn't think at all. When she tried to sleep, her nerves turned the smallest sound into firecrackers, and what sleep she found brought no rest.

Mister Al would wake to the sound of her tormented voice. At first she refused to believe that she was talking in her sleep, so he taped her and played the recording back in daylight. Then she broke down and sobbed, cursing her father.

In her dreams, she was a child again, and her father was mounting her. With the nightmares came the conviction that Lamont himself was the result of that terrible coupling.

Lamont kept asking about his father. Prentis Smith had abandoned her, she said. It would be a mistake for him to seek him out. She tried to change the subject. Her son would be nineteen on June 4. She urged him to spend his birthday with her, and he agreed. She would take him out to celebrate, she promised. She even telephoned him the day before to make sure he was really coming over this time. But when he showed up, she had vanished.

IN THE FOURTEEN YEARS since Alicia Fils-Aime had given up Lamont, she had finished college at night, earned a master's degree in divinity from Duke University, and become a Methodist minister at the Spanish-speaking congregation of Fordham United Methodist Church and Saint Stephen's in the Bronx.

But when she heard Lamont's name from a reporter, she began to weep. She didn't care what had happened in between. She wanted to tell Lamont that she loved him, that she had never stopped loving him.

"Lamont was a beautiful child, a loving, very happy child, and everywhere I took him, people loved him," she said. "He was like my child. And still, to this day, people ask me, 'Have you heard about Lamont?' I would like to see him, because the only reason I didn't adopt him is that I was going through a divorce at that time, and I wanted him to have a mother and a father."

For weeks, Lamont promised and then dodged a meeting with Alicia. Finally, in a quiet sitting room at Mind-Builders, the reunion took place. Alicia brought with her the talismans she had kept for all those years: a drawing he had made in nursery school, his favorite placemat shaped like a dog, the turquoise infant sleeper he was wearing when she brought him home from the hospital.

"That's tiny, tiny," he marveled, fingering the brushed cotton.

She was older, of course, and not as slim, but she looked and sounded the same as he remembered. He looked the same too, she said, just grown up. He studied the photos she had brought, especially one of himself at less than a year, holding a teddy bear in a white crib and smiling. The face was his. Only the expression seemed truly alien, a wide-eyed joy without reserve that seemed to him the essence of lost innocence.

She had brought other photographs, too, including a roll from the family's Disney World vacation that had been forgotten in the camera for five or six years before she had it developed. When the pictures came back, she had cried out as though she were seeing ghosts.

The awkwardness between them eased when he took her upstairs to the piano studio and played her the opening bars of "Für Elise." She gave him the two poems she had written for him so many years earlier.

"Didn't I get lost once?" Lamont asked her. Yes, they both remembered the time Alicia had called the police because she couldn't find him. All the while, it turned out, he had been playing with a little boy who lived on the Grand Concourse. Stammering, he asked her, "Was I bad when I was young?"

"You were very good," she told him gently, leaning over the piano. "You were very curious; you were very, very bright, and you asked questions like, 'Does anyone live in the moon?' And 'What keeps the clouds up?' "

He shook his head like a bewildered child. "I don't know what happened," he said. "I don't remember being bad."

Before they parted, she revealed that the church was relocating her to another state: at the end of the month, she would be moving to Connecticut. He must come and visit her there, she said. As soon as she had the telephone number, she would call him with it. No matter where she was sent in the future, he would always be able to find her through Methodist headquarters in New York.

Lamont did not know how he should feel. The only emotion he really knew how to feel was anger. This was the way the system had damaged him, he thought. It had made him really good at feeling angry, and confused by any other emotion.

Alicia's face brought back shameful memories that he had tried to forget since he and Missi shared their secrets of sexual exploitation in the Wassermans' backyard. His mind accepted that she had been powerless to protect him, that her decision to give him up had been understandable under the circumstances. But that reasoned judgment did nothing to untangle the nameless feelings that throbbed into a knot of controlled anger inside him.

"The system kind of trains you to base everything on thought," he told someone later. "No one's ever really telling you the truth. No one is telling you the entire story. A lot of times they're trying to tell you things to see what your reaction is. You have to learn to be just as calculative as they are. So I kind of trained myself. For every question, I've got two answers."

SHIRLEY RETURNED to Mister Al's later that summer, and she confessed her addiction to her son. Spending the night at their place for the first time, Lamont made her promise to quit drugs cold turkey. Again he pressed her to tell him about his father. He rejected her warnings that his father's family was no good, that her silence was meant to protect him. Finally, near daybreak, she told him how she and Peanut had met at Sam's Soul News, his uncle's store in Harlem.

THREE

T HE STORE WAS STILL CALLED SAM'S SOUL NEWS. WHEN LA-
mont walked in, he found the dark and rancid-smelling place
almost empty. Eyeing him from behind the counter was a skinny middle-
aged man with straightened hair that clung in long strands to the sweat
on his yellow skin. Once, Sam Seay had owned several businesses in
Harlem—a fish-and-chips restaurant, a newsstand, a variety store. But he
had lost nearly everything to bad times and his twelve-year cocaine habit.
The last store was hanging on with a meager stock of outdated sodas and
dirty magazines, cheap liquor sold under the counter to winos, cheap
hookers sold down the block.

"I'm looking for Prentis," Lamont told him. "I'm his son."

"My God, you look just like him!"

That was all Lamont needed, it turned out, to enter the life of a family
surviving at the inner-city intersection of crack, low-wage labor, and subsidized poverty. In 1993, one out of four young African American men
was in jail, in prison, on probation, or on parole. Among these, he soon
learned, were all of his father's brothers.

He was welcomed into his father's extended family with southern barbecue and sweet-potato pie on the Fourth of July weekend of 1993. In a
haze of sunshine and grill smoke, thirty relatives and neighbors jammed
a communal sixth-floor terrace overlooking train tracks fringed with
weeds and broken glass in the Morrisania section of the Bronx. The party
at the housing project on Webster Avenue spilled into hallways and flowed
through other apartments (one the stop for collard greens and ham,
another for home-churned ice cream), propelled by the pulse of a boom-

box, running children, and the raucous, liquored-up laughter of strangers who shared his blood.

Everyone was drunk on that day that thrust him raw into the realities of project life—his fifty-four-year-old grandmother, Betty Washington, his father, Prentis Smith, the many uncles who went downstairs to smoke their weed. The reunion was fun, Lamont thought, but disappointing: "Everybody was drinking and drugging like it was normal. You expect people to put on a show for you when you first meet them, and they didn't."

Then his mother walked in like a specter of the street, strung out and disheveled in a yellow netted shirt, old jeans, and soiled sneakers.

"Go change your clothes," someone told her. She shot back a defiant refusal, and the exchange of words quickly escalated to curses. Lamont ducked out, gratefully accepting the invitation of a distant cousin to watch her VCR eleven flights up. They were deep into Francis Ford Coppola's *Dracula* when the cousin's boyfriend walked in. He was a drug dealer, he had a gun, and he began to beat her up.

After he beats her, Lamont thought, he's going to shoot me. He ran all the way down to his grandmother's apartment from the seventeenth floor, jumping from flight to flight.

OVER THE NEXT TWO YEARS, Betty Washington's dark and crowded four-room apartment would repeatedly serve as Lamont's refuge even as he longed to leave it behind.

At first he slept on a couch in the living room, under a large triptych of Nelson Mandela, Martin Luther King, and Malcolm X. His father, who slept on the facing couch, took credit for introducing his mother to Africanism; once, he said, she would have had a big white Jesus on the wall instead.

Prentis Smith was a former postal worker who said he had conquered past problems with alcohol and drugs and spoke vaguely of starting computer training for a new job. He never did start. At thirty-six, he was smaller than Lamont, with lighter skin but a similar mustache and pencil-thin outline of a beard around his chin. He often wore an African dashiki and a fezlike cap, and he could speak at length about black civilizations ransacked and erased from black collective memory by white oppressors.

But he told the family's story as a descent from southern decency to northern degradation.

Betty Washington was Betty Seay Smith and only eighteen years old when she left her two small children in Memphis with her mother and headed to New York with her young husband in 1957. "They got here and it tore the family up," Smith would say. "That's when the nightmare began."

He was five and his sister, Brenda, six when Betty fetched them. By then she was an alcoholic and remarried to a man who beat children in the face with his fists. Prentis was eleven when his stepfather left, and his four half-brothers—Jeff, Stevie, George Junior, and Greg—were between infancy and six. Child welfare workers periodically visited the household but never removed the children. Those were the days of the so-called paper-bag test, when children with skin darker than a grocery bag were unlikely to be accepted by any foster-care agency; besides, the children did not want to be separated. "We used to cover it up so good," Lamont's father recalled of the way he and his brothers prepared for the social workers' visits. "We would have the house clean, the windows shining. But they knew."

Prentis's sister, Brenda, became a heroin addict as a teenager like her boyfriend, Christopher, and had two sons with him. The first baby, Chris, was born addicted and sent back to Memphis to be adopted by an aunt and uncle. The second, Troy, was a toddler when Shirley was pregnant with Lamont. While Lamont went into the foster-care system, Troy grew up in and around Betty Washington's household—the same household that had so appalled Shirley's child protective services worker. Troy's father eventually died of a drug overdose; his mother, Brenda, died of AIDS when Troy was about fifteen. By the age of twenty-one, Troy was known as the drug dealer who supplied Washington Avenue from 170th to 177th and the projects where his grandmother lived. He had the reputation for ruthlessness that had become critical in the crack trade: he was said to have shot and killed his best friend in public over drug money. Only days after Lamont met him at the family barbecue, Troy was busted by the cops with half a kilo of cocaine and twenty thousand dollars in cash.

Prentis's half-brothers Jeffrey, thirty-two, and Stevie, thirty-one, had already spent twelve to fifteen years each in prison, and George, twenty-seven, had recently been sent back for a three-to-six-year term. The youngest of Prentis's half-brothers, Greg, twenty-five, was a gay man addicted to crack who was now dying of AIDS; he had never held a job. Prentis himself had spent the least time in jail—just six months on Riker's Island at seventeen, awaiting trial on a homicide and unable to make the fifteen-thousand-dollar bail. That was where he had been when Shirley gave birth, it seemed, not on an army base in New Jersey. He had beaten up a wino "protecting my mother's honor"; a week later, the wino had died. Luckily, an autopsy eventually indicated that a brain tumor had contributed to the man's death, and Smith was released.

Seven years after Betty Washington had been rejected as incompetent to raise Lamont, Smith, now married, looked to her to rear his second son, Prentis Junior, and his fatherless stepson, Rashim. The boys were four and five, and their own mother had suffered a manic-depressive breakdown. It was scary to entrust his sons to a "real cursing malicious drunk" whose alcoholism had blighted his own childhood, Lamont's father acknowledged. But he felt he had nowhere else to turn.

"I wasn't in a position to care for them, and the BCW was trying to take them away from me," he recalled, using the familiar initials of the old Bureau of Child Welfare. "But I think my kids motivated her toward change. She did a real turnaround—no AA or anything, just southern wits and willpower. She is sober eighty-five percent of the time now."

Betty Washington had been caring for the boys for most of five years by 1987, when new policies spurred by the lawsuit known as *Eugene F.* allowed her to apply for foster-care benefits; her home was finally certified in 1989. Those two years were the height of the foster-bed crisis, when boarder babies languished in hospitals, children slept on caseworkers' desks, and a boy with "special needs" like Rashim, who had suffered brain damage in a fall from a six-story window as a young child, could have been churned through dozens of different "placements" at a cost of more than a hundred dollars a day. No one was going to second-guess a relative's home where the children had been living for years. And as was typical of many kinship foster-care cases, especially those originating in the overwhelmed Bronx field office, this one remained in the city's direct-care caseload with little or no supervision or services, to be recertified automatically.

Lamont and his father were among at least seven people who slept in the cramped apartment now. Besides Prentis Junior, sixteen, Rashim, seventeen, and their grandmother, there was Greg, the gay uncle with AIDS; Vernon, an elderly alcoholic boarder whose Social Security check helped pay the rent; and sometimes Aunt Sylvia and her kids. Sylvia was not really an aunt, but she was considered a member of the family because one of her children had been fathered by a Memphis cousin, one in the stream of Tennessee relatives who periodically came north and stayed awhile.

Betty Washington was the mainstay of this household, the one who held the lease, pooled the food stamps, shopped and cooked, and always found room for one more. She often worked as a home health-care aide, but she was between jobs that first summer. Day labor of various kinds—painting jobs, moving, and construction for the men, baby-sitting and temp work for the women—accounted for the cash flow to the household beyond public-assistance, foster-care, Social Security, and disability checks. Prentis Junior had a part-time job at a White Castle fast-food counter. Rashim scalped tickets. Lamont had the only full-time work—an eight-dollar-an-hour summer job as a day-camp counselor at Mind-Builders, funded through government youth-employment grants. He had resolved not to return to his Leake & Watts group home, where another resident had attacked him with a stick and bitten him so badly he'd needed stitches. But when his grandmother began to demand fifty dollars a week for his room and board, he felt hurt. It did not fit his idea of family.

Sometimes that summer Lamont had to sleep on the floor. In the blue glow of the TV set, roaches crawled through greasy cartons of leftover Chinese takeout and into the dregs of malt-liquor bottles. The smoke of Greg's crack pipe seeped from beneath the bathroom door. Once a prostitute came in to service a muscular southern visitor, quick and dirty under a blanket for the price of a high. All the while, one little orange fish darted to and fro in his grandmother's aquarium, sending flickering shadows over her knickknacks—the gilt plaster hands in prayer, the family photos, the red-hearted pink teddy bear kept sealed in a zippered plastic bag. By morning Lamont tried to imagine it all as a kind of prelude to a grander destiny and talked bravely about the lucrative music gigs and show-business connections that put him at the threshhold of fame.

Then one night, while Lamont slept, his uncle Greg crept into the room and stole his last fifty dollars for crack. Betty Washington reimbursed Lamont herself, but she cursed him roundly, too.

"You're a fucking fool for leaving your money in your pants," she screamed.

He felt like an innocent. Where else did you leave your money? Where he had grown up, it was normal to take your pants off before you went to sleep, and when you woke up in the morning, your cash would still be in the pocket.

"Living at Grandma's is scary," he told his father. "I love my family, but I can't live with you all."

Still, he stayed on.

It was, in fact, commonplace for children who had grown up in foster care to go back to their birth family in the end. They usually had nowhere else to go. The pattern had horrified Judy Schaffer in the 1970s when she pored over stacks of children's files to help Marcia Lowry make the case for adoption in a lawsuit called *Child* v. *Beame*. Children might be removed as toddlers from the worst mothers in the world and medicated with psychotropic drugs to keep them docile (in one unforgettable case, two children aged one and a half and three had been put on Thorazine after their foster mother complained that they were climbing on her white sofa), "but as soon as the kids were sixteen and would act up they would be sent right home to mommy monster who had a forty IQ and a drug habit and lived in an apartment with roaches." Yet eventually Schaffer would wonder whether their younger siblings who had never been removed were not better off.

Looking at Prentis Junior Lamont saw a teenager who was doing OK in high school, keeping away from reefer and alcohol, and working at the local burger joint. His grandmother gave him $180 a month out of his foster-care grant, which let him buy the latest sneakers without working for some drug dealer. "I'm not going to turn out like the rest of the family," Prentis Junior told his half-brother firmly. "It might be hard, but I'm strong-minded."

Was Lamont strong-minded? If destiny was not waiting in the wings, he would have to fall back on himself. It was a thought that could make him feel hollow and shopworn, like one of those dolls of painted wood that only hide smaller, empty versions of themselves.

THE FIRST TEST CAME when Uncle Jeff emerged from prison. In earlier years Uncle Jeff had taken a long-running game of three-card monte from New York to the Kentucky Derby and the New Orleans Mardi Gras, his hand perpetually quicker than the eye, his feet never quite quick enough to stay out of jail for long. But this was the 1990s, and he began running a crackhouse one floor up from Betty Washington's apartment. When Lamont's paycheck from Mind-Builders stopped in the fall, Uncle Jeff offered him a job selling crack.

It was easy to refuse him at first. Instead of going into business with his uncle, Lamont accepted Leake & Watts's invitation to enter its in-dependent-living program. With a twenty-year-old roommate who had also spent his life in foster care, he shared a spacious two-bedroom apart-ment owned by the agency in Parkchester, a huge housing complex in an eastern section of the Bronx. The rent was paid, and he had fifty-nine dol-lars a week for expenses.

Then everything began to fall apart. In the fall, Lamont's best friend's little brother was shot and killed by another teenager. His father, still unemployed, borrowed a hundred dollars from him and used most of it to get high. A few times they set dates to play chess together at the Park-chester apartment, and one night Lamont even cooked dinner—fish, steamed broccoli, and rice. But his father never showed. His mother, after a brief stint in drug detox, her third or fourth in seven years—quickly relapsed. This time Mister Al left her on the street, cut off from public assistance, so Lamont knew she had to be hooking to support her habit.

He himself kept setting up job interviews and not showing up, as though unable to face the possibility of rejection. He gave up his music lessons at Mind-Builders and joined its theater troupe, only to drop out just when rehearsals were beginning. Finally he started cutting hair in a Bronx barbershop.

On Christmas Eve 1993, Lamont went down to LaFamille, a jazz club at 125th Street and Fifth Avenue in Harlem. A girl he barely knew kept pushing him to play, and at last he sat in on keyboard for one set of the blues. It felt pretty good. But when he left the club to go home, the cold night air sliced away his sense of satisfaction. Walking to the subway past Park Avenue, he stared into the shadowy underpass beneath the elevated Metro North train tracks. Metro North was like the white man's safari car through the jungle, he and his father had joked that summer. As they watched the train speed through the Bronx from the vantage of his grand-mother's apartment house, Lamont had put on his best tour-guide voice and intoned, "To your left you have your crack spots and basketball courts, and over there are the projects." But the suburban commuters were missing the real underbelly of their journey home to Westchester County, he thought now. Here in the dark spaces below the hulk of steel and mortar, the living dead of the drug plague peddled their bodies for as little as three dollars a trick. Lamont could no longer walk by without peering in, involuntarily searching for a face that looked like his.

When he got back to his Parkchester apartment that Christmas Eve, it was full of his roommate Reggie's friends, guys from the group homes or the projects getting drunk and stoned, blasting the radio through the night. He joined the party until he felt good again, and at daybreak he fell asleep. The telephone woke him. It was his mother, calling from Mister Al's. She was back from the street, this was Christmas Day, and she wanted to see her son.

Unlike Christmases past, this one had brought Lamont more family invitations than he could handle—from his father, who still owed him money; from Alicia Fils-Aime in Connecticut; from his best friend's bereaved mother in the Bronx. The last was the only one he had felt comfortable accepting. But in the end, at about five or six o'clock, he went down to see his mother.

Mister Al's place was full of people. They had already eaten, but the table was still laden with leftovers of ham, turkey, and collard greens. He always felt uncomfortable at such family gatherings, a stranger spacing out amid the noise and chatter, and he had come empty-handed. But Shirley seemed to be eating, at least, maybe even to have gained a little weight.

She smiled, revealing a missing bottom tooth.

"I think I'm pregnant," she told him.

Mister Al, drunk on Christmas cheer, already knew and seemed unperturbed. All Lamont could do was urge his mother to go into long-term inpatient rehabilitation as soon as possible. "I don't want to lose my sister or brother," he said.

She agreed that seven-day treatment programs were no good. She promised to go into a forty-five-day program in the first week of the new year. Perhaps the bitter cold would help keep her inside. "I'm scared of going into a rehab," she confessed. "I'm scared of the challenges. It's like giving birth to a baby. This baby, I don't want it to get lost in the system."

She embraced Lamont, and he felt that she was rubbing up against him.

"Watch how you behave with me," he told her sharply. "I'm your son. You can't behave like that."

In no time they were in an angry argument. She complained that he had not come by or called on Thanksgiving Day, which had also been her thirty-fourth birthday, and suggested that his neglect had helped drive her back to drugs. She accused him of showing up only when he was broke and wanted something.

She had been so proud of her son the day they met. Now she no longer believed what he said about his life. "Lamont can be a good con man," she told someone later with a short laugh. "When I see Lamont, I see myself, so I see it coming."

LAMONT'S CONTEMPT FOR the foster-care agency grew as his self-esteem declined. "The program's just a big joke. It's easy to get over," he bragged one day in late February 1994 as he swept up hair from the black-and-white-checkered floor of the Starling Clippers barbershop in the Bronx. "I just give them all that boojie stuff, and they eat it up. They are so easy."

The barbershop was a small, out-of-the-way place with six red-vinyl-and-aluminum barber chairs and a hand-lettered sign on the wall that read The Way You Speak Says Alot About You. The best day he'd ever had there financially was during the Thanksgiving holidays, when he cut thirteen heads and made $189. Often he took home less than a hundred dollars a week, and business was slow these days. Besides, the weather had been so warm that he had taken a good many days off to play basketball with Reggie's friends. He had a girlfriend now, too, and she liked to party.

That spring, one of Leake & Watts's rare inspections turned up contraband beer bottles and marijuana blunt ends from a weekend party in the apartment. On another visit, a caseworker caught Lamont's girlfriend, Kisha, in his bed.

Lamont just wasn't ready for independent living, the agency decided, and it ordered him back to a group home. Instead, shortly before his twentieth birthday, he returned to Betty Washington's. By then he knew that Shirley wasn't pregnant after all. But Kisha was.

A SMALL, STRONG-WILLED WOMAN six months older than Lamont, Kisha had grown up in the projects and had never known her father. Her mother, who had a job with the Transit Authority, hated Lamont with a passion and often flew into rages at her daughter. Once Lamont had seen her beat Kisha with her shoe. After graduating from Truman High School in 1991, Kisha had taken some business courses, but she had trouble keeping office jobs. Christmas week she had been fired for insubordination from a job processing money for an armored-car company, and now she was shuttling between temp jobs or cashing a general-assistance check for $215 a month. Before moving into Lamont's Leake & Watts apartment, against the agency's rules, she had left her mother's home because they kept fighting. Now she was determined not to have an abortion, but instead to get her own place and keep the baby.

"I'm not ready for a child," Lamont argued. "I don't want to be one of those families on welfare."

For months the talk on TV and radio had been about ending welfare, about the government getting tough on unwed mothers and requiring all able-bodied adults to work off their relief checks. Welfare and child welfare debates were suddenly converging in arguments of a sort that had not been heard for three quarters of a century. Children without private economic support should be put up for adoption or placed in orphanages, Charles Murray, a conservative intellectual, had declared in a *Wall Street Journal* opinion piece in October 1993. "Those who find the word 'orphanages' objectionable may think of them as twenty-four-hour-a-day preschools," he wrote. "Those who prattle about the importance of keeping children with their biological mothers may wish to spend some time in a patrol car or with a social worker seeing what the reality of life with welfare-dependent biological mothers can be like."

After Republican leaders proposed an end to all government cash assistance to poor women and children, early in 1994, various versions of Murray's formulation, with its startling call for an orphanage revival, were embraced by Republican state and local politicians around the country. Newt Gingrich, the Republican whip of the House of Representatives, picked up the orphanage theme that May, focusing specifically on teenage mothers. If they could not support their children, Gingrich said, America should tell them, "We'll help you with foster care, we'll help you with orphanages, we'll help you with adoption"—but not with money to keep mother and child together. The same concept was part of the Republican "Contract with America," the centerpiece of Republican congressional campaigns, though there the word *orphanage* was softened to "children's homes."

Whatever you called them, Lamont wanted no child of his consigned to one. "My child will never go in the system," he vowed. But he was really broke now, living on cornbread and coffee by day, so depressed and scared of the future when night fell that he just stared at the television screen, drinking beer and smoking marijuana to zone out on ads that promised to make him a better person if he chose the right credit card.

Sometimes his father exhorted him to go to Morehouse College and be a doctor, though Lamont still had not secured his GED. In the next breath, Smith would mock Lamont's upbringing by white people and say it had made him think like a little rich kid. "If you can't learn to be a nigger in the projects, you won't survive," his father admonished him. If legitimate avenues to success were closed to him, his father was saying, Lamont's psychic survival demanded that he embrace his outcast status and test himself by a different set of values.

Every day on Webster Avenue Lamont walked past numbers gambling holes and corner drug spots, crossing paths with menacing young men who lived by "Watcha lookin' at?" and made respect a killing matter. In one doorway, a friendlier fellow named Ed would send up a crooning cry as soon as he saw Lamont coming: "I got weed, I got weed." Ed was a "turnout man" who selectively laced the marijuana he sold with crack to turn out new customers for Uncle Jeff's crackhouse. Later, in the night, Lamont would hear the calls echo down the stairwells: "Oh-ee," and "O-hoo," signals that meant "Come upstairs, they're selling crack." Then the crackheads would start moaning and groaning, like zombies who smelled blood.

One night Lamont was caught in a crowd that had gathered to watch a twenty-two-year-old man punish a thirty-year-old female crackhead. She had stolen his girlfriend's welfare money, and he beat her "like she was a man." With two black eyes, she was begging the guy, "Please, mister, I hear you, I'm sorry." She tried to hide behind Lamont, grabbing his shirt and ripping it as she fell. But the guy stomped her with his boots, stomped and kicked her while fifty people looked on.

"Right now I'm experiencing things I heard about and acted like I knew, but never knew," Lamont told someone that summer. "I know stuff I never wanted to know. It's like in order to be down, what people consider the essence of blackness, you got to be a project kid, you got to know the streets. That group-home stuff is fake. Now I'm learning what life really is."

As a kid, Lamont had avidly watched the *Oliver Twist* movie whenever it appeared on television. He felt the story related to him in a special way. Like Oliver, he had grown up in a kind of orphanage with other boys. Like Oliver, he had always been different from his peers, his origins more mysterious, his speech and bearing a little out of sync. In Dickens, that was a sign that blood would tell before the story ended. But what if Oliver had discovered that his blood tie was to Fagin, the pickpocket, or to Bill Sikes, the murderer? What if Oliver's mother, instead of dying at his birth, had turned up belatedly as one of the gin-soaked wretches of the London slums?

HIS MATERNAL GREAT-AUNT Carrie Powell lived a different kind of life, but it held little appeal for him. When Lamont met her at last, Shirley's aunt Carrie was sixty-three and for nineteen years had worked as a room attendant at the Sherry-Netherland Hotel, rising at five every morning and taking two buses and a subway from the Bronx to scrub, vacuum, and dust for meager wages amid thousand-dollar knickknacks and diamond rings. The Sherry-Netherland, on Fifty-ninth Street and Fifth Avenue, was one of the most elegant and exclusive hotels in the city, known for its large cooperative apartments that the very rich maintained as pieds-à-terre or as trysting places.

"This type of work, it does make you mad," she allowed. "They try to make you do more than you're suppose to do. They try to cheat you out of your money. You got to raise hell."

The staff union had been pretty good once, but it wasn't anymore, Aunt Carrie said. Now the management took advantage of those new girls from Africa, Asia, Poland, Romania, and other places she'd never even heard of. They were supposed to get the same pay as veterans like her after only ninety days, but they needed jobs so bad they were afraid to claim their rightful wages.

For herself, she planned to go back down south when she retired. "Hotel work is hard," she said. "I'm tired. I've been working all my life. But I'm so close to sixty-five, I said, 'I'll make it, if I get good health.' "

Trudging down the hill toward home, her body stiff, her knees too sore for subway stairs, she would nod politely to the young drug dealers at the corner of 167th and Grant. "I get along good with the dope pushers," she told a visitor. "I don't try to bother with them so they'll put no contract out on me, darling. The police have to catch them on their own."

In her one-bedroom apartment in a Bronx high rise, pictures of children in caps and gowns covered much of one wall. In the middle was a painting that a Muslim boy had made of her wedding, on December 12, 1946. The marriage hadn't lasted, but she had nine grandchildren, four great-grandchildren, and lots of stepgrands, too, she told Lamont. Of her three children, one worked for the post office, another had a job as a home health attendant, and her son was married and going to college.

But when Lamont raised the possibility that he and Kisha could get a place together and live as a family after the baby was born, even Aunt Carrie Powell told him that wasn't a good idea. "Maybe if both of you was older and had a better job," she said. "You can't afford to put food on the table and pay the rent, why should you live with a person? How can you support a family, in school and trying to work and you don't have a stable job? Being a barber, you don't know what money you're going to make during the week. Even if she's on welfare, she should be getting her check by herself."

It was the kind of economic common sense that made two-parent families an endangered species in poor black communities. A man without a solid, steady job could easily become an extra dependent instead of a provider, even if he briefly earned enough to disrupt benefits. It made no sense to tie the baby's subsistence to such a relationship.

ONE DAY LAMONT FINALLY AGREED to report for duty at his uncle Jeff's crackhouse. "Open the door and give 'em what they want," his uncle instructed him. "If the cops come, just pretend to be a crackhead."

But on the night that was supposed to be his first on the job, he just couldn't go through with it. He did not want to go to jail, not even for a day. He did not want to end up shot by a rival drug dealer, crumpled up somewhere in a pool of blood. So he just went to sleep on his grandmother's couch. At six the next morning he was awakened by the noise of cops raiding the crackhouse. Everyone was arrested, including Uncle Jeff.

FOR WEEKS LAMONT'S FATHER had talked of driving him to Memphis for an annual family reunion, to be held the weekend of July 8, 1994. These reunions drew up to a thousand people, all members of a far-flung kinship network descended from Sam and Elizabeth Seay, a Pickens, Mississippi, farm couple. Lamont really wanted to go, hoping to find in his father's Memphis clan the sense of family that still eluded him. Prentis Smith backed out of the trip at the last minute, but Lamont went anyway, his ticket bought for him by the newspaper reporter who had witnessed his reunion with his mother.

He felt a heady sense of freedom at first, walking down Beale Street like a tourist, far from his grandmother's housing project. But as he headed up Jackson Avenue toward North Memphis, where he was to stay with Betty Washington's sister Susie Paige, his mood abruptly darkened. At first, under towering trees, large brick and stucco houses sat above the broad boulevard on raised lawns where the eucalyptus ivy ran like water. Then a seedy strip of stores and burned-out houses intervened, and beyond the first of two weedy railroad crossings, the blight began in earnest. The main artery in North Memphis, like the neighborhood around it, was called Hollywood. The name seemed almost like a cruelty. The only glamour to be found there was in the giant, freestanding billboard advertisements for liquor, cigarettes, and hair relaxer. They towered over the street in place of trees, sprouting images of a universe inhabited by sleek and carefree black people. Below the billboards, in a low-slung, spreading cinderblock version of the bodega strip on Webster Avenue, stood a hodgepodge of such marginal local businesses as the Hollywood Car Wash, with its four brick and frame stalls and vending-machine water hoses, where self-service cost twenty-five cents and young black men without cars sold their labor for a few quarters more, or peddled something else in the bushes behind. The premier sales product of this Hollywood was brand-name liquor, from Cora's Hollywood Liquors, with its flashing E&J Brandy bottle sign, to the Hollywood Deli & Sundry annex, where ads for Seagram's V.O., Seagram's Gin, and Canadian Mist competed with a small, hand-lettered addition reading Milk and Bread.

Susie Paige's single-story white house had pink flamingos on the lawn and metal furniture on the porch. She was waiting to welcome him, weary-faced at the end of a long shift as a nurse's aide at Saint Joseph's Hospital, where she had worked for thirty-four years. Family photographs, plaques, dolls, dishes, and souvenirs jammed the shelves of glass-front cabinets and every other surface in the house. A massive fifty-four-inch television set framed in wood and topped by two VCRs sat in one corner of the parlor. Hanging on one wall was an old picture of a white Jesus with flowing hair. It had thirty-six pennies taped around its perimeter, each marking the birth of a child in the extended family. Lamont's name was missing, of course, but Chris Smith, Brenda's son, was represented by a bright 1970 penny. It was like the token of some lost legacy.

Chris had just escaped having Lamont's life. Born heroin-addicted at Mount Sinai Hospital in October 1970, he had already been assigned by the city to the Sheltering Arms foster-care agency when he was claimed instead by his great-aunt Gertrude Seay Redditt, a nurse's aide at the hospital where Martin Luther King had died. Her husband, Willie B. Redditt, was one of the sanitation strikers whose struggle had brought King to Memphis. They were eager to raise Chris as their own, and in North Memphis he had grown up envied as the only child of steadily employed parents. He was fifteen before the Redditts formally told him that he was not their son. But at twenty-one, he was orphaned anew: the Redditts, separated and reunited during his childhood, died within a few months of each other in 1992. Like so many kinship-care arrangements among blacks, even those sanctioned by foster-care systems, his "adoption" apparently had never been legalized. Neither a will nor formal adoption papers were found, so Chris was forced to leave the home where he had lived all his life. At first he set up house with Charlene Every, his girlfriend since eighth grade, and their two children, a six-year-old girl and a five-month-old baby boy. But after he lost his job cutting metal for five dollars an hour, Charlene and the kids moved back in with her parents.

"It don't make no sense for us to be staying together and him not working," Charlene said flatly as Chris cradled his infant son, Chris Junior, during a visit to her parents' ramshackle house. "There's not enough to support all of us and him, too."

Chris, who had a GED, a year of community college, and no car, had become one more member of Susie Paige's hard-pressed household, which periodically expanded to take in grown sons and nephews between jobs. Susie herself was a widow with seven grown children, whose husband, a cab driver, had been murdered on the job in 1990 at the age of fifty. Finding work was hard in Memphis, which, like the rest of the country, had lost thousands of manufacturing jobs during the 1980s. Black unemployment was officially running at more than 15 percent, triple the white rate.

"It's temporary services now, mostly," said Lamont's cousin Teddy Paige, thirty. "The job pays the service ten to twelve dollars an hour, but they only pay you five. And it costs you two-forty a day in bus fare to make it there and back. Temporary services, it's a form of slavery."

The night before the big family-reunion barbecue, Lamont saw Teddy Paige use the few dollars he had made cutting lawns in the neighborhood to buy crack. He smoked some and resold the rest for as much as he had paid.

"People are selling crack from their mama's porch, drinking lemonade with their feet up," Lamont said later in astonishment. "I couldn't believe it. Sitting on the porch in Hollywood, it's like the projects, with the crackheads walking by. This place is just like my grandmother's."

For better or for worse, he and Chris had lived out very different versions of childhood. But in the end, how much difference had it really made? Whether in Memphis or in New York City, they had come of age as young black men in the same time of widening economic inequality, surrounded by the same corrosive consumer poverty. They both seemed like social scrap.

The whole system was a setup, Lamont thought. It was designed so the rich would win and the poor would fail. "Then when they fail and put out their hands, it's like everybody throws up their arms and says it's their fault." Maybe belonging even to the most flawed and threadbare family could still serve as a buffer against society's disregard. But that first night in Memphis, he felt more alone than ever.

The next afternoon, an American idyll of family ties unfolded around Lamont at the reunion picnic, held a few miles north of the city limits. On a great green expanse of lawn surrounded by lush trees, a state-park summerhouse held tables piled with enough roasting pans and coolers to hold a feast for hundreds: barbecued ribs and fried chicken, black-eyed peas and baked beans, hamburgers, coleslaw, peach pie. From under the maples came the clang of horseshoes and the wheeze and rumble of male laughter. Happy shrieks rose from the sack races, and adult voices urging on the children who tumbled, panting, to the grass. Babies were burped and dandled in the shade while aunties had just one more piece of pecan pie over another tidbit of family news.

The organizing, middle-class side of the Memphis family found Lamont a reunion T-shirt. He was quickly dubbed Peanut Junior and introduced to two of the event's organizers, a schoolteacher who had just been named principal of a Memphis elementary school and a man who had retired from the air force and now worked as a medical technologist. In the great flat stretch before the trees, a softball game was starting. Yes, family problems were there, too. Uncle Dwight, drunker than usual, was interfering with the pitching. An impulsive eighteen-year-old girl with a crying five-month-old son handed him off so she could play, too. Uncle Waddell, whippet-thin and red-eyed, provoked shaken heads and whispers: "He need to go to a rehab. . . ."

But there was room for everybody. A cousin invited Lamont to join the batting lineup. "Let's see your arm, man," someone yelled to the pitcher when Lamont stepped up to the plate. On the first pitch, Lamont swung and missed. On the second he swung harder and missed again. Would he be embarrassed before them all, these strangers whose blood he claimed to share? The next pitch was so low he let it pass, his bat still on his shoulder. One and two. Now he needed to swing, he had to swing, and he hit a foul, then another foul, and still another. Watching from the sidelines, observers were steeled for the strikeout.

Instead came the smack of the softball against the metal bat, and full-throated cries as it soared toward the trees over the heads of the outfield: "Hit it, Peanut Junior! Hit it, Peanut Junior!" Lamont was running hard around the bases, low to the ground as he rounded the grassy curve, past second, past third, and then sliding, sliding home, just before the ball.

"He's safe, he's safe!" they yelled, the cousins, the uncles, and the aunts, slapping high-fives in celebration.

WHEN LAMONT GOT BACK to New York, his grandmother told him to leave the apartment if he couldn't pay his way. The best option he had, he realized, was to return to a group home. In July 1994, exercising a right won by the 1985 lawsuit *Palmer v. Cuomo,* he signed himself back into foster care one last time.

FOUR

THE BABY WAS OVERDUE. FOR WEEKS THAT WINTER LA-
mont had expected Kisha to go into labor. Now, in late January
1995, he just wanted it to be over. Their relationship had always been
stormy, but he hoped they would get along better after the baby was born.
Everyone told him women were subject to crazy mood swings while they
were pregnant, and he kept telling himself that must be the reason for
Kisha's tirades. He could not have stuck it out this long without encouragement from Mo Gadsen, the counselor at the Leake & Watts group
home on St. Peter's Avenue, where he had been since the summer of 1994.

"Big Mo" Gadsen lived up to his reputation as the best group-home
counselor at Leake & Watts. He was a tall, lean, thirty-eight-year-old man
with a graying beard and coffee-colored skin who saw right through Lamont when he tried to "front" with bravado or excuses. Gadsen had worked
at Leake & Watts for six years, but as the firstborn son among twelve children raised by a single mother on and off welfare, he would say, "I been
running a group home all my life." From Gadsen's perspective, Lamont
arrived with no money, no place to live, and, in effect, no GED. He
wasn't interested in the young man's story about some bureaucratic error
on his test scores. Lamont had to enroll in a GED program at Bronx
Community College, the counselor insisted, because with a GED, he
could apply to a two-year college, get the educational grants available to a
ward of the court, and live on campus. What else could he possibly
achieve in six months' time that would assure him of a place to live and an
education? And six months was all he had. At that point his placement
would expire, and coincidentally, he would become a father.

Lamont's ability to provide for the coming child seemed uncertain at best. Between remedial classes at Bronx Community College, he was still cutting hair at a barbershop on Westchester Avenue. Nevertheless, Aunt Carrie had been shocked when Lamont told her that Kisha did not want to give the baby his last name.

"Put the baby under Daddy's name," she urged Kisha. "The baby's his, right? That's important."

Kisha just giggled.

Seeing Lamont's hangdog look, Aunt Carrie told him, "You can go to the hospital with her. You can coach her. Do you want to be in the delivery room?"

Yes, he did. But it was not clear that he would be granted the chance.

"She act like a teenager," Aunt Carrie said of Kisha later. "She don't act like a twenty-year-old girl. Both of them are kids."

In Lamont's eyes, Kisha was tough. She never admitted she was scared of childbirth. Her grandfather died during her pregnancy, and her mother moved to New Jersey to help her widowed grandmother with the house payments, but Kisha was determined to stay in New York and get her own place. She had started from scratch in the emergency shelter system. For a while that winter she had lived in a city prenatal shelter, sharing a tub with sixty-seven other pregnant women. But then she had been sent to Siena House, a city-funded residence for twenty-seven homeless young mothers and their newborns, run by Catholic nuns in the Bronx. That was where she and the baby would go from the hospital. Eventually, the staff would help her get a subsidized apartment. Then she planned to find a baby-sitter and a Midtown office job and get off welfare.

The old blond-brick convent where Kisha and the baby would be housed stood behind wrought iron gates and a small statue of the Madonna and child. It was struggling with social-services cuts now, and with the backlash against women on welfare. "They say, 'Send them back to their relatives,' " Sister Mary Doris, the director, explained. "But many of their mothers are in prison, or they've died of AIDS, or they're drug addicts.

"Our social workers can't counsel them in seeking birth control. I don't totally agree with the teachings of the church on this issue because I'm here on the firing line, and it's really tough."

Fathers were not much of a factor at Siena House, she added. Some were in jail, and others ought to be. It was unusual for a mother to want the father involved, and a rare man who came up the convent steps to visit.

DOCTORS AT MOUNT SINAI HOSPITAL finally induced Kisha's labor at 7:00 A.M. on January 25, 1995. That was five days before Lamont was due to leave his group home, and the morning after President Clinton's State of the Union address to Congress.

"I want to work with you, with all of you, to pass welfare reform," the President had said. "But our goal must be to liberate people and lift them up from dependence to independence, from welfare to work, from mere childbearing to responsible parenting. Our goal should not be to punish them because they happen to be poor."

Kisha did not summon Lamont to the hospital until evening, when she had already been in labor for ten hours. Her labor was what the doctors called vigorous, but slow, and he stayed at the hospital most of the night. In the morning, Kisha's older sister arrived, and the nurses suggested that Lamont go home, get some rest, and come back later. On the subway ride back to the group home, wired from lack of sleep, he thought about his future as a father and about the lost family his baby would enter at birth. "I'm gonna do what I gotta do to feed me and my kid," he resolved.

He had to find a real job. Other kids at Leake & Watts were always telling him their problems and saying he should be a counselor. Perhaps a career in child care was his true vocation, he thought as the elevated subway lurched through the Bronx in the early-morning light. You had to be twenty-one to do such work, he knew, but meanwhile maybe he could volunteer in a homeless shelter somewhere. Maybe Shirley's Marcia Lowry would help him with a letter of reference. The ACLU, now that was clout!

"If everything goes how I want it to, I could seriously be holding down a good job after my twenty-first birthday," he told himself. Working as a counselor in a children's institution, maybe even at Astor Home—he could probably handle that. You could even say it was the place he'd been trained to fill.

By the time he reached his stop, he had decided he should extend his stay in foster care until he turned twenty-one. As soon as he crossed the threshold of the group home on St. Peter's Avenue, he signed the necessary agency documents to get those last five months, like a man applying for a stay of execution.

Lamont was about to go to bed for a couple of hours when Sefus Henderson called. Still running on adrenaline and caffeine, Lamont went into a riff about his new career plans. But Henderson had heard too many other short-lived scenarios from him.

"Lamont, you have great ideas, you're a great thinker, but you have a problem seeing things to completion," Henderson said.

Lamont's mood could not be dampened. When he thought of the impending birth of his child now, he felt an otherworldly excitement, almost a sense of awe. All he lacked was Henderson's blessing. In the end, Henderson softened. This was one of Lamont's big fears, he knew—being a father, being the parent he himself had never had. This was a big step for him. Lamont always blamed his past for his problems; it was easy, but it was also true. What did Lamont have to change to stop the cycle for his own son or daughter? he wondered. What did Kisha have to change? Well, Henderson told himself, sometimes because of the love of the baby, new parents do straighten out and come up to snuff.

"I really hope you have a healthy baby and everything works out," he said before he hung up.

LAMONT RETURNED TO THE HOSPITAL and stood by Kisha as she labored into another night, hooked up to a fetal monitor that beeped and clicked. But in the wee hours of January 27, when the nurse said the time for delivery was near, Kisha told Lamont to leave. Only one relative was allowed in the delivery room. Her mother wanted a tape of the birth, she said, and her sister was downstairs with the video camera. Lamont should wait downstairs while her sister recorded the big event.

An icy rage filled his heart. "What?" he asked, his voice dead cold. "What?"

She repeated her dismissal.

Her family always came first with her. Nothing he did was enough. She had threatened more than once that if they broke up, she would cut him out of his child's life.

Lamont stood his ground. Whatever else happened, at least he would always be able to say that he was there. When the moment came, he saw the blood, felt Kisha's nails dig into his arm, and heard the cry of the small, slippery creature who was his newborn son. Lamont was the first person to hold him, all six pounds, eleven ounces.

"He looks like me," he whispered.

FIVE

MARCIA LOWRY WAS EXPECTING LAMONT, BUT SHE WAS astonished when he walked into her office.

"You look like your mother," she said. "You have your mother's smile when she was thirteen."

She took him to lunch at a restaurant next door on West Forty-third Street. The place was unpretentious by Midtown standards, but the clientele was nearly all white, and Lamont felt acutely aware of his dark skin when they walked in. His Guess shirt, black jeans, and khaki vest suddenly seemed inadequate. After they were seated in an upstairs section, he pointedly examined his spoon and found it dirty. "I hate that," he said coolly.

"See, I take you out to a fancy place with dirty silverware," Lowry responded. They both laughed, and the tension eased. Lamont settled back.

"So tell me about this lawsuit," he said. "I still don't understand it."

"It's a long story." Lowry sighed and gave the briefest of summaries. "It wouldn't have fixed everything in foster care, just a piece of it," she concluded. "But it would have been better, except that the city hasn't done what it was supposed to do."

Lamont leaned forward, eager now. "Could I get a copy of the lawsuit?"

"Well, the complaint. It's been amended four times—"

"See, I live in the system," he interrupted. "Most kids in the system don't even know there's a lawsuit that affects them. If I knew what the lawsuit says—I mean, I see a lot of stuff. There are so many things that are wrong. I'm asking, like, what can I do? I thought maybe I could get like an inspiration from you."

Lowry was touched, almost humbled. "It is very hard to figure out what to do. *Wilder* is difficult—" She broke off, smiling at him. "You must think, Why is she talking about me? It's kind of funny because *Wilder* has a separate identity for me."

Their conversation soon shifted to him. "It's amazing how you can treat a kid like they treated you and have him turn out together," she marveled. She was blown away by his charm, his energy and animation. They agreed that his first five years in a loving home had probably been the saving grace. But he tried to hint that he was not all he seemed: "I'm pretty together, but kids do stupid things sometimes." Asked point blank if he earned enough at his job to support himself, he grew evasive, then blustered, "If I play my cards right, I can make a killing," and stammered out a plan to illegally combine public assistance and student loans while working at the barbershop off the books. A little later he spoke harshly of his mother—his mother the crackhead. His mother the prostitute.

The contempt for Shirley was like a blow. Lowry instinctively came to her defense: "Your mother was very lively and bright and enthusiastic, and she had a smile like you do. She had a lot of potential."

"I get a lot of stuff from her," he allowed.

"She had a lot of hard times, but she was terrific."

"I'm kind of upset with her. She doesn't even know she has a grandson now."

Lowry recognized hurt behind the anger and shifted to meet it. "That has much more to do with her own problems than the way she feels about you."

He shrugged. "My parents, they live their lives, and I live my life."

Lowry's voice became husky and urgent. To plead for Shirley at the bar of her son's harsh judgment was also to advocate for Lamont himself, to try to put balm on his wounds. "I know Shirley's always felt bad about you. At various times she called me and asked me about you. She couldn't get her life together, but in her own way, she cares."

"I don't blame her," Lamont replied quickly, seeing that Lowry's eyes were moistening. "I don't know who to blame." He wanted to smooth things over, but his anger and confusion wouldn't let him. "My mother, she lies. You can't believe anything she tells you. I can see that motherliness in her, but her life just won't let her act on it. I tried to be there for her, but I can't."

Lowry grew gentle. "It is sometimes appropriate to take care of your parents, but not when you're twenty," she said. She thought of her own parents; just in the last year, after a series of strokes, her father had become like a cranky, retarded child, frightened and agitated when he didn't recognize her ailing mother. But Lamont was a father himself. She asked about his three-week-old son.

"My name is on the birth certificate," he told Lowry proudly.

Her face registered concern. "They'll come after you for support."

"I know," he said. "That's my kid, and I know what it's like not to have a father." He spoke faster now. "There are things I can't be that I want to be to him. It's exciting and scary, 'cause I'm thinking if I were to slip and give up, he could end up just like me. But I'm gonna make it—" He stopped short, catching Lowry's eye. "I'm pretty sure you heard my mother say the same thing."

"I don't think she was so clear on what she wanted," Marcia said carefully. "I think she was more confused."

"I'm still confused about a lot of things—about life," he confessed. "That's what can get you in trouble. Now my mother is trying to wake up, and it's too late. She's what, thirty-five?" He shook his head, looking at Lowry in her wool vest and tailored slacks and thinking of the tunnel under Metro North. "You live in a different world," he said, "eating lunch in restaurants."

"Most days I eat a yogurt at my desk," Lowry protested.

Dessert defused the conflict. Lamont had ordered warm apple and pear crisp with ice cream, and it arrived in a soup plate, decorated with a sprig of mint. "This is the kind of food that's asking to have its picture taken," he mocked. A little later, as if making a peace offering, he told Lowry, "Once I thought of being an attorney."

Her response was heartfelt: "Well, Lamont, a lot of people go through school at night. If you decide you want to do that and need a reference, call me."

"Actually, I'd really like to get into child care."

"You'd be wonderful!" Her eyes were glowing now, and she offered to help with contacts. "You go to college at night, become the head of an agency, and I'll sue you!" she joked.

He sparred back in good humor: "Oh, yeah, 'This is my dream, kid, grow up so I can sue you.' I'll sue you back."

He was in the groove now, ready to give his life the con-man spin. "I think the whole experience has been good, you know, 'cause I learned to adapt. I'm versatile like that. I know how to talk to different people so they're not on their guard."

Lowry nodded. "Psychologists say people who have had adversity and overcome it are stronger." She paid the check. "It's such a pleasure meeting you, Lamont, such a great pleasure. If I can help you to find a job—"

"I'll adapt," he put in. "I'll learn."

". . . Anybody named Wilder!"

He knew this was the way to end it, light and upbeat, but he couldn't help himself. "You know what's scary?" he blurted out. "Whoever doesn't get into college now and on welfare now probably won't make it. Seven years from now, they'll be nowhere."

She asked him back to the ACLU building; there, striding ahead, she realized a moment too late that he was being stopped by the security guard. "No, he's with me," she said, embarrassed. Upstairs she pointed out the rows of cabinets lining a narrow corridor, all labeled *Wilder:* "See, your name's all over this place." She called to an assistant, "Rosemary, here's a famous person." She drew him into a side office and showed him the bulging accordian folders: *Wilder* correspondence, *Wilder* résumés. "Yes, the city even has a Wilder Unit," she told him.

Lamont put on a serious face and deepened his voice: "Excuse me, I'm Lamont Wilder, take me to my unit!"

They both laughed again, but Lowry felt a pang go through her heart. For a fleeting moment it was as though she really had seen Shirley look out from Lamont's eyes, like a lost child or an unquiet ghost.

SHIRLEY WILDER DID LEARN of her grandson's birth. But when she thought of him, he was like another piece of herself, lost beyond the crack smoke. Even her body was lost to her now. One night in 1994, she had stood before a big mirror at Metropolitan Psychiatric Hospital and been terrified to see herself fully naked. She had assumed she was still pretty, but instead of the lush curves she expected, she saw drawn skin and wasted flesh. The locked psychiatric ward had been her last resort; every drug-rehab program she called was full, and at Mister Al's suggestion she had threatened suicide to get past the waiting lists. But her misery was not make-believe, and the image in the mirror was unforgettable.

In November 1996, forty-five pounds below her normal weight, Shirley was arrested in a police sweep at 115th and First Avenue. The charges were one count of drug possession and another of drug sale. She had been helping a street dealer in exchange for crack; she was now smoking up to five hundred dollars' worth of the drug a day. After going through withdrawal in one of the low-slung brick-and-cinderblock buildings that make up the city's jail on Riker's Island, she was shuttled to Elmhurst Hospital for tests to explain the abnormal uterine bleeding that had followed her phantom pregnancies. Shirley learned then that she had cancer of the cervix.

The doctor said an operation would kill her. Instead, he put radiation implants inside her womb to shrink the tumor, which was the size of a four-month fetus. By the end of 1996 she was having seizures and unexplained blackouts. One psychiatrist told her that part of her brain had probably been burned out by crack.

Riker's was hellish: the clashes with other inmates who made fun of her when she forgot, midsentence, what she was saying; the power of the guards to put her in the hole when she lost it; the rancid smell of confinement that reminded her of juvenile detention at Manida. Once, on the television set in a common area of the jail, she saw Marcia Lowry on the news. Marcia was stubborn, Shirley thought with a kind of pride. She had filed a new lawsuit against the city in the name of a five-year-old girl called Marisol who had been returned to a home where she was beaten, locked in a closet for months, and nearly starved to death. Looking down at the orange prison jumpsuit that strained over her swollen abdomen, Shirley thanked God Marcia didn't know she was in jail. Marcia would be so disappointed. A sense of shame and regret came over her like the uterine cramps that seized her belly and made her rock and weep.

Between her illness and court delays, Shirley was not sentenced until June 1997, to one to three years in state prison. She was transferred to Bedford Hills, the state prison for women located in the Hudson Valley, in November 1997. By then she had been clean of drugs for a year, and her face was full and smooth again, her hair braided tight, the way her grandmother used to do it when she was very little. At thirty-eight, she had only one tooth left in the middle of her bottom gum, giving a jack-o'-lantern glint to the broad smile she still flashed. But at Bedford Hills her memory lapses grew worse. For ten minutes at a time she would forget where she was and what she was saying. When she came out of a blackout, she would be agitated and distraught; when other inmates mocked her, she would get angry. After conflicts with her cellmate, she begged for a room by herself. She was glad when prison officials separated her from the general population, placing her on a unit where she had her own little cubicle, bed, and locker. Then she realized there was something weird about the others on that unit. They walked around like zombies, their movements stiff, their eyes glazed.

On this unit, it was mandatory for her to take psychotropic medication. If she refused, she went to the "lock"—isolation. If she took the pills, all she could do was sleep. They made her body heavy and sluggish, and when she tried to talk, the words did not come out right. She wasn't a violent person, she told the doctor; she only lashed out when she felt threatened. She didn't trust people, and the medication just made it worse. She hated the feeling that something was controlling her, and she felt herself becoming more hostile and aggressive. But he said he couldn't cut down her dose.

She would not be in prison long, though. Her parole officer at Bedford Hills said he was surprised they had bothered to send her up at all. With a year already served in Riker's, she would be on conditional release soon after Christmas. He seemed incredulous when she told him she wanted to go straight into an inpatient drug-treatment program from prison. Why did she want to incarcerate herself again?

"I think I need it," she said. "The desire to use drugs is still there."

But in January, when her release date was imminent, she learned that no treatment plan had been arranged; the terms of her parole were for her to live at Mister Al's and stay out of trouble. She was furious. "They know you have a problem," she told the parole officer. "They send you upstate and then they just cut you loose, knowing you have this problem. How can I not violate? You're just going to put me back in the same spot I was, and I'm telling you I need help."

"Ms. Wilder, you're very high-strung," he said. "Did you take your medication today?"

A few days before she was released, late in January 1998, the parole officer would ask Shirley if she had ever had an HIV test. No; she had always refused, avoiding what she didn't want to know. But here in prison the blood test had been a mandatory part of a physical exam, and now he told her the results: she was HIV-positive. In fact, he said, citing her low T-cell count, she had AIDS.

SIX

O NE OF THE BABY'S FIRST WORDS WAS *DADDY*. LAMONT loved that. It was like proof that what he did counted. He was very conscious that everything he had done for his son was something his own father had not done for him, from signing paternity papers in the hospital to bottle-feeding the baby before dawn. But no matter what he did, he felt he could not satisfy Kisha, because she held against him everything she had not received from her own father.

He remembered Memorial Day weekend of 1995 as a rare oasis in their rocky relationship. For a long time Alicia Fils-Aime had been asking them to come up to her and her second husband's house in Connecticut, a large parsonage with a two-car garage in an affluent neighborhood of northern Stamford, and finally they agreed to stay overnight. Alicia thought Kisha a very good mother, and told her so. The baby was exceptionally friendly, loving, and good-natured, just the way Lamont used to be as an infant, down to the way he sucked two fingers. Alicia told stories about baby Lamont, and they all laughed, Lamont with some embarrassment. On their second evening there, Diane, the niece who had carried Lamont down the stairs when he was a toddler, came over with her own children and her husband, and they ate Puerto Rican–style rice with peas, a dish Alicia remembered Lamont loving as a child. Later they saw Alicia's nephew Johnnie——little Johnnie who had jumped the waves with Lamont in Puerto Rico. Little Johnnie was big now, and a New York City cop. He and Lamont gripped each other, and Johnnie started to cry. "We're family, man," Johnnie said.

But they were not. Lamont's final exit from foster care came a few days later, on June 3, 1995, the day before his twenty-first birthday. He had all of nine dollars in his pocket, enough to pay a cab to ferry a few boxes of jumbled clothes, old schoolbooks, and laundry soap to the room he had rented in a lady's house in the Bronx. The arrangement lasted only two weeks. Her bedroom was next to his, and she didn't want girls or babies visiting him. He had a bad week at the barbershop and was late with the rent. After she turned him out, he stayed with friends. His welcome soon wore thin. He still made too little at the barbershop to cover a security deposit and a month's rent for a place of his own.

With the help of Siena House, Kisha was accepted into the so-called Section 8 voucher program, which allowed her and the baby to move out of the shelter and into a small apartment. Reluctantly, she agreed to let Lamont stay over. She threw him out a week later. To Lamont, it seemed she was berating him for every piece of lint shed from his pants onto her couch, every drop of water his shower left on the bathroom tiles. To Kisha, it was as though she had to run after another child, but one with no claim on her tolerance.

"I had urine on my bathroom floor," she would recall later, her voice full of resentment. "I had to tell him, 'Lamont, you don't leave piss on the toilet seat.' 'You don't leave a dirty bowl in the sink.' 'Lamont, put down the toilet seat—the baby, he could fall in.' " When she asked Lamont to get her a jar of baby food, she complained, he gave her a dollar instead. "That's not enough to buy baby food," she told him.

"That's all I have right now," he replied, but then he turned around later and asked, "You want to smoke?"

"No, nigger, look through the house," she raged. "I need Infamil—necessities, not bullshit."

When he tried to assert himself, she did not hold back. "You have no rights here," she declared. "I went through hell getting this apartment. You don't come here and rule."

Everything she did for the baby was like ammunition, he thought. If he did ten things, she let him know that she had done fifteen. "If you ain't going to be there, I'll just get another man who can," she said. "You're not doing for your son."

He could not even do for himself. By the time he made some cash at the barbershop, where half of his take went to the boss, he already owed the money twice over—not counting the child-support debt that had been mounting against him ever since his son was born onto welfare.

Nevertheless, just to feel good for half an hour, he would sometimes buy enough weed and beer to get buzzed, or to share with someone who had a place where he could spend the night. Other times, when no friend could take him in, he began to stay in cheap flophouse hotels like the Riverview, a twenty-one-dollar-a-night place on Jane Street that had once been a women's detention center. The rooms were just big enough to fit a cot and a TV, and he had to wear cheap plastic sandals into slimy showers shared with homeless people.

Alicia had invited him to think of her house as his home, and for two weeks or so, he did crash there. But why did it feel so wrong? At first he put it down to the forty-five-minute commute and wanting to stay close to his son. Then he admitted to himself that he found it hard even to look Alicia in the face without feeling uneasy. He thought it must be because of the secret that still lay between them—the secret of his molestation. But when he finally told her, he felt worse. She listened to his account of having been sexually fondled by Frantz and she was diplomatic, but he realized that she did not believe him. Eventually, Lamont's accusation would reach Frantz indirectly, and he would deny it. By then Lamont's uneasiness had become bleak, muted anger.

To outside eyes, it seemed clear that deep down, he would never really forgive Alicia for not adopting him. But an Alicia of the 1990s would have found it even harder to make a different decision. At the time there had been little value accorded to her love for Lamont. Her fear, that as a single mother she would have to turn to welfare to support him, had been sharpened by the stigma and meagerness of the public assistance then available. Now such assistance was even more stigmatized and even less adequate to stave off poverty. More than ever, economic self-sufficiency was considered the first duty of every adult, and mothers, like fathers, were judged wanting if they were unable to provide for their young.

In hindsight, what looked like government thrift had proved very expensive. Lamont's twenty-one years in foster care had cost the public $531,021. And now he couldn't afford the price of a bed.

Kisha had no sympathy for him. "You smell," she told him one time when he came by to see his son. "Homeless? Who gives a damn? My child was born homeless," she told someone else. "Lamont's a damn man. He's an able-bodied man. He has no excuses." Not long after that, she took the baby and moved without leaving an address.

Lamont tried to shrug off the loss of his son: "If I'm going to sit here and bleed my heart out and you don't want to let me see my son, then fuck you and fuck him. I don't want to see him." Then he comforted himself by envisioning a future reunion: "I guess I'm going to be one of those daddies where I meet him when he's twenty and we do the whole lost-daddy thing."

He was lost, all right. One cold night early in 1996, not long after he heard on the street that his mother was deeper than ever into drugs, he went back to the projects and knocked on Betty Washington's door. She wouldn't let him in. "Grandma, can't I just stay till the morning?" he pleaded. It was 2:00 A.M. and twenty degrees outside, and he was wearing only a thin little denim jacket, carrying a knapsack and a duffle bag.

"No," she told him. "The shelter's up the hill."

He went looking for it, but there was no shelter there. She had said that just to get rid of him, he realized. He went to the rectory of the big church on Boston Road, thinking maybe the priest would let him crash there. But there had been a recent rash of church robberies in the neighborhood, and they weren't letting anybody in. In the end he descended to the subway. That was the first of many nights he would spend in Grand Central Station, riding the train back and forth to the Bronx so he could catch a few winks or sitting upstairs in the waiting room until six in the morning. He had long since dropped out of college classes. For a time, even when he had not slept or showered, he made it to work at the barbershop. But the day came when another man was cutting hair at his station when he walked in, and the manager told Lamont not to come back.

Once, during the countdown to his exit from foster care, the reporter had taken him and Kisha to lunch at Jimmy's, reputed to be the best restaurant in the Bronx. It was perched on the heights overlooking the bridge to Manhattan and the Major Deegan Expressway. The servers wore black-tie uniforms, the menus featured thirty-dollar entrees of lobster and shrimp, and at the best tables, male diners sported heavy gold chains. But looking out the window, Lamont had picked out, far below and tiny in the distance, a squeegee man in a bright-red cap working the cars on the ramp to the expressway. Fear had gripped him then, as though he were witnessing a vision of his own future. In that moment he had felt he would rather sell drugs or even rob people than be that abased creature in the abyss of an indifferent urban landscape.

Now he was in a free-fall.

KISHA HAD RESOLVED to get off welfare after leaving the shelter, and she did, by working as a stripper. She started in a girlie joint in Times Square early in 1996, about the time Lamont was sleeping in Grand Central Station. Soon she was strip-dancing at clubs in Queens, on Long Island, and in New Jersey, getting bookings through a man who acted as a bouncer. His sister took care of the strippers' kids for $25 a day each. The year she stripped, she felt she barely slept at all. Sometimes the work paid good money. The best take she remembered was $298 on New Year's Eve. The worst was $75 for lap-dancing the whole night at a dive in New Jersey, and out of that she had to hand over a share to the place where she'd performed, come up with money for the cab ride home with the other dancers, and pay the sitter besides. As time passed, the places that booked her got worse and worse, and the good money was only for those willing to do more than strip. "Everybody else is going to be fucking and sucking, and I don't get down like that," she would say later. "I stopped because I was getting real sick of that crap."

In 1997, when Shirley was in Riker's, Kisha went from stripping to sales, hawking what she was taught to call "vacation ownership." Commissions were slim and seasonal. By the middle of 1997, when her son was eighteen months old, she decided that she had to go back to school or she'd never get a better job. Somehow she would have to juggle college business classes, a toddler, and work. To do that, she might have to call on Lamont again.

EARLY IN 1997, Lamont had noticed a sign in a small barbershop window near the Castlehill subway station in his old neighborhood: "Barbers wanted." Eventually he made an arrangement with the manager to sleep on a cot in the shop's back room, paying a flat $150-a-week rent on a barber chair. After four months the relationship soured over unpaid rent, but by then Lamont had enough loyal customers to move to another barbershop around the corner, Danny's Hair Palace. Danny, a Haitian immigrant in his forties, let him lock up the place each night. After pulling down the shades so people passing by wouldn't see him, Lamont slept on the shop floor or in one of the barber chairs.

The work itself could still sometimes lift him out of his depression. Patient and painstaking, his tongue pointed between his lips like a child, his maroon barber's jacket on and electric clippers in hand, Lamont felt in control. He liked the rhythm of a barbershop: the slow mornings, with time to read the daily newspapers; the trickle of retirees talking gossip and politics; the cops and drug dealers succeeding each other in the same barber chair. But the middle-aged white owner of the neighborhood shoe store, who had let him buy Timberland shoes on the installment plan, was waiting to collect his cash the moment the customer, spritzed and brushed, put the bills into Lamont's hand. That was the problem: Lamont had to cut sixteen heads just to make the rent on his chair. Nine- and twelve-dollar haircuts didn't add up fast enough in a neighborhood where practically every block had a barbershop staffed with free-lancers like him. But Lamont was afraid to work for a paycheck.

It had taken only five minutes in the summer of 1995 for him to stand up in family court and proclaim his fatherhood; he had not understood the endless consequences. He'd been told to pay thirty to forty dollars a month, but he could not spare even that sum most months, and even if he could, he saw no point in paying it to the city to defray the cost of Kisha's welfare checks. A welfare allowance was too small to support a mother and child. Most women on welfare preferred to have their child's father pass them whatever money he could under the table, or buy things for the baby outright. But however much a father contributed in this way, it did nothing to shrink his official child-support debt. And as long as he was four months in arrears on child support, Lamont discovered, he was prohibited from getting or renewing a legitimate barber's license—the document he would need to work in any better hair salon. Eventually the court could issue an enforcement order. If he worked on the books he would be found out, arrested, maybe even jailed. He made plans to go to court and try to explain, but he never did. He thought, too, about seeking another line of work—at the florist's shop down the street, as a bail-bondsman, even as a soldier. But Danny's was not just his work; it had become the only place he felt at home.

In September 1997, he did find a place of sorts to live. He heard that Betty Washington had kicked his father out of Webster Avenue, and that he and his Memphis cousin Chris had moved into a two-room apartment on Boynton Avenue in the Bronx. He knew they had to be broke. "I can feed you guys," Lamont told his father, who agreed to let him sleep on an old black couch for fifty dollars a week. Lamont had no illusions about his father anymore. He had seen the man earn eight hundred dollars by doing carpentry work and painting and smoke it up in crack in three hours. Prentis was down to 120 pounds. Lamont knew enough now to keep his money on him when he slept, but sometimes his father's crackhead friends would come through the apartment in the middle of the night, stop at his couch, and try to take his earnings off him anyway. He simply had no better place to go.

When Kisha called him at the shop later in September 1997 and challenged him to reenter his son's life, Lamont felt as though the high wall around his own life had suddenly revealed a gate.

WHAT A GREAT KID HIS SON WAS. He could be too loud and crazy sometimes, squealing and running around to be chased, his big eyes scrunched up with laughter, his little legs pumping. But he was so funny, so smart and cute, how could anyone resist the feeling of tenderness that washed up at the sight of him?

Lamont grew close to his small son through the fall of 1997 as he visited him three times a week, but he tried to hold back in Kisha's presence. "As soon as she sees he's really attached to me, she'll take him," he worried. Not that he could knock Kisha as a mother. They were getting along better now. Lamont began to see the three of them bonded as a family and felt happy that his son actually had both a mom and a dad.

Lamont's relationship with his own father hit bottom late that fall of 1997. Chris was gone. The unpaid utility bills were up to twelve hundred dollars. The cable TV alone came to three hundred because his father's friends had flipped through a dozen pay-per-view channels at once when they were high. The inside doorknob was gone, and you had to open the door with a knife to get out. One night his father let in a drug dealer, and the place literally became a crackhouse. The next night Lamont stayed out until morning to avoid the crowd, falling into an exhausted sleep on his couch at 5:00 A.M. Half an hour later, Prentis woke him up, stealing his cigarettes and demanding five dollars.

"I'm your father," he said when Lamont objected, as though that word would beat him into obligation. Lamont called his father an old crackhead. They were nose to nose, cursing each other out. There was nothing to eat in the place, not a bean, not a grain of rice, not Kool-Aid, nothing but tap water and ketchup.

"I only have one son," Lamont said. "I shouldn't be raising my father. Either you go into rehab or I'm shutting it all down."

It was shutting down anyway. The landlord had had enough. But he saw that Lamont was a workingman, and he was willing to draw up a new lease in his name if he would get rid of his father and come up with two months' rent by December. Just before that deadline, Prentis left for a rehab program, and an unexpected windfall put money in Lamont's pocket: compensation for driving up to Astor Home with the reporter who had introduced him to his mother.

They left early on Monday, December 1, drove up the Taconic Parkway to Rhinebeck, and arrived before noon. The place looked smaller—even the front rooms where maintenance men were trimming an artificial Christmas tree. Walter Joseph welcomed Lamont warmly and led the two visitors on a tour from the basement laundry bins where Lamont used to hide, to the annex where children still lived and went to school. Lamont remembered how much he had hated being displayed to strangers, and he hung back at the open classroom doors. In one corridor, a woman was talking to a small boy who had shifted restlessly from one wall to the other. "You need to wait for Joe to tell you to move," she instructed the child. Later they passed what was called a crisis room, with a padded floor and bare walls. No child was left alone there, Joseph stressed; Lamont knew better. The children's rooms were very stark and small, and throughout the living quarters still ran the beige and brown linoleum he remembered, but the chapel, renamed Founder's Hall, was now carpeted; it was used mainly for staff meetings. Lamont left feeling chilled. He had never quite realized it, but now he knew: he had grown up in a psychiatric institution.

Lamont had missed his son's first two Christmases. He had never really bought him anything, not even for his birthday. On Christmas Eve 1997, he went shopping for toys. Going from store to store, he kept buying: two remote-control cars, a game-playing Mickey Mouse with Velcro attachments, a big plush teddy bear, a Batman, a Joker, even a "Bananas in Pajamas," one of those three-foot humanoid bananas that made the children in the television ads that year laugh with delight. All told he spent two hundred dollars on presents for his son. The next month's rent was due on

January 1, but he would still have ten days to get the money together, he told himself.

It felt wonderful to arrive at Kisha's place loaded with packages. Their son, nearly three now, loved the remote-control speeder car so much he didn't open anything else. He could only make it go forward, not backward, so he would run to get it, shrieking with glee, and start over. But Kisha was miffed that Lamont had not known his child's sneaker size. She did not invite him to stay for Christmas dinner, and as soon as her mother arrived, he left. He ended up alone at a bad movie, filling up on popcorn and soda.

IN THE NEW YEAR KISHA asked Lamont to help with child care by keeping their son over the weekend sometimes. Soon she was demanding that he also pick him up from the baby-sitter during the week. The new sitter, a woman with a licensed day-care home in the Castlehill projects, lived closer to Lamont, she said, refusing to listen to his objections about his own schedule. "Three years you didn't do nothing for your son," she shouted. "I keep giving you chances. If I don't hear something different, we don't need you." Sometimes she would leave the child with him overnight, promising to pick him up promptly the next day, only to call and say Lamont had to keep him another night because she was too tired to come and get him. When Lamont protested that he had to go to work, she got angry.

"Fuck, I've been working all day. You try carrying a child out of his bed at four A.M. to go to a sitter so you can be at the job at eight A.M. I get home from school, I'm tired. I've got to keep a B average to keep my loan. I got no time to do my homework without hearing, 'Mommee, Mommee, Mommee.' "

It wasn't easy for Lamont to take care of a three-year-old, either. The apartment wasn't equipped for a kid. Lamont's eighteen-year-old cousin Shawn had moved into the bedroom to help with the rent, paying two hundred dollars a month from her SSI disability check, and Kisha saw no reason that Shawn couldn't watch his son, but Lamont knew she was a party girl.

Business was very slow after the holidays. At the end of January 1998, just after his son's third birthday, Lamont learned that Danny was going to close the business unless he could sell it. He offered it to Lamont for twenty-six hundred dollars, and Lamont briefly thought of it as a possibility, remembering that Walter Joseph had said a kid could always turn to Astor Home for help later in life. But in his heart he knew that Walt had not meant money help. He had to find another job fast.

On Friday, February 6, the child had been staying with him for more than a week. The boy kept asking for his mother. "She's gonna come tomorrow," Lamont said. But when he called Kisha's number, he just got the answering machine. He took the boy to the baby-sitter, who was mad because she hadn't been paid.

Lamont started work at one o'clock that afternoon, keeping a knit cap on his head because he had a cold. At six, when he was supposed to pick up his son, he still had customers waiting. His feet and throat ached, but he kept cutting hair until a high school friend arrived to give him a ride to the sitter's. The round trip in a gypsy cab would have set him back ten or twelve bucks, the price of a haircut.

"I'm coming right back—I just have to pick up my son," Lamont told the waiting customers.

The Castlehill projects rose forbiddingly at the water's edge in one of the farthest corners of the Bronx. The elevators smelled of urine. But the sitter had transformed her living room into a day-care-center classroom with big colorful letters and numbers on the wall. Lamont's child was the last to be picked up this day, and the sitter was cooking dinner for her own children, eight and five. When Lamont's son saw him at the door, he laughed and ran to the bathroom to hide. It was one of his favorite games, being chased by his father. Eventually he let himself be caught, noisily imitating a machine as Lamont dressed him in a dark-blue down winter jacket and black ski cap.

"Isn't he big? He's a little man. Come on, Sheemie," Lamont said, calling the child by his nickname. He scooped him up for the walk through the dark grounds of the housing project. The little boy bounced shoulder-high in his arms as he strode. Frozen mud and a rough residue of grass were hard as ice underfoot. At the sidewalk Lamont stopped, scanning the night streets anxiously until his friend's car appeared. When they got back to the shop, only one customer was left, a black man of thirty-five in a business suit, and Danny was cutting his hair.

"Sheemie, you want some food?" Lamont asked. "What do you want?"

"Ice cream."

Lamont laughed. "Naw, not ice cream." He went out and bought buttered English muffins and a cup of vegetable soup at the diner down the block. Sitting on one of the folding chairs in the barbershop, the child ate the bread blissfully, tilting up his little face. He didn't want the soup, so Lamont ate it, his own face weary. Catching his reflection when he stood up to sweep the store, he thought he looked thin and old. He was 23.

In the gypsy cab riding back to the apartment, Sheemie dozed off. Lamont and the driver argued over the fare before settling on six dollars, but the boy did not wake. Lamont carried the sleeping child into the bedroom, clearing away crumpled cigarette wrappers from the large bed and straightening a sheet over the torn mattress with one hand before he laid him down. An open forty-ounce bottle of beer stood on the bare floor in the middle of the room. Boxes and a shopping cart full of clothes stood against the walls, and rock CD covers were taped everywhere. It was Shawn's room, but she was out; Sheemie shared her double bed. Lamont gently took off the child's shoes and coat and covered him.

The apartment's galley kitchen was rank with the debris from a party the weekend before. Trash from the crackhouse days still stood in the short hallway; the window in the bathroom was broken, and there were holes in the walls where the mice came in. But Lamont had reclaimed the living room's bare, scarred floor with a big blue piece of carpeting bought from a crackhead for fifteen dollars, laying it down with a twenty-dollar staple gun and a borrowed hammer. One of his father's friends had shown him how to do it, almost the way a guy might teach his own son. Lamont had put up a discarded set of fleur-de-lis drapes, hanging them upside down as curtains by the hems. He had a small black leather couch, battered but intact, a TV set, and even an artificial plant. He kept his own bed folded behind the couch; it had been passed on to him by a guy he had known in the group home. He had arranged one corner of the room especially for Sheemie, with small toys lined up on top of a light-blue trunk, just dime-store plastic things; the good Christmas toys were all at Kisha's.

Kisha was supposed to pick up the kid the next morning, but she didn't show. Finally Lamont telephoned her sister, Naomi, and she got Kisha on a three-way call. He said that the barbershop was closing, he was trying to moonlight in an East Village hair-salon job at night, and he just couldn't do the pickup at the sitter's anymore. She went crazy.

"You're a single person with no serious problems," she said. "I stripped for a year and let men fondle my fucking body to feed your child. I don't need your sob stories."

Kisha raged, out of her mind from pain in her mouth. She needed a thousand dollars' worth of dental surgery—two root canals and a surgical extraction—and she had held out working for one of the world's biggest assholes for four months, waiting to qualify for dental insurance. But her boss delayed putting in the insurance papers, so she started interviewing for other jobs. Before she could land one, she and the boss had clashed over the time she was missing at the office. Now she was unemployed again, and maybe blacklisted at the temp agency, too. She was going to have to withdraw from school and lose her loan. Had Lamont at least paid the baby-sitter the seventy dollars for the week, like he promised? No. Had he asked his aunt Sylvia to watch his son? No. Had he bought his son the new shoes he needed? No. He was a worthless, selfish nigger who needed reality to hit him in the face like a mug. Well, she just wasn't coming to pick up the boy. "You keep him," she said.

Her sister came and got the child. It wasn't good for him, she said. They might not realize that he knew what was going on, but he probably felt sometimes that nobody wanted him.

In the empty apartment, the stillness made the pain sharper. Lamont suddenly remembered hints from Kisha's family that maybe the child could have a better life somewhere else. He couldn't let that happen. He couldn't let Sheemie go into the system. And that was exactly what would happen, he realized, if one of them didn't take him. He fought panic, trying to review his options. If he had to, he could turn to welfare for emergency help to feed and clothe his son and pay the rent, get the kid on Medicaid, buy time to get his life together. Or could he? With the new crackdown you practically had to be missing a limb to qualify for welfare, and even then it took weeks and weeks. An able-bodied man like him, they'd take one look and assign him to work off his grant in Brooklyn. He wouldn't be able to cut hair anymore, and welfare paid only $215 a month for rent, less than he earned.

Long before now, Kisha had asked, "Why don't you send him to your stepmother?" She meant Alicia. But Lamont couldn't turn to Alicia. The last time they had spoken was before Christmas, when she'd called to tell him her Connecticut church had burned down—arson, apparently, perhaps by one of the homeless men she had sheltered there. Lamont, stammering condolences, was immediately struck by the thought that she suspected him, that she might be listening to his voice for sounds of guilt. And his own mother, fresh out of prison, had left Mister Al's within two days. Someone had told Lamont only the day before that she was now in the hospital. He just didn't have anyone to run to and tell, "This is what I'm going through, and I need your help."

Kisha had insisted that Lamont had to pick up the kid and his stuff at her place on Sunday night or never see him again. What would happen if he didn't? He knew she was starting to stress out. Recently, in front of him, she had hit the three-year-old for wetting his pants. She had not mentioned foster care, but there had been talk of Sheemie's living with his aunt for a while. Other living arrangements—that's the way it starts, he thought. Then the aunt goes through her own problems, loses her job or her man, has trouble with her own kid. It all went to the same thing in the end.

In his mind's eye, he saw Sheemie's little face tilt up at him with perfect trust while a black hole opened under his feet. His heart raced. "I am not going to let him go through everything I went through," he said. "He wouldn't be able to take it like I did."

Walking to the barbershop, he built his pitch to Kisha as though words were bricks that could wall out this invasion of helplessness and pain. "We don't have to be together, but we made this boy. We have to work together. We have to find another alternative. I'm willing to stop partying and bust my ass to try to make it work. 'Cause I love him. I really do. He's a good kid, and he's mine."

That night, for the first time in many years, he broke down and cried.

IN A HOSPITAL GOWN with her hair braided back, Shirley Wilder looked much younger than thirty-eight. But like a very old woman, she had to lie down after crossing the room. She didn't know how long she had left now. More than anything, she wanted to do something for her grandbaby. She was entitled to a small living allowance from the Department of AIDS Services. She wanted to set aside a hundred dollars a month for a certificate of deposit for the baby, and she couldn't do it on her own. She needed someone who could be the payee for the stipend so she wouldn't blow it all.

She was afraid to tell Marcia Lowry that she had AIDS. "It would crush her. She, like, raised me from a child. I don't want to hurt her." Shirley didn't want Lamont to know, either. "I don't want him to feel sorry for me. I don't want him to feel I'm dependent on him." The reporter who had come to visit her was the only possibility, she said.

"My grandmother was there for me. I want to be there for my grand-baby. It's the only thing I can do for him." Her large eyes filled with tears that spilled silently down the sides of her smooth cheeks. "I want him to have something from me because he won't know me."

Then she heard what was happening in Lamont's life. "Oh no, not that," she cried out, and began to sob uncontrollably. "The baby. I don't want my grandbaby to go in the system. If it's the only thing I do, at least one of us can be free." She was gasping, shaking with grief.

She had to talk to Lamont. They were in a position to help each other. "If it's the only thing we do," she kept repeating, "we have to keep the baby from going in the system."

But she had no benefits in place yet, not even a completed application pending. And soon the pain came shooting down her spine again, pain worse than childbirth, pain stronger than the morphine.

IT WOULD HAVE BEEN EASIER if he'd never met his son, Lamont thought as he walked up the stairs to Kisha's apartment the night of Sunday, February 8. For three years he had hoped that one day he and Kisha could work it out and be a family. Yet, he had decided, for all his own failures, what was happening had nothing to do with him. Kisha had a boyfriend, a guy with a phone-company job who wanted to move to Maryland. The kid was probably in the way. All her girlfriends did the same thing, dumping their first baby on the father or their family. Knowing Kisha, she would probably get pregnant with the boyfriend, marry him, and then turn around and say, "I want my son back." So even if he could take Sheemie now, there would be more turmoil later.

He tried to buy time. "This is a bit much for me to take him right now, with no transition period, no time to set up," he said.

"There's nothing I can do for him here," she retorted. "I'm not working. I don't have any food for him. Your son is eating dinner for breakfast. And I am not going back on welfare. I can't stay on top of my bills on welfare."

"I'm in between jobs right now," Lamont said. "I got no food in the house either. On the weekend I lived on macaroni and cheese out of the box. I haven't even paid my rent yet."

It was as though she hadn't heard him. "You've got two jobs," she said. "You've got money coming in from everywhere. You are to take responsibility for him."

"You got to understand, we have to do this together," he pleaded. "If you're stressed out, imagine how stressed I'm going to be. I'm not going to take him in the middle of the night."

"Why not?" she insisted. "That is your blood. That is your seed."

And all the while, Sheemie kept running in and out of the bedroom. He knew something was wrong.

"Where's Daddy?" he asked when Lamont was gone. "Where's Daddy?"

SEVEN

S HIRLEY WILDER WAS READY FOR HOSPITAL DISCHARGE, THE woman on the phone told Lamont on March 17, 1998. Couldn't his mother spend one night with him? Just one night, until she could apply to the Department of AIDS Services for a place?

He felt like running away. But the nurse made it seem that if he didn't say yes, he was some kind of an asshole.

He put Shirley where his son used to sleep. All night, every few minutes, she called Lamont's name. Could he turn out the light? Could he pass her the glass of water? At four o'clock in the morning she was still calling to him, maybe just to make sure she was not alone in the dark. He felt like he was dealing with a needy kid. By morning, when she said the pain was coming back too strong for her to make it over to the Department of AIDS Services that day, it was clear that she did not want to leave. He called an ambulance to take her to the nearest hospital.

"I'm not willing to take on somebody dying right in front of me," he said later. It had nothing to do with anger or trying to get even. In fact, he felt he was starting to get over a lot of his anger. "When you go through life yourself and you see you can't keep all your commitments because life keeps throwing you curve balls, you understand what you didn't understand as a little kid," he said.

BY THE YEAR 2000, Mayor Giuliani vowed in a speech he delivered on July 20, 1998, "New York will be the first city in the nation, on its own, to end welfare." Since April his administration had begun converting the city's thirty-one Income Support Centers into Job Centers, where people seeking aid would be deterred from applying for government benefits. They would be told to look for work instead, or to turn to friends, relatives, and charities. If they insisted on applying for aid, they would be required to come to the Job Center or go to a private contract agency and do a daily job search for thirty-five days as a condition of having their application processed. If they missed an appointment, they would have to start over. Those who did not find jobs would be assigned to work off their grants in city workfare assignments. The results were dramatic: 54 percent of people who had sought assistance each month at Income Support Centers between March 1997 and April 1998 had received benefits, but at the Job Centers, the figure had dropped to 19 percent by July.

Jason Turner, Mayor Giuliani's welfare commissioner, said these sweeping changes were not the result of lengthy planning followed by implementation. Rather, "we acted first and worried about the consequences later," Turner declared on November 17, 1998, in a speech he gave at a forum on welfare reform, sponsored by the Nelson A. Rockefeller Institute of Government. The idea that poverty itself hurt family well-being was a "serious mistake," he explained. Even with very low incomes, families with two parents and a working head "are usually stabilized and seem to do well overall." To push welfare applicants toward such self-reliance, he added, "we need to create, if you will, a personal crisis in individuals' lives."

ON THE NIGHT OF DECEMBER 7, 1998, Kisha took stock of the food she had left in the house: some chicken, two cans of vegetables, three tangerines, some hot cereal, a little rice, some carrots. There was less than a dollar in her purse, and her phone and electricity were about to be shut off. She and her boyfriend had broken up, and without his contributions, she was falling seriously behind in her rent of $307 a month. In the morning she would go to the local welfare center and ask for help. She knew it was a long process, but at least she could start with emergency food stamps. She had a child to feed, and she had never had any intention of putting him in foster care. "When the shit hits the bricks, it's not your daddy, it's your mommy. I'll manage, even if it means I've got to sell my ass again," she swore.

The Hamilton Income Support Center in her Harlem neighborhood had a new name on the door: Hamilton Job Center. Anyone who needed immediate help with food was in the wrong place, a caseworker told several dozen would-be applicants in a speech that gave a grim description of the city's workfare program. Kisha waited all day long to talk to a caseworker.

Expedited food stamps no longer existed, the worker said. Kisha would have to wait for thirty to thirty-five days before she could get any help to purchase food. Meanwhile, the caseworker gave her a referral to a private charity's food pantry. When Kisha got there, she was informed that the supply of food had run out.

Back at the center, two people from the Legal Aid Society attracted Kisha's attention. They said the city workers were turning away people who had a right to food stamps and Medicaid. Legal Aid was looking for plaintiffs to join a class-action lawsuit against the practice, which violated federal law. Was she interested in signing up?

THAT DECEMBER LAMONT, TOO, turned to the city for help. While he was at housing court trying to contest an eviction, the landlord put all his belongings out on the street and padlocked the door. Everything was taken. For a few nights Lamont climbed in through the broken bathroom window and slept on the floor of the empty apartment. An old group-home buddy stole him some blankets from a Bronx homeless shelter. Finally Lamont asked to stay in the shelter himself. But he was advised that he had to go through the city shelter system's central intake in Manhattan, near Bellevue Hospital.

His first night was the worst. Many of the other men at intake were mentally ill, and a lot of the younger ones just out of prison. At midnight, one dude in leather pants threw feces on the floor. Another man seemed catatonic, standing stock-still for hours without blinking. The guards were rough, and Lamont kept telling himself to be real, real quiet. He waited on a wooden chair until three in the morning. Finally he was bused to a distant armory and given a cot in a military-style barracks, only to be awakened at five and told he had to leave. After cutting hair until nine that night, he had to start the process all over again.

This was the overnight circuit. To get a steady bed assignment, a worker explained, he had to spend twenty-one days in an assessment bed. But simply getting an assessment-bed assignment was not easy for a man who couldn't get to the Bellevue intake shelter until after work. He related his situation to day-shift shelter staff, and some of them were sympathetic enough to promise to help. But every time he returned to intake, the night-shift staffers would say that there was nothing they could do, that he just had to keep trying.

That winter, full-time stock clerks, short-order cooks, and $5.50-an-hour Wall Street messengers were among the men left to shuttle through the overnight circuit with Lamont. As the now-booming economy increased employment opportunities for low-wage workers, it also drove up rents, sending more single workingmen to the shelter system to bridge the gap. Homeless people in the city still had a court-ordered right to shelter, but that right now clashed with the mission of the city's poverty administrators: to eliminate government entitlements and to prod the poor to work for any wage.

For more than a year, city officials had been meeting with representatives of a for-profit company that wanted to turn the Bellevue shelter building into an upscale assisted-living residence where the elderly would pay rents of five thousand dollars a month. When it emerged that the developer had been paying the wife of the mayor's chief of staff a three-thousand-dollar monthly retainer to lobby for his project, officials insisted that the decision to close the men's shelter was quite independent of any development plan. Instead, it was tied to the mayor's support for the $28 million renovation going on in a building across the street: Nicholas Scoppetta's new Administration for Children's Services (ACS).

Scoppetta had separated Child Welfare from its parent agency, the Human Resources Administration, in a reorganization emblematic of a larger shift in ideology. Now the former morgue of Bellevue Hospital was being refitted with marble and glass to serve as headquarters for the free-standing children's agency. Besides management offices and a caseworkers' training academy, the landmark building would house the city's emergency-intake center for abused and neglected children. And neither the mayor nor Commissioner Scoppetta wanted their children's shelter to be so close to a shelter for homeless men.

On Christmas Eve 1998, Lamont gave up on the shelter system. He had been through seven or eight nights of the overnight circuit and was no closer to landing an assessment bed. That night he checked into a cheap hotel, drank enough to dull his senses, and slept for ten hours straight. On Christmas Day, he went to see his mother.

He had not seen Shirley since the day she left his apartment. For months she had been in a hospice for people with AIDS. Lamont was shocked when he saw her. She looked to weigh no more than forty pounds now. Her skin was taut against her bones, her eyes enormous. When she saw Lamont, she got mad. "You were supposed to come and talk to my worker," she said. "You were supposed to cosign for my benefits."

There was no way he could have done that, he told her. Now she was too sick to live outside the hospice anyway. Privately, he figured she had wanted a copay arrangement only so she could wheedle cash out of him for drugs. In the absence of a copayee, the city sent money straight to the landlord and to the food-voucher service, because a drug addict couldn't be trusted with cash, AIDS or no AIDS.

Shirley drifted in and out of consciousness. When she opened her eyes again, she asked about her grandbaby. What could he tell her? He had not seen his son in months. "It was sad," Lamont said later. "It was hard. It was really, really difficult to spend Christmas like that." When she asked him to go buy her some cigarettes, he said he would be back in five minutes. Instead, he escaped without saying good-bye.

MARCIA LOWRY, TOO, began asking about Shirley's whereabouts that winter. After two decades as head of the ACLU's Children's Rights Project, she had struck out on her own late in 1995 and set up Children's Rights, Inc., an independent, national nonprofit advocacy organization. She had a staff of six lawyers, nine class actions filed around the country, and a projected $1.4 million annual budget that sometimes kept her lying awake in terror at all the bills to be paid out of legal fees and foundation grants not yet awarded. She had filed *Marisol* v. *Giuliani* on December 13, 1995. Working on the legal papers late at night in her rambling house in Chappaqua, where Avi had an extra room for his electric trains and Legos, she had suddenly found herself weeping over her own account of "Marisol," a child who had almost starved to death in a dark closet at the age of four while the city ignored evidence of her mistreatment. The *Marisol* lawsuit was her second chance, Lowry felt, a way to fulfill the original promise of *Wilder*.

Marisol argued that the city had already shown itself incapable of fixing the system from within, and demanded that the court appoint an outside receiver to take over the whole $1.2 billion operation. When the mayor named Nick Scoppetta to restructure and reform the agency a month later, Judge Ward himself asked Lowry, "What more do you want?" Scoppetta was seen as the ultimate good guy—a prosecutor of dirty cops, twice the city's investigation commissioner, and a longtime trustee of the Children's Aid Society, whose own childhood in an orphanage made this job his calling.

Scoppetta's ambitious reform plan, unveiled in December 1996, all but equated child protection with child removal. His own views were certainly more sophisticated, but his personal history and the politics of his patron overdetermined the thrust of his agenda. "Any ambiguity regarding the safety of the child will be resolved in favor of removing the child from harm's way," a boxed mission statement at the start of his 163-page reform plan declared. "Only when families demonstrate to the satisfaction of ACS that their homes are safe and secure, will the children be permitted to remain [in] or be returned to the home." Accountability was to be the hallmark of the agency's new culture, built around "outcome and performance measures" that would track the system's progress. "Stopping the killing of children" was the first goal Scoppetta listed.

Yet any child-abuse fatality was an aberration. The highly publicized death of a child often brought a surge in removals, a defensive kind of casework that swept many children needlessly into an already chaotic and crowded system in which they were anything but safe. And an overwhelmed system typically saw a rise, rather than a reduction, in the number of children known to the child protection agency who died of abuse.

To be sure, Scoppetta's plan did also make neighborhood-based foster care central to the blueprint for a better system, and at public hearings, Scoppetta himself had stressed the need for more drug-treatment options for parents and more preventive programs to make the removal of children unnecessary; he reiterated old prescriptions including better caseworker training and pay, reduced caseloads, and computerized case files. But as Dale Russakoff put it in 1997 in a *New Yorker* profile of the commissioner, "Scoppetta's plan is like an appealing destination to which no roads have been built."

Preventive programs had been severely hurt by Giuliani budget cuts. By definition, parents who could not provide for their children were suspect in the era of welfare reform. In New York City, the same sorts of child neglect cases that other cities still treated as matters for counseling and assistance were being prosecuted as crimes. Poor mothers were led away in handcuffs because they had left a child unattended while trying to buy milk at the grocery store, or because a child had wandered away during a family eviction. One severely depressed mother in Brooklyn was actually criminally charged with endangering the welfare of a child after she notified the authorities that she had taken an overdose of sleeping pills in a suicide attempt; had she died, prosecutors said, her three-year-old would have been left alone in the apartment.

Lowry was not blind to the new criminalization of poverty. She could not fix poverty, she had always said, but surely she could fix foster care. In a way, she and Scoppetta were collaborators in the same fiction—the belief that the two realms could be separated.

Both Lowry and Scoppetta saw fixing the system as a personal mission, but in Scoppetta's view, litigation consumed vast resources and time, fostered disconnected decision making, and overshadowed more important needs. "The continued failure of the agency to achieve stability and safety for children, notwithstanding all the efforts of attorneys and judges in these cases, calls into question the value of litigation as an effective tool to make a difference in the lives of children," he wrote. His reform plan pledged to "aggressively pursue resolutions of all lawsuits."

Wilder, which he had once supported, was his first target. It was all about legal fees, he charged. Early in 1998, city lawyers claimed that the *Wilder* decree had expired in December 1997, when Lowry wasn't looking. She had failed to petition for an extension of the settlement decree by the date cited in a long forgotten sunset clause. Lowry replied that the sunset clause could not be invoked because of her unanswered contempt motions and the city's bad faith. Eventually Judge Ward agreed, noting that the city had never come close to implementing *Wilder.* It was a hollow victory. And it all made others wonder, since traditional court enforcement had been so glaringly unsuccessful in *Wilder,* why should she expect it to work in *Marisol?*

She had begun to think harder about a *Marisol* settlement when Ward ruled that he would let the city lawyers keep introducing fresh evidence to demonstrate that all the problems she had cited were now being fixed. That would mean a very long trial against a moving target. Even though Lowry believed Ward would have to rule that the city was liable for having violated the rights of the *Marisol* children, she knew he would never take the agency away from Scoppetta. People were so desperate for things to be fixed that when someone like Scoppetta came in and said, "I'm doing it," they wanted to believe him. The problem was that she now had thirty-five hundred pages of depositions showing that it just wasn't true.

The solution, she had decided, was to bring in independent national experts—experts without the adversarial taint that made her own points harder for Ward to accept, experts who could show from within how to repair this long-crippled tanker and begin to steer it in a new direction. The Annie E. Casey Foundation offered to fund such a panel, and the city consented to open itself to its unprecedented scrutiny for the next two years. The panel would issue periodic reports and help Scoppetta accomplish his planned reforms. If it determined that the city was acting in bad faith, Lowry would be free to reopen the litigation, with the ready ammunition of the panel's new information. The city agreed to pay her legal fees, an amount to be decided by the court. As part of the deal, the *Wilder* principles would be folded into the *Marisol* settlement, but the *Wilder* decree itself would be dissolved. This was as good an outcome as she could hope to win at trial, Lowry felt.

She had not balked long at an unexpected concession the city had also demanded: a moratorium on new class-action lawsuits against Scoppetta's agency. The city insisted that the settlement should release it from all claims "known or unknown, foreseen or unforeseen, matured or unmatured, accrued or not accrued, direct or indirect," that Lowry's sweepingly defined plaintiff class "ever had, now has, or can, shall, or may hearafter have . . . from the beginning of time through December 15, 2000." Lowry knew the provision would draw fire from other children's advocates who had their own, smaller lawsuits in the works. Her critics would later say that in her arrogance, she had sacrificed the immediate legal interests of real children for the mere potential of future systemic reform. But piecemeal litigation could not be the answer, she believed. Other people's lawsuits served one interest at the expense of others.

Lowry seemed unconscious of how closely her thinking had come to parallel Scoppetta's condemnation of all class-action litigation. She had long committed herself to the idea of litigation massive and sustained enough to fix foster care. Now, in this settlement, she was stepping back from litigation, deferring to a group of child welfare professionals answerable to no one and devoid of political power. For at least two years—a lifetime for flesh-and-blood children—the city children's agency would be immune to legal pressure. Legal Aid lawyers would later call this a dramatic change in course. In fact, it was more like an implosion.

BY THE TIME MARCIA LEARNED where Shirley was, the signed stipulation of settlement in *Marisol* was waiting for court approval. Marcia traveled down to the hospice on Rivington Street in the quiet week between Christmas and New Year's, buying a cheerful bouquet for Shirley on the way. "Oh, I'm so glad somebody brought her flowers," the nurse at the duty station said.

Shirley was asleep. She was so small under the sheet, smaller than she had been at the age of thirteen. But when Marcia called her name and she opened her eyes, all of her was there.

"Marcia, I saw you on TV!" she said with her old smile. She asked after Marcia's son and praised the snapshot of him in Marcia's wallet; then hesitated, asking "Oh, may I look at the other pictures?"

It was one of those small, polite gestures Marcia remembered, the imprint of the well-brought-up little girl her grandmother had left behind. Yes, of course she could look, Marcia told her, and she leaned close to explain her other family photos.

There were no photos in the bare and narrow room where Shirley lay. A small television set on an accordion arm nestled against the sharp angle of her hipbone, its vibration and warmth a defense against loneliness. In the end, Marcia couldn't bring herself to tell Shirley that the *Wilder* lawsuit was dying, too. When Shirley asked for cigarettes, Marcia gladly ran out to the bodega across the street and brought back a forbidden pack. They hugged each other and said good-bye.

"I love you," Shirley told her.

At the nurse's station, Marcia paused, struggling with the emotion of those unexpected words. Composing herself, she left her business card. They should call her when the time came, she said. She did not want Shirley to have to die alone.

The reporter visited a few days later, on January 2, 1999, bringing a framed photograph of a little boy with a wide smile and laughing eyes. Shirley was too weak to sit up, but as the picture of her grandson came close, she started and stared. She did not smile. "I tried so hard to hold out," she whispered, her fierce eyes devouring the image. "But I'm not going to make it to see him."

There were no more visitors. On Sunday, January 17, when the hospice staff called Marcia Lowry's number, an answering machine picked up. Marcia was in Florida that evening. She had flown down from New York, and her sister in from California, to surprise their widowed mother, Sophie, on her eighty-second birthday. "I'm so lucky to have such wonderful children," their mother said.

As night fell in New York, Shirley called for Cora—Corazon Alino, the nurse with the gentle voice and Filipino accent. Cora brought Albert, another nurse, and injections for the pain. Together they prayed for Shirley. She was restless. She wanted to sleep, she kept saying, she just wanted to sleep. She asked for a cigarette, and they gave her one, just to hold and smell. She begged not to be left alone, and so Corazon Alino stayed and prayed the rosary. "Just say Amen," she told Shirley.

Near the end, Shirley cried out that she was afraid. She saw Jesus, she said; she saw Mother Mary. "OK, you have to be happy," Corazon Alino told her. "You're going to be with them. Relax, and just be comforted."

She died at 9:30 P.M. Albert took the body down to the morgue. In the morning, the hospice social worker began making calls, trying to find someone to bury Shirley Wilder. Otherwise she would go to windswept Hart Island, to a common grave with no marker in the city's potter's field.

"She wasn't my mother in any real sense," Lamont said when he was reached at his latest barbershop. "But if nobody else wants to do it, I might as well."

In the end, Shirley's aunt Carrie applied for the modest welfare burial grant, since Lamont, a workingman with no proper ID, probably could not have qualified. There was no money for flowers or a minister, but they made arrangements for cremation. The ashes would be mailed to California, to Shirley's estranged younger sister, Virgie, who sobbed bitterly when she learned of her death. "I was angry, but she still was my sister," Virgie said. "I didn't intend to cut her off forever. I didn't want her to leave this world thinking she wasn't loved."

FIVE DAYS AFTER SHIRLEY'S DEATH, Marcia Lowry stood before Judge Ward, urging him to approve the settlement in *Marisol*. Fighting back tears, she invoked Shirley's fate. "Being in foster care shouldn't mean that you grow up to die alone," she said. The *Marisol* settlement was the "best chance for making sure that other children don't have the experience Shirley had." Critics called its promise wholly illusory, but Ward overruled their objections and approved all the terms of the settlement. On January 22, 1999, after twenty-six years of litigation, *Wilder* was finally over.

But in the same federal courthouse, on the same day, in a class-action lawsuit called *Lakisha Reynolds* v. *Giuliani,* a different judge was determining that the tough new welfare practices of the city's Human Resources Administration had endangered needy children, and specifically a three-year-old child named Wilder. Even the Legal Aid lawyers who had chosen his mother as their lead plaintiff had no idea that he was Shirley Wilder's grandson.

POSTSCRIPT

SHIRLEY WILDER'S GRANDSON turned five in the year 2000. He lives with his mother, who is still struggling to make ends meet. His father cuts hair at a barbershop in the Bronx, and is deeper in debt since he spent a night in jail for failing to pay child support. Teachers have considered calling in child protective services to investigate the boy's family; they wondered why he wrecked his classroom one morning and cried, "My mommy put my daddy in jail." But he has changed schools since then. He and his mother have moved in with her sister's family in the Bronx, not far from his father's barbershop. And these days, on weekends, father and son can sometimes be found there together.

NOTES ON REPORTING
AND SOURCES

BY 1993, *WILDER* HAD OVERFLOWED the file cabinets and filled much of the basement at the American Civil Liberties Union with depositions, expert reports, court transcripts, and proposed findings-of-fact. Marcia Robinson Lowry generously made herself, and almost everything else, available to my inquiries, eventually even letting me take home a set of bound legal papers in fifteen volumes totaling 6,718 pages. What saved me from drowning in all that material, however, was meeting Shirley Wilder, who told me about the "hole" at Hudson, and urged me to help her find her son.

Early in the project I saw that part of my task would be to reconstruct the past: Shirley's childhood and Lamont's; the lawsuit's course to that point; and the deep history underlying both. The other challenge was to follow the Wilders' lives and the lawsuit itself as each unfolded in real time. For years, the work seemed to keep expanding in both directions.

Overall, I adhered to the same standards of journalism that I have followed at the *New York Times* and before that at *Newsday*. No facts or names have been changed. In the reconstruction of events that I did not witness, I have relied mainly on official records and on in-depth interviews with as many participants as possible. References to what people thought or felt reflect what they told me they were thinking or feeling at the time, or what they expressed in written or transcribed records. For reasons of narrative style I used direct quotations from such interviews sparingly, but passages recounted from the point of view of particular participants—Nann and Bill Miller, for example, Margaret Martin, Lowry, and Lamont himself—often closely follow the exact wording that they used in describing the events. And when I quote what protagonists "would say later," or later told "someone," I am the person to whom they made the remark.

My interpretations are my own, of course. I have tried to flag the few instances when I interjected an analysis—for example, in saying that one of Shirley's sexual encounters sounded more to an outsider's ears like a rape than an assignation, and in offering in the form of a question a suggestion as to why Bill Miller would demand Lamont's immediate removal.

AT FIRST, PIECING TOGETHER a narrative of Lamont's early years from remembered fragments was like detective work. For example, I located the right Millers, among dozens of families by that name in Minnesota, after Lamont recalled that their son's name was Ian, and a clerk at the Minnesota Department of Motor Vehicles combed computerized lists to find the correct address. Such help was almost as crucial in the early stages as the cooperation of the Millers, the Wassermans, and the Fils-Aimes when I reached them.

Confidential child welfare records about Shirley and Lamont became key sources. Shirley gave Lowry permission to hand me her file, which included family court proceedings, psychiatric assessments, detailed caseworker narratives, Sister Dorothy Gallant's social service notes, and correspondence by Holy Cross Campus officials concerning Shirley's request for birth control.

Much later, the bulging folders containing Lamont's complete foster care record were carried to me in the dead of night in two shopping bags by someone who worked inside the child welfare administration. With Lamont's approval, I photocopied every scrap. The detailed, contemporaneous accounts by caseworkers started when he was a newborn and continued, with few gaps, all the way through his adolescence in a Bronx group home. They included psychiatric reports from Golden Valley, a rich social services chronicle from Astor Home, an account of his stay with Ms. Martin, even a March 28, 1990 letter from city investigators corroborating his complaint that his savings had been stolen by a staff person. Combined with Lamont's own recollections, the records allowed me to identify and interview additional witnesses from nearly every stage of his placement history, including caseworkers, teachers, and contemporaries: Gertrude Kihara and Susan Leaf; Rev. Cesar Ramos and Ruby Alomar (of the Mount Eden parish); Jonathan Sulds; Sister Dorothy; Myrna Otte and Ann Sinott; Joyce Storla (his teacher at Robert Fulton); Janet Young (his teacher at Adams); Al, Kevin, and Missi (Vera Ellen James) Wasserman; Sister Theresa Kelly at Foundling; Walter Joseph, Reuben Contero, Jan Weido, Mary Zuvic, Mrs. Martin, Frank D., Sean P., James R. and others from Astor; Sefus Henderson; Mo Gadsen, James Campbell, and Daphne Stevens of Leake & Watts, and Andre Dell, his high school friend.

Lamont himself I interviewed too many times to count. He repeatedly renewed his commitment to the project, and brought to it extraordinary honesty, intelligence, and insight. Time and again I found that his memories—of Astor Home children who had died, for example, or a psychologist arrested for molesting his charges—could be tracked down and fully corroborated. My sources for the David A. Hoffman case include interviews with state police investigators, victims, and staff members; a copy of the state police investigation report, local newspaper articles, and Dutchess County Court records, especially the transcript of Hoffman's July 24, 1986 guilty plea and a September 23, 1986, sentencing memo from Gerald J. Pisanelli, his lawyer, with attached letter from Howard S. Susser, the senior psychologist at Astor Home. Erica's death, which so haunted Lamont, was confirmed in detail by a former staff member who witnessed it. The drowning of Marcus Little is memorialized in the *Rhinebeck Gazette Advertiser,* YOUTH DIES AFTER POOL MISHAP, Thursday, June 9, 1983, and the *Poughkeepsie Journal,* April 16, 1988, RHINEBECK TOWN BOARD PAID $45,000 IN OUT OF COURT SETTLEMENT IN DEATH OF CHILD WHO DROWNED.

OVER LONG PERIODS Lamont and I had almost a running conversation about what I was discovering and about his current life. In several key scenes in the book, of course, I was present and taking notes. Examples include Lamont's reunions with Shirley and Alicia in 1993; the Memphis family reunion in July of 1994; the lunch with Lowry in February 1995; the evening in January 1998, when he picked up his son at the baby-sitter's. Lamont sometimes waited until he had emerged from his most desperate times—his first bout with homelessness, for example—before sharing the details with me. But at other times he related his experiences almost as they occurred. Sections describing his life in the projects, his son's birth, and clashes with Kisha and with his father are based on such accounts, as well as on interviews with other participants.

Although Shirley dropped out of sight for long periods, I had more than a dozen interviews with her, including: on a tour of Mister Al's garden and the roof in east Harlem, in long telephone calls when she was in prison, and in a bedside visit two weeks before she died. She was always proud of her role in the *Wilder* lawsuit, and I believe she saw this book as another dimension of that legacy.

Nearly all sections of the book draw on a mix of interviews and other research. The chapters on the training school at Hudson are a good illustration. Interviews with former staff members, and a trove of old news clippings, photographs, and original research shared by a local historian, Margaret B. Schram, provided a picture of the place beyond the published historical and sociological accounts, including Giallombardo's valuable book, *The Social World of Imprisoned Girls* (Wiley, New York, 1974). Gloria McFarland, the institution's former psychologist, put me on the trail of nineteenth- and early-twentieth-century inmate records that had been boxed and shipped away shortly before the institution became a men's prison. When the prison superintendent showed me the old graveyard in the woods, I became obsessed with tracking down the missing records to learn more about the girls buried there.

It turned out that the ledgers had been forgotten for years, uncatalogued, in a back room of the New York State Archives in Albany. As the first person in close to a century to read them, I thrilled to the discovery of names that matched the ones fading from the old headstones and of life stories that fit the dates I'd gleaned from microfiche death records.

Another three years would pass before I could ask Shirley Wilder about the old cemetery; then, as we sat in the crowded visiting area of the Riker's jail, she recounted the terror she'd felt as a thirteen-year-old when she stumbled on it during her flight.

SEVERAL OTHER SECTIONS of the book also rely on collections of primary sources and the published or unpublished work of other people.

The Justine Wise Polier Manuscripts at the Schlesinger Library at Radcliffe, in Cambridge, Massachusetts, were an important source of reports, correspondence, and court transcripts that documented her own role as a would-be reformer during four decades on the bench; policies and practices at Louise Wise Services; and the uproar among board members of the sectarian philanthropies and the Legal Aid Society after *Wilder* was filed. Particularly valuable was documentation on the jockeying over amicus briefs; the fight over James Dumpson's appointment; the tension between Legal Aid and the NYCLU over Lowry's conduct of the *Wilder* case, and the Hunter College forum. My account of that event, largely based on Frances FitzGerald's memo, was supplemented with participants' recollections and Dumpson's own copy of his "Statement in Support of *Wilder*."

I also quote from *The Personal Letters of Stephen Wise,* Justine Wise Polier and James Waterman Wise, eds., Beacon Press, Boston, 1956; from Polier's first book, *Everybody's Children, Nobody's Child: A Judge Looks at Underprivileged Children in the United States,* Scribners, New York, 1941; and her last, *Juvenile Justice in Double Jeopardy: The Distanced Community and Vengeful Retribution* (Lawrence Erlbaum Associates, Hillsdale, N.J., 1989), which contains her own account of the Shirley Wilder case. Elizabeth T. Schack, Kathryn McDonald, Irene Arnold, Viola Bernard, Trude Lash, Trudy Festinger, Debra Bradley, Stephen Wise Tulin, and Don Cohn were also helpful with memories of Polier. The Polier report that helped inspire Ira Glasser's Children's Rights Project was produced with Schack, who was full of additional information and encouragement. The complete title is *Juvenile Justice Confounded: Pretensions and Realities of Treatment Services* (Committee on Mental Health Services Inside and Outside the Family Court in the City of New York, National Council on Crime and Delinquency, Paramus, N.J., 1972).

AT THE TRAINING SCHOOL, besides Tom Tunney and Gale Smith (who offered the toilet paper anecdote), and others named in the narrative, Beulah Crank, who remembered when Ella Fitzgerald was an inmate, was very helpful (see Nina Bernstein, "Ward of the State: The Gap in Ella Fitzgerald's Life," *New York Times, Week in Review,* June 23, 1996). For more on the lost colonies of runaways, see Tim Mulligan, *The Hudson River Valley, a History and Guide* (Random House, New York, 1981, 1985). For more on prostitution in the town of Hudson, see Bruce Edward Hall, *Diamond Street* (Black Dome Press, Hensonville, N.Y., 1995). A reference to the Hudson as a "drowned river" comes from Robert H. Boyle, *The Hudson River: A Natural and Unnatural History* (Norton & Co., New York, 1979).

For the visit to Shirley at Hudson and an account of the earliest days of the litigation, I am indebted to the vivid recollections of Risa Dickstein, who spoke to me at her Wall Street firm, in her fifty-fourth-floor corner office, where she then conducted a flourishing practice in art law, intellectual property, real estate, regulatory, and matrimonial matters. Besides Lowry herself, with whom I had many interviews about *Wilder's* early years, information came from Paul Dickstein, Carl Weisbrod, Marilyn Shaffer, Ira Glasser, Paul Chevigny, Bruce Ennis, Carol Sherman, Martin Guggenheim, Peter Bienstock, Steven Shapiro, Jule Sugarman, Barbara Blum, Karin Perez, Carol Parry, Leonard Sand, David Roth, Sister Mary Paul, Linda Schleicher; David Rudenstine; Sanford Solender, Gerald Bodell, and others. Lowry's account of John Lowry's trial was supplemented by William Kunstler, *Deep in My Heart* (Morrow, New York, 1966), and by Dick Scupi, who also provided court records in the case.

MY ACCOUNT OF LITIGATION in *Smith* v. *OFFER* in Part Two draws heavily on the work of Michael Wald and David L. Chambers in *In the Interest of Children,* Robert H. Mnookin, ed. (W. H. Freeman, New York, 1985), as well as on articles in the *New York Times* in 1976 about Pamela Wallace and her daughters, and interviews with Lowry, Louise Gruner Gans, Susan Kaiser, Parry, Guggenheim, Weisbrod, Dorothy Lhotan, and Danny Greenberg.

The *New York Times* editorial that caused Judge Tyler to take *Wilder* seriously was written by Roger Wilkins. Several *Wilder* adversaries brought up the fact that he and Lowry also were romantically involved at some point in this period. "It was only after I wrote the editorial that I ever talked to Marcia," Wilkins, who declined to talk about Lowry, told me. "Everything that I learned subsequently supported my initial view of the lawsuit." He added: "Marcia was suing all the good people of New York, and a lot of the good people were people who had relations at the *Times* and they made their views known. My editor, who was a principled man, John Oakes, relayed the conversations, and humorously twitted me for stirring up the hornets' nest, but never suggested the issue be reconsidered or the opinion changed."

CHARLES SCHINITSKY S DESCRIPTION of family court is from Peter S. Prescott, *The Child Savers* (Knopf, New York, 1981). The development of child protection is documented in Barbara Nelson, *Making an Issue of Child Abuse: Political Agenda Setting for Social Problems* (University of Chicago Press, Chicago, 1984). The discussion of shifting attitudes toward sexual delinquents and children, including the quotation from Marion E. Kenworthy in Part Two, chapter 3, is from Robert Mennel, *Thorns and Thistles* (University Press of New England, Hanover, N.H., 1973). For more on the public outcry over juvenile institutions and the interstate traffic in children at the time, see Kenneth Wooden, *Weeping in the Playtime of Others* (McGraw-Hill, New York, 1976); Ronald B. Taylor, *The Kid Business* (Houghton Mifflin Co., Boston, 1981); and Willard Gaylin, Ira Glasser, et al., *Doing Good: The Limits of Benevolence* (Pantheon, New York, 1978).

FOR THE HISTORY of the Children's Center, which Polier investigated and Parry closed, I greatly benefited from David Rosner and Gerald Markowitz, "Race and the Politics of Abandonment: New York City and African-American Children," a draft article provided by the authors in 1994, and their *Children, Race and Power: Kenneth and Mamie Clark's Northside Center* (University Press of Virginia, Charlottesville, Va., 1996). See also Murray Schumach, "Gangs of Girls Terrorize Staff and the Retarded at Children's Unit Here." *New York Times*, September 8, 1974; and "Children in Limbo," the reprint of a five-part series from the *New York Herald Tribune*, 1965.

The last was part of the valuable personal file of clippings, memos, and manuscripts on foster care, adoption, and race provided to me by Patricia G. Morisey. Judy A. Schaffer's personal files on transracial adoption and her intimate knowledge of the foster care field were equally useful. The most important published source for my accounts of racial issues in adoption and foster care in the 1950s and 1960s is Andrew Billingsley and Jeanne M. Giovannoni, *Children of the Storm: Black Children and American Child Welfare* (Harcourt, Brace, New York, 1972). Also valuable, especially for the Minnesota chapters, were Joyce Ladner, *Mixed Families* (Anchor Press, Garden City, N.Y., 1977); Rita James Simon and Howard Alstein, *Transracial Adoption* (John Wiley & Sons, New York, 1977); and *Adoption, Race and Identity from Infancy Through Adolescence* (Praeger, New York, 1992).

THE DISCUSSION OF FOSTER CARE reform politics in the late 1970s is based largely on the unpublished Ph.D. dissertation by David M. Tobis, "The New York City Foster Care System, 1979–1988; the Rise and Fall of Reform," provided by its author, who helped in many other ways.

IN THE WASSERMAN CHAPTERS, background on Vera Ellen James's ancestors is based on Edmund Jefferson Danziger, Jr., *The Chippewas of Lake Superior* (University of Oklahoma Press, Norman and London, 1979). Documentation on Golden Valley includes copies of the Minnesota State Health Department complaint investigations cited and a videotape of "Tortured Teens," produced by Peter Wilkinson for *60 Minutes* and broadcast April 28, 1985, which depicts abuses at Golden Valley a few years after Lamont's stay. Also useful were articles on widespread problems in child psychiatric hospitals nationwide, provided by Barbara Demming Lurie, director, Patient Rights Bureau, Los Angeles. For more on the child in the Parham case, see Louise Armstrong, *And They Call It Help: The Psychiatric Policing of America's Children* (Addison-Wesley, Reading, Mass., 1993).

THE CHAPTERS ON THE RISE AND FALL of the *Wilder* settlement would have been impossible without the cooperation of most of the principal players, but especially Fritz Schwarz, who, besides interviews, gave me access to memoranda, appointment books, and even his Harvard College thesis on John W. Davis. Likewise, Burt Neuborne graciously opened himself to my sometimes uncomfortable questioning and supplied copies of his speeches and articles. Robert Ward allowed me to pore over clipping scrapbooks and other memorabilia in his chambers, to interview his past clerks, and to ask him questions about his personal background as well as the case. "I think it's unconstitutional," he said in 1995 of the statute that had been upheld before he got the case. "These children were not having made available to them equality of care. [But] I never was in a position to write a decision on a fresh slate." Most of his other thoughts on *Wilder*, however, are taken from his decision or court transcripts.

Besides Lowry, Mushlin, Hansen, Eli Gilbert, and Stephen Michelson, others who were particularly generous with their time, or especially forth-coming, included Monsignor Robert Arpie (who had retired to Florida in poor health when I caught up with him), Thomas Aquilino, who took time from the bench to meet with me (he was by then a judge at the U.S. Court of International Trade in Manhattan); Gail Kong (by then executive director of the Asian Pacific Fund in San Francisco); Stanley Brezenoff; Eric Brettschneider; Diane Morgenroth, Michele Ovesey, and Gary Shaffer; Flo-ran Fink and Richard Nolan (who, when asked about accounts that in the heat of the infamous czarina incident he had lunged at Lowry as though to strangle her, allowed that "I probably got a little hot," but dryly added, "The conference tables at Davis, Polk are wide enough that I wouldn't have reached her.").

For my interpretation of Edward I. Koch's response to *Wilder*, besides *His Eminence and Hizzoner: A Candid Exchange,* with Cardinal O'Connor and *Citizen Koch: An Autobiography* (St. Martin's Press, New York, 1994), and my own reporting at *New York Newsday* after 1986, I drew on the political analysis of the Koch coalition in John Hull Mollenkopf, *A Phoenix in the Ashes: The Rise and Fall of the Koch Coalition in New York Politics* (Princeton University Press, Princeton, N.J., 1992). See also Irving Howe's stinging portrait, "Social Retreat and the Tumler," in *Dissent* (Fall 1987). For more on the municipal scandal mentioned in passing, see Jack Newfield and Wayne Barrett, *City for Sale* (Harper & Row, New York, 1988).

I relied on both Tobis and Brettschneider for the account of the foster bed crisis and on Dinitia Smith's excellent piece in *New York Magazine* (December 1986). For the rise and demise of PAS and to answer many questions about foster care, John Courtney, who ran the assessment system in its heyday, was an invaluable resource, as were Rose Firestein, Cohn, and Tulin. For the strategies of the religious agencies in the face of the settlement, see Iron Hill Associates, "Wilder and Beyond, Planning Foster Care System Expansion Short and Long Term," prepared for the New York City Human Resources Administration, November 1987. For more information on the overnighters who churned through Lamont's group home in the 1980s, see my article in *New York Newsday*, May 16, 1990, "Abandoned by the City," and the Legal Aid suit, *Doe* v. *New York City Department of Social Services*.

THE MOST INSIGHTFUL constitutional discussion of *Wilder* is by Guggenheim, "State Supported Foster Care: The interplay between the prohibition of establishing religion and the free exercise rights of parents and children: *Wilder* v. *Bernstein*," *Brooklyn Law Review* 56: no. 2 (1990), p. 603–55. For accounts of the case and other child welfare litigation by the participants, see especially Lowry's "Derring-Do in the 1980s: Child Welfare Impact Litigation After the Warren Years," *Family Law Quarterly* XX: no. 2 (Summer 1986); Burt Neuborne and Frederick A. O. Schwarz, Jr., "A Prelude to Settlement of *Wilder*," in *Consent Decrees: Practical Problems and Legal Dilemmas,* the University of Chicago Legal Forum, 1987; Chris Hansen, "Making It Work: Implementation of Court Orders Requiring Restructuring of State Executive Branch Agencies," in *Child, Parent & State: Law and Policy* (University of California, Berkeley, 1994); Michael B. Mushlin, Louis Levitt, and Lauren Anderson, "Court-Ordered Foster Family Care Reform: A Case Study," in *Child Welfare,* March–April 1986.

The article I cite by Brenda McGowan and Edward Delaney, "The *Wilder* Case, A Different View," was a response to John P. Hale's articles on the lawsuit in *America,* April 20, 1974, and December 28, 1974. Also useful for my understanding of the Catholic perspective was John T. McGreevy, *Parish Boundaries, The Catholic Encounter with Race in the Twentieth Century Urban North* (University of Chicago Press, Chicago, 1996); Charles Morris, *American Catholic* (Times Books, New York, 1997); John Cooney, *American Pope: The Life and Times of Francis Cardinal Spellman* (Times Books, New York, 1984); Nat Hentoff, *John Cardinal O'Connor: At the Storm Center of a Changing American Catholic Church* (Scribners, New York, 1988); and conversations with Monsignor Henry J. Byrne.

Telling details about John W. Davis came from both J. Harvie Wilkinson III, *From Brown to Bakke* (Oxford University Press, New York, 1979) and Richard Kluger, *Simple Justice* (Knopf, New York, 1976), which also informed my larger themes.

To write about Lowry's twentieth anniversary party, I corroborated Glasser's account with Bienstock, Mushlin, Hansen, Shapiro, Kaiser, and others who were present. I am the reporter to whom Robert L. Little complained that Lowry's contempt motion in *Wilder* was a racial power play. But after reading my *New York Newsday* series about the lawsuit (July 13 and 14,

1993), he expressed great sympathy for Lamont and told me, "I am personally incensed every time I go into that courtroom in the *Wilder* case. What a strange place I'm in, defending the indefensible!" Little died in 1999.

Besides my own interviews with him, including several after he returned to Michigan, I drew on "Robert Little and the Kinship Foster Care Program in New York City," prepared in 1993, with his cooperation, by Esther Scott and David Eddy Spicer for use at the John F. Kennedy School of Government, Harvard University; and a transcript of an interview he gave to foster teenagers at *Foster Care Youth United*. Other sources include Joel Berger, Doug Lasdon, and Theodore Stein; Douglas J. Besharov, ed., *Children and Youth Services Review*, "Reforming Child Welfare Through Demonstration and Evaluation," vol. 14, nos. 1–2, 1992; and my own reporting on child welfare during this period for *Newsday*. See "A Neglected Life" (October 17, 1993) and "Crack Kids: City Cheats the Children" (January 23, 1994).

OF BOOKS I CONSULTED on issues of crack, poverty, welfare, and homelessness for Part V, particularly useful were Elliott Currie, *Reckoning: Drugs, the Cities, and the American Future* (Hill and Wang, New York, 1993); Craig Reinarman, ed., *Crack in America* (University of California Press, Berkeley, 1997); Linda Gordon's *Pitied, But Not Entitled: Single Mothers and the History of Welfare* (Free Press, New York, 1994); Kathryn Edin and Laura Lein, *Making Ends Meet: How Single Mothers Survive Welfare and Low-Wage Work* (Russell Sage Foundation, New York, 1997); Christopher Jencks, *The Homeless* (Harvard University Press, Cambridge, Mass., 1994); and the work of Dennis Culhane. On shelter development, see Dan Barry and Nina Bernstein, "Questions Clouding Future of Men's Shelter at Bellevue," *The New York Times*, January 2, 1999.

FOR DELVING INTO early child welfare history, the single most valuable source was Robert H. Bremner's *Children and Youth in America: A Documentary History* (Harvard University Press, Cambridge, Mass., 1970–74). Also important were David M. Schneider & Albert Deutsch, *The History of Public Welfare in New York State, 1867–1940* (University of Chicago Press, Chicago); and Kenneth T. Jackson, ed., *The Encyclopedia of New York City* (Yale University Press, New Haven, 1995). Although published too late for most of my research, I also used Edwin G. Burroughs and Mike Wallace, *Gotham: A History of New York City to 1898* (Oxford University Press, New York, 1999).

HELPFUL PRIMARY SOURCES, besides those in Bremner, included: Henri Julius Browne, *The Great Metropolis* (1869); Robert W. De Forest, et al., *In Memoriam, Josephine Shaw Lowell, The Charity Organization Society of the City of New York* (1916); Edna Bullock, *Selected Articles on Mother's Pensions* (H. W. Wilson Co., White Plains, N.Y. and New York City, 1915); William B. Farrell, "A Public Scandal: The Strong Commission" (February 18, 1916) and other documents from the Kingsbury charities scandal in the Rare Book and Manuscript Library of Columbia University.

THE ORPHAN TRAIN SECTIONS draw on Marilyn I. Holt, *Placing Out in America* (University of Nebraska Press, Lincoln and London, 1992); Miriam Langsam, *Children West* (University of Wisconsin Press, Madison, 1964); Janet Liebl, *Ties that Bind: The Orphan Train Story in Minnesota* (Southwest State University, Marshall, Minn., 1994); Matthew Josephson, *The Robber Barons* (New York, 1934); and publications of the Orphanage Heritage Society of America, especially first-person accounts in *Orphan Train Riders: Their Own Stories*, vol. 1, 1992. New since my research is Stephen O'Connor, *The Orphan Trains: The Story of Charles Loring Brace and the Children He Saved and Failed* (Houghton Mifflin, New York, 2001). I also highly recommend a novel by Joan Brady, *Theory of War* (Ballantine Books, New York, 1993), about a four-year-old white boy sold into slavery after the Civil War.

THE CHAPTER ON NEW YORK FOUNDLING is indebted to the unpublished Ph.D. dissertation of Maureen Fitzgerald, "Brigit's Profession: Irish Catholic Nuns, Cultural Resistance and the Origins of New York City's Welfare System, 1840–1920; research on foundlings by Julie Miller; and is also based on Peter C. English, M.D., "Pediatrics and the Unwanted Child in History: Foundling Homes, Disease, and the Origins of Foster Care in New York City, 1860 to 1920," in *Pediatrics* 73: no. 5 (May 1984); Jacqueline Bernard, *The Children You Gave Us: A History of 150 Years of Service to Children* (Jewish Child Care Association of New York, 1972); and the work of Deborah A. Frank, M.D., Boston University School of Medicine, who gave me her draft article on orphanages and the failure to thrive.

Besides John Bowlby's work (Basic Books, New York, 1982), and J. Goldstein, A. Freud, and A. Solnit, *Beyond the Best Interests of the Child* (Free Press, New York, 1973), I was helped by Clara J. Jewett, *Helping Children Cope with Separation and Loss* (Harvard Common Press, Boston, 1982) and *Adopting the Older Child* (Harvard Common Press, Boston, 1978); Selma H. Fraiberg, *The*

Magic Years, Understanding and Handling the Problems of Early Childhood (Scribners, New York, 1959); draft articles by Tim Hacsi; and an unpublished autobiographical account of life inside the Hebrew Orphan Home by Maurice Bernstein. A quoted critique of the diagnosis of childhood schizophrenia is from Jeanne Smith, M.D., who reviewed the issue for the *Archives of Pediatrics* in 1951. The Des Lauriers Method is described by its author in *The Experience of Reality in Childhood Schizophrenia* (International Universities Press, New York, 1962).

SECTIONS ON VINCENT ASTOR and the history of Astor Home draw from Sari B. Tietjen, *Rhinebeck, Portrait of a Town* (River Press, Rhinebeck, N.Y., 1990); Monica Randall, *Phantoms of the Hudson Valley: The Glorious Estates of a Lost Era* (The Overlook Press, New York, 1995), as well as documents provided by Kay Verrilli and Nancy Kelly of the Dutchess County Historical Society. Data on the tenements is from Eric Homberger, *The Historical Atlas of New York City* (Henry Holt, New York, 1994); see also, Jacob A. Riis, *How the Other Half Lives* (Scribners, New York, 1890; Dover, New York, 1971).

MUCH SOCIAL WELFARE HISTORY INFLUENCED ME, but I am particularily indebted to the work of Linda Gordon, whose central argument, that the definition of child welfare problems is a historical and political construction, was crucial to my analysis of Shirley Wilder's case. See especially *Heroes of Their Own Lives: The Politics and History of Family Violence, Boston, 1880–1960* (Penguin Books, New York, 1988); and also *Woman's Body, Woman's Right: Birth Control in America* (Penguin Books, New York, 1974/1990). Also influential have been Richard Hofstadter, *Social Darwinism in American Thought* (Beacon Press, Boston, 1944, 1983); Michael B. Katz, especially *In the Shadow of the Poorhouse: A Social History of Welfare in America* (Basic Books, New York, 1986); and David J. Rothman, including *Conscience and Convenience: The Asylum and Its Alternatives in Progressive America* (Little, Brown and Co., Boston, 1980) and *Willowbrook Wars*, written with Sheila Rothman (Harper & Row, New York, 1984).

Among many studies that helped me think historically about key issues were Eric C. Schneider, *In the Web of Class: Delinquents and Reformers in Boston, 1810s–1930s* (New York University Press, New York, 1992); Christine Stansell, *City of Women: Sex and Class in New York, 1789–1860* (Knopf, New York, 1986); Timothy Gilfoyle, *City of Eros: New York City, Prostitution and the*

Commercialization of Sex, 1790–1920 (Norton, New York, 1992); Barbara Brenzel, *Daughters of the State: A Social Portrait of the First Reform School for Girls in North America, 1856–1905* (The MIT Press, Cambridge, Mass., 1992); and Patricia T. Rook and R. L. Schnell, *Discarding the Asylum: From Child Rescue to the Welfare State in English-Canada, 1800–1950* (University Press of America, Lanham/New York/London, 1983); Ellen Chesler, *Woman of Valor: Margaret Sanger and the Birth Control Movement in America* (Simon & Schuster, New York, 1992); Viviana A. Rotman Zelizer, *Pricing the Priceless Child: The Changing Social Value of Children* (Basic Books, New York, 1985); Frances Fox Piven and Richard Cloward, *Regulating the Poor* (Pantheon, New York, 1977). Nicholas Lemann, *The Promised Land: The Great Migration and How It Changed America* (Vintage Books, New York, 1991); and Gerald N. Rosenberg, *The Hollow Hope: Can Courts Bring About Social Change?* (University of Chicago Press, Chicago, 1991).

A SCRUPULOUSLY FOOTNOTED CRITIQUE of foster care policy that was very valuable is Richard Wexler, *Wounded Innocents: The Real Victims of the War against Child Abuse* (Prometheus Books, Buffalo, N.Y., 1990). I am particularly indebted to Wexler for highlighting the fact, to which I refer in the Introduction, that foster care rates dropped from 59 out of every 10,000 children in 1933 to 38 per 10,000 in 1960, but reached 75 per 10,000 by 1977, after changes in federal financing in 1961 rewarded placement. See also Mark Courtney, *Child Welfare in the Context of Welfare 'Reform,'* S. Kamerman and A. Kahn, eds., Cross-National Studies Research Program, Columbia University School of Social Work, 1997; and Nina Bernstein, "Deletion of Word in Welfare Bill Opens Foster Care to Big Business," *New York Times*, May 4, 1997, A-1.

FOSTER CARE HAS ALWAYS DRAWN a multitude of commissions and audit reports, and I used many for data about the system at various stages of the narrative. The most useful were made available by Peggy Ayers of the Robert Sterling Clark Foundation, especially Judy A. Schaffer, *Compendium of Foster Care Research*, for the Office of the President of the City Council, New York, 1979. See also, "Redirecting Foster Care," Mayor's Task Force on Foster Care, N.Y. 1979–80; "Whatever Happened to the Boarder Babies?" Office of the Comptroller of the City of New York, January 1989; "Now We Are Four, Boarder Babies Growing Up in Foster Care, A Follow-Up Study (December 1989); "Foster Care, Adoption Assistance, and Child Welfare

Services," prepared for the Committee on Finance, U.S. Senate, September 1990. "A National Evaluation of Title IV-E Foster Care Independent Living Programs for Youth, prepared for the Department of Health and Human Services Administration for Children and Families by Westat, Inc., Rockville, Md., in 1993; and Thomas P. McDonald, et al., *Assessing the Long-Term Effects of Foster Care: A Research Synthesis, Institute for Research on Poverty* (University of Wisconsin, Madison, 1993). Throughout, first hand insights about life in foster care were invaluable. My thanks especially to June Carolyn Erlick, who was steadfast and generous in her responses.

CASE REFERENCES

Aguilar v. Felton, 473 U.S. 402 (1985).

Black v. Beame, 550 F. 2nd 815, 2d Cir. (1977).

Brown v. Board of Education, 347 U.S. 483 (1954).

Caban v. Mohammed, 441 U.S. 380, 99 S. Ct. 1760, 60 L. Ed. 2d 297 (*U.S.N.Y.,* April 24, 1979) (No. 77 6431).

Child v. Beame, 412 F. Supp. 593 (S.D.N.Y. 1976) 425 F. Supp.

Committee of Public Education and Religion v. Nyquist, 93 Supreme Court 2955 (1973).

Doe v. NYCDSS, 670 F. Supp. 1145 (S.D.N.Y. 1987).

Eugene F. v. Gross, index no. 1125/86 Sup. Ct. N.Y. County.

Goldberg v. Kelly, 397 U.S. 254 (1970).

Grand Rapids v. Ball, 473 U.S. 373 (1985).

In the matter of Ellen Bonez, 272 N.Y.S. 2d 587 (1966).

In the matter of Ellery C. 32 N.Y. 2d 588.

In re Gault, 387 U.S. (1967).

In re Vardinakis et al., 289 N.Y.S. 355, 160 Misc 13 (1936).

Jesse E. v. NYDSS, 90 Civ. 7274 (S.D.N.Y. 1990).

Joseph A. v. New Mexico Department of Human Services, 575 F. Supp. 346 (D.N.M. 1983).

Kirkpatrick v. Christian Homes of Abilene, Inc., 459 U.S. 1145, 103 S.Ct. 784 74 L. Ed. 2d 991 (U.S.Tex., April 23, 1983).

Levitt v. Committee for Public Education and Religious Liberty, 93 Supreme Court 2814 (1973).

New York State Association for Retarded Children, Inc. v. Rockefeller, 393 F. Supp. 715, 718 (E.D. N.Y. 1975) (Willowbrook).

Marisol v. Giuliani, 929 F. Supp. 662 (S.D.N.Y. 1996).

OFFER v. Dumpson, 418 F. Supp. 277 (S.D.N.Y. 1976).

Palmer v. *Cuomo*, 503 N.Y.S. 2d 20 (N.Y. App. Div. 1986).

Parham v. *J.R.*, 442 U.S. 584 (1976).

Plessy v. *Ferguson*, 163 U.S. 537 (1896).

Reynolds v. *Giuliani*, 35 F. Supp. 2d 331 (S.D.N.Y. 1999).

Roe v. *Wade*, 410 U.S. 113 (1973).

Sinhogar v. *Parry*, 53 N.Y. 2d 424, 442 N.Y.S. 2d 438 (1981).

Smith v. *OFFER* (Organization of Foster Families for Equity and Reform), 431 U.S. 816 (1977).

State v. *John C. Lowry*, 263 N.C. 536, 139 S.E. 2d 870 (1965).

Tinker v. *Des Moines School District*, 393 U.S. 503 (1969).

Wilder v. *Sugarman*, 73 Civ. 2644 (S.D.N.Y. June 14, 1973) 385 F. Supp. 1013 (S.D.N.Y. 1974).

Wilder v. *Bernstein*, 499 F. Supp. 980 (S.D.N.Y. 1980). The history of the litigation is recounted in 645 F. Supp. 1292, 1297–1304 S.D.N.Y. 1986 (approving settlement).

Wisconsin v. *Yoder*, 406 U.S. 205 (1972).

OTHER RELATED LITIGATION by Marcia Robinson Lowry: *Baby Neal* v. *Casey*, 43 F. 3d 48 (3d Cir. 1994), filed Philadelphia, 1990; *Brian, A., et al.* v. *Sundquist, et al.*, Civ. Action No. 3-00-0445 (M.D. Tenn., May 10, 2000); *Charlie and Nadine H.* v. *Whitman*, 83 F. Supp. 2d 476 (D.N.J. 2000); *Foster Children Bonnie L., et al.* v. *Bush*, 00-2116-CIV-Huck (S.D. Fla. 2000); *G.L.* v. *Zumwalt*, 564 F. Supp. 1030 (W.D. Mo. 1983) and *G.L.* v. *Stangler*, 873 F. Supp. 252 (W.D. Mo. 1994); *Jeanine* v. *Thompson*, 877 F. Supp. 1268 (E.D. Wisc. 1995); *Jeremy M., et al.* v. *Guiliani, et al.*, 00CIV.6498 (S.D.N.Y. August 30, 2000); *Juan F.* v. *Weicker*, 37 F. 3d 874 (2d Cir. 1994); *LaShawn* v. *Barry*, 762 F. Supp. 959, 985 (D.D.C. 1991); *Martin A.* v. *Gross*, 524 N.Y.S. 2nd 75 (N.Y. Sup. Ct. 1987) affirmed, 153 A.D. 2d 812 (N.Y. App. Div. 1989); *Sheila A.* v. *Finney*, No. 89-CIV-33 (Kan. Dist. Ct., filed Jan. 8, 1989); *In re P.*, 7 Family Law Rep. 2722, Louisville, Ky., approved 1981.

ACKNOWLEDGMENTS

A BOOK SEVEN YEARS in the making incurs debts too deep to be forgotten and too numerous to name. Generous, even courageous help came from people who lived through the events that it chronicles, and many of them figure in its pages, or in the notes on sources. But the book could not have been written without the assistance of many others who also shared recollections, insights, or records.

Along the way, I have had more than my share of institutional and editorial support. At *New York Newsday,* Robert Friedman edited the two-part series that began the project in 1993, kept listening on countless homeward subway rides, and encouraged me to write a book.

Gloria Loomis, my agent, taught me how to craft the proposal, found the right publisher, and gave me Joan Brady's *Theory of War: A Novel*—an inspiration.

The Alicia Patterson Foundation granted me a crucial 1994 fellowship, thanks to the strong support of Tony Marro and Don Forst, my *Newsday* editors, who extended the year's leave by six months when I asked for more time. The leave expired in July of 1995, on the same day that the Times Mirror Company announced it was closing *New York Newsday.* Without that newsroom's nurturing mix of idealistic expectations and upstart glee—"Truth, Justice and the Comics," as the slogan had it—I would surely never have set out on such an ambitious project.

When I joined the *New York Times,* my editors, Joe Lelyveld and Dean Baquet, graciously agreed to another book leave down the road and, meanwhile, gave me the chance to pursue several projects for the paper that widened my grasp, including an investigation of the Elisa Izquierdo case, and of a one-word change in child welfare law that permitted money earmarked for poor children to flow into orphanage profits.

Two newspapers, two leaves of absence, and in the end, two book editors without whom this book would not be. Linda Healey brought the project to Pantheon, practically breathed her belief into me whenever I seemed to lose heart, and swept me from my journalistic tics toward an authorial voice. She mixed high praise with a demand for detail that deepened my reporting. And when I was in a moral crisis of the kind only writers of nonfiction encounter, she gave me wise and humane advice.

Dan Frank inherited an unwieldy, incomplete draft and a discouraged writer after Linda left Pantheon at the end of 1998, and devoted his amazing skill and discernment to summoning forth the book I had wanted to write all along. He is simply, as a colleague of mine said, the Joe DiMaggio of book editors.

The champions of patience, however, are Andreas, Daniel, David, and the other members of my family. Nothing so intensified my understanding of what lost children lose than the loving support that buoyed me through the darkest waters. And nothing made clearer how brave Lamont had to be without it. In grateful respect, I hope this book redeems his trust.

INDEX